Francophone Literatures

'will help students find their way around this culturally diverse and complex body of writing, providing accessible points of entry and stimulating a thirst to read more.'

Alec G. Hargreaves, Loughborough University

Francophone Literatures: a literary and linguistic companion is an accessible and student-friendly guide to the key literary texts of the French-speaking world.

The book is in four sections corresponding to the major divisions of the francophone world – North Africa, Black Africa and the Indian Ocean, the Caribbean, and North America. Each section comprises:

- A brief introduction outlining the political and literary history of the francophone zones.
- Seven key extracts from major literary works. The extracts have been carefully selected to present a chronological picture of the development of the literature and to represent writing by both men and women.
- A Text and Context commentary which provides a literary and historical background to each extract and outlines its principal aesthetic, social, cultural and political features.
- A Language and Style commentary which demonstrates the most significant linguistic and stylistic characteristics. The commentary is based on a detailed analysis of five linguistic levels – phonology, graphology, lexicology, syntax and the text as a whole.

Francophone Literatures: a literary and linguistic companion will be an invaluable resource for all students of French.

Malcolm Offord is Reader in French at the University of Nottingham. His most recent book is *French Words: past, present and future.* **Laïla Ibnlfassi** is Senior Lecturer in French Studies at the London Guildhall University. She is co-editor, with Nicki Hitchcott, of *African Francophone Writing: a critical introduction.* **Nicki Hitchcott** is Lecturer in French at the University of Nottingham. She is the author of *Women Writers in Francophone Africa.* **Sam Haigh** is Lecturer in French Studies at the University of Warwick. She is the author of *Mapping a Tradition: francophone women's writing from Guadeloupe.* **Rosemary Chapman** is Senior Lecturer in French at the University of Nottingham. She is the author of *Siting the Quebec Novel.*

Francophone Literatures

A literary and linguistic companion

Malcolm Offord, Laïla Ibnlfassi, Nicki Hitchcott, Sam Haigh and Rosemary Chapman

First published by Lawrence Erlbaum Associates, Inc., Publishers
10 Industrial Avenue
Mahwah, New Jersey 07430

Reprinted 2010 by Routledge

Routledge

270 Madison Avenue
New York, NY 10016

2 Park Square, Milton Park
Abingdon, Oxon OX14 4RN, UK

Routledge is an imprint of the Taylor & Francis Group

Typeset in Baskerville and Gill Sans by
RefineCatch Limited, Bungay, Suffolk

British Library Cataloguing in Publication Data
A catalogue record for this book is available from the British Library

Library of Congress Cataloging in Publication Data
Francophone literatures : a literary and linguistic companion / Malcolm Offord . . . [et al.].
p. cm.
Includes bibliographical references and index.
ISBN 0–415–19839–9 – ISBN 0–415–19840–2
1. French language – Readers – French literature. 2. French literature–French-speaking countries. 3. French language – Textbooks for foreign speakers – English. I. Offord, M. H.
PC2117 .F7925 2001
843.008′091754 – dc21 00–051744

ISBN 0–415–19839–9 (hbk)
ISBN 0–415–19840–2 (pbk)

Contents

Acknowledgements

We wish to thank Peter Hawkins and Emily Allport for their help with the commentary on Axel Gauvin's *L'Aimé*.

Permission given by the following copyright holders and authors is gratefully acknowledged:

Le Passé simple, Driss Chraïbi © Editions Denoël, 1954; *La Statue de sel*, Albert Memmi © Editions Gallimard, 1966; *Le Fleuve détourné*, Rachid Mimouni © Editions Robert Laffont, 1982; *Le Thé au harem d'Archi Ahmed*, Mehdi Charef © Mercure de France, 1983; *L'Enfant de sable*, Tahar Ben Jelloun © Editions du Seuil, 1985; *La Nuit sacrée*, Tahar Ben Jelloun © Editions du Seuil, 1987; *Le Gone du Chaâba*, Azouz Begag, © Editions du Seuil, 1986; *La Voyeuse interdite*, Nina Bouraoui © Editions Gallimard, 1991; *Une vie de boy*, Ferdinand Oyono © Julliard, 1956; *Les Bouts de bois de Dieu*, Ousmane Sembène © Presses de la Cité, 1960; *Les Soleils des Indépendances*, Ahmadou Kourouma © Editions du Seuil, 1970; *Une si longue lettre*, Mariama Bâ © Les Nouvelles Editions Africaines de Sénégal, 1979; *La Vie et demie*, Sony Labou Tansi © Editions du Seuil, 1979; *Le Petit Prince de Belleville*, Calixthe Beyala © Editions Albin Michel, 1992; *L'Aimé*, Axel Gauvin © Editions du Seuil, 1990; *Gouverneurs de la rosée*, Jacques Roumain © Editions Désormeaux, 1944; *La Rue Cases-Nègres*, Joseph Zobel © Présence Africaine, 1974; *Pluie et Vent sur Télumée Miracle*, Simone Schwarz-Bart © Editions du Seuil, 1972; *L'Isolé Soleil*, Daniel Maximin © Editions du Seuil, 1981; *Chronique des sept misères*, Patrick Chamoiseau © Editions Gallimard, 1986; *Traversée de la mangrove*, Maryse Condé © Mercure de France, 1989; *Pays sans chapeau*, Dany Laferrière, Lanctôt Editeur, 1996; *Menaud, maître-draveur*, Félix-Antoine Savard, Bibliothèque Québécoise, 1992 © Fides; *Bonheur d'occasion*, Gabrielle Roy © Fonds Gabrielle Roy, 1993; *Une Saison dans la vie d'Emmanuel*, Marie-Claire Blais © Editions du Boréal, 1991; *La Grosse Femme d'à-côté est enceinte*, Michel Tremblay © Leméac, 1978, 1996; *Pélagie-la-Charrette*, Antonine Maillet © Bibliothèque québécoise 1990 and Editions Bernard Grasset; *La Québécoite*, Régine Robin © XYZ Editeur, 1993; *Volkswagen Blues*, Jacques Poulin © Leméac, 1988.

Every effort has been made to contact copyright holders. We apologize for any inadvertent omissions.

Introduction

General

First coined by French geographer, Onésime Reclus, at the end of the nineteenth century, the term 'francophone' originally denoted nothing more than people who spoke French in countries other than France. During the twentieth century, the term evolved to connote not only a shared language but also shared experiences and ideals, culminating in the concept of a Francophone Community, initially promoted by the Senegalese president, Léopold Sédar Senghor, in the 1960s. In 1969, the first conference of francophone states was held in Niamey, Niger, and led to the creation of the ACCT (Agence de Coopération Culturelle et Technique) to encourage cooperation and solidarity between the French-speaking countries of the world. It was, however, not until the 1980s and the arrival of French President François Mitterrand that the formal institutionalization of *la francophonie* began to take place, with the establishment of the Haut Conseil de la Francophonie in 1984. In 1986 the first Francophone Summit was held in Paris, and in 1992 the international Conseil Permanent de la Francophonie was created, headed by fifteen heads of state or government. *Francophonie* now signifies a vast institutional apparatus with members in all continents of the world. The majority of these members are former colonies of France.

Outside the European French-speaking nations (France, Belgium, Switzerland and Luxembourg), there are four major francophone geographical zones: North Africa (the Maghrebian countries of Algeria, Morocco and Tunisia); Black Africa and the Indian Ocean (Benin, Burkina Faso, Burundi, Cameroon, Central African Republic, Chad, Ivory Coast, Democratic Republic of Congo (formerly Zaïre), Gabon, Guinea, Madagascar, Mali, Mauritania, Mauritius, Niger, Republic of Congo, Réunion, Rwanda, Senegal, Seychelles and Togo); the Caribbean (Martinique, Guadeloupe and Haiti); and North America (Canada and parts of the USA). Not all areas share the same relationship with France. For example, all the African nations gained independence in the 1950s and 1960s whereas the Caribbean islands of Martinique and Guadeloupe have remained French *départements d'outre-mer*. Even within the zones differences exist: the Indian Ocean island of Madagascar has been independent since 1960 whereas its neighbour, Réunion, is a *département* of France. With the exception of Algeria, in each of these countries, *départements* or provinces, French is an official, co-official or administrative language. There are also a number of countries which are members of the Francophone Community but in which the French language has no special status. Egypt, for example, attends the Francophone Summits but has a francophone population of less than 0.5 per cent of the total. Algeria, on the other hand, has refused to join the community despite the fact that over six million Algerians speak French.

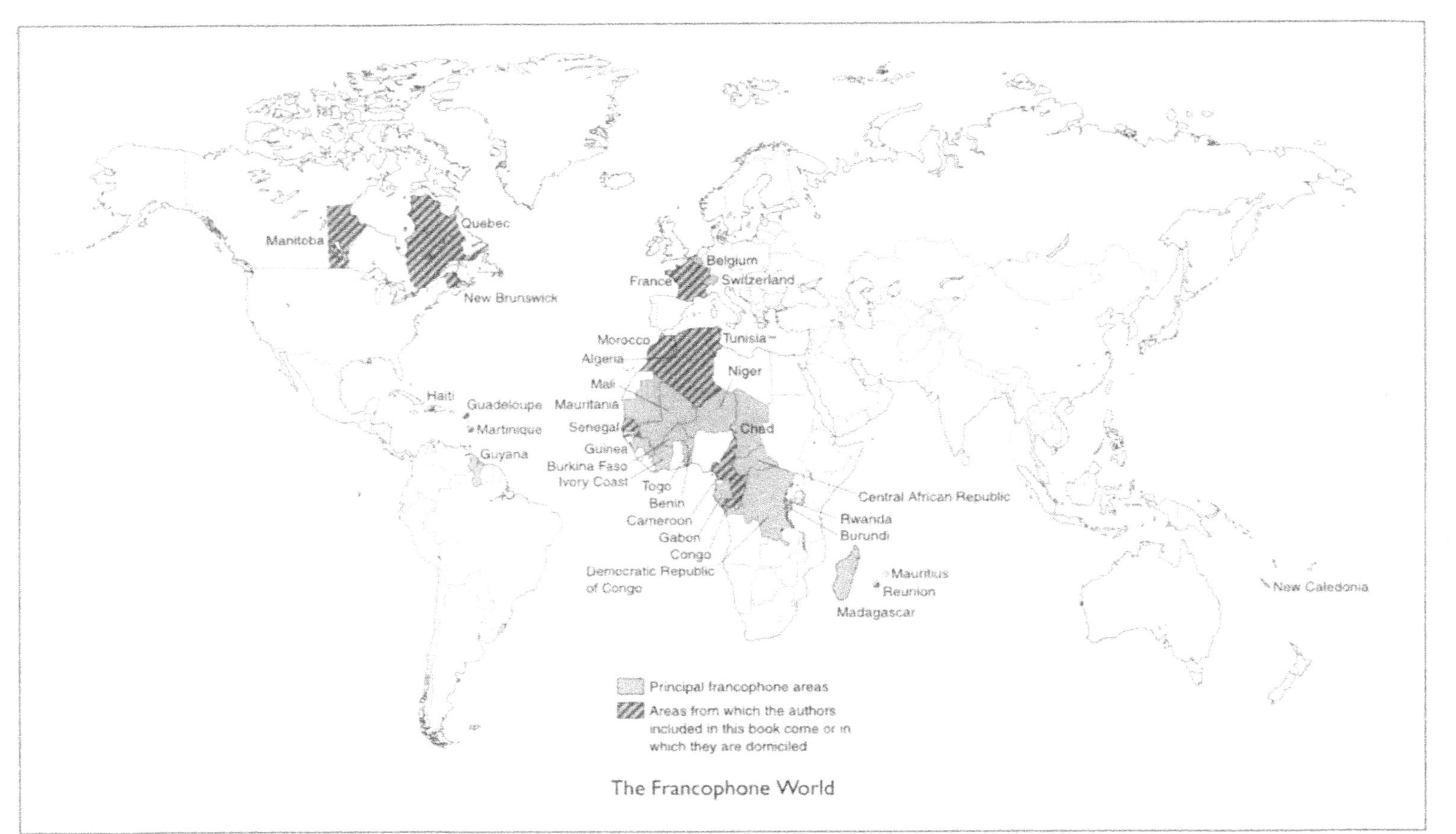

The Francophone World

Having fought a long and bloody war to gain independence, Algeria introduced a policy of arabization, rejecting linguistic and institutional *francophonie* as a continuation of French colonialism. Only very recently (in June 2000) has Algerian President Bouteflika attempted to renew diplomatic relations with France.

In spite of Algeria's rejection of *francophonie*, many Algerian authors have published and continue to publish in French. This raises some interesting questions for the reader of francophone literature, questions that can be applied to any of the extracts in this volume. Why has the author decided to publish a text in French (rather than, for example, Arabic)? How might this decision be influenced by such contextual considerations as time and place of writing? What are the implications of publishing in French? Who is the implied reader of the text and how is this affected by the author's choice of language? Are indigenous languages and dialects incorporated into the French text? How does *oralité* transform the written language? In what ways is the text marked by the experience of colonization? How are the effects of colonial histories described? Such issues are considered in the introductions to each of the four parts of this book, as well as in the 'Text and context' commentaries on the extracts themselves.

It is hoped that the reader will be helped in his or her consideration of the above questions and issues by the ways in which the extracts chosen for commentary have been selected. The division of the *Companion* into four parts – North Africa, Black Africa, the Caribbean and North America – is not, of course, meant to imply that these are the only regions of the world in which francophone literature has been produced, or that these are the only francophone literatures worthy of close analysis. Rather, the authors have attempted to focus upon those non-European regions whose literature is most likely to be readily accessible to readers and is already taught at university level throughout the anglophone world. Exhaustive coverage would obviously have been impossible, and the provision of a wider range of francophone literatures (from the Middle or Far East, for example) would inevitably have resulted in a much slighter coverage of those texts and regions included. Rather than risk superficiality by including a larger number of shorter extracts and commentaries, we have therefore aimed to provide extracts which, because there are fewer of them, are of sufficient length to give a feel for the nuances and complexities of the original text and to allow for detailed and meaningful analysis. Each of the extracts has therefore been selected because it forms a self-contained episode within the novel from which it is taken, while at the same time raising issues, both thematic and formal, which are representative of those present in the rest of that novel.

That all of the extracts included here are taken from novels, rather than from other literary genres, raises another issue which was important when the selection of texts was considered. Not only is the novel the predominant written francophone genre in most of the countries under consideration here, but it is also the genre which is most frequently taught on courses in francophone literature at university level. Thus, although poetry is an important genre in *québécois* literature, for example, and while theatre is of increasing importance in the French Caribbean, it is hoped that the inclusion of extracts from only one literary genre will make it easier for the reader to draw comparisons across and within the different geographical zones. Indeed, it is hoped that this will also enable the reader to become aware of the many innovations and experiments within the genre that have taken place in all of the different literatures examined.

Such innovation and experimentation are typical features of those novels published most recently. Consequently, and while almost all of the extracts included are taken from novels published during the second half of the twentieth century, there is considerable chronological spread within each zone and across them. This should allow the reader to track the evolution of each literature and, once more, should encourage comparison – between the literature of different historical periods, as well as from different geographical regions and cultural contexts. Finally, it is this same desire to provide an insight into the richness and variety of francophone writing of the late twentieth century which has meant that care has been taken to include texts written both by men and by women, as well as by writers from different areas within each of the wider zones (from Acadie in the case of Canada, for example; from the dependent and independent islands of the French Caribbean; from a variety of the countries which make up North and Black Africa). Questions of exile, migration and displacement are also raised by the inclusion of texts by writers such as Dany Laferrière, Régine Robin and Calixthe Beyala.

The inclusion of such a diversity of literature and the authors' desire to facilitate comparison across this varied corpus lead to the question of how best to use this *Companion*. The structure of the book has been devised to enable the reader to gain an insight into the texts in as effective a way as possible. The chosen extracts are arranged chronologically by date of composition within each of the four geographical areas. This means that the reading of each part should give some sense of the development of that region's literature. The individual extract and its two commentaries – 'Text and context' and 'Language and style' – are conceived as a unit and should be read as such. 'Text and context' aims to offer a close textual reading of the chosen passage, a reading which will situate the passage perhaps within a specific literary development, in relation to a historical context or in terms of some cultural phenomenon. Each commentary aims to construct an individual interpretation of the particular episode or section of the novel. The interpretation put forward does not claim to be definitive. Rather, it is hoped that the readings offered here will serve as a springboard for other readings of the extract, and eventually of the novel as a whole. Each 'Text and context' commentary is accompanied by a short list of further reading. Typically, 'Further reading' will include both a few other texts by the same author and a selective list of secondary reading. In some cases the writers concerned have already been the subject of extensive critical analysis, whereas in others very little secondary material is currently available. These suggestions for further reading are therefore not exhaustive, nor can they be representative of the entire critical field. They do, however, indicate a way forward for those wishing to pursue their study of an author's work.

The second commentary is entitled 'Language and style', and the rationale for these analyses of the texts is explained fully in the next part of this Introduction. However, readers should look out for cross-references between the paired commentaries, evidence of the ways in which the division between textual and stylistic (or linguistic) analysis is not necessarily clear cut. So, for example, a particular author's use of *oralité* may well be an issue treated in both commentaries, thus creating a dialogue between the different methodological approaches adopted. In order to gain the most from their reading of each extract, readers should also refer to the Part's Introduction, where the broad historical, cultural and literary context has been outlined and where they will find a short list of background reading relating to the specific geographical area.

Different readers will doubtless find different routes through the *Companion* according to the breadth of their own interests and existing knowledge. While some may find it interesting to concentrate on a particular zone, others may decide to follow through a specific thread that crosses the divisions between sections. Comparisons might be drawn between texts written in a particular decade, between texts written by men or women, between texts approaching a similar issue or set in the same historical period (such as the period immediately prior to decolonization). Equally the reader may wish to follow through common stylistic features, such as the use of a first-person narrator or the incorporation of indigenous languages or dialects. Whatever the path chosen, it is hoped that the combination of explanatory and analytical material provided in the commentaries will encourage the reader to consider the range of literature written in French both more closely and more widely.

Language and style

The heading 'Language and style' to describe the second commentary for each passage reflects the fact that there is a distinction between the two phenomena as well as a relationship. It is our conviction that there is no language without style, and style results from a deliberate choice of linguistic features. In preparation for the production of the commentaries, the language component of the texts is examined in detail. This involves an objective analysis of the various linguistic levels listed below, quantifying usage and in fact virtually establishing a data bank for each text. The style component, on the other hand, involves an evaluation of those data, an attempt to discover the intentions behind the linguistic choices made, an endeavour to offer an interpretation of the linguistic evidence. One object is to discover in what ways the linguistic and stylistic profile of a text confirms and complements what has been established in the 'Text and context' commentaries. Another is to identify and evaluate any special linguistic effects created by the authors, any distinctive, individual characteristics that they employ (deviations from the standard, repetitions, parallelisms, use of high- or low-level register, imagery and so on).

The linguistic analysis is undertaken at five levels. Together they provide the instruments for extracting what is of linguistic and/or stylistic significance from the texts. However, as explained below, not all will necessarily be mentioned in the final analysis in every case.

1 Phonology

At the phonological level, the features that are identified for potential comment are such matters as alliteration, onomatopoeia, rhyme, echoic effects. Since we are dealing with written prose works, it is not to be expected that these features will figure as prominently as if we were studying poetry or dramatic literature. However, a number of texts drawn from North Africa and the Caribbean are influenced by oral traditions and contain features associated with story-telling and folk tales. In addition, in certain texts, especially in the North America group, a quasi-phonetic representation of the speech of certain individuals with strong regional or local speech habits is used – see especially Michel Tremblay and Antonine Maillet; this happens to a lesser extent in the texts by Calixthe Beyala and Azouz Begag.

2 Graphology

Phonology, important in oral texts and also in those which attempt to reproduce speech directly, has graphology as its counterpart in texts which decline to do so. In order to replicate the modulations and idiosyncrasies of speech, the array of devices available in punctuation may be exploited. Exclamation marks, question marks, *points de suspension*, parentheses, breaks in speech, incomplete speech acts may all be used to represent the way someone speaks without recourse to phonetic transcription – see Axel Gauvin and Marie-Claire Blais in particular. These may be supplemented by specific comments on how the speech was delivered. Other graphological devices may also be used to guide the reader's reading of the text – indentations, paragraph length, spaces between paragraphs, scene divisions, and, as in the case of Régine Robin, the flow of text may be disturbed, for literary and ideological reasons, through the use of columns and lists.

3 Lexicology

The third level of analysis is the lexical level, the examination of the actual words used in the passages. The main focus here is upon register. In certain texts a low-register lexis is adopted. By gradating the degrees of low-register lexis – familiar, colloquial, slang – the narrator is able to make distinctions between the various age groups and social classes involved in the narrative (this is especially the case for Mehdi Charef, who even allows slang words to spill over into the narrator's account; see Calixthe Beyala also). In other cases the narrator adopts high-register lexis to confer a sense of authority or dignity on the text. A particular sociolect may also be exemplified through the use of an appropriate lexis (see Michel Tremblay). Regional speech is also reproduced, not only through phonological means, but also through introducing local words into the passages. This is apparent at a number of levels – descriptions of localities (for example Rachid Mimouni), flora and fauna (in the Caribbean and Réunion passages in particular), clothing (the Caribbean passages again), social hierarchies (the black African and Caribbean passages), local practices. Many such words are not recorded in standard French dictionaries, and translations are provided in the commentaries as necessary. The controversy over whether to write in French or in the vernacular language of the authors is addressed in certain of the Caribbean commentaries and also in the Réunion commentary. The lexical examination also deals with such matters as wordplay and malapropisms (see Axel Gauvin), hyperbole, repetition of words, often exploited for rhetorical purposes.

4 Syntax

On the syntactic level, the main focus is upon the ways in which the authors manipulate such topics as major and minor sentences, types of sentences, sentence structure, word order, use of tenses, use of subordinate clauses, adjectives, participles and adverbs. It is informative to note whether the author majors on simple and compound sentences, or whether complex sentences are also used, and, therefore, what role subordinate clauses play. The nature of the first element in a sentence may also be revealing: is it always the subject or are other parts of speech involved or, if it is the subject, is it always the same as in the previous clause? Climax, suspense, anticlimax may also be produced by varying the order of words in a sentence. The use of the historic present tense often confers a sense of drama upon the narrative; the use of the past historic suggests a more measured account.

5 The complete passage

Other devices apply to the passage as a whole and are not constrained by textual proximity. These include such phenomena as narratorial voice, overall textual structure, imagery, balance/contrast of items, free indirect discourse, stream of consciousness, textual cohesion and coherence, which are often more indicative of a narrator's intention than features identified at the other levels.

As intimated above, not all features are present in each text, and, even when they are, they are not always necessarily relevant to the discussion or significant enough to warrant comment. Space does not permit discussion of all features, and it is the minor ones in a particular passage that will have to be set aside. It is not our intention to make all commentaries follow the same pattern: the approach to the commentaries is not rigid or prescribed in advance. What appears to be significant will be concentrated upon. Each text will be considered as a separate entity with its own distinctive features. Consequently, particular studies may illustrate different facets or aspects of linguistic and stylistic analysis in general, and each will constitute a unique exercise.

The following technical terms, presented in alphabetical order, are used in the 'Language and style' commentaries:

aphaeresis	the loss of one or more sounds or letters at the beginning of a word, e.g. 'Bartine' for 'Albertine' (Tremblay, l. 4).
attributive adjective	an adjective which immediately precedes the noun it qualifies.
chiasmus	the repetition of words or elements in reverse order, e.g. 'les blancs immeubles de la ville blanche' (Kourouma, l. 11).
closed question	a question expecting the answer *oui* or *non* (cf. open question).
complex sentence	a sentence with one main clause and one or more subordinate clauses, e.g. 'Elle a mis un pantalon gris prince-de-galles qui lui fait un cul indescriptible, vu que ça prend toute la place' (one main + two subordinate clauses) (Beyala, l. 64).
compound-complex sentence	a combination of at least two main clauses and at least one subordinate clause, e.g. 'Elle l'a de l'Afrique et elle le garde pour des raisons sentimentales que j'connais bien' (Beyala, l. 67).
compound sentence	a sentence with two or more main clauses and no subordinate clauses, e.g. 'Et là, Soumana passe son cure-dent de l'autre côté de la joue et se fâche' (Beyala, l. 62).
decorative adjective	an adjective which is not essential to the understanding of the noun qualified but which adds extra information to it, e.g. 'Il prend la lourde valise à deux mains pour la faire glisser' (Charef, l. 38) (cf. functional adjective).
free indirect discourse/speech	the representation of the thoughts or utterances of a protagonist which involves combining features of direct speech as from the protagonist with features of indirect report as from the narrator.
functional adjective	an adjective which contributes essential information for the understanding of the noun qualified, e.g. 'Ils n'en sont pas à

leur première tentative' (Charef, l. 4) (cf. decorative adjective).

high register — highly formal, intellectual language, often marked by the use of abstract, poetic, slightly archaic lexis and/or sophisticated syntactic constructions, e.g. balancing of clauses, embedding of subordinate clauses in main clauses, using inversions and the less common tenses.

il-/ne- deletion — the omission of *il* or *ne* in verbal groups, usually associated with the representation of low-register speech.

imagery — includes simile, metaphor, metonymy, tenor, vehicle.

largonji — a lexical process whereby the syllable *lar-* is placed in initial position in a word, e.g. 'larfeuille' (Charef, l. 84).

lexical cluster — a group of words closely related semantically, e.g. 'rire, s'esclaffer, éclater, se tenir les côtés' (Oyono).

low register — informal language, often marked by the use of slang words and/or departures from the norms of standard French in syntax, e.g. *il-* and *ne-* deletion.

major sentence — a sentence with at least one main finite verb; major sentences may be simple, compound, complex or compound-complex.

malapropism — unintentional misuse of a word, confused with one of similar sound, often with humorous effect, e.g. 'Le riche ça peut pas te colloquer [communiquer] ses microbes' (Gauvin, l. 127).

metaphor — a comparison between objects or concepts based on similarity, e.g. 'Il avait retrouvé ses ailes' [= ready to embark on a new adventure, like a bird] (Savard, l. 30).

metonymy — a comparison in which the referent is indicated by an attribute or some other association, e.g. 'la menace de l'intervention policière. Quelques-unes [des femmes] désorientées, effrayées, se précipitèrent dans la rue, mais, là aussi, il y avait des uniformes' [= police epitomized by their distinctive clothes] (Sembène, l. 12).

minor sentence — a sentence without a main finite verb: with no verb at all, e.g. 'Vélocement. Un instant bref' (Chraïbi, l. 10); with verb in a subordinate clause, e.g. 'Elle luttait pour un peu d'argent. Un peu d'argent qu'il lui enlevait' (Roy, l. 44).

ne- deletion — see *il-/ne-* deletion.

open question — a question expecting a more extensive answer than a closed question, usually introduced by an interrogative word (cf. closed question).

oxymoron	a compressed paradox often containing contradictory terms, e.g. 'de joyeuses funérailles' (Bouraoui, l. 9).
parataxis	the linking of clauses or sentences by juxtaposition rather than by a specific linking word or device, e.g. 'La valise semble lourde pour le type, il change souvent de main' (Charef, l. 17).
popular etymology	an etymology which is not sound historically, based on some fanciful analysis and association of terms, e.g. 'Le Thé au harem d'Archi Ahmed' [= le théorème d'Archimède] (Charef, title).
register	the level of formality of the language (pronunciation, lexis and syntax) used; see low register and high register.
reprise	repetition in anticipation or recall by a subject or object pronoun or other part of speech, e.g. 'Toute sa ménagerie, Gaby la fourrait donc dans son bocal' (Gauvin, l. 51).
simile	a comparison between two objects or concepts expressed explicitly, e.g. 'Les élèves ricanaient, faisaient éclater Alexandre comme un coup de trompette: Alexan-ndre!' (Memmi, l. 8).
simple sentence	a sentence with only one main clause and no subordinate clauses, e.g. 'A la maison, les femmes parlent' (Beyala, l. 54).
sociolect	the collection of speech habits associated with a particular social group, as in the case of the *joual* of Quebec (Tremblay).
stream of consciousness	the representation of thought processes as they occur within the protagonist, based on free association and random ordering.
syllepsis	a construction in which one word (usually a verb) is applied in two differing senses to two other words or phrases, e.g. 'elle a vingt ans de plus que ma mère, un fils adipeux et des chucots dorés qui flamboient dans l'obscurité' (Bouraoui, l. 74).
tenor	the subject or starting point of an image (see vehicle for illustration).
vehicle	the analogy which is the basis of an image, e.g. 'Fama [tenor] avait comme le petit rat de marigot [vehicle] creusé le trou pour le serpent avaleur de rats' (Kourouma, l. 100).
verlan	a lexical process, typical of young, often marginalized, people, as a result of which words consisting of two syllables reverse the syllables, e.g. *tromé* from *métro*, and words consisting of a single syllable reverse their sounds (often accompanied by other adjustments), e.g. *beur* from *arabe*.

Part I

North Africa

Chapter 1

Introduction

Francophone Maghrebian literature arose out of the French presence in North African countries. It is a relatively new literature, emerging in the 1950s; by contrast, Arabic and Berber literatures – the latter exclusively oral – had existed for centuries prior to the onset of French colonization.

Although each of the three countries of the Maghreb (Morocco, Algeria and Tunisia) lived under French colonial rule, their experiences and the character of that rule differed markedly from one country to another. Under the second colonial empire, France launched a policy of expansion, conquering Algeria in 1830. Under the Third Republic, Tunisia and Morocco became French protectorates, in 1881 and 1912 respectively. The contact between North Africa and the French went hand in hand with the latter's policy of assimilation which imposed French educational and cultural systems upon the colonies. The impact of this policy was stronger in Algeria than in the neighbouring countries. The imposition of French as the sole language in education resulted in a number of future generations of Algerians being illiterate in their own native languages: Arabic and Berber. This phenomenon also explains the great number of Algerian writers who write in French in comparison, for example, with Tunisia where Arabic retained its official place in education despite the French colonial presence.

The early writing which emerged from Algeria was by *Pieds-noirs* – white settlers of French, Italian, Maltese and other Mediterranean origins who settled or were born in Algeria. Their writing was distinguishable from metropolitan French literature as it deployed images and expressions reflecting the settlers' experiences in North Africa. The writers of this period gathered in a movement called *Algérianisme* founded by Robert Randau. As such, they aimed to highlight their difference from France while at the same time taking pride in their western origins. The *Algérianistes* excluded Arabo-Berber cultures and peoples from their ranks and did not see the colonization of Algeria as an act of aggression that might reasonably be condemned.

Another group, more tolerant towards the indigenous people and more sympathetic to their struggle for liberation, brought to life a movement known as the Ecole d'Alger. Unlike Robert Randau's restrictive *Algérianisme*, the members of the Ecole d'Alger (among whom were Henri Kréa, Albert Camus, Gabriel Audisio and Jules Roy) advocated an Algerianist movement which celebrated a Mediterranean typology encompassing the whole melting pot of languages, cultures, ethnic groups and creeds that Algeria had become.

However, when the Algerian War broke out in 1954 under the banner of the FLN (Front de Libération Nationale), a new literature sprang into life. It was constituted by writers of Arab and Berber origins. Unlike the generation before, these writers were from the colonized ranks of society and their writing was fuelled by anti-colonial sentiments and the dream of a free Algeria.

The Algerian War was the bloodiest and most brutal and destructive war in the history of French colonization. Disillusioned and fed up by France's unfair discrimination against them, the Algerian Muslims, who made up the majority of the population, took up arms and sought independence and self-determination. The French policy of assimilation which promised equal education for all, provided it only to Algerians of western origin and a few privileged Muslims. The rest – the Muslim majority – were dismissed as second class and those who owned land were dispossessed in favour of settlers (a major fact to which a passage from Rachid Mimouni's *Le Fleuve détourné*, studied here (Chapter 4), alludes). What emphasized the unequal division between the settlers and the colonized in all three countries of the Maghreb was the manner in which Arabs and Berbers saw their status managed by a Bureau des Indigènes while the settlers enjoyed a similar administrative system to the French in France.

The denunciation of the French by pro-independence Algerians took place in writing, as well as on the ground. As most of the educated Algerians were illiterate in their native languages, when it came to their written forms, it was no surprise that French was the language in which they wrote. Though using French became a matter of great controversy for Algerians, Moroccans and Tunisians alike, it was nonetheless the majority's chosen idiom of expression. At first, it was hard for some to accept the use of French, considering its association with colonization, and those who used it often were subjected to heavy criticism for embracing a language epitomizing oppression. As a consequence, very early writing by Muslim North Africans, like that of the Algerian M'Hammed Ben Rahhal who published a short story, *La Vengeance du Cheikh* in 1891, was dismissed by generations of Maghrebians and went unnoticed. For others, like Jean Amrouche, his sister Taos Amrouche and mother Fadhma Amrouche, the situation was different. They belonged to a Kabyle family which had been converted to Christianity by missionaries, but lived and studied mainly in Tunisia. Jean Amrouche later became involved with the Ecole d'Alger. He published mainly poetry. His collection of poems *Cendres* (1934) dealt with the humiliation of the Algerian people brought about by the colonizers. His work also highlighted Berber culture and its oral literary tradition. Taos Amrouche was the first North African woman to publish a novel in French, *Jacinthe noire*, in 1947. Like her brother, she suffered the consequences of acculturation and tried to recapture her roots by her performances of Berber songs and dance.

The language question became less controversial as it became clear that French could be used to spread the message of anti-colonial struggle beyond North Africa. French thus became for the Maghrebian writer the means to communicate with western audiences and to share the experience of colonization with other colonized peoples.

Thus in the 1950s, at the height of the Algerian War, literary production soared in the Maghreb. The nuances of the new literature differed between countries. While in Algeria the tendency was geared more towards a literature of resistance and combat, Morocco and Tunisia produced a literature which exposed the alienation and hybridity of the colonized subject. Two such literary figures are Driss Chraïbi (Morocco) and Albert Memmi (Tunisia), whose work is analysed in this *Companion* (see Chapters 2 and 3). These writers' concern was to voice their alienation from their communities and respective Jewish and Muslim backgrounds, an alienation which stemmed from their close contact with the French educational system. That system was later criticized by Memmi in his essay on the effects of colonization, *Portrait du colonisé précédé du portrait du colonisateur* (1957), as a source of a cultural void for the colonized. For Algerian writers, however, there was no room to dwell on the conservative and religious restraints of their upbringing. They were intellectually engaged with the war and made it their prime concern. Kateb Yacine's canonical text *Nedjma* (1956) not only highlighted the case of colonized Algeria but also gave a new aesthetic dimension to the Maghrebian novel by subverting the linear structure of the Realist novels which preceded its publication. Two decades after Algeria's independence, Kateb Yacine ceased writing in French (Malek Haddad similarly did so) to show his opposition to the institutionalization of *francophonie*, which was perceived as a cultural imperial policy on the part of the French.

Other writers similarly engaged with the war, like Mouloud Mammeri and Mohammed Dib, used their writing to celebrate patriotic commitment and to chant war heroism. The determination of all three North African countries to gain independence figured largely in the literature of the period, to the extent that criticism was heaped upon any writer not addressing the question of resistance and war in his or her work. Such was the case for the Algerian Mouloud Feraoun and the Moroccan Ahmed Sefrioui, whose respective novels *Le Fils du pauvre* (1950) and *La Boîte à merveilles* (1954) were branded as self-exotic and ethnographic.

The declaration of independence of Morocco and Tunisia in 1956 and that of Algeria in 1962 saw the literary movement take a different direction with a different focus. Writers' main concerns centred on the internal situation of their newly autonomous countries. They focused their attention on the abuse of power by their leaders who took over the running of the countries after the French left. In Algeria, the FLN became the sole party, and in Morocco the monarchy held absolute power. Tunisia, by contrast, appeared less troubled under the reformist leadership of Habib Bourguiba.

In Algeria and Morocco, censorship inhibited freedom of expression and in some cases resulted in imprisonment. Consequently, it became common for writers to seek publication of their work outside their countries, mainly with French publishers, and to live in exile to safeguard their liberty of expression.

In Morocco, under the stewardship of the poet Abdellatif Laâbi, the literary review *Souffles* (and its Arabic equivalent *Anfas*) was founded in 1966. It became the forum for a new wave of Maghrebian literature. Among the contributors to the review were young writers and poets who later gained international acclaim. They included Tahar Ben Jelloun, Abdelkébir Khatibi, Mostafa Nissaboury and Mohammed Khaïr-Eddine. *Souffles*, however, was banned in the middle of the 1970s on the grounds of its Marxist overtones, and its founder Laâbi was jailed, not to be released until 1988.

In the 1970s and for most of the 1980s, North African writing was marked by a new style. Philosophical and semiological dimensions characterized the publications of such writers as Abdelkébir Khatibi (*La Mémoire tatouée*, 1971) and Abdelwahab Meddeb (*Talismano*, 1979). In this new writing, the French language was subverted and given highly sophisticated Arabo-Berber and Islamic characteristics. Language, history, identity and sexuality became key themes in the literature of this period.

From the 1980s to the present, North African women's writing has gained more prominence. In the Maghreb, women publish significantly less in French. However, the same is not necessarily true for arabophone and berberophone literatures. In Tunisia, for example, where Arabic has a wider audience, women have been prolific in publishing and cover most literary genres. Filmic texts, for instance, have been the object of interest for a number of women in the Maghreb, including more established women writers such as the Algerian Assia Djebar. For the latter and others, films seemed to be more accessible and an ideal medium to communicate with women, among whom the rate of illiteracy is considerably higher than for men in the Maghreb.

Women's writing in the 1990s witnessed a new surge. More women than before were published, with Algerian women being the majority. The dramatic political events that shook Algeria in the 1990s provided women with more opportunities to express themselves. Indeed, the cancellation of the 1992 elections by the Algerian army-backed government resulted in bloody confrontations between the state and the Islamists (led by the FIS, Front Islamique du Salut), which were to last for most of the 1990s. The dramatic escalation of the events spared no one in Algerian society. Women, in particular, were targeted for daring to question the patriarchal and authoritarian methods of Muslim fundamentalists and the military. Such views are voiced in the writing of Malika Mokeddem (*L'Interdite*, 1993), Leila Marouane (*Ravisseur*, 1998) and to some extent in the work of Nina Bouraoui, an extract from whose *La Voyeuse interdite* (1991) is studied here (see Chapter 8).

The Algerian civil war of the 1990s hindered the work of many intellectuals who found themselves unable to exercise their freedom of expression without falling prey to either the army-led government or to the intolerant factions of Islamists. A number of journalists and writers were assassinated – including the novelist Tahar Djaout and the Berber activist and poet-singer Lounès Maatoub – for defending and practising the right to freedom of expression.

On the contrary, in Morocco, the last part of the 1990s witnessed a loosening of the reins of governmental power. Political prisoners and exiles, including Abraham Serfaty, were granted their freedom and were able to return from exile. Fictional themes, which very often stemmed from real-life experiences, such as corruption, repudiation and an unfair legal system, were backed by factual journalistic reports owing to the newly acquired freedom of the press. Accordingly, Morocco is undergoing considerable political and cultural reform, making progress on its commitments to democratic values and the respect of human rights.

The policy of arabization which swept through North Africa in the aftermath of independence did not hinder the progress of Maghrebian literature written in French. If anything, the enforcement of the Arabic language and culture provided additional value to a literature whose founders primarily relied on their knowledge of French culture. Arabization provided Maghrebian writers, whether of the older or the newer generation, with an in-depth knowledge of Arabo-Muslim philosophy and arts. In turn, by incorporating their newly acquired knowledge of Arabic thought into their writing, these writers enriched the French literary scene with innovative ideas and approaches.

Further to Maghrebian writers' output in French, authors born into North African immigrant families in France launched in the 1980s what is currently known as *beur* fiction. Such literature distinguishes itself by its thematic approaches, which highlight the identity and socio-economic problems young people of Maghrebian origins encounter in France. The duality and hybrid status of the *Beurs* remain, for publishers, critics and academics alike, problematic and difficult to classify. While some believe in the integration of *beur* fiction into mainstream French literature, others see it as emanating from the Arabo-Berber and Islamic cultures of North Africa and, consequently, link it with francophone Maghrebian literature. Arguably, however, *beur* fiction is best classified as a bridging literature between cultures – French and North African – which are so different and yet are so closely tied by history.

Further reading

Arnaud, Jacqueline, *La Littérature maghrébine de langue française* (Paris: Publisud, 1986).

Chikhi, Beïda, *Maghreb en textes* (Paris: L'Harmattan, 1996).

Déjeux, Jean, *Situation de la littérature maghrébine de langue française* (Algiers: Office des Publications Universitaires, 1982).

Djaout, Tahar, *Les Mots migrateurs: écrivains francophones du Maghreb* (Algiers: Office des Publications Universitaires, 1984)

Hargreaves, Alec G., *Voices from the North African Community in France: Immigration and Identity in Beur Fiction* (Oxford: Berg, 1991).

Jack, Belinda, *Francophone Literatures* (Oxford: Oxford University Press, 1996).

Khatibi, Abdelkébir, *Maghreb pluriel* (Paris: Denoël, 1983).

Mortimer, Mildred, (ed.), *Maghrebian Mosaic: a Literature in Transition* (Boulder, Colo.: Lynne Rienner, 2000).

Research in African Literatures, Special Issue on North African Literature 23, 2 (1992).

Segarra, Marta, *Leur pesant de poudre: romancières francophones du Maghreb* (Paris: L'Harmattan, 1997).

Stora, Benjamin, *La Gangrène de l'oubli: la mémoire de la guerre d'Algérie* (Paris: La Découverte, 1995).

Chapter 2

Driss Chraïbi

Le Passé simple (Paris: Denoël, 1954), pp. 42–6.

Je ne sais si j'ai rêvé ou simplement somnolé. Tout d'abord je me sentis coupable de m'être apitoyé sur un passé – fût-il le mien – puis je repris ma lucidité et tout me frappa simultanément, comme autant de notes suraiguës: le mendiant ne hurlait plus, l'horloge sonnait onze heures et le Seigneur était debout, face à Camel qui se déchaussait. Manifestement, Camel était ivre.

Tout de suite après, je perçus les corollaires et je sus que mes sens étaient aux aguets. La nuque du Seigneur était rouge, par la fenêtre entraient des bolées d'air frais et le visage de mon frère, tel que je le voyais de mon coin, était insolite. J'annihilai tout ce qui n'était pas ce visage, analysant, définissant, supputant, essayant de prévoir. Vélocement. Un instant bref. Effet de l'éthylation ou bien résultat de cet éclairage faible? Deux arcades sourcilières, deux pommettes, un appendice nasal, une mâchoire et des zones d'ombre, cette tête avait quelque chose de brutal.

Une phrase de Roche me revint à l'esprit:

– L'habit fait le moine. Persuade-toi un quart d'heure que tu as mal aux dents. Un quart d'heure après, tu as effectivement mal aux dents.

C'était peut-être cela: depuis le parc Murdoch, tout avait été dramatique et tout devait me sembler ainsi. Mais Camel releva la tête et je fus certain que c'était une tête de révolté. Je vis que la nuque du Seigneur était devenue violette. Mon échine suinta froid. Je plongeai le poing dans ma poche. Le fermai sur mon couteau à cran d'arrêt.

Je souriais. Ce couteau avait tout coupé: les feuillets de mes livres, le cou des coqs de l'Aïd Seghir (32 au total), la gorge des moutons de l'Aïd El Kébir (10 au total) et, une fois, à la naissance d'Hamid, le ventre de ma mère. Après ce dernier exploit, on s'en était débarrassé dans une des caisses du grenier où je le découvris, le dérouillai, fourbis et aiguisai – si minutieusement qu'il avait pris l'aspect d'un tranchet. Puis le mis dans ma poche, persuadé qu'il pourrait encore servir, d'autres moutons à égorger, une autre césarienne à opérer – et, un jour parmi les jours créés par Dieu, avec un peu d'adresse, un peu de sang-froid, le lancer vers le Seigneur, quelque part vers le corps du Seigneur, vers sa nuque par exemple, où il se planterait jusqu'au manche, comme une aiguille.

– Femme!

Un claquement avait jailli de ses paumes. Sa nuque se décongestionnait. De ma poche le couteau sortait à demi. Je l'enfouis précipitamment. «Celui dont tu ne veux pas voir le visage dans la rue te montrera son derrière au bain maure», disent les Bédouins. J'étais un peu déçu, mais résigné.

Ma mère fut présente comme si elle eût émergé d'une trappe, vêtements amples, tête des dimensions d'une main ouverte, chevelure coulant lourde sur ses hanches.

– Maître . . . commença-t-elle.

Elle souscrivait à toutes les catastrophes éventuelles. Qu'était-elle, sinon une femme dont le Seigneur pouvait cadenasser les cuisses et sur laquelle il avait droit de vie et de mort? Elle avait toujours habité des maisons à portes barricadées et fenêtres grillagées. Des terrasses, il n'y avait que le ciel à voir – et les minarets, symboles. Une parmi les créatures de Dieu que le Coran a parquées: «Baisez-les et les rebaisez; par le vagin, c'est plus utile; ensuite, ignorez-les jusqu'à la jouissance prochaine.» Oui, ma mère était ainsi, faible, soumise, passive. Elle avait enfanté sept fois, à intervalles réguliers, deux ans. Dont un fils qui ne pouvait qu'être ivrogne et moi, qui la jugeais.

Il ne lui accorda pas un regard et je compris que Camel était gracié, provisoirement.

– Tout le monde est-il encore en ablutions?

C'était une question rituelle. Ce soir elle tombait avec deux heures de retard, voilà tout. Mais oui! mes frères n'ont pas pété, ma mère est en perpétuel état de grâce . . . ah si! Camel a bu et je suis un parjure, mais qu'est cela? La foi est sauve et Dieu très puissant et très miséricordieux.

Nous nous plaçâmes en triangle isocèle et la prière commença. Le canard de tête était naturellement le Seigneur. Nous nous agenouillions, prosternions, lui sur son tapis de prière, nous sur la mosaïque froide. Il déclamait un verset, puis un autre, choisissant les plus longs, les plus rythmés, les plus monotones. Nous psalmodions «Dieu est grand» à chaque agenouillement et «Gloire au Très-Haut» à chaque prosternation. J'écoutais cette voix grave dénuée du moindre friselis. Elle était celle d'un homme qui parlait à Dieu d'égal à égal.

Nous . . . bien sûr! même moi, nous remuions les lèvres, accomplissions consciencieusement notre mimique et récitions mentalement ce que le Seigneur disait tout haut. Mais nos véritables prières étaient:

Camel: bordel de bordel! Quelle correction il va m'allonger! J'aurais dû rester au bordel.

Ma mère: . . . dévoués à mon Seigneur et maître . . . Saints des Grecs et des Russes, un petit accident, une chute dans l'escalier, un microbe inédit ou une bombe allemande, n'importe quoi, je veux mourir . . . Saints des Grecs et des Russes . . .

Mes autres frères: Rien.

Moi: qu'est-ce qu'il peut donc avoir?

Et par-dessus, comme la fanfare de l'Archange, la clameur du mendiant revenu soudain à la charge:

– M'entends-tu, m'entends-tu? . . .

Nous nous agenouillions une dernière fois, crevâmes l'œil de Satan, dîmes «Amen» et le Seigneur se leva, saisit Camel à bras le corps, le projeta contre le mur.

– Ceci, appuya-t-il, pour le vin que tu as honoré.

Le ramassa littéralement, le lança de nouveau.

– Et ceci pour l'idée de révolte que tu viens d'avoir à l'instant.

Et lui tourna le dos, me fit face.

– Le couteau!

J'étais encore agenouillé. Je me levai.

– Quel couteau?

Il plongea la main dans ma poche.

– Celui-là.

Le tenant entre le pouce et l'index, il fit un geste bref. La lame jaillit blanche, fine, longue, un vrai tranchet.

– Prends.

Je le pris.

– Je vais te tourner le dos et compter jusqu'à 10. A 10, tu le lanceras.

Il sourit.

– Vers la nuque par exemple, tu la jaugeais tout à l'heure.

Son sourire se résorba.

– A moins, ajouta-t-il, que tu ne puisses pas attendre jusqu'à 10.

Et se retourna, se mit à compter. La demie de onze heures sonna. Le mendiant entonna le chapitre des malédictions.

– . . . 2 . . . 3 . . .

Je regardai le couteau, regardai Camel, regardai ma mère. Camel était tombé, près du pain d'orge, à la place qu'il occupait tous les soirs. Il demeurait immobile, me regardait sans me voir. Il avait eu son compte. Le reste, tout le vaste reste lui importait peu. Il saignait du nez, des lèvres, d'une coupure à l'arcade sourcilière.

Ma mère non plus ne bougeait pas. Sa tête était obstinément penchée. Ses lèvres balbutiaient comme les lèvres d'un prêtre, mais probablement étaient-ce les saints des Grecs et des Russes qu'elle continuait d'invoquer. Puisque tout était écrit, même l'assassinat de son époux.

Cinq paires d'yeux suivaient mes gestes: un geste et cinq estomacs seraient calmés, cinq existences s'épanouiraient au soleil.

– . . . 6 . . . 7 . . .

Je considérai le couteau. Que disait Roche?

– Depuis l'époque des Califes, vous autres, Arabes, n'avez cessé de digérer et de dormir. Ce qu'il vous faut, c'est une bonne petite guerre.

Au bout de ma main, il y avait l'acte – qui nous accomplirait tous. Je fermai le couteau.

– . . . 9 . . .

– Arrête!

Ma mère se dressait devant moi. Je lui présentai l'arme devenue inoffensive. Sa bouche se tordit: reconnaissance ou dégoût? Je n'eus pas le temps de décanter, le couteau était déjà entre les mains du Seigneur.

– Bien, femme.

Text and context

Driss Chraïbi's *Le Passé simple* tells the story of a son rebelling against his father. The story takes place in 1930s Morocco with the French protectorate still in place. The violent revolt of the protagonist against his father is to be understood as a revolt both against the biological father as head of the family and against the French protectorate whose 'protection' was a thin disguise for colonization.

The extract describes the violence which dominates the entire narrative of *Le Passé simple* . It illustrates the hatred of the son for his father. The scene of the knife in this passage is the culmination of years of abuse the protagonist, his mother and brothers suffered under the father's authority. The desire to stab the father and kill him is described in this passage as a liberating act which the protagonist feels compelled to carry out.

The extract, like the novel as a whole, is narrated in the first person. The narrator/protagonist is called Driss (the same first name as the author) which, along with other factual elements relating to the writer's life throughout the novel, suggests that the story has a significant autobiographical dimension. From the opening sentence of the extract, the reader is made aware of the fact that the narrator is telling his past. Like most autobiographies, and especially those which deal with a past life and past experiences, the tone used is often elegiac, hence the narrator's words: 'm'être apitoyé sur un passé' (l. 2). The past that the narrator recounts starts on a day of Ramadan. Ramadan is a month in the Muslim calendar during which Muslims, from puberty, must abstain from food and drink from dawn to sunset. Other activities are also prohibited during this month, such as sex and gambling. In general, the Muslim is expected to observe fasting as well as adhere to a pious code of behaviour. Camel, one of the protagonist's brothers, breaks all rules in one act: he is drunk during the month of Ramadan. The consumption of alcohol is strictly forbidden by the Muslim religion. Drinking during Ramadan is a double sacrilege in the eyes of Muslims. To underline the extent of Camel's offence to his family and religion, the narrator informs the reader that while awaiting his father's punishment for turning up late and drunk, Camel wished he had stayed where he spent most of his day: in a brothel ('J'aurais dû rester au bordel'; (l. 66)). In the eyes of the father, Camel has committed a serious crime for which he has to be punished. However, for the narrator, Camel's attitude provokes empathy. For him, Camel's act is not a crime but a revolt, as expressed in the statement: 'Mais Camel releva la tête et je fus certain que c'était une tête de révolté' (l. 17).

An atmosphere of fear permeates this passage – fear of the punishment the father is reserving for Camel. The father appears to hold absolute power over his family; this is expressed by the generic appellation 'le Seigneur'. Le Seigneur appears as a Godlike figure, but rather than being compassionate as one would expect of someone with godly attributes, he is described as brutal, harsh and violent. In describing him thus, the passage seems to offer the reader the two characteristics associated with God in Islam. He is a compassionate God, yet one who punishes those who deviate from the right path. Ironically, the latter is the dominant characteristic of le Seigneur. His violence shows in the brutal punishment he inflicts on Camel. Camel is thrown across the room twice: the first time for drinking and the second time for having expressed disrespect to the law of le Seigneur. The violence of such physical punishment is witnessed helplessly by the narrator: 'Il saignait du nez, des lèvres, d'une coupure à l'arcade sourcilière' (l. 104).

Unlike his brothers and mother who seem resigned to their fate and submissive to the authority of le Seigneur, the protagonist is less inclined to obey the rules. He is, indeed, ready to bring to an end the tyrannical situation he, his siblings and mother have to endure. The murder of the father appears to be the only way to freedom from suffering. What the passage shows, however, is that murdering the father is not a spontaneous decision on the part of the protagonist. It is a premeditated and calculated act. He is in possession of a knife, which he has scrupulously polished and sharpened, with the conscious wish that it will serve him to carry out the killing. The scene is highly Freudian. The knife as a phallic symbol entails a quest for power that will inevitably lead to the sought-after freedom. By asking the following question: 'qu'est-ce qu'il peut donc avoir?' (l. 73), the protagonist implicitly wonders about the power le Seigneur holds. The extract hints at the despotic nature of this power. This could be understood, for example, through the metaphor of the triangle ('Nous nous plaçâmes en triangle isocèle'; l. 56) the family forms in order to pray. It shows a hierarchical structure whereby one person is placed at the head and others line up behind. While in the context of prayer it displays the notion of the *imam* (leader) leading his congregation in prayer, the strongest sense of this metaphor is the noticeable inequality between le Seigneur and the other members of the family. In connection with his abusive power, the triangular structure is therefore one which pertains to despotism and absolutism: one tyrannical figure as a master on top and the powerless masses forming the base. As a master, le Seigneur enjoys privileges, as is suggested by him sitting on a rug while the others pray directly on the bare cold floor.

Killing the father would not only mean putting an end to his misuse of power but would also free the rest of the family from their miserable existence. This is expressed by the protagonist who feels that the future depends on his act: 'un geste et cinq estomacs seraient calmés, cinq existences s'épanouiraient au soleil' (l. 109). The protagonist sees himself as playing the role of a saviour. Being in possession of a knife provides him with the strength to protect his brothers and mother. Though the extract does not display it as much as does the whole of *Le Passé simple*, the mother is the central preoccupation for the protagonist.

The passage shows the reader how women, alongside children, have no say in their own life within a society entrenched in religion and tradition. The patriarchal climate which dominates in the passage is one which subjugates the protagonist's mother. She is enslaved by le Seigneur and his power. He commands her by the appellation 'femme' and a click of fingers. In return she obeys him and calls him 'maître'. So, rather than being a husband and wife relationship, theirs is that of master and slave. The protagonist sees her as a shapeless being. She is described as wearing clothes much larger than her (l. 36), which hints at the Muslim tradition whereby a woman's body should be effaced and asexual. She is no more than an object to serve le Seigneur and to satisfy his sexual needs. He has the power of life and death over her. The reader is also told that she is confined to her home. To be prisoner in a house is part of her lot as a woman.

The fact that the reader is told that the mother has always lived a confined life strengthens the idea of woman as a commodity. She has been passed from the authority of a father to that of a husband. The only access she has to the outside world is through the house terrace, but even then the symbolic minarets which dominate the view are there to remind her of the patriarchal order. Far from being completely resigned to her fate, the mother seeks salvation from her endurance by wishing for death. The irony here is that her prayers are directed to other than Muslim saints (l. 68). This could probably be understood as her way of rejecting anything that has a connection with the religious traditions which bestow on le Seigneur the power to subjugate her.

Death, whether hers or her husband's, is for the mother the key to freedom. However, the failure of the protagonist to carry out the act leaves him wondering about his mother's attitude to the whole incident: 'Sa bouche se tordit: reconnaissance ou dégoût?' (l. 119). Though the passage might suggest that she is the one who stopped her son from killing his father and receiving thus the approval of the latter, it is in fact the protagonist's own decision not to do so. He closes the offensive weapon before le Seigneur finishes the countdown. What the passage shows is the unshakeable patriarchal power le Seigneur represents. It is the kind of power which not only enslaves the individual but also dispossesses him or her of the ability to rebel. The individual is thus unwilling, if not incapable, to alter his or her destiny.

Further reading

Chraïbi, Driss, *Succession ouverte* (Paris: Denoël, 1962).
—— *La Civilisation, ma Mère!...* (Paris: Denoël, 1972).
—— *La Mère du printemps* (Paris: Seuil, 1982).
—— *L'Inspecteur Ali* (Paris: Denoël, 1991).

Basfao, Kacem, 'Pour une relance de l'affaire du *Passé simple*', *Itinéraires et contacts de cultures* 11, 2 (1990), pp. 57–66.
Benchama, Lahcen, *L'Œuvre de Driss Chraïbi* (Paris: L'Harmattan, 1994).
Ibnlfassi, Laïla, 'Chraïbi's *Le Passé simple* and a theory of doubles', in L. Ibnlfassi and N. Hitchcott (eds), *African Francophone Writing* (Oxford: Berg, 1996), pp. 59–67.
Kadra-Hadjadji, Houaria, *Contestation et révolte dans l'œuvre de Driss Chraïbi* (Paris: Publisud, 1986).
Laâbi, Abdellatif, 'Défense du *Passé simple*', *Souffles* No. 5 (1967), pp. 18–21.
Meyer, Martine, 'A reinterpretation of Driss Chraïbi's trilogy: shrinking the father', *The Maghreb Review* 18, 1–2 (1993).

Language and style

Prominent from a lexical point of view are the quantity and exploitation of vocabulary describing parts of the body of the protagonists. Certain words acquire particular significance. Foremost among these is 'nuque' with reference to le Seigneur, a metonym for his power. It occurs on five occasions. Le Seigneur's suppressed anger at Camel's behaviour in holding up the family's daily prayers is shown by the change in the colour of the back of his neck: from red (l. 7) to violet (l. 18); his anger is released as prayers begin – 'Sa nuque se décongestionnait' (l. 32). Le Seigneur's omniscience is revealed as he reads Driss's thoughts – 'tu le [le couteau] lanceras . . . Vers la nuque par exemple, tu la jaugeais tout à l'heure' (l. 95; compare l. 29). His power is also seen in references made to his hands, which take possession of the knife (ll. 32, 87, 89, 121), and his arrogant physical movements, e.g. 'tourner le dos' (ll. 83, 93) and 'faire face' (l. 83). Le Seigneur's overweening despotism contrasts strikingly with the submissiveness and passivity of the rest of the family. Whereas he has a voice – 'cette voix grave dénuée du moindre friselis' (l. 61) – which confers authority upon him, the others are denied such a possibility; they, especially Driss's mother, are portrayed as simply lips (ll. 63, 105) or a mouth (l. 120). This lack of an identity is echoed in other references to the members of the family. They become an undifferentiated group, consisting only of eyes and stomachs (l. 109). The description of Driss's mother is more detailed but at the same time emphasizes her subordinate position as producer of children – 'elle avait enfanté sept fois' (l. 46) – as sexual tool, as most of the words relate to her lower body, 'ventre' (l. 23), 'chevelure' (l. 37), 'hanches' (l. 38), 'cuisses' (l. 41), 'vagin' (l. 45). Her head is described as 'des dimensions d'une main ouverte' (l. 37) and is lowered (l. 105) in respect of her husband. As for Camel, it is his head which is focused on – his face fascinates Driss (ll. 8–12) and shows his revolt (l. 18, where 'tête' is repeated). His facial features mentioned earlier as a gesture of revolt are bleeding as a result of le Seigneur's brutal attack (l. 104). As for Driss, he attempts to stay in the background and out of sight of his father – the words relating to his body are 'échine' (l. 18), 'poing', moving surreptitiously (l. 19), 'main' impotent to act (l. 115). To return to the matter of speech, the dominance of le Seigneur is emphasized by the fact that, apart from three minor utterances, his is the only voice that is heard. Two of the minor utterances come from Driss's mother: a subservient 'Maître' (l. 39), an ambiguous 'Arrête' (l. 118); the other is a disingenuous 'Quel couteau?' (l. 86) from Driss himself.

The passage is characterized by a number of unusual syntactic features, many of them related to the drama of certain events, the speed of the action or the passing of time. On five occasions, Chraïbi omits the subject pronoun at the beginning of a sentence if it would be the same as in the preceding sentence, e.g. 'Je plongeai le poing dans ma poche. Le fermai sur mon couteau' (l. 19, also l. 26). More unusual still are the sections ll. 80–3 and 96–8, where passages of speech from le Seigneur cut into the narrative constructed in exactly this way. The purpose is no doubt to convey graphically the speed of the sequence of events, as le Seigneur attacks Camel and taunts Driss. The dynamic piling up of verbs is used to indicate the intensity of a situation, e.g. 'J'annihilai tout ce qui n'était pas ce visage, analysant, définissant, supputant, essayant de prévoir' (l. 9), 'dans une des caisses du grenier où je le découvris, le dérouillai, fourbis et aiguisai' (l. 24, also ll. 63, 77, 78). A similar effect is produced by the use of triplets, which abound in the passage, e.g. 'Il déclamait un verset, puis un autre, choisissant les plus longs, les plus rythmés, les plus monotones' (l. 58, also ll. 4, 7, 36, 46, 63, 89, 101). Minor sentences have the effect of suggesting impending doom about to crash in on the family, e.g. 'Vélocement. Un instant bref. Effet de l'éthylation ou bien résultat de cet éclairage faible?' (l. 10), as does the sequence of three short simple sentences a little later (l. 18). The absence of conjunctions linking clauses and groups of words also contributes to the tension of the drama, e.g. 'Nous nous agenouillions, prosternions, lui sur son tapis de prière, nous sur la mosaïque froide' (l. 57, also ll. 67, 77). The use of the apposition of 'symboles' to 'les minarets' (l. 43) is another very economical way of expressing the dominant religious and sexual position of le Seigneur.

Repetition allows for the painstakingly precise reporting of an incident, e.g. 'Je regardai le couteau, regardai Camel, regardai ma mère' (l. 101); this may even be achieved through the repetition of a preposition, e.g. 'le lancer vers le Seigneur, quelque part vers le corps du Seigneur, vers sa nuque' (l. 28). The pace of the passage slows down in the paragraph devoted to Driss's mother (beginning l. 40): she is summed up in a very few words, 'ma mère était ainsi, faible, soumise, passive. Elle avait enfanté sept fois, à intervalles réguliers, deux ans' (l. 46) – scarcely human.

Time is also significant with the use of certain single-word, polysyllabic adverbs ending in *-ment*, placed at strategic points in the passage: the adverbs may constitute a minor sentence, e.g. l.10, be sentence initial, e.g. l. 5, clause/sentence final, e.g. ll. 3, 33, 50, 81, occur after a dash, e.g. l. 25, create symmetry, e.g. '[nous] accomplissions consciencieusement notre mimique et récitions mentalement ce que le Seigneur disait' (l. 63). The use of these long adverbs is like the tolling of a bell (compare ll. 4, 98) and parallels the shouting of the beggar (ll. 3, 74, 98).

The passage opens with an alliterative sentence (l. 1), where the *s*-sounds suggest drowsiness, and later there are two sentences with a preponderance of *p*-sounds (ll. 19, 26), which, through their plosive quality, imply determination on Driss's part. Furthermore most of the imagery in the passage is concentrated on a single theme – sound (the symbolism of voices, the effect of the bell striking and the beggar shouting have already been mentioned): Driss is roused from his drowsiness by events around him 'comme autant de notes suraiguës' (l. 3); the beggar's shout is 'comme la fanfare de l'Archange' (l. 74), his mother's lips mumble 'comme les lèvres d'un prêtre' (l. 106). The remaining image, relating to Driss's fantasy about stabbing his father, echoes the first one with its reference to sharpness: 'le [couteau] lancer vers le Seigneur . . . vers sa nuque . . . où il se planterait jusqu'au manche, comme une aiguille' (l. 28).

A combination of many features make this a skilfully crafted text – alliteration, imagery, use of repetition, triplets, absence of conjunctions and subject pronouns, all used in a very economical manner. The title of the book *Le Passé simple* obviously refers to Driss's attempt to relate his autobiography, but the syntactic allusion is inescapable. The novel is written mainly in the past historic tense – *le passé simple* – which accords well with the high tone of the narrative and which allows the narrator a certain detachment from the events and the possibility of judging his own actions.

Chapter 3

Albert Memmi

La Statue de sel (Paris: Gallimard, revised edition 1966), pp 107–11.

La Ville

Je m'appelle Mordekhaï, Alexandre Benillouche.

Ah! ce sourire fielleux de mes camarades! A l'Impasse, à l'Alliance, j'ignorais que je portais un nom si ridicule, si révélateur. Au lycée, j'en pris conscience au premier appel. Désormais, le seul énoncé de mon nom, qui accélérait mon pouls, me faisait honte.

Alexandre: claironnant, glorieux, me fut donné par mes parents en hommage à l'Occident prestigieux. Il leur semblait traduire l'image qu'ils avaient de l'Europe. Les élèves ricanaient, faisaient éclater Alexandre comme un coup de trompette: Alexan-ndre! Alors je détestais mon prénom de toutes mes forces et aussi mes camarades. Je les détestais et leur donnais raison, et en voulais à mes parents de ce choix stupide.

Mordekhaï, Mridakh en diminutif, marquait ma participation à la tradition juive. C'était le nom redoutable d'un glorieux Macchabée, celui aussi de mon grand-père, débile vieillard, qui jamais n'oublia les terreurs du ghetto.

Appelez-vous Pierre ou Jean, et changeant d'habit vous changerez de statut apparent. Dans ce pays, Mridakh est si obstinément révélateur, qu'il équivaut à clamer «je suis juif!» et plus précisément «j'habite le ghetto», «je suis de statut indigène», «je suis de mœurs orientales», «je suis pauvre». Et j'avais appris à refuser ces quatre titres. Il serait facile de me le reprocher et je n'y ai pas manqué depuis. Mais comment ne pas avoir honte de sa condition, après avoir été méprisé, moqué ou consolé depuis l'enfance? J'ai appris à interpréter les sourires, à deviner aux chuchotements, à lire dans les yeux, à reconstituer les raisonnements au hasard d'une phrase, d'un saisi au vol. Quand on parle de moi, *a priori* je me sens agressé, mon poil se hérisse et j'ai envie de mordre. Bien sûr, on arrive à tout accepter, au prix de grands efforts ou d'une complète lassitude. Mais d'abord on se refuse et l'on se déteste ou bien, pour défier les mépris des autres, on revendique même ses laideurs, on s'exagère et l'on grimace.

Au lycée, rapidement, j'ai pris l'habitude de sauter Mordekhaï dans mes copies;

et bientôt je l'oubliai comme une vieille peau. Mais cette peau traînait, bien collée. A propos des appels officiels, des convocations, de tout événement extra-quotidien, elle se rappelait à mon attention. A la fin de ma scolarité, le jour du baccalauréat, je devais être un des triomphateurs. J'attendais, certain, à peine angoissé au milieu d'une foule nerveuse, lorsque l'appariteur grimpa sur une chaise: j'étais le premier de la liste. Mais rétablissant l'ordre exact de mon état civil, l'appariteur avait crié, dans le silence tendu:

– Mordekhaï, Alexandre, Benillouche!

Alors je ne bougeai pas. La foule étonnée de ce calme chercha des yeux l'heureux candidat. Il n'y eut aucune explosion de joie, personne ne jeta ses cahiers en l'air, ne fut entouré, embrassé. Je n'aimais pas que mes parents m'assistent dans les événements publics de ma vie et je ne les avais pas avertis de l'heure des résultats. Je me contentai de sourire aux camarades qui me félicitaient du regard. Chacun, d'ailleurs, était occupé de son propre destin.

Mordekhaï, Alexandre, Benillouche. Benillouche enfin, Ben-Illouche ou le fils de l'agneau en patois berbéro-arabe. De quelle tribu montagnarde mes ancêtres sont-ils sortis? Qui suis-je enfin?

Scrutant mes traits aux angles nets, fouillant l'état civil, j'ai essayé de retrouver quelque fil qui me conduirait à ce que je suis. Un jour, je crus me découvrir issu d'une famille de princes berbères, judaïsés par la Kahéna, cette reine guerrière qui fonda un royaume juif en plein Atlas. Je me réjouis de sortir du cœur de ce pays. Une autre fois, je me trouvai descendant d'un peintre italien de la Renaissance. Je découpai l'article du gros Larousse et montrai à mes amis les toiles de mon aïeul. La philologie rendait compte de la transformation, et Sitboun, le meilleur en latin, m'approuva. Même, il me signala un homonyme en un bienfaiteur d'un poète latin. Mais la science philologique est fragile et le passé trop lointain. Descendrais-je d'une tribu berbère que les Berbères ne me reconnaîtraient pas, car je suis juif et non musulman, citadin et non montagnard; porterais-je le nom exact du peintre que les Italiens ne m'accueilleraient pas, car je suis africain et non européen. Toujours je me retrouverai Alexandre Mordekhaï Benillouche, indigène dans un pays de colonisation, juif dans un univers antisémite, Africain dans un monde où triomphe l'Europe.

Si je croyais aux signes, ne pourrais-je dire que mon nom renferme déjà le sens de ma vie? Comment faire une synthèse, polie comme un son de flûte, de tant de disparités?

Et ma ville natale est à mon image. Par la rue Tarfoune, l'Impasse conduisait à l'école de l'Alliance; de la maison à la cour de l'école, l'atmosphère restait homogène, familiale. Nous étions entre juifs et de même classe, sans conscience douloureuse ni grimaces. Nous parlions patois, malgré les affiches du directeur qui exigeaient le français à l'école. Je traversais quelquefois un quartier musulman, comme on traverse une rivière à gué. En allant au lycée, j'allais faire connaissance avec la ville. J'avais cru que, par une faveur insigne, on m'ouvrait les portes du monde, je n'aurais qu'à y entrer pour être accueilli avec joie: je me découvris irréductiblement étranger dans ma ville natale. Et, comme une mère, une ville natale ne se remplace pas.

Un homme voyage, s'étonne, se diversifie, devient un inconnu pour ses parents et même pour ses amis; mais au cœur il garde un noyau dur: son appartenance certaine à quelque village anonyme. Vaincu, aveugle, par l'imagination il se réfère à cette borne; ses mains, ses pieds en connaissent les contours, ses nerfs miraculeusement s'y accordent. Moi, je suis un bâtard de ma ville natale. O ville prostituée, au cœur fragmentaire, qui ne t'a eue pour esclave? Quand je sus un peu d'histoire, j'en eus le vertige: Phéniciens, Romains, Vandales, Byzantins, Berbères, Arabes, Espagnols, Turcs, Italiens, Français, j'en oublie et je dois en confondre. Cinq cents pas de promenade et l'on change de civilisation. Voici la ville arabe, ses maisons aux visages fermés, ses longs conduits de silence et d'ombre débouchant sur des foules compactes, les ruelles juives, agitées, sordides et familières, creusées d'échoppes, boutiques et bistrots, entassant au mieux leurs maisons difformes; la petite Sicile où la misère attend aux pas des portes, les fondouks collectifs des Maltais, bizarres Européens au parler arabe, de nationalité britannique, l'église russe orthodoxe, enluminures et coupoles, conçue un soir de rêve moscovite, le petit train belge, électrique et propre, net comme un intérieur flamand, les buildings de la Standard Oil, l'aérodrome et le cimetière américain, matériel perfectionné, jeeps et camions au service exclusif des morts, la Shell Company ou le pétrole anglais, la résidence des ambassadeurs de Sa Majesté britannique; voici les maisonnettes des rentiers français, toits couverts de tuiles rouges et jardins plantés de choux, tout comme dans une chanson.

Et dans cette diversité, où n'importe qui se sent chez soi et personne à l'aise, chacun enfermé dans son quartier a peur de son voisin, le méprise ou le hait. La peur et le mépris, nous les avons connus dès l'éveil de notre conscience, dans cette ville malodorante, sale et débraillée. Et pour nous défendre, pour nous venger, nous méprisions, nous ricanions . . . entre nous; espérant être craints autant que nous craignions. Dans cette atmosphère, nous vivions à table, à l'école, dans la rue. Lorsque, trop neufs, sceptiques, nous espérions encore, on nous promettait des trahisons et des aubes sanglantes. Lentement, comme par un poison absorbé goutte à goutte, ma sensibilité, mes sentiments, toute mon âme fut envahie, repétrie, j'appris à faire l'odieux inventaire. Au-delà d'une politesse cérémonieuse, chacun reste sournoisement hostile aux autres et définitivement ulcéré par sa propre image qu'il découvre chez eux.

On peut rater son enfance ou sa vie. Lentement, douloureusement, je compris que j'avais raté ma naissance à ma ville.

Text and context

Along with Driss Chraïbi and others, Albert Memmi is a co-founder of North African literature expressed in French. His first novel, *La Statue de sel* , first published in 1953, is a canonical text in the study of colonized nations and individuals. At the time of the publication of *La Statue de sel*, Tunisia (home of the author and the setting for the novel) was still under French rule. The country became independent in 1956. The major theme Memmi explores in the text is the destructive long-term effect of colonization on the colonized individual, especially the problems of alienation and assimilation.

La Statue de sel is quasi-autobiographical. Narrated in the first person, it is an account of the life of a Jewish Tunisian boy growing up in the Jewish quarter in Tunis. Memmi's life story, as embodied by his fictional counterpart, Alexandre, is structured in the *Bildungsroman* style. The whole novel is a kind of *bilan* whereby the narrator/protagonist assesses his life. In so doing – as is common in autobiographical writing – he tries to locate and define an identity for himself within a society fragmented by the effects of colonization. In such writing, there is an inevitable return to one's past life – a return that the writer warns about, as it can be detrimental. The dangers of introspection are hinted at in the title of the novel. The biblical allusion to the plight of Lot's wife, who turned into a pillar of salt for looking back, is a reminder that delving into past memories can have petrifying consequences and can profoundly disable the quest for identity. In other words, the search for identity can lead to a destructive realization of the self, as the narrator discovers at his own expense: 'je meurs pour m'être retourné sur moi-même' (p. 368).

The passage here is extracted from the second part (of three) of the novel, entitled 'Alexandre Mordekhaï Benillouche', the name of the narrator/protagonist. In this passage, from the chapter 'La ville', the narrator introduces himself to the reader against the background of the city where he was born and grew up. The city, as revealed in this extract, displays a hybrid structure which parallels the hybrid identity of the hero.

The hero's father has Italian origins and his mother is Berber. His very name – Alexandre Mordekhaï Benillouche – is a caricatured identity of the colonized. The three components of his name represent his alienated status. Respectively, they represent his closeness to the West ('Alexandre . . . en hommage à l'Occident prestigieux'; l. 6), his Jewishness ('je suis juif . . . j'habite le ghetto'; l. 17) and his ethnic group ('Benillouche . . . le fils de l'agneau en patois berbéro-arabe'; l. 43). But rather than being a source of cultural wealth and diversity, the narrator's name is at the root of his anguish. It fragments his identity and categorizes him politically, religiously and geographically. As the narrator puts it himself, he is 'indigène dans un pays de colonisation, juif dans un univers antisémite, Africain dans un monde où triomphe l'Europe' (l. 58).

The narrator's split identity provokes feelings of exclusion, alienation and inadequacy. He develops a sense of inferiority in the face of the colonizer's culture and a sense of displacement concerning his own culture. In short, he displays common afflictions of the colonized as depicted and analysed in Memmi's book *Portrait du colonisé précédé du portrait du colonisateur* (1957), an essay on colonization.

Memmi's protagonist has no pride in his name or in his origins. In the passage, the reader learns that he deliberately keeps his parents away from school, as he is ashamed of them (l. 39). This situation, according to Memmi (and to Frantz Fanon who dealt with similar issues in *Peau noire, masques blancs* (1952)), is inevitable for the colonized. In an attempt to be accepted by and within the colonizing culture, the colonized detaches himself from and revolts against his own parents before marking his total rupture from the community as a whole.

The protagonist of *La Statue de sel* shows that he has no sense of belonging and no place in his city. He justifies to the reader as much as to himself the reasons for denigrating his city. Like him, the city is split, 'ma ville natale est à mon image' (l. 64). It is a city where colonizers, settlers, indigenous Muslims and indigenous Jews cohabit but do not interact. The city is divided into quarters, each is closed on itself and hostile to the others. Between the different communities there is hatred, prejudice, fear and suspicion. The gulf is widened even more by the injustices of the divisive colonial rule.

Consequently, the protagonist feels a stranger in his own city. It is a city where he encounters racism, rejection and the inability to identify with the hierarchical communities. The description of the city in this passage is highly oedipal. The different conquests and rules ('Phéniciens, Romains, Vandales, Byzantins, Berbères, Arabes, Espagnols, Turcs, Italiens, Français' (l. 80)) the city has been subjected to are felt by the protagonist as consecutive rapes. It is the rape and violation of a city/mother-figure. As such the hero is burdened by the history of his own city for which he laments: 'O ville prostituée, au cœur fragmentaire, qui ne t'a eue pour esclave?' (l. 78) He is unable to cope with the fragmentation of his city and sees himself as its illegitimate product, 'Moi, je suis un bâtard de ma ville natale' (l. 78). As a consequence, he feels compelled to reject his city, for the same reasons, later on, he denigrates his own mother (p. 181).

The only possible cure for the protagonist's alienation is to find salvation in the colonizer's culture, namely French. All along in the depiction of his city, community and family, the protagonist implicitly reveals an admiration for the French culture and language. Such an attitude is highly symptomatic of the colonized, who harbours an inferiority complex before a culture he views as modern and intellectually superior.

By embracing the French language, the protagonist attempts to find for himself a place in a culture he glamorizes. In his own community, the language that is spoken is an Arab-Berber patois. It is a dialect which, like the name of the protagonist and the structure of his native city, mirrors a sense of division. It reflects his linguistic hybridity. However, despite his efforts to excel in French (he is first when the examination results are announced (l. 34)) in the hope of becoming accepted and assimilated, he faces rejection. His use of French is reduced by the spiteful remark of his teacher that it is a 'langage de concierge' (p. 126). This disdain and rejection on the part of the colonizer are emphasized later in the novel when, during the Vichy regime in the Second World War, the French he admires and yearns to be like put him in a concentration camp: 'J'avais refusé l'Orient et l'Occident me refusait. Que serai-je donc? Qu'allais-je devenir?' (pp. 352–3).

The end of the novel shows the protagonist's heightened awareness of his identity and linguistic dilemma and inadequacy. His only solution is to leave and not to look back lest he be petrified in his past.

Further reading

Memmi, Albert, *Agar* (Paris: Buchet-Chastel, 1955).

—— *Portrait d'un Juif* (Paris: Gallimard, 1962).

—— *Le Scorpion* (Paris: Gallimard, 1969).

Arnaud, Jacqueline, *La Littérature maghrébine de langue française* (Paris: Publisud, 1986).

Dugas, Guy, 'An unknown Maghrebian genre: Judeo-Maghrebian literature of French expression', *Research in African Literature* 23, 2 (1992), pp. 21–32.
Hand, Sean, 'Don't look back: Albert Memmi's *La Statue de sel*', in L. Ibnlfassi and N. Hitchcott (eds), *African Francophone Writing* (Oxford: Berg, 1996) pp. 93–101.
Saltani, Bernoussi, 'De quelques figures du juif dans la littérature arabo-berbère d'expression française', in Y. Benayoun-Szmidt, H. Bouraoui and N. Redouane (eds), *La Traversée du français dans les signes littéraires marocains* (Toronto: La Source, 1996), pp. 41–54.

Language and style

Although the passage is entitled 'La Ville', sixty-one of the 106 lines (well over half the narrative) are devoted to the narrator himself, who in many ways, as we will discover, sees himself as a microcosm of the town. The theme of the passage is the search for identity, and the key word is 'image', which occurs at three significant points. The first reference is to the narrator's parents' wish to encapsulate their view of Europe in their son's name – 'Il [Alexandre] leur semblait traduire l'image qu'ils avaient de l'Europe' (l. 7). The second reference occurs at the beginning of the section devoted to the town itself, where Mordekhaï says, 'ma ville natale est à mon image' (l. 64). The racial diversity enshrined in his full name, Mordekhaï Alexandre Benillouche – 'Toujours je me retrouverai Alexandre Mordekhaï Benillouche, indigène dans un pays de colonisation, juif dans un univers antisémite, Africain dans un monde où triomphe l'Europe' (l. 58) – is a reflection of the situation in the town itself: 'Voici la ville arabe . . . les ruelles juives . . . la petite Sicile . . . les fondouks collectifs des Maltais . . . l'église russe orthodoxe . . . le petit train belge . . . la résidence des ambassadeurs de Sa Majesté britannique; voici les maisonnettes des rentiers français' (l. 82). This sentence, thirteen lines long, by the mass of details it contains and the multitude of references it includes, matches the ethnic diversity of the town itself. The final occurrence transcends Mordekhaï's own confusion and evokes the alienation and hostility experienced by the town's ethnically mixed inhabitants: 'chacun reste sournoisement hostile aux autres et définitivement ulcéré par sa propre image qu'il découvre chez eux' (l. 105). Contrasts between expectation and reality run parallel to this negative view of identity. As far as Mordekhaï's name is concerned, his parents gave him as his second forename Alexandre 'en hommage à l'Occident prestigieux' (l. 6), whereas for him it was 'un nom si ridicule' (l. 3) and was mocked so much by his school friends that 'je détestais mon prénom' (l. 9). His first forename Mordekhaï was 'le nom redoutable d'un glorieux Macchabée' (l. 13), but was also the name of his grandfather, 'débile vieillard qui . . . n'oublia les terreurs du ghetto' (l. 14). And as far as his status in the town is concerned, '[j']avais cru que, par une faveur insigne, on m'ouvrait les portes du monde' (l. 70), but 'je me découvris irréductiblement étranger dans ma ville natale' (l. 71).

Parallels of a more genuinely linguistic nature help cement the link between the two major divisions of the passage, for example the repetition of 'certain' = 'sure' (l. 32 and l. 76), of 'cœur' (l. 49 and ll. 75, 79), and more especially the repetition of 'l'Impasse' and 'l'Alliance' at the beginnings of the two sections (l. 2 and l. 64). The backgrounds, current situations and destinies of Mordekhaï and the town are inextricably interlocked.

Imagery – metaphors but especially similes – plays an important role in the passage. The similes, indirect, almost detachable, dispensable, centre on two tenors. The major tenor is provided by the narrator himself – his school friends make fun of his name which they shouted out 'comme un coup de trompette' (l. 8) and he himself tries to eliminate another of his names, Mordekhaï – 'je l'oubliai comme une vieille peau' (l. 29); he is unable to reconcile the diverse sides of his nature, 'Comment faire une synthèse, polie comme le son d'une flûte, de tant de disparités?' (l. 62), and later he is similarly unable to reconcile the diverse sides of the town's make-up 'Lentement, comme par un poison . . . toute mon âme fut envahie' (l. 102). This further parallel between him and the town is also brought out in another simile, 'comme une mère, une ville natale ne se remplace pas' (l. 72). The undercurrent of danger of living in such a hybrid town is illustrated in another simile: 'Je traversais . . . un quartier musulman comme on traverse une rivière à gué' (l. 68). The second group of similes is much more incidental: 'le petit train belge . . . net comme un intérieur flamand' (l. 89) and the French landowners' gardens, planted 'comme dans une chanson' (l. 94).

There is a striking accumulation of metaphoric imagery centred on the town, imagery which is much more emotional and visceral and, if detached, as the similes could be, would lead to a disintegration of the text:

> Vaincu, aveugle, par l'imagination [un homme] se réfère à cette borne [son village]; ses mains, ses pieds en connaissent les contours, ses nerfs miraculeusement s'y accordent. Moi, je suis un bâtard de ma ville natale. O ville prostituée, au cœur fragmentaire, qui ne t'a eue pour esclave?
>
> (l. 76)

The language of the passage in general is of a high register, often rhetorical and emotional. Significant features are the use of inverted questions (e.g. ll. 44, 45, 61), questions with 'comment' + infinitive (ll. 20, 62), past historic tense, doublets (e.g. ll. 2, 3, 6, 9), triplets (e.g. ll. 20, 21, 23, 30), adjectives preceding the noun, e.g. 'l'odieux inventaire' (l. 104, also ll. 14, 25, 87), abstract, abstruse vocabulary, e.g. 'fielleux' (l. 2), 'judaïsés' (l. 48), 'homonyme' (l. 53), 'fondouks' (l. 86), use of appositions (e.g. l. 58, quoted above), repetition and short, similarly constructed clauses or expressions, e.g. 'Alors je détestais mon prénom de toutes mes forces et aussi mes camarades. Je les détestais et leur donnais raison, et en voulais à mes parents de ce choix stupide' (l. 10), 'On peut rater son enfance ou sa vie. Lentement, douloureusement, je compris que j'avais raté ma naissance à ma ville' (l. 107, also ll. 23, 25, 38, 95, 99), use of enumerations, e.g. 'J'ai appris à interpréter les sourires, à deviner aux chuchotements, à lire dans les yeux, à reconstituer les raisonnements au hasard d'une phrase, d'un saisi au vol' (l. 21), 'ma sensibilité, mes sentiments, toute mon âme fut envahie, repétrie, j'appris à faire l'odieux inventaire' (l. 103). Repetition, doublets and triplets are all well illustrated in the following section:

> chacun enfermé dans son quartier a peur de son voisin, le méprise ou le hait. La peur et le mépris, nous les avons connus dès l'éveil de notre conscience, dans cette ville malodorante, sale et débraillée. Et pour nous défendre, pour nous venger, nous méprisions, nous ricanions . . . entre nous; espérant être craints autant que nous craignions. Dans cette atmosphère, nous vivions à table, à l'école, dans la rue.
>
> (l. 96)

An unusual feature is the use of inversion to express hypothesis, e.g. 'Appelez-vous Pierre ou Jean, et changeant d'habit vous changerez de statut apparent' (l. 15), 'Descendrais-je d'une tribu berbère que les Berbères ne me reconnaîtraient pas' (l. 54, also l. 56). The sophistication of the passage is underlined by the variety of sentence-initial elements – only in the narrative passages does a subject begin more than one sentence in sequence. Similarly the sentence structure is highly varied: taking a typical section, ll. 15–36, one discovers one minor sentence, seven simple sentences, three compound, two complex and two compound-complex. This, combined with the alternations of adverbs, subjects, participles, subordinate clauses as initial elements, testifies to skilfully planned internal sentence structure. What is seen as vibrant and a matter for rejoicing in Régine Robin's *La Québécoite* (see Chapter 31 below) – ethnic diversity – becomes a source of anxiety and alienation in *La Statue de sel*, but in both novels the search for identity is expressed in powerful, sophisticated language.

Chapter 4

Rachid Mimouni

Le Fleuve détourné (Paris: Robert Laffont, 1982), pp. 43–9.

J'étais bien content de rentrer au pays. Une vive allégresse hâtait mes pas, à la descente du train. Il faisait chaud et j'ôtai ma veste. Je marchais sans rencontrer âme qui vive sur mon chemin. Les campagnes semblaient désertes. Les champs de vigne qui autrefois verdissaient le flanc des collines avaient disparu. La terre restait en friche et je me demandai pour quelle obscure raison les paysans refusaient désormais de la cultiver.

Après un détour du chemin mon douar natal m'apparut. Rien n'avait changé parmi ces masures plaquées sur le flanc de la colline et une grande bouffée de tendresse envahit mon cœur. Un instant, j'eus envie de couper à travers champ pour courir me précipiter dans les bras de ma femme. Mais je sentis que cela aurait manqué de dignité. Une pudique retenue est le corollaire de la virilité de nos hommes. Je refrénai mon désir et me dirigeai à pas lent vers l'entrée du douar pour que tous les vieux de la *djemaâ* pussent me voir et me saluer. A mon approche, deux hommes armés de fusils de chasse se levèrent. Ils me saluèrent poliment et s'enquirent de la raison de ma venue. Je leur appris que j'étais le fils de Mohamed et que je revenais au pays après de longues années d'absence. Ils répondirent qu'ils ne me connaissaient pas et que je ne pouvais pas entrer au douar. Je leur demandai la cause de cette interdiction.

– Aucun étranger ne doit pénétrer dans le douar.

Soudain, un groupe d'hommes, débouchant de la place, arriva sur nous. Quatre d'entre eux portaient un cercueil. Nous nous reculâmes pour leur laisser le passage. Quand le cortège se fut éloigné, je me retournai pour regarder le cimetière, niché au creux de la vallée. Il grouillait d'une foule bigarrée qui allait et venait parmi une dizaine de tombes ouvertes.

– Que se passe-t-il ici? leur demandai-je.

Ils me répétèrent que je ne pouvais pas aller plus avant. Comme j'insistais et commençais à m'agiter, un des deux hommes releva le canon de son arme vers ma poitrine. En dépit du geste menaçant, je ne lus aucune hostilité dans son regard, mais une immense lassitude, comme s'il se contentait d'appliquer une vieille consigne mystérieuse et nécessaire.

– Puis-je voir mon père?

Après une courte réflexion, l'un d'eux répliqua.

– Il est là-haut, au sommet de la colline. Tu peux y aller, à condition de contourner le douar.

Je les quittai sans les saluer.

Mon père était en train de labourer son petit lopin de pierrailles. Le cheval qui tirait la charrue était si maigre et si chétif qu'à chaque pas on craignait de le voir s'effondrer. L'homme qui tenait les manches de l'outil n'avait pas meilleure mine. C'était miracle de les voir, l'un et l'autre s'arc-boutant pour rassembler leurs forces, parvenir à tracer un sillon hasardeux.

La charrue eut soudain un brusque sursaut et les manches échappèrent des mains de l'homme qui trébucha et se retrouva sur ses genoux.

J'étais debout près de lui.

L'homme, accroupi, observait avec une immense tristesse le soc brisé de sa charrue. Il avait envie de pleurer. Comme, de rage impuissante, pleurent les hommes dépossédés de leur outil, et qui doivent rester les bras ballants.

Il finit par relever la tête dans ma direction.

– Tiens, fit-il en se redressant, c'est toi?

Il avait terriblement vieilli, comme si pendant mes années d'absence il avait dû vivre son temps et le mien. Ses moustaches avaient blanchi. Je fus bien triste de le voir occupé à user le peu de forces qui lui restaient dans l'espoir de tirer une maigre subsistence de cette terre ingrate.

– Tu as beaucoup vieilli, lui dis-je.

Je fis un pas pour l'embrasser, mais il ne bougea pas et je n'osai pas achever mon geste.

– Comment ça va au pays? demandai-je.

– Tout le monde te croit mort, éluda-t-il.

Puis il se tourna à nouveau vers sa charrue brisée.

– C'est la deuxième fois cette semaine. Cette terre est infestée de rocaille. On a l'impression qu'elle nourrit la pierre au lieu de l'orge semé. J'ai beau redoubler d'attention, il y a toujours une pierre traîtresse qui vient heurter le soc. Il va falloir arrêter le travail, emprunter un âne et emmener la charrue chez le forgeron. Il ne sera pas content. Je ne l'ai pas encore payé pour la dernière réparation. Il va faire traîner les choses. Et si la pluie se met à tomber, le labour est fichu.

– Je vois que rien n'a changé, lui dis-je.

Il me lança un regard étonné, comme s'il venait à peine de découvrier ma présence.

– Tu te trompes. Beaucoup de choses ont changé.

Un instant, il eut envie d'ajouter quelque chose, mais se ravisa et se tut.

– Pas ici, pas pour toi, complétai-je.

Je le questionnai sur les deux hommes armés qui m'interdirent l'entrée du douar. Il demeura longtemps silencieux.

– Une terrible malédiction pèse sur les membres exilés de la tribu. Beaucoup sont morts pendant la guerre. D'autres nous ont quittés pour devenir des vagabonds, des commerçants, ou des employés dans les administrations. Et, régulièrement, d'étranges maladies viennent éclaircir nos rangs déjà clairsemés. Tu ne dois pas pénétrer dans le douar. La malédiction ne manquerait pas de s'abattre sur toi aussi.

Je lui répondis que je voulais voir ma femme.

– Ta femme nous a quittés. Un jour, elle est partie en emmenant ton fils.

– Où est-elle allée?

– Je ne sais pas. Je ne veux pas le savoir. Elle a rejeté la protection parentale.

Il me scruta longuement et ajouta:

– Ces Temps Modernes ont bouleversé bien des choses. Je ne suis qu'un pauvre paysan. Je ne peux pas comprendre. Toi, tu comprendras, peut-être.

Puis il ajouta que je devais aller à la mairie pour régulariser ma situation, car tous me croyaient mort.

– Ton nom est inscrit dans le monument aux morts du village.

Puis, comme à regret, il acheva:

– C'est ton cousin Ahmed, le fils de Messaoud de la branche d'en haut, qui est le maire.

Je fixai longuement mon père. Il y avait une grande tristesse dans ses yeux. Je compris que depuis longtemps il avait perdu tout espoir. En la vie. En sa descendance. En l'avenir de la branche exilée de la tribu.

Il tourna le dos et me laissa partir sans même un geste d'adieu. Je ne devais jamais le revoir.

– La malédiction ! clame Vingt-Cinq.

Il est debout sur le seuil de la porte, prophétique, barbe au vent, et menace de sa canne l'obscurité du ciel.

– La malédiction!

Encore ivre? Une réelle frayeur se lit pourtant dans ses yeux. C'est l'heure intime où l'homme oublie ses vanités pour se retrouver face à ses craintes.

Omar se balance d'un pied sur l'autre, hésitant entre la colère et la pitié. Il choisit de rassurer le vieillard.

– Nos populations ont toujours recherché une quelconque malédiction à l'origine des catastrophes et fléaux naturels. Tout a un sens. Le mal ne peut être gratuit. Il est pourtant des faits qui sont le résultat d'une nécessité ignorée, la simple conséquence de lois physico-chimiques ou biologiques qui régissent le monde et la vie. Il n'y a aucune malédiction, vieillard. Il s'agissait sans doute d'une épidémie de choléra, qui, à cette époque, a ravagé beaucoup de nos villages. De rien d'autre.

– Pourquoi m'ont-ils interdit l'entrée?

– Pour t'éviter tout risque de contagion. Hommes désolés et fraternels, ils ne t'ont renié que pour te préserver.

Vingt-Cinq n'est pas convaincu. Il parle d'une femme aux cheveux dénoués.

Sur mon chemin vers le village, j'empruntai un pont flambant neuf, large et solide, campé avec assurance sur ses piliers, avec l'arrogance d'un homme aux ambitions réalisées. En me penchant au-dessus du parapet, je m'aperçus qu'il n'enjambait pas le moindre filet d'eau. Je me demandai pourquoi la rivière était morte.

– N'y a-t-il plus de pluie au pays? Les sommets des montagnes refusent-ils les neiges de l'hiver?

Le lit asséché servait de dépotoir. Des camions énormes venaient y déposer des montagnes d'ordures. Un vieillard était assis à l'ombre du pont. Je descendis le saluer. Je lui demandai pourquoi on construisait des ponts sur des rivières mortes.

– Des planificateurs arrogants et lointains ont quadrillé leurs cartes de traits rectilignes et puissants, à l'encre de Chine, indélébile, de façon à rendre leurs projets définitifs et l'option irréversible. Des engins étrangers sont venus éventrer nos collines afin de tracer la ligne droite requise. Mais le fleuve coulait ailleurs, serein et libre. Ils ont maintenu que son cours se trouvait à l'endroit exact de leurs calculs, et ont entrepris de la détourner pour confirmer leurs dires.

Je lui demandai ce qu'il faisait sous le pont.

– Les hommes et les oueds de ce pays se ressemblent: ils ne connaissent pas la mesure, ils sont à sec ou débordent. J'attends la crue imprévue, irrésistible et violente, qui viendra balayer tous ces monceaux d'immondices.

Text and context

Rachid Mimouni's *Le Fleuve détourné*, from which this passage is extracted, is his third and most acclaimed novel. Though the novel deals partly with the period of the Algerian War of Independence from French rule, Mimouni uses the war solely as a backdrop to focus attention on his main concern: political lethargy and corruption in Algeria since independence.

The main technique used in the novel is the flashback. In the present-moment narrative, the unnamed hero/narrator is held prisoner in makeshift, dilapidated barracks. Earlier in the novel, it is understood that the prisoners' crime has been to question the ruling authorities – they are accused of having subversive thoughts. Mimouni makes his readers understand that his focus is in fact on the leaders of the ruling FLN (the National Liberation Front: the single party in Algeria after independence), especially their harsh treatment of anyone challenging their methods. Powerful metaphors, such as 'l'Administration' and 'les Sioux', are used throughout in the novel to refer to the FLN and its army. Similarly, the protagonist's fellow prisoners bear symbolic names, such as l'Ecrivain or Vingt-Cinq, suggesting either their intellectual background or the number of times they have been arrested. The flashbacks, which occur constantly and interact with the present-moment narrative, consist of the protagonist's recalling to his fellow prisoners the events which resulted in his arrest.

The extract begins with the hero returning to his hamlet ('douar'). The sense of happiness expressed in the first line suggests his long absence from his homeland. The reason for his absence is explained earlier in the novel: he was involved in the war for independence, in the maquis in the mountains fighting the French army. But during an air raid he was hurt and, as a result, suffered temporary amnesia. When he recovered, he decided to return to his community and family. His feelings of excitement and happiness were to be short-lived. This is suggested in the text by the ominously desolate landscape which greets him. The green hillsides he longed to see again were replaced by what seemed to him an abandoned land. This was the first of many scenes of desolation he was to encounter. Mimouni's clear message here is about his vision of the whole of Algeria in the aftermath of independence. As he himself is of peasant origins, the land and how it is cared for are matters close to his heart.

When the protagonist meets his father, the latter is portrayed as struggling to plough his 'petit lopin de pierrailles' (l. 36). The small plot of land owned by an individual peasant, as portrayed in this passage, describes the reality of North African peasantry. During French colonization, most fertile lands – which were usually cultivated by extended families or communities – were confiscated by the French and either sold or offered to settlers as part of the policy of expansion. After independence, rather than returning the lands (known as *Terres du Domaine*) to their original owners, the ruling indigenous governments took over all the recovered land for their own benefit, leaving the legitimate owners struggling with what small plots they were allowed to possess. Despite the hardship, the father persists in cultivating crops from the rocky and barren land. Here, the FLN leaders' mismanagement of Algeria is caustically targeted by Mimouni; this is clearly evident in his description of the poverty-stricken land and people. As the father points out, the land – and by implication Algeria – is 'cette terre ingrate' (l. 52). The very land whose liberation the people fought for confines them to poverty. By the same token, the resistance leaders they fought alongside confine them to hardship. The text directly links the barren earth and the actions of the Algerian leaders, whose corruption led to the destruction of the land and those who depend on it for their livelihood. As the father states: 'Cette terre est infestée de rocaille' (l. 59) and 'On a l'impression qu'elle nourrit la pierre au lieu de l'orge semé' (l. 59). In Voltairian style, Mimouni brands those who lack respect for the land and its people, and who destroy the country's economy, as 'pierre[s] traitresse[s]' (l. 61).

The returning hero's expectations are shattered. Instead of receiving a freedom-fighter's welcome, he is prevented from entering the *douar* at gunpoint. Later he learns that he is believed by all to be dead, and that his name is listed on the village monument to the dead. Rather than taking their attitude as a sign of hostility, the hero sees the two armed guards as wary and powerless. Their attitude, tinged with 'une immense lassitude' (l. 29) is reiterated by the hero's father's 'immense tristesse' (l. 44). This contradicts conventional views of the Algerian peasant man who is normally depicted as epitomizing masculinity and pride.

The community portrayed in this passage is founded on the supremacy of male power. This power is built on the assumption that men are rational, and do not indulge in emotions. Mimouni is critical of such attitudes, which deprive men of a means to express their emotional needs and compel them to adhere to a stereotypical image of masculine virility. For example, the hero's first reaction on his return is to take a short cut as he is impatient to embrace his wife; however, the dictates of social expectations among men make him pause, as to rush would have 'manqué de dignité' (l. 11). He represses his true feelings, slowing down and reminding himself, as well as the reader, that: 'Une pudique retenue est le corollaire de la virilité de nos hommes' (l. 11). Similarly, he restrains himself from holding and kissing his father as the latter's lack of reaction (l. 54) – due also to his subdued resignation to his fate – is another reminder that expressing and showing one's emotions is unmanly.

Mimouni's depiction of men in this passage suggests that they are helpless, powerless, subdued beings. The sadness in which they seem trapped is indicative of heroes who have been dispossessed of their most cherished assets: pride and honour (in a subsequent novel, *L'Honneur de la tribu* (1989), Mimouni deals further with this issue). Men in this passage are deprived of the source of their pride – the land – and exiled into a hostile environment. Their isolation is deepened by numerous epidemics. Through the eyes of the narrator, the reader witnesses the busyness of the villagers in the cemetery, burying their dead in numbers. At the hero's inquiry, his father explains that, apart from diseases villagers could not understand, an evil spell has struck the village and rendered all powerless (l. 76).

The villagers seem deeply prone to ignorance and superstition. Mimouni advocates the people's right to education to combat these ills. It is with this focus (through a university student, Omar) that a rational explanation for the numerous deaths is given: 'Il s'agissait sans doute d'une épidémie de choléra' (l. 109). Thus, Omar epitomizes the rational educated individual as opposed to Vingt-Cinq, the embodiment of an older, illiterate generation weakened by their beliefs in supernatural forces. The woman with loose hair Vingt-Cinq alludes to in this passage is a reference to a mythical ogress who, in Maghrebian culture, is believed to render men powerless.

In depicting his characters as resigned to their fate and dispossessed of their rights and power, Mimouni portrays a people who have been deprived of their revolution. This deprivation represents the loss of their freedom, which is the core of the protagonist's quest in the remainder of the novel. This is translated allegorically into his search for his missing wife, Houria (meaning freedom in Arabic). Earlier in the novel, the reader learns that Houria was victim of a rape. By marrying her, not only does the protagonist act as a protector but also as someone who acknowledges her status as a victim. Later, when he finds her, he learns that during his absence she has been repeatedly raped by dignitaries promising her a better life. On the level of allegory, one could see how the two rapes of Houria are representative of the Algerian man's dispossession of his freedom by the French and the FLN leaders respectively. The freedom the Algerian revolutionaries thought they had achieved is depicted by Mimouni as a sham, a fake freedom one has to fight for in order to 'arracher son masque colorié pour découvrir enfin le vrai visage de Houria' (p. 168).

The last scene in this passage provides the central theme and contextualizes the title of the novel. With the help of foreign powers, the Algerian authorities undertook to build a new bridge, only to find out later that it has been built away from the course of the river. Rather than acknowledge their mistake, they decide to divert the river so as to justify their actions. Like the river, the reality Mimouni highlights is the diversion of the Algerian revolution from the people who fought for their political and economic independence. Finally, in a passage hailed as visionary by some readers, Mimouni prophesies that the diverted course of the river will wash away the accumulated waste under the new bridge: 'J'attends la crue imprévue, irrésistible et violente, qui viendra balayer tous ces monceaux d'immondices' (l. 132). His prediction came true when the diverted revolution ended in chaos. Indeed, ten years after the publication of *Le Fleuve détourné*, an uprising against the one-party government and a civil war erupted in Algeria.

Further reading

Mimouni, Rachid, *Tombeza* (Paris: 1984).
—— *L'Honneur de la tribu* (Paris: Robert Laffont, 1989).
—— *De la barbarie en général et de l'intégrisme en particulier* (Paris: Le Pré aux clercs, 1992).
—— *La Malédiction* (Paris: Stock, 1993).

Adam, Jeanne, '*Le Fleuve détourné* de Rachid Mimouni', *CELFAN Review* 4 (1984).
Desimeur, Martine, '*Le Fleuve détourné* ou le pélérinage calamiteux', in J. Bardolph (ed.), *Le Temps et l'Histoire chez l'écrivain: Afrique du nord, Afrique Noire, Antilles* (Paris: L'Harmattan, 1987).
Fabre, Thierry, 'L'Algérie traumatisée: entretien avec Rachid Mimouni', *Esprit* 152 (1989).
Grenaud, Pierre, *La Littérature au soleil du Maghreb* (Paris: L'Harmattan, 1993).
Redouane, Najib, 'Au-delà de la peur: *La Malédiction* de Rachid Mimouni', in N. Redouane and Y. Mokaddem (eds), *1989 en Algérie: Rupture tragique ou rupture féconde* (Toronto: La Source, 1999), pp. 203–15.
Verheyen, Gunther, 'Rachid Mimouni: visionnaire d'une autre Algérie', *Etudes littéraires maghrébines* 10 (1995).

Language and style

Although the three episodes constituting this extract – the narrator returning to his native village and meeting his father, Vingt-Cinq and his ignorance concerning the epidemic, the narrator and the bridge over the dry river-bed – inform us through flashbacks of events in the narrator's earlier life, they also have allegorical value. In the two episodes where he is present (the first and third), he is presented as a Candide-like figure, innocently seeking to understand situations which he meets on his journey. He asks simple questions, e.g. 'Que se passe-t-il ici? leur demandai-je' (l. 25), 'Puis-je voir mon père?' (l. 31), 'Comment ça va au pays?' (l. 56), 'N'y a-t-il plus de pluie au pays? Les sommets des montagnes refusent-ils les neiges de l'hiver?' (l. 119). Indirect questions also occur – 'Je leur demandai la cause de cette interdiction' (l. 17, also l. 71), 'Je me demandai pourquoi la rivière était morte' (l. 118, also l. 130). Various techniques used in the first-person narrative underline the innocence of the traveller. An analysis of the section from the beginning of the extract until his father speaks (ll. 1–47) shows that of the forty-three sentences, twenty-nine (two-thirds) are simple in structure and another four are compound. Subordinate clauses (ten examples) occur in only nine (one-fifth) of the cases; only one sentence (l. 36) contains more than one subordinate clause. This sense of simplicity of general sentence structure is echoed in the internal structure of the sentences; most of them are very short and all but five of the simple sentences (83 per cent) begin with the subject. Those with a different initial element involve short adverbial expressions, four of time, one of place ('Après un détour du chemin' (l. 7), 'Un instant' (l. 9), 'A mon approche' (l. 13), 'Soudain' (l. 20), 'Après une courte réflexion' (l. 32)). Syntactically, therefore, the passage reflects the candour of the traveller returning home and, unlike the other two episodes, his gentleness and filial respect as he meets his father again – and for the last time (l. 95).

The first allegory focuses on the aridity and desolation of Algeria – no green where vines used to grow (l. 4), land untilled (l. 5), the narrator's father's 'petit lopin de pierrailles' (l. 36), 'cette terre ingrate' (l. 52), 'Cette terre . . . infestée de rocaille' (l. 59, also ll. 60, 61). Not only is the land in a parlous state but so are the father (ll. 38, 49–51) and his horse (l. 36). The condition of the land and its inhabitants symbolizes the disastrous consequences of the government's policies. The most striking sentences in this episode are the minor sentences, which serve the purpose of summarizing the themes. The first, poetically via a simile and through inversion of adjective and complement and of verb and subject, describes the fate of the disenfranchised – 'Comme, de rage impuissante, pleurent les hommes dépossédés de leur outil, et qui doivent rester les bras ballants' (l. 45); the others describe their despair – 'Je compris que depuis longtemps il avait perdu tout espoir. En la vie. En sa descendance. En l'avenir de la branche exilée de la tribu' (l. 92).

The lament of the narrator's father – 'Une terrible malédiction pèse sur les membres exilés de la tribu' (l. 73) – anticipates the central pivot of the second allegorical episode, beginning 'La malédiction! clame Vingt-Cinq' (l. 97). The theme of the ignorance and superstition of the populace, epitomized in Vingt-Cinq's unwillingness to accept the explanation of the epidemic, seen as a curse, is expressed in much more discursive language than the first episode. The description of the old man is much more vigorous than that of the father: 'Il est debout sur le seuil de la porte, prophétique, barbe au vent, et menace de sa canne l'obscurité du ciel' (l. 98). The language of the enlightened Omar contrasts with Vingt-Cinq's unenlightened outbursts, in its philosophico-scientific content:

> Tout a un sens. Le mal ne peut être gratuit. Il est pourtant des faits qui sont le résultat d'une nécessité ignorée, la simple conséquence de lois physico-chimiques ou biologiques qui régissent le monde et la vie. . . . Il s'agissait sans doute d'une épidémie de choléra.
> (l. 106)

The third episode also has a vigour in its language absent from the first. The narrator hits out at the arrogance of the authorities, symbolized in the bridge they have built over a non-existent river: 'un pont flambant neuf, large et solide, campé avec assurance sur ses piliers, avec l'arrogance d'un homme aux ambitions réalisées' (l. 115), an impressive structure, bestriding – rubbish (l. 121). As with Omar in the second episode, the sage beneath the bridge also speaks in a pseudo-scientific way: 'Des planificateurs arrogants et lointains ont quadrillé leurs cartes de traits rectilignes et puissants, à l'encre de Chine, indélébile, de façon à rendre leurs projets définitifs et l'option irréversible' (l. 124). The imagery associated with the river, also expanding the title of the novel, *Le Fleuve détourné*, represents the Algerian people (l. 131 explicitly links the two), who, though constrained by the authorities – 'il [le pont] n'enjambait pas le moindre filet d'eau . . . la rivière était morte' (l. 117, also ll. 121, 123, 129) – are still free – 'le fleuve coulait ailleurs, serein et libre' (l. 127; the use of 'fleuve' rather than 'rivière' to denote the people suggests superior power and vitality). The three adjectives used to describe the flood to come – 'imprévue, irrésistible et violente' (l. 132) – and the relative clause – 'qui viendra balayer tous ces monceaux d'immondices' – serve as a powerful climax to the extract.

There is a twist in the presentation of the allegories, which lies in the contrast between initial expectations and the reality of the situations. In the first, the narrator is happy and full of joy on reaching his home (l. 1), but disillusionment soon engulfs him in the form of the armed guards forbidding his progress, his ageing father and decrepit horse, his absent wife. In the second, Vingt-Cinq thinks that a curse has befallen the country, to be told that it is in fact an outbreak of cholera which is perfectly explicable in scientific terms. In the third, the narrator sees a dead river, but it is an artificial river.

The author uses few specific stylistic devices in the extract. The most obvious concerns the use of adjectives. They are relatively few and far between (only two attributive adjectives for fifteen nouns in the first paragraph) – the sparse use of adjectives reflects the bare landscape.

Consequently those which do occur are invested with particular power (ll. 8, 23, 28, 40, 45, 52, 58, 61), the more so when they occur in pairs (ll. 30, 37, 112, 124, 125, 128) or a triplet (l. 132) or quartet (l. 115), and when they are pre-posed (ll. 1, 5, 11, 32, 41, 44, 101 – the double use of 'immense lassitude' (l. 29) and 'immense tristesse' (l. 44) conveys the pitiful plight of the peasants). Another device is the use of high-register expressions instead of more standard ones: abstract nouns for more normal verbal constructions – 'Ils . . . s'enquirent de la raison de ma venue' (l. 14); 'Je leur demandai la cause de cette interdiction' (l. 17) – and high register verbs for standard ones – 'Je refrénai mon désir' (l. 12), 'd'étranges maladies viennent éclaircir nos rangs déjà clairsemés' (l. 76, also l. 119), as well as the past historic tense throughout.

Although the author makes little effort to reproduce conversational informality, the passage varies in tone from the first episode with its direct, straightforward structures (discovering a new situation) to the other two episodes where technical jargon is used to counteract ignorance (situations being explained). In this novel allegory becomes a potent weapon to attack political incompetence and the superstition and apparent backwardness of the ordinary people.

Chapter 5

Mehdi Charef

Le Thé au harem d'Archi Ahmed (Paris: Mercure de France, 1983), pp. 103–8.

Pat et Madjid arrivent finalement sur le quai, et ils prennent place sur une banquette. Ils restent là un bon moment à regarder, guettant le sac à main propice ou le portefeuille qui dépasserait d'une poche. Pour eux, c'est un moyen comme un autre de se faire du pognon. Ils n'en sont pas à leur première tentative.

«Se faire un métro» voulait dire dans leur jargon: faire le pickpocket en sous-sol. Puis, quand on est chômeur et pas aidé, on ne regarde pas aux moyens de se payer un sandwich et un paquet de cigarettes. Vivre au jour le jour et se taper le coquillard de ce que pourra être demain! Tels les animaux.

Voilà qu'un gros type, balaise, la quarantaine, sort d'une voiture stoppant à quai, avec une énorme valise à la main droite. Il sue. Une femme, certainement la sienne, l'accompagne, qui tient un sac de voyage. Sur le quai, le gars s'arrête, sort son mouchoir de sa poche et s'essuie le front. Sa femme l'attend. Il porte un blouson en skaï qui lui arrive à la ceinture, si bien qu'on voit son portefeuille dépassant de la poche arrière de son pantalon. Pat le voit et le montre à Madjid qui aurait plutôt tendance, lui, à regarder les filles.

Le gros suant et sa femme se dirigent vers le couloir de correspondances. Madjid et Pat aussi. La valise semble lourde pour le type, il change souvent de main. Visiblement sa femme a de la peine pour lui. Elle profite qu'il s'arrête pour lui passer un coup de mouchoir sur le front. Madjid et Pat les suivent à distance, marquant le pas quand il faut, faisant mine de regarder les affiches publicitaires sur les murs du couloir.

A une intersection de correspondances, le gros et sa femme prennent la direction Mairie d'Issy. Sur le quai, ils marchent jusqu'au milieu: les premières classes.

Le gros pose sa valise en soupirant. Il sort une nouvelle fois son mouchoir et s'essuie le front, le cou. Il regarde sa montre et dit quelque chose à sa femme, qui répond d'un geste affirmatif de la tête. Pat arrive seul et s'assoit sur la banquette juste derrière le gros.

Le portefeuille est remonté de la poche arrière du gros quand celui-ci s'est baissé pour poser la valise. Madjid arrive à son tour, les mains dans les poches de son blouson. Tranquille, il regarde une pub à quelques mètres de Pat et du gros. Quelques voyageurs patientent aussi.

Il est déjà presque quatorze heures, heure creuse.

La rame montre son nez. Madjid s'avance discrètement derrière le gros. Celui-ci prend sa valise et fait un pas vers le bord du quai. Pat se lève et descend à moitié la fermeture éclair de son blouson.

La rame stoppe, quelques voyageurs descendent. Le gros monte, suivi de sa femme. Il prend la lourde valise à deux mains pour la faire glisser. Madjid monte à son tour, frôlant le plus possible le gros au moment où il se baisse pour reposer son bagage. Madjid en profite pour tirer prestement le portefeuille de sa main gauche et, vite, se retourne contre la portière.

Entre Pat et Madjid, il y a une fille, une belle minette comme Pat les aime, qui s'admire dans la vitre de la portière, plaquant de sa main ses longs cheveux. Madjid passe le portefeuille discrètement à Pat sur sa gauche. Celui-ci quitte sa place, les yeux fixés sur le plan de la ligne de métro au-dessus de la portière.

Pat se dégage doucement, mine de rien. Madjid reste où il est, dos tourné au gros. Les portières fermées, la rame prend son élan. Le gros et sa femme consultent le trajet de la ligne. Ils parlent à voix haute. L'homme s'éponge une nouvelle fois le visage.

Madjid regarde le couple reflété dans la vitre. Le gros enfouit son mouchoir humide dans une poche avant de son pantalon. Brusquement il porte la main sur sa poche arrière, du même côté.

Il regarde sa femme, l'air affolé.

– Mon portefeuille!

– Tu ne l'as plus? Tu es sûr?

– Non. Regarde dans ton sac.

La dame ouvre son sac, évidemment pour rien. Elle demande:

– Tu ne l'as pas oublié à la maison?

– Je suis sûr que je l'avais: j'y ai mis mes tickets de métro.

Il regarde par terre au cas où . . .puis se retourne vers Madjid.

Il le dévisage de haut en bas sans se gêner: un Arabe!

Il prend l'Arabe par le colbac et l'attire vers lui:

– Mon portefeuille, fumier!

Madjid se fait tout petit, tout tremblant, trouillard. Murmure:

– Ça va pas, non? je vous ai rien fait, moi.

Et finalement crie:

– Il est fou, ce mec, il est dingue!

Il voit Pat qui se marre, là-bas. Il continue de crier:

– De quel droit, hein? Je m'en fous, moi, de ton larfeuille. Mais ça y est: ils voient un Arabe, c'est un voleur!

Le gros le plaque contre la portière et Madjid se laisse fouiller tout en protestant. Le gros fouille bien comme il faut, devant, derrière, le froc et tout.

Tu veux pas que j'enlève mes pompes aussi? demande Madjid. Et mon slip, peut-être?

Le gros se retrouve comme un con. Il s'excuserait presque. Quand ils voient l'Arabe s'avancer vers lui, quelques voyageurs, par peur, reculent.

Madjid, au gros:

– Et maintenant?

La rame arrive à une nouvelle station, des gens descendent. Madjid aussi, fixant le gros et sa femme avec méchanceté. Pat est sorti par une autre portière et s'en va vers la sortie du quai. Le gros, vexé, glisse quelques mots à sa femme. Madjid, jouant le jeu à fond, l'insulte une dernière fois du quai, et suit Pat.

Pat l'attend en haut des marches. Il sourit. Ils sont à «Madeleine». Pat sort le larfeuille de sous son blouson, et après avoir jeté un œil autour de lui, pas de flic, fouille. Deux billets de cent francs, pas plus.

– Tu parles d'un fauché! On ira pas loin, avec ça!

Ils se dirigent vers Strasbourg-Saint-Denis par les grands boulevards. Faubourg Saint-Martin, ils cassent la croûte au bar d'un bistro. Sandwich aux merguez avec harissa pour Madjid et un jambon-beurre pour Pat. Et de la bière. Ensuite, ils flânent le long du Sébasto jusqu'au Châtelet. Ils font un tour rue Saint-Denis pour mater les putes. Pat va même demander le prix à l'une d'elles, montée comme une danseuse qui passe à la télé. Trop cher pour lui. Pat discute le prix avec la fille, puis, montrant Madjid:

– Mon copain, il a une réduction familles nombreuses. Ça marche pas chez vous?

La fille:

– Allez, barrez-vous, laissez-moi bosser.

– Salope! dit Pat en continuant son chemin.

La fille ne répond pas. Elle les regarde de travers.

Dès qu'ils voient une belle des plus dénudées, ils vont vers elle. Ils se rincent l'œil pour tuer le temps . . .

– Ça me donne envie de baiser, dit Pat. J'ai la barre à mine.

– On rentre, dit Madjid, on va se taper Joséphine.

– Okay, mec, avant que son Jules rentre du boulot.

Ils reprennent le métro, puis le train jusqu'à la cité.

Pat monte directement chez la Joséphine en se pressant.

Madjid n'y va pas. Tout compte fait, il préfère rentrer chez lui.

– A tout à l'heure! dit Pat.

– Ouais, dit Madjid.

Text and context

Mehdi Charef's *Le Thé au harem d'Archi Ahmed* is the first published work by a *beur* writer to gain a wide audience. It set off a new wave of writing in French that was to become known as *beur* fiction. The word *beur* was originally coined by the descendants of North African immigrants in France. It stems from *verlan*, a speech code among French youth which consists of reversing the first and second syllables of words. Thus *beur* is *verlan* for *arabe*. When the term *beur* was appropriated by the media and began to be used in a derogatory manner which separated French youths of Maghrebian origins from 'Français de souche' (authentic French), it was dropped by its originators.

The identity issue is a core concern for those whose parents are North African immigrants in France. The 'second generation' of immigrants (so-called even though many of them were born in France) possess French nationality. They have achieved integration, generally speaking, into French society, yet refuse assimilation. They see their right to be culturally different constantly threatened by a political and social system which offers them a restricted choice: either to assimilate to the French people and culture, which means denial of their origins, or to be categorized and marginalized like the generation before them.

In general, the *Beur* is confined in the French collective imagination to the notion of the Other. The publication of *Le Thé au harem* provoked a strong reaction because the Other, in the person of Charef, had taken the pen and written his own story. *Le Thé au harem* is an autobiographical account of Charef's youth in the *cité* (working-class suburbs on the outskirts of Paris, such as Nanterre where Charef grew up and which is the setting for his novel). It depicts the deprived life he and his peers went through, ignored by the State other than to be labelled as troublemakers. *Le Thé au harem* was originally written as a film-script. After the publication of the novel, the film *Le Thé au harem d'Archimède* came out in 1985, directed by Charef himself and produced by Costa-Gavras. Unrelated to Charef, though on the same theme, the film *La Haine*, which appeared a decade later in 1995, directed by Mathieu Kassowitz, portrayed for an international audience the fragmentation of modern French society and the predicament of dispossessed and impoverished working-class youths first encountered by readers of *Le Thé au harem*.

The passage under study here shows that the Other is not necessarily the Arab, but those who are economically and socially deprived irrespective of their origins. By writing, Charef is considered a trail-blazer in breaking the silence which he and his generation had endured.

This extract depicts a scene where two youths, Madjid and Pat, go pickpocketing in the Paris Métro. Though the episode is about theft, it neither dwells on the morality of the act nor glamorizes it. The focus is, unexpectedly, on the harmony and unity between the two teenagers in carrying out the offence. Throughout the whole narrative, Charef gives equal place to his co-protagonists. Madjid and Pat are inseparable friends with identical lives though ethnically different (from a different angle, they could be representatives of Charef's bi-cultural status). Madjid is a Muslim of Algerian origin, while Pat is a Christian 'Français de souche'. For an outsider, this difference in cultural backgrounds would be sufficient to trigger a divide between them. But this is not the case for Madjid and Pat, or any of the youths who belong to the same *cité*. Their being culturally different is a *fait accompli* and irrelevant to how they relate to one another.

Despite their ethnic differences, Madjid and Pat stand out, in this passage and in the novel as a whole, as very similar. They are the same age and both unqualified school drop-outs with no prospects. Through them, Charef portrays a bleak image of the working-class people and the dilapidated housing estates in which life is an everyday struggle for survival.

Feeling trapped and bored, Madjid and Pat indulge themselves in idleness and to kill time they go on sprees of petty crime. Thus the scene in this passage is for them a time-killing activity, which would also provide them with the necessary money for a day: 'quand on est chômeur et pas aidé, on ne regarde pas aux moyens de se payer un sandwich et un paquet de cigarettes' (l. 6). To symbolize the economic gulf that separates the capital city and its suburbs, Charef shows the two companions leaving their poverty-stricken *cité* and descending on Paris with its rich pickings.

The victim-to-be – fat, sweaty and carrying a heavy suitcase – is a caricature of the rich who epitomize the ugly face of wealth. Though Madjid and Pat are the wrongdoers in this scene, the reader's sympathy remains with them. The reason for this is because, overall, it is they who are the victims. They belong to a class which is economically deprived and discriminated against. The State's lack of action to improve life in the *cité* and to provide the youths with adequate opportunities shows in the desperate cry: 'Ça chante pas, le béton, ça hurle au désespoir comme les loups dans la forêt' (p. 63). Consequently, it is justifiable in the eyes of the two companions to steal from the rich.

This passage offers a minutely detailed account of the act of robbery, from the moment Madjid and Pat spot their victim right up to their escape. What is striking in this scene is the lack of speech between the accomplices. They exchange only glances (and eventually the stolen wallet). On the one hand, the professionalism with which they carry out the theft reflects their long-standing experience in pickpocketing; on the other, it shows their knowledge of each other and their harmoniously united actions, almost as if they were the same person.

This harmony between the co-protagonists symbolizes and reinforces the solidarity between those who experience in common the feeling of being let down by a governing system whose only intervention tends to create an ethnic gap: 'Quand on veut s'occuper d'eux, c'est pour mieux les détruire, proprement. Pour les séparer. En horde ils attaquent. Ils dérangent' (p. 64). However, Madjid and Pat do not hesitate to exploit the inherent racism in French society for their own ends. When the victim realizes that his wallet is missing, he does not hesitate to accuse Madjid. Unlike the reader, the victim does not know that Madjid is really the thief. For the victim, Madjid is the guilty one simply by the fact that he is the only Arab in the compartment. This is to enhance the racist stereotypical attitude towards the Other – the Arab in this case. Madjid is conscious of this and has the effrontery to use it for his advantage. He plays the innocent and lets himself be searched while at the same time crying out his outrage: 'Mais ça y est: ils voient un Arabe, c'est un voleur' (l. 69). And by not apologizing to Madjid for suspecting him – 'Il s'excuserait presque' (l. 75) – the victim implicitly agrees with the veracity of these preconceived ideas of the Arab.

Racism and the suspicion surrounding North African immigrants and their families are brought up and highlighted in *Le Thé au harem* with a degree of black humour. Pat's pleading with the prostitute, at the end of this passage, for a special concessionary rate on the grounds of Madjid's 'famille[s] nombreuse[s]' status, echoes the general view among French people that the large North African families burden and abuse the generosity of the welfare state.

The novel, in general, offers an optimistic and positive view about the young in France. It shows that, for the deprived, the social gap is economically rather than racially grounded. Though the end of the novel is pessimistic, showing how bleak is the future for the likes of Madjid and Pat, it nonetheless indicates a flicker of hope for harmony among the younger generation. When Madjid is arrested by the police, Pat gives himself up – 'J'étais avec lui' (p. 185). Their struggle for a better life and future is to remain united.

Further reading

Charef, Mehdi, *Le Harki de Meriem* (Paris: Mercure de France, 1990).

Achour, Christiane, 'Ancrage, identité et dérision: l'humour dans le récit "beur"', in *Humoresques: l'humour d'expression française* (Paris: CORHUM and Université Paris 8, 1990).
Djaout, Tahar, 'Ecriture au "beur noir"', *Notre librairie* 103 (1990).
Hargreaves, Alec G., *Voices from the North African Immigrant Community in France: Immigration and Identity* (Oxford: Berg, 1991).
Jay, Salim, 'Mehdi Charef, *Le Thé au harem d'Archi Ahmed*', *L'Afrique littéraire* 70 (1983).
Laronde, Michel, *Autour du roman beur: immigration et identité* (Paris: L'Harmattan, 1993).
Sessa, Jacqueline, 'Le "Beur" dans les romans de Mehdi Charef et d'Azouz Begag', *New Comparison* 10 (1990).

Language and style

This text is written in everyday narrative mode: no pretension, little ornamentation, straightforward, ordinary prose. The language may be sited at the lower end of the register scale; that is to say it avoids the sophistication of the upper registers present in most of the other passages studied, but exploits different layers of familiar usage. The content is undemanding and very little analysis or interpretation of what is being recounted is undertaken, either by the narrator or the protagonists. The storyline simply recounts a day in the life of two adolescents from a *cité* in an underprivileged part of Paris.

The lack of intellectual analysis is epitomized in the title of the novel – *Le Thé au harem d'Archi Ahmed* – formed by popular etymology from *le théorème d'Archimède:* the boys have no concern about the finer points of geometry – and, unwittingly or deliberately, present a distorted version of one of its central hypotheses – or about conventional education in general. Just as they show no interest in things of the mind, so the narrator seems to have no interest in understanding the workings of their minds. Linguistically this lack of analysis is illustrated in a number of ways.

The narrator uses the 'familiar' style throughout. Lexically, it may be seen first in the fact that the vocabulary used is as ordinary as could be, involving generally basic, concrete terms, eschewing the abstract, and with a very limited range of reference, and second in the inclusion of a number of fairly restrained slang words in the narrative, e.g. 'pognon' (l. 4), 'coquillard' (l. 8), 'balaise' (l. 9), 'type' (l. 9), 'une pub' (l. 31), 'minette' (l. 42), 'mine de rien' (l. 46), 'se marre' (l. 68), 'flic' (l. 84), 'Ils se rincent l'œil' (l. 99). From time to time one can hear echoes of the boy's language in the narrative itself – e.g. 'Le gros se retrouve comme un con' (l. 75), 'larfeuille' (l. 84) (an example of *largonji*, a particular brand of slang formation), 'Sébasto' (l. 90), 'pour mater les putes' (l. 90).

Their 'jargon' (l. 5) is more robust and descends a notch on the register scale into the 'popular' category, e.g. 'mec' (ll. 67, 103), 'dingue' (l. 67), 'je m'en fous' (l. 69), 'larfeuille' (l. 69), 'un fauché' (l. 86), 'salope' (l. 97), 'la barre à mine' (= erection, l. 101), 'se taper' (l. 102), 'son Jules' (l. 103), 'boulot' (l. 103). The language of the prostitute they approach is similarly vigorous – 'Allez, barrez-vous, laissez-moi bosser' (l. 96). In his fury, thinking that he has been pickpocketed, 'le gros' also uses a 'strong' word, calling Majdid the highly insulting 'fumier' (l. 63).

Syntactically, the 'familiar' register appears in the use of the historic present as the main tense throughout, in the sparse use of adjectives, in the predominant use of simple and compound sentences, in the infrequent use of subordinate clauses, in the use of 'Voilà que' (l. 9) to introduce a new stage in the story's development, in the use of 'que' with 'profiter' (l. 18).

As far as adjectives are concerned, they are few in number and narrow in range: from the first half of the text come a small number of functional adjectives: 'première' (ll. 4, 23), 'droite' (l. 10), 'arrière' (ll. 14, 29, 52), 'publicitaires' (l. 20), 'nouvelle' (ll. 25, 48), 'seul' (l. 27), 'gauche' (l. 41), 'haute' (l. 48), 'avant' (l. 51), 'même' (l. 52); and a few decorative ones, referring in the main to 'le gros' and his case – 'bon' (l. 2), 'gros' (l. 9) (which becomes substantivized to refer to their victim), 'énorme' (l. 10), 'suant' (l. 16), 'lourde' (ll. 17, 38), 'belle' (l. 42), 'longs' (l. 48), 'humide' (l. 51). On the other hand, a small group of adjectives is clearly of a higher register – 'propice' (l. 2) 'affirmatif' (l. 27), 'creuse' (l. 33), 'affolé' (l. 53) – and hint at the narrator's own intervention and evaluation of events, as are the adverbs 'visiblement' (l. 18), 'discrètement' (ll. 34, 44), 'prestement' (l. 40), 'doucement' (l. 46).

An examination of the sentence structures present in the first half of the text reveals that there are three minor sentences, thirty simple sentences (60 per cent of the major sentences), nine compound (18 per cent, but only one with more than two clauses), nine complex (again 18 per cent) and two compound-complex (4 per cent). Minor sentences are more numerous in the second half of the text (e.g. ll. 77, 79, 84, 85, 88, 89), providing an appropriate narrative accompaniment to the conversational sections. Of the major sentences in the first half of the text, therefore, forty-eight (78 per cent) do not contain a subordinate clause. Indeed there are comparatively long stretches of text, especially at particularly dramatic points, where no subordinate clauses occur at all (e.g. ll. 30–8, 47–66). In all there are twelve subordinate clauses, eight of which are relative and three temporal. The remaining subordinate clause is consecutive and occurs in what could be seen as the sentence which is the catalyst of the action of the text – the observing of the wallet (l. 13). This is the only sentence where cause and effect are specifically mentioned; on other occasions cause and effect are simply hinted at by juxtaposition of clauses (parataxis), e.g. 'La valise semble lourde pour le type, il change souvent de main' (l. 17). The fact that there are actually fifty-three sentences in fifty-three lines of text, an average of one sentence per line, proves that generally they are very short and lack complexity. An examination of the first item of the fifty major sentences shows that forty (80 per cent) begin with the subject, one with a complement of the subject (l. 31), the other nine with an adverb (e.g. ll. 3, 22, 23). Taken together these syntactic phenomena create an impression of simple, even simplistic story-telling, direct and unsophisticated, confirming the impression gained from the lexical analysis and reflecting the reluctance of the boys to indulge in any sort of cerebral reflection.

One or two other devices warrant mention. First, three very blunt similes occur, appropriate to the overall limited style of the narrative and specifically to the preoccupations of Pat and Madjid, e.g. 'Tels les animaux' (l. 8), 'Le gros se retrouve comme un con' (l. 75), '[une fille] montée comme une danseuse qui passe à la télé' (l. 91). Second, a highly alliterative sentence, describing Madjid's obsequious submission to the body search, occurs amid a very dramatic section, where a compound sentence seems to be split into three: 'Madjid se fait tout petit, tout tremblant, trouillard. Murmure: – Ça va pas, non? je vous ai rien fait, moi. Et finalement crie' (l. 64). Finally comes a microcosm of the relationship between the two boys: their racial contrast is brought out in their choice of food – 'Sandwich aux merguez avec harissa pour Madjid et un jambon-beurre pour Pat' (l. 88) – and their social unity in their choice of liquid refreshment – 'Et de la bière'.

Chapter 6

Tahar Ben Jelloun

L'Enfant de sable (Paris: Seuil, 1985), pp. 25–7.

Je vous disais . . .

Toute la famille fut convoquée et réunie dans la maison du Hadj dès le mercredi soir. La tante Aïcha s'activait comme une folle. Les deux frères, avec femmes et enfants, étaient arrivés, inquiets et impatients. Les cousins proches et lointains furent aussi invités. Lalla Radhia s'était enfermée avec l'épouse du Hadj. Personne n'avait le droit de la déranger. Des femmes noires préparaient le dîner dans la cuisine. Vers minuit on entendait des gémissements: c'étaient les premières douleurs. De vieilles femmes en appelaient au Prophète Mohammed. Le Hadj faisait les cent pas dans la rue. Ses frères tenaient un conseil de guerre. Ils se parlaient à voix basse dans un coin du salon. Les enfants dormaient là où ils avaient mangé. Le silence de la nuit n'était interrompue que par les cris de douleur. Lalla Radhia ne disait rien. Elle chauffait des bassines d'eau et étalait les langes. Tout le monde dormait sauf le Hadj, la sage-femme et les deux frères. A l'aube, on entendait l'appel à la prière. Quelques silhouettes se levèrent, tels des somnambules et prièrent. La femme hurlait à présent. Le jour se leva sur la maison où tout était dans un grand désordre. Les cuisinières noires rangèrent un peu et préparèrent la soupe de la naissance et du baptême. Les frères durent partir à leur travail. Les enfants se considèrent en vacances et restèrent jouer à l'entrée de la maison. Vers dix heures du matin, le matin de ce jeudi historique, alors que tout le monde était rassemblé derrière les pièces de l'accouchement, Lalla Radhia entrouvrit la porte et poussa un cri où la joie se mêlait aux you-you, puis répéta jusquà s'essouffler: c'est un homme, un homme, un homme . . . Hadj arriva au milieu de ce rassemblement comme un prince, les enfants lui baisèrent la main. Les femmes l'accueillirent par des you-you stridents, entrecoupés par des éloges et des prières du genre: Que Dieu le garde . . . Le soleil est arrivé . . .C'est la fin des ténèbres .. Dieu est grand . . . Dieu est avec toi . . .

Il pénétra dans la chambre, ferma la porte à clé, et demanda à Lalla Radhia d'ôter les langes du nouveau-né. C'était évidemment une fille. Sa femme s'était voilé le visage pour pleurer. Il tenait le bébé dans son bras gauche et de sa main droite il tira violemment sur le voile et dit à sa femme: «Pourquoi ces larmes? J'espère que tu pleures de joie! Regarde, regarde bien, c'est un garçon! Plus besoin de te cacher le visage. Tu dois être fière . . . Tu viens après quinze ans de mariage de me donner un enfant, c'est un garçon, c'est mon premier enfant, regarde comme il est beau, touche ses petits testicules, touche son pénis, c'est déjà un homme!» Puis, se tournant vers la sage-femme, il lui dit de veiller sur le garçon, et qu'elle ne laisse personne s'en approcher ou le toucher. Il sortit de la pièce, arborant un grand sourire . . . Il portait sur les épaules et sur le visage toute la virilité du monde! A cinquante ans, il se sentait léger comme un jeune homme. Il avait déjà oublié – ou peut-être faisait-il semblant – qu'il avait tout arrangé. Il avait bien vu une fille, mais croyait fermement que c'était un garçon.

La Nuit sacrée (Paris: Seuil, 1987), pp. 55–7.

Je crois que tout était en ordre la veille de la vingt-septième nuit du ramadan.

Tout devenait clair en moi. Je ne peux vous dire que mes dispositions étaient prises, mais je savais qu'après la mort du père, j'allais tout abandonner et partir. Je laisserais tout aux filles et je quitterais pour toujours cette maison et cette famille. Avec la disparition du père quelque chose devait aussi s'achever. Il emporterait avec lui dans sa tombe l'image du monstre qu'il avait fabriqué.

Après l'enterrement je perdis tous les repères. Pendant quelques jours je ne savais pas où j'étais ni avec qui j'étais. Je vous ai raconté cette aventure qui avait tout pour être merveilleuse et qui finit dans la peur et l'errance.

Comme vous le savez je retournai une nuit à la maison. J'y entrai par la terrasse des voisins. Les filles étaient revenues. Elles étaient très bien habillées, maquillées à outrance et portaient les bijoux de leur mère. Elles riaient et jouaient avec d'autres femmes venues du quartier. L'enterrement et le deuil furent pour elles une libération et une fête. A la limite je comprenais leur réaction. Des filles frustrées, longtemps tenues à l'écart de la vie, découvraient leur liberté. Alors elles se déchaînaient avec l'hystérie qu'elles avaient en réserve. Toutes les lumières étaient allumées. On passait des disques sur un vieux phonographe. La fête battait son plein. Il ne manquait plus que des hommes pour assouvir leur désir. J'eus un sourire; de toute façon plus rien ne me concernait, j'étais déjà une étrangère. J'ouvris discrètement la porte de ma chambre, pris quelques affaires que j'entassai dans un sac et repartis par la terrasse.

Habillée d'une djellaba, un foulard sur la tête – mes cheveux étaient longs –, je me dirigeai en cette nuit claire vers le cimetière. J'enjambai un muret pour ne pas être vue du gardien et allai sur la tombe de mon père.

La nuit était calme et belle. C'était la veille de l'Aïd. Le ciel était particulièrement étoilé. La terre recouvrant la tombe était encore fraîche. Mes mains creusaient avec rapidité et méthode. Il ne fallait pas déranger le mort ou attirer l'attention du gardien ou d'un profanateur. Quand un morceau de linceul blanc m'apparut, je dégageai doucement avec mes doigts la terre. Le corps était glacial. Le linceul était mouillé par l'humidité de la terre. J'eus un frisson. Il ne faisait pas froid. C'était un sentiment où la crainte était mêlée à quelque appréhension. Je m'arrêtai un instant et je fixai la tête du mort. Au niveau des narines il me sembla que le tissu blanc bougeait. Respirait-il encore, ou n'était-ce qu'une hallucination? Je vidai très vite le sac qui contenait presque tout ce que je possédais, une chemise d'homme, un pantalon, un extrait d'acte de naissance, une photo de la cérémonie de circoncision, ma carte d'identité, l'acte de mariage avec la malheureuse Fatima, les médicaments de mon père que je lui faisais prendre de force, des chaussettes, des chaussures, un trousseau de clés, un ceinturon, une boîte de tabac à priser, un paquet de lettres, un livre de registres, une bague, un mouchoir, une montre cassée, une ampoule, une bougie à moitié entamée . . .

Au moment de fermer la tombe, je m'accroupis pour bien tasser les objets et j'eus mal à la poitrine. Quelque chose me serrait les côtes et le thorax. Les bandelettes de tissu étaient encore autour de ma poitrine pour empêcher les seins de sortir et de grossir. Je retirai avec rage ce déguisement intérieur composé de plusieurs mètres de tissu blanc. Je le déroulai et le passai autour du cou du mort. Ensuite je serrai très fort et fis un nœud. J'étais en sueur. Je me débarrassais de toute une vie, une époque de mensonges et de faux-semblant. Avec les pieds et les mains j'entassai les objets sur le corps que je piétinai un peu au passage. Je remis de la terre. La tombe avait changé de volume. Elle était grosse. Je calai le tout avec des pierre lourdes, me recueillis un moment, pas pour prier ni pour demander à Dieu miséricorde, mais afin de m'imprégner de l'air nouveau que je respirais. Je dis quelque chose comme: «Salut!» ou: «Adieu gloire factice, à nous deux la vie, l'âme nue, blanche, vierge, le corps neuf même si la parole est ancienne!»

Text and context

This extract is made up of two passages taken respectively from Tahar Ben Jelloun's *L'Enfant de sable* (1985) and its sequel *La Nuit sacrée* (1987). The latter won the author the prestigious Prix Goncourt. The two texts tell the story of the androgynous character Ahmed/Zahra. The first accounts for twenty years of the protagonist's life as a man with the name of Ahmed. The second sees the protagonist regaining her female identity and bearing the name Zahra.

As in a number of Ben Jelloun's works, the narrative style of both extracts borrows heavily from the oral tradition of story-telling. Accordingly the reader is put into the position of a listener. The 'vous' of the opening sentence of the extract is a direct address to the reader. What follows is therefore the story-teller's account of the circumstances of the protagonist's birth.

The gathering of the extended family, as described in the beginning of the passage, seems too formal: more like a family council meeting than relatives coming together. The perplexity here is that an event, such as a birth, does not require the extended family to be present; customarily the family gathering would occur after the birth. However, the gathering is a calculated part of Hadj's scheme: whatever the gender of the expected baby, he is going to announce the birth of a boy. He is determined that his brothers know that he has a male heir. Ben Jelloun depicts here an aspect of the Muslim tradition which privileges boys over girls. The *Shari'a* dictates that male heirs receive twice as much as females in the inheritance of their father (of the three countries of the Maghreb and the whole of the Muslim world, only Tunisia, under the leadership of the late President Bourguiba, saw a reform in the *Shari'a* concerning women's inheritance). Where there is no male heir, it is a male next of kin who inherits. In the case of Hadj, it would be his brothers.

Hadj is a wealthy man with seven daughters but no son. His brothers are jealous of his wealth and rejoice at the idea of being his inheritors. This prompts him to plot the birth of a son. As his wife goes into labour the atmosphere becomes tense. While Hadj paces the street, his brothers connive ('tenaient un conseil de guerre' (l. 9)). The only person allowed with Hadj's wife is Lalla Radhia, the midwife. She is the only one besides Hadj and his wife involved in the deception. Although the newly born baby is a girl, ululating, Lalla Radhia declares to the assembly: 'c'est un homme, un homme, un homme . . .' (l. 22).

The new daughter is thus brought up under a false gender identity. She is named Ahmed and inculcated with the norms of masculinity. *L'Enfant de sable* describes her life as a man and her silent suffering. For his own masculine pride and for the sake of social prejudices against women, the father imposes on his daughter a fraudulent life. The novel, in this sense, provides the reader with an idea of how powerful patriarchy can be. By his law and power, the father is able to dictate everything, even his daughter's identity, in order to realize his wishes. The androgynous daughter learns how to suppress her femininity. Indeed, the novel shows her enjoyment of the privileges of masculinity. Ironically, instead of being understanding to her sisters, who are oblivious of her real gender, she exercises her male power sadistically, punishing them for their passivity. Like her father, she manages to suppress the woman in her ('Il avait bien vu une fille, mais croyait fermement que c'était un garçon' (l. 39)).

The second part of the extract is narrated by the protagonist herself. Twenty years have passed since her birth. But on the eve of the twenty-seventh day of Ramadan her life is going to change again. The eve of the twenty-seventh day of Ramadan is considered by Muslims to be the time when one's destiny is sealed. It is a sacred night for Muslims, hence the title of the novel. In this novel, the protagonist's destiny is, indeed, going to take a different turn. Just before dying, her father liberates her from her false identity. He asks for her forgiveness, names her Zahra (meaning flower in Arabic and suggesting the beginning of spring and a new life) and tells her that she is free to live her life the way she was supposed to: as a woman.

The father's death is not only a liberating moment for the protagonist but also the end of the monstrosity she had become when leading life as a man. This is suggested by her own statement: 'Il emporterait avec lui dans sa tombe l'image du monstre qu'il avait fabriqué' (l. 5).

For the sisters, the departure of the father and the patriarchal order he embodies also means their rebirth, albeit symbolic. His death is celebrated rather than mourned. To salute their newly acquired freedom, as the protagonist observes, the sisters light up the whole house and play loud music (l. 13). It is as if the long-suffering daughters are finally taking their revenge on the father by not respecting the customary mourning period. Rather than interfere and bring back order in the household, Zahra's reaction translates into a smiling detachment. With her new self, she feels a stranger to her family and surroundings.

To be able to start a new life, Zahra is aware that she has to break completely from her past. Consequently she visits her father's grave, not to pay her last respects, but to mark her total rupture and divorce from the past and the father who created that past for her. The macabre scene of the graveyard describes her opening up the freshly dug grave of her father. Once the shrouded body is reached she adds all her possessions which she secretly smuggled out of her home that night. In a symbolic way she buries with her father's corpse all that was part of her life as a man. Among her male clothes and possessions are her birth certificate, a photograph of her 'circumcision' and a marriage certificate.

All of these documents are proof that she existed as a man. Though her identity was a fraud, their existence underlines Hadj's great efforts to legitimate the falsified identity of his daughter. For example, the photograph from the circumcision ceremony is one slice in the protagonist's corrupt and illicit past. This does not relate to female circumcision, for the latter is not practised in the Maghreb, but to the fake circumcision the protagonist supposedly had when she was believed by all to be a young boy. In reality, the bloodstained clothes the guests saw were soiled by Hadj's blood (he cut his own finger). The marriage of Zahra to her cousin Fatima is another instance of masking her false identity. In the eyes of society and family, her marriage is yet another convincing disguise. However, the choice to marry Fatima is also a calculated act. The latter was crippled, suffered frequent epileptic seizures and died soon after the marriage, taking with her the secret of Zahra's identity .

To free herself totally from the grip of her past, the protagonist performs one final act – that of executing the father. By imposing on her a false identity for twenty years, the father also deprived her of her womanhood. Her body, for instance, was not allowed to develop naturally. Under the father's orders, she had to wear firm bandages around her chest so as to flatten her breasts. Symbolizing both sexuality and motherhood, it is significant that it is these very parts of a woman's body that the patriarchal order wants to 'silence'. The protagonist's regaining of her identity translates also into releasing her body from this 'silence'. Tying a knot with the bandages around the neck of her dead father is her way of punishing him by his own weapon. His double death will grant her both bodily and spiritual freedom.

The father, as the embodiment of law and order, is Ben Jelloun's metaphor to show the abuse of power in a male-dominated society. Women, in the very core of their being, are oppressed. They seem to have no right or status, as is the case of the protagonist's mother and sisters, hence their lack of names in this extract and in both novels. Similarly, the protagonist's predicament is the means whereby the author portrays women's servitude in a society where religion and traditions underlie and justify the privilege of one gender over the other. Though the reader might see Ben Jelloun's writing as critical of Islamic traditions, in reality his story is more relevant to pre-Islamic customs when newly born girls were buried alive. This brutal suppression of new-born life was considered precautionary: because girls were seen as more likely to bring shame and dishonour to the family, it was deemed right to be rid of them before they could do so.

Ben Jelloun's texts are not only a reminder of such pagan, abhorrent acts, but also show that Islamic laws have failed to change well-embedded customs. The physical murder of girls might have been suppressed in theory by Islam, but in reality women, in most Muslim communities, are subjected to various 'deaths', be they arranged marriages as in Bouraoui's *La Voyeuse interdite* (see Chapter 8 below), forced silence and obedience as in Chraïbi's *Le Passé simple* (see Chapter 2 above), or denial of femininity as in the present passage.

Further reading

Ben Jelloun, Tahar, *Harrouda* (Paris: Denoël, 1972).
—— *La Prière de l'absent* (Paris: Seuil, 1981).
—— *La Nuit de l'erreur* (Paris: Seuil, 1997).

Boughali, Mohammed, *Espaces d'écritures au Maroc* (Casablanca: Afrique-Orient, 1987).
Cazenave, Odile, 'Gender, age and narrative transformations in *L'Enfant de sable* by Tahar Ben Jelloun', *The French Review* 64, 3 (1991).
Edson, Rosa Da Silva, 'Tahar Ben Jelloun: identité arabe/expression française', *Présence Francophone* 34 (1989).
Elbaz, Robert, *Tahar Ben Jelloun ou l'inassouvissement du désir narratif* (Paris: L'Harmattan, 1996).
Ibnlfassi, Laïla, 'Whose voice is it anyway?', *Bulletin of Francophone Africa* 6 (1994), pp. 25–31.
M'Henni, Mansour (ed.), *Tahar Ben Jelloun: stratégies d'écriture* (Paris: L'Harmattan, 1993).
Novén, Bengt, *Les Mots et le corps: études des process d'écriture dans l'œuvre de Tahar Ben Jelloun* (Uppsala: Acta Universitatis Upsaliensis, 1996).

Language and style

The narrator, one of many to contribute to the telling of the story of 'Ahmed', presents the circumstances of 'his' birth in a structurally repetitive, machine-like manner, reflecting the meticulous organization and manipulation of the event by Hadj. The first twenty-four sentences (ll. 1–18) follow a very similar pattern. Nineteen are simple in structure and short in length; four others (ll. 7, 12, 14 and 16) are compound, all except the first being again extremely similar, consisting of only two clauses each, with the same subject governing both verbs and with non-repetition of the subject; they also bear a close structural resemblance to the simple sentences. For the first seven sentences, the first element is the subject: in each case the subject is a different member of the assembled group (except perhaps for the sixth sentence, with 'Personne' (l. 5)). Significantly, the brothers and Lalla Radhia are both the subjects of successive sentences (l. 9 and l. 11 respectively): no one else has two sentences devoted to them. They are key players in Hadj's scheme, and the sentences produce a sort of symmetry since the brothers are unaware of Hadj's machinations whereas Lalla Radhia is an integral component of them. The next sentence (l. 7) is the first compound sentence. Its structure contrasts strikingly with the previous seven sentences and succeeding nine, and marks a highly important turning point in the narrative – the announcement of the onset of Hadj's wife's labour pains. Hadj's plot has reached the point of no return. Thereafter the earlier pattern of simple sentences and an occasional compound sentence, with a subject indicating a person as first element, is resumed, with only slight departures from this pattern (compare sentences beginning ll. 10, 13, 15). Three sentences begin with an adverbial expression of time and track the sequence of events during the period of labour – 'vers minuit' (l. 7), 'à l'aube' (l. 13), 'vers dix heures du matin' (l. 18); this is reinforced by the two sentences without a personal subject, since the subjects there are 'le silence de la nuit' and then 'le jour'.

The announcement of the birth (l. 21) brings about a radical departure from the previous pattern of sentence structure: the floodgates of emotion are opened. The sentences are more complex and longer. The two principal protagonists who put the fraud into effect have a sentence each, and the effect of the announcement is revealed in the last sentence of the paragraph. The second paragraph concentrates on Hadj's policy of deliberate self-delusion – brought out by the frequency of 'il' as subject and the slightly more complex structure of the sentences. His wife has only one sentence devoted to her (l. 28), which describes her anguish at giving birth to her eighth daughter.

The imagery of the passage (four similes only) is, like the sentences of the first paragraph, very simple and terse; those relating to the effect of the birth on Hadj are particularly significant: 'Hadj arriva . . . comme un prince' (l. 22); '[Hadj] se sentait léger comme un jeune homme' (l. 38). The other images occur at ll. 3 and 14.

Another feature which acquires stylistic and literary significance through its repetition at strategic points in the episode is the use of 'c'est/était/étaient': 'on entendait des gémissements: c'étaient les premières douleurs' (l. 7); 'Lalla Radhia . . . répéta . . . c'est un homme . . .' (l. 20); 'C'est la fin des ténèbres' (l. 25); 'C'était évidemment une fille' (l. 28); 'c'est un garçon . . . c'est un garçon, c'est mon premier enfant . . . c'est déjà un homme' (l. 31); '[il] croyait fermement que c'était un garçon' (l. 40). This last clause forms part of the concluding sentence which is striking in its symmetry and encapsulates the deception which is being perpetrated, not only on the assembly but also on Hadj himself.

Narratorially and syntactically, the second passage continues the practice of the first. Although the narrator is no longer the anonymous narrator of the previous passage but Ahmed/Zarah herself, the readership is still addressed as if in oral mode: 'vous' occurs in ll. 2, 8 and 10, and questions are asked of the audience later (l. 33). Syntactically there is again a strong predominance of simple and compound sentences (thirty-seven, 65 per cent, and ten, 18 per cent, respectively) with a minimum of complex and compound-complex sentences (eight, 14 per cent, and two, 4 per cent, respectively): this pushes the main storyline along and concentrates exclusively upon the most significant events following Hadj's death: first, Ahmed's resolve to resume life as a woman, but especially the effect of their father's death upon his daughters and Ahmed's visit to the house and then the graveyard. Subordinate clauses are not called upon to provide subsidiary details. The longest sentence begins in l. 34 and lists the items Ahmed collects to bury in the grave – and in some ways parallels and cancels the sentence in the previous passage where Lalla Radhia (l. 20) had announced the birth of a 'male'; now the masculine accoutrements which had accompanied the deception are to be buried for good: the deception is at an end. Ahmed's determination to bring the deception to an end is conveyed linguistically through the frequent use of 'tout' in the opening lines: 'Je crois que tout était en ordre . . . Tout devenait clair en moi . . . je savais qu'après la mort du père, j'allais tout abandonner et partir. Je laisserais tout aux filles et je quitterais pour toujours cette maison et cette famille' (l. 1).

There are other contrasts between the two passages. The first is the reversal of the normal emotion evoked at the most momentous events in human existence: birth and death. The tension and anxiety experienced by everyone waiting for news of the sex of the baby contrasts powerfully with the joyful celebration of the daughters after their father's death. Another concerns the manipulation of events at Ahmed's birth by Hadj which are replicated in Ahmed's obliteration of all marks of her/his previous life through burying the evidence in Hadj's grave – the circle of deceit is completed. The language of rebirth and a new beginning accompanies this act: 'Je . . . me recueillis un moment . . . afin de m'imprégner de l'air nouveau que je respirais. Je dis quelque chose comme: « . . . à nous deux la vie, l'âme nue, blanche, vierge, le corps neuf même si la parole est ancienne!»' (l. 49); 'imprégner, nouveau, vie, nue, blanche, vierge, neuf' all look forward to a radically different new life.

It is difficult to avoid noticing the large number of doublets used in the passage. These vary from the pairs of main clauses constituting the compound sentences – all but one of the ten contain two clauses only (the exception being l. 18 with three clauses) and in all but one case (l. 33), the same subject governs both verbs, e.g. 'Je le déroulai et la passai autour du cou du mort. Ensuite je serrai très fort et fis un nœud' (l. 45), to a pair of relative clauses in a complex sentences, e.g. 'Je vous ai raconté cette aventure qui avait tout pour être merveilleuse et qui finit dans la peur et l'errance' (l. 8) – to pairs of nouns, adjectives and infinitives, e.g. 'j'allais tout abandonner et partir . . . je quitterais pour toujours cette maison et cette famille' (l. 3), 'La nuit était calme et belle' (l.25, also ll. 27, 28, 42, 44, 47). The most striking example is 'L'enterrement et le deuil furent pour elles une libération et une fête' (l. 13), where the symmetrical structure of the sentence represents the fundamental change occurring in the daughters' lives, and the passage finishes with an appeal to 'nous deux' (l. 52) – body and soul are invited to start afresh. These recurrent doublets may be seen as a means of expressing the past and future duality of Ahmed/Zarah's life.

Chapter 7

Azouz Begag

Le Gone du Chaâba (Paris: Seuil, 1986), pp. 96–103.

J'ai dû m'asseoir au bureau de Jean-Marc Laville, à contrecœur. J'aurais pourtant bien voulu montrer à Moussaoui et aux autres cousins que je ne le désirais pas, mais c'était impossible parce que la suggestion venait du maître et que, si je voulais un jour être premier de la classe, il fallait que je le fasse.

Ils m'ont tous regardé avec mépris lorsqu'ils sont allés rejoindre le fond de la classe, comme s'ils attendaient de moi que je brave l'autorité du maître, ce matin.

Jean-Marc a essayé de me parler. Je crois qu'il me demandait si je voulais être à droite ou à gauche de notre bureau commun, et je lui ai répondu de se taire parce que M. Grand parlait. En réalité, je ne voulais pas que mes cousins me voient échanger des mots avec lui.

Tout le monde est assis à présent. Le maître se lève à son bureau et prend la parole:

– Aujourd'hui, leçon de morale sur l'hygiène, dit-il.

Et pendant quelques minutes, il parla de la propreté, posa des questions du genre: Faut-il être propre? Combien de fois faut-il se laver par jour? Les élèves français répondirent avec zèle à toutes ces choses qu'ils connaissaient bien chez eux. Ils parlèrent de baignoire, de lavabo et même de brosse à dents et de pâte dentifrice. Au Chaâba, si l'on avait su que les règles de la propreté nécessitaient une telle minutie, on aurait beaucoup ri. Pour se laver la bouche, tous les grands de chez nous prennent un verre d'eau, gardent le liquide dans la bouche, contractent leurs mâchoires pour le faire circuler entre les dents, passent un doigt sur les incisives afin de nettoyer la surface, provoquent à nouveau des vagues dans la bouche et recrachent enfin un grand coup pour évacuer l'eau sale. On les entend ensuite racler les parois du fond de leur gorge pour en extraire les impuretés de la journée précédente et les propulser sur le bitume. Puis ils recouvrent de leur pied cette substance pour ne pas dégoûter leurs voisins. Et voilà. Pas besoin de brosse à dents ni de Colgate.

– Que faut-il faire pour bien se laver? demande à nouveau le maître.

Trois élèves lèvent le doigt.

– M'sieur! M'sieur! gazouillent-ils comme des nouveau-nés dans un nid d'oiseau.

M. Grand attend un instant que d'autres demandent la parole, puis il reformule sa question:

– Avec quoi vous lavez-vous les matins?

– M'sieur! M'sieur! sifflent toujours les téméraires.

– Jean-Marc, fait le maître en le désignant du doigt.

Il se lève:

– Une serviette et du savon!

– C'est bien. Et quoi d'autre?

– Du shampooing! dit un autre.

– Oui. Quoi d'autre encore?

Une idée jaillit dans ma tête. Instinctivement, je lève le doigt au ciel, ignorant les reproches que m'ont adressés les cousins il y a quelques minutes.

– Azouz! autorise M. Grand.

– M'sieur, on a besoin d'un chritte et d'une kaissa!

– De quoi??! fait-il, les yeux grands ouverts de stupéfaction.

– Un chritte et une kaissa! dis-je trois fois moins fort que précédemment, persuadé que quelque chose d'anormal est en train de se passer.

– Mais qu'est-ce que c'est que ça? reprend le maître, amusé.

– C'est quelque chose qu'on se met sur la main pour se laver . . .

– Un gant de toilette?

– Je sais pas, m'sieur.

– Comment c'est fait?

Je lui explique.

– C'est bien ça, dit-il. C'est un gant de toilette. Et vous, vous dites une kaissa à la maison?

– Oui, m'sieur. Mais on l'utilise seulement quand on va aux douches avec ma mère.

– Et un chritte, alors, qu'est-ce que c'est?

– Et ben, m'sieur, c'est comme beaucoup de bouts de ficelle qui sont entortillés ensemble et ça gratte beaucoup. Ma mère, elle me frotte avec ça et je deviens même tout rouge.

– Ça s'appelle un gant de crin, conclut-il en souriant.

Je rougis un peu mais il m'encourage:

– C'est bien de nous avoir appris ça, en tout cas!

Un bref silence s'ensuivit. Puis il se mit à nouveau à nous exposer la théorie de l'hygiène. Je me rendis compte qu'au Chaâba nous étions de très mauvais praticiens, mais je ne le dis pas.

– Maintenant, reprend-il après avoir parlé pendant une demi-heure, vous allez tous enlever vos chaussettes et les mettre à plat sur vos tables. Je vais vérifier la propreté de chacun d'entre vous.

Une terrible angoisse me prend à la gorge. Mais elle s'atténue rapidement lorsque je me souviens que ma mère m'a fait mettre des chaussettes propres ce matin. Autour de moi, c'est le silence total, puis tous les élèves se baissent pour dénouer les lacets de leurs chaussures. Je m'exécute, mets le nez dans mes chaussettes pour en tester le parfum. Hum! ça va. Je ne serai pas trop ridicule! A côté de moi, Jean-Marc allonge sur la table les couleurs pures de ses chaussettes en Nylon. M. Grand passe dans les rangs, cueille ici et là quelques échantillons; se garde bien de les renifler trop profondément, mais les tourne dans tous les sens pour analyser la nature des taches et des trous.

– Pas très propre, ça! Très bien! dit-il à quelques-uns.

Tandis que certains sont fiers d'être conformes à la morale, d'autres se maudissent de n'avoir pas pensé à changer de chaussettes ce matin.

M. Grand parvient auprès de Moussaoui et de son équipe. Pas de chaussettes sur la table.

– Moussaoui, ôtez vos chaussettes et posez-les immédiatement sur le bureau, fait-il calmement.

L'élève hésite quelques instants, pose son regard sur la fenêtre et, finalement, se décide à parler en fixant le maître.

– Mes chaussettes, je les enlève pas, moi. Pourquoi que je les enlèverais, d'abord? C'est pas le service d'hygiène ici? Et pis d'abord, vous êtes pas mon père pour me donner des ordres. J'enlèverai pas mes chaussettes. C'est pas la peine d'attendre ici!

M. Grand vire au rouge d'un seul coup, paralysé par la surprise. Ça doit être la première fois de sa vie d'instituteur qu'il a à faire face à une telle rébellion.

Moussaoui résiste, plus déterminé que jamais. Peut-être est-il respectueux des narines de son adversaire, après tout?

– Tu as les pieds sales. C'est pour ça que tu ne veux pas ôter tes chaussettes, rétorque le maître qui, sans s'en rendre compte, tutoie son élève.

Alors, l'incroyable se produit. Moussaoui, le rire jaune, le foudroie d'un regard méprisant, avant de lui lancer:

– T'es rien que un pédé! Je t'emmerde.

Un froid givrant mortifie la classe. Pendant quelques secondes, on entend le maître balbutier. Les mots ne parviennent pas à ses lèvres. Il est décontenancé. Moussaoui s'enhardit. Il se lève, se place dos à la fenêtre, de profil par rapport au maître, poings serrés, et lui crie:

– Si tu veux te battre, pédé, viens. Moi, tu me fais pas peur!

M. Grand ne parvient même plus à rire de cette situation grotesque. Il retourne à son bureau et, sans regarder Moussaoui, lui dit:

– On règlera ça chez le directeur!

Le cousin se rassied en desserrant sa garde.

– Le directeur? Je le nique, avertit-il avant de se situer à un niveau plus général. Et d'abord, je vous nique tous ici, moi, un par un.

– Vous serez expulsé de l'école, pauvre idiot.

– Tu sais où je la mets, ton école?

– Bon, ça suffit maintenant, dit le maître, sinon je vais me fâcher pour de bon!

– Fâche-toi! Fâche-toi! s'excite à nouveau le rebelle en sautillant sur ses jambes, à la Mohamed Ali. Viens! Viens! je t'attends!

– Mais, c'est qu'on va être obligé de l'enfermer, ce forcené! suggère M. Grand en se tournant vers nous.

– Pédé! réitère Moussaoui en raclant le P dans sa gorge.

– Continuez! Quand vos parents ne toucheront plus les allocations familiales, vous serez content!

Ces derniers mots assomment Moussaoui. L'argument est de taille. Qu'on l'expulse de l'école, soit, mais qu'on touche au portefeuille de son père parce qu'il ne veut pas montrer ses chaussettes au maître, non! La peur apparaît sur son visage et ses yeux retombent sur son bureau, vaincus. Le moribond grommelle encore dans sa bouche quelques mots incompréhensibles, puis, soudainement, une lueur jaillit de son corps tout entier.

– Vous êtes tous des racistes! hurle-t-il. C'est parce qu'on est des Arabes que vous pouvez pas nous sentir!

M. Grand a les cartes en main. Il attaque:

– Ne cherchez pas à vous défendre comme ça. La vérité, c'est que tu es un fainéant et que les fainéants comme toi ne font jamais rien dans la vie.

– Quel pédé! fait Moussaoui en se tournant vers Nasser. Il croit qu'on n'a pas compris pourquoi il nous mettait toujours dernier au classement.

Peureux comme il est, Nasser ne sait où cacher son regard. Il ne tient pas du tout à couper les allocations familiales à ses parents.

– Menteur! poursuit M. Grand. Regardez Azouz . . . (Toutes les têtes se retournent alors vers moi.) C'est aussi un Arabe et pourtant il est deuxième de la classe . . . Alors ne cherchez pas d'alibi. Vous n'êtes qu'un idiot fainéant.

La réplique me cloue sur ma chaise. Pourquoi moi? Quelle idée il a eue, là, le maître, de m'envoyer au front? Moussaoui a la bouche ouverte sur son cahier. Il était sur le point de riposter encore une fois, de prouver au maître qu'il était raciste, et voilà qu'il reçoit en pleine face une vérité implacable. C'est fini. Il agonise. Et cheikh au roi! A cause de moi!

Text and context

Following the success of Mehdi Charef's *Le Thé au harem d'Archi Ahmed* (see Chapter 5 above), a number of young people of immigrant descent took up the pen to express their own experiences. Azouz Begag is one of them. He has at various times acknowledged the impact Charef's book had on him and how it influenced him to write his own story. The influence is obvious in as much as the two writers share similar ethnic, economic and social backgrounds. Like his role model, Begag spent all his childhood and most of his adolescent years in poverty along with his family. The family lived in squalid conditions, first in a shanty-town near Lyon, then in HLMs (low-rent housing on the outskirts of big cities where most immigrant and French working-class families live). *Le Gone du Chaâba*,

Begag's first novel, is thus an account of a child's life and upbringing in such places and conditions.

Begag's *Le Gone du Chaâba*, like most *beur* fiction, is highly autobiographical. However, in this novel, Begag uses the diegetic elements to the full: the narrator/protagonist bears the same name as the author; the other characters represent real people known to the author, even appearing in the text under their real names. Further, the different locations in the narrative stand for real places in Begag's life. The little boy at the centre of the novel is the undisguised counterpart of Begag. It is clear that *Le Gone du Chaâba* is, on the whole, the author's own personal journey.

'Le Gone', a slang word meaning boy from the region of Lyon where the author was born and grew up, leads a life limited to two spaces: the family and the school. The two worlds these spaces represent are totally different from each other. The family is for the narrator a reminder of his origins: Algerian, Muslim, poor and (most importantly) largely illiterate. The school, however, is the opposite: widely populated by French pupils and teachers whose standards of living are better, a place for education and knowledge matching the most important of the narrator's aspirations, especially given the extensive illiteracy of his family and community.

The extract studied here shows a scene at school during a lesson, a moment when the protagonist's two conflicting worlds come into contact, resulting in a violent outburst. The classroom lesson is about hygiene – not something the children of immigrants, the classroom's minority, identify with, hence the loud reluctance of one of them to participate.

Azouz, the narrator, and all other Maghrebian children around him, come from an environment where hygiene is almost non-existent. The *chaâba* where they live is a poverty-stricken health hazard. The word *chaâba* comes from Algerian Arabic dialect meaning an uninhabited, isolated and desolate place. It is a word which stresses wilderness and detachment from urban life. With these wilderness-like characteristics, *chaâba* is a highly suggestive metaphor in the novel. It describes a compound of tin huts – commonly known in French as *bidonvilles* – where a great number of families live in crowded conditions. The *chaâba*, home for the protagonist, has none of the facilities, such as electricity and water, that French people take for granted. The shanty-town has one water pump which all families share to fill buckets they then take to their respective huts. There are no bathrooms but one communal pit (with no septic tank) shared and used by all as a toilet. Furthermore, not only is the *chaâba* a hard place in which to maintain strict hygiene, but is also adjacent to the city's main rubbish tip where, once a week, the children go digging in the new refuse for whatever could be useful for them or their homes.

The gulf between school and home and communal life is so huge that a lesson in hygiene is the ultimate insult for Moussaoui, the protagonist's cousin and classmate. He refuses to obey the teacher and display his dirty socks, knowing that he will be scolded for a lack of cleanliness he did not choose to live in. By asking the children to show whether their socks are clean or not, the teacher demonstrates a lack of sensitivity towards his ethnic-minority pupils. The act is perceived by Moussaoui and his Arab friends (all seated at the back of the classroom) as humiliating. The whole episode ends with a hysterical Moussaoui insulting the teacher and defying his authority.

The violent, abusive behaviour displayed by Moussaoui in this scene has its counterpart in other episodes in the novel in humour, irony and self-mockery. In all cases, the latter behaviour is perceived as a defence mechanism. To avoid humiliation, Moussaoui counter-attacks before the teacher has a chance to condemn his lack of hygiene. For Moussaoui, it is not so much his own person, but his whole community which is at risk of being humiliated and disgraced. He represents a community which struggles to maintain its sense of pride in spite of its degrading lifestyle.

This extract, like most of the novel, does not display the narrator's judgement or explanation of any specific incident. The novel generally relies on dialogue. The narrator's interjected comments amount to simple and subtle remarks, such as when the teacher M. Grand (probably a coincidence but nonetheless a significant and symbolic name for the one who has authority) drops the formal *vous* and addresses Moussaoui with the *tu* form; he thus reinforces the latter's unequal status. Similarly, in signalling to Moussaoui that his misconduct will result in his family's loss of child allowance, the teacher not only shows implicit knowledge of the financial struggle of families like Moussaoui's, and hence their reliance on child allowances, but also demonstrates the latent attitude in French racist discourse which accuses immigrant families of having many children for the sole purpose of pocketing more allowances.

In shock, like the rest of his class, but happy not to be involved in the incident, the narrator is nevertheless drawn in and implicated by the teacher who points him out as an example of a high-achieving Arab pupil. Unknowingly, in so doing, the teacher isolates the protagonist from his own ethnic group. Azouz is indeed an exemplary hard-working pupil. He is eager to learn, not only because he is motivated but also because his father is strict in seeing that his children achieve and take the opportunity to gain an education he himself never had.

But, typically for his generation, Azouz faces trying to accommodate two antagonistic worlds. His eagerness to learn drives a wedge between his culture and the French one; to his misery he realizes that he cannot progress in his learning without alienating his own culture and group. His desire to learn leads him at times to being ridiculed. For example, he contributes during the lesson on hygiene by giving examples of items used for cleaning the body but uses Arabic words such as 'kaissa' (toilet glove) and 'chritte' (loofah) showing thus his alienation from the French concept of cleanliness and the French language in general. To his embarrassment, rather than being encouraged by the teacher, he becomes a source of amusement. Also, when he achieves the grade of second best in a class test, his good work turns against him when the teacher puts him next to a French pupil in the front row, thus isolating him from the other Arab boys, sitting in the back row, 'le coin des bourricots' (p. 104).

So, when he is used as an example by the teacher, he is filled with apprehension. He fears the reprisals of Moussaoui who lost the argument because of him: 'et voilà qu'il reçoit en pleine face une vérité implacable' (l. 144). Not only is the teacher's statement true, but it is detrimental to Azouz, as it is going to ostracize him further from his group. His determination to do well at school and be accepted is offset by the Arab boys rejecting him: 'Si t'en étais un [Arabe], tu serais dernier de la classe comme nous' (p. 106). As such, Azouz's dilemma stems from his awareness that being an achiever from a minority group comes at a price: mutual alienation and rejection between him and his group.

Further reading

Begag, Azouz, *Béni ou le paradis privé* (Paris: Seuil, 1989).
—— *L'Ilet-aux-vents* (Paris: Seuil, 1992).
—— *Les Chiens aussi* (Paris: Seuil, 1995).

Benarab, Abdelkader, *Les Voix de l'exil* (Paris: L'Harmattan, 1995).
Bonn, Charles (ed.), *Littératures des immigrations* (Paris: L'Harmattan, 1995).
Djeghloul, Abdelkader, 'Souvenirs d'enfance d'un algéro-lyonnais', in *Actualité de l'émigration* (Paris: Amicale des Algériens en Europe, 1986).
Hargreaves, Alec G., *Voices from the North African Immigrant Community in France: Immigration and Identity in Beur Fiction* (Oxford: Berg, 1991).
—— 'Writers of Maghrebian immigrant origin in France: French, Francophone, Maghrebian or Beur?', in L. Ibnlfassi and N. Hitchcott (eds), *African Francophone Writing* (Oxford: Berg, 1996), pp. 33–34.
Laronde, Michel, *Autour du roman beur: immigration et identité* (Paris:L'Harmattan, 1993).
Mdaghri-Alaoui, Abdellah, 'Interculturel et littérature beur', in M. Bencheikh and C. Develotte (eds), *L'Interculturel: réflexions pluridisciplinaires* (Paris: L'Harmattan, 1995).
Rosello, Mireille, 'The "Beur nation": toward a theory of "departenance" ', *Research in African Literatures* 24 (1993).

Language and style

The clash of cultures implied by the title – 'gone' = 'boy', a dialectal word from the Lyon area, and 'chaâba' = wasteland, an Arabic word – is painfully experienced by the narrator, Azouz, in this passage. His dilemma over whether to identify with the educational aspirations of his French classmates or remain loyal to his Maghrebian 'cousins' is poignantly portrayed in the first three paragraphs through a stream of consciousness technique – the reader shares the narrator's anxiety. Linguistically this is brought out in the frequent use 'vouloir/désirer' (ll. 2, 3, 7, 9, the interplay of negative and positive polarity (ll. 2, 3, 9), the use of 'mais/à contrecœur', the conditional tenses and the subjunctive mood (ll. 1, 4, 6, 9), as he tries to justify his behaviour and convince himself that he has made the right decision in moving to the front of the class. A similar sense of uncertainty – and use of 'mais' – occurs later (l. 67) when the clash of cultural hygienic practices is brought home to Azouz. The culture clash is also symbolized in the use of proper names: M. Grand, the teacher, an expression of superiority and authority over Azouz and his 'cousins', and Jean-Marc Laville, whose name represents mainstream France and contrasts with the *chaâba*.

The three past tenses – perfect, past historic and historic present – are skilfully manipulated to convey three aspects of past action in the narrative. The perfect tense is used (ll. 1–9) for internal reflection, as Azouz describes his reluctance to move to the front of the class and goes over in his own mind his reasons for doing so. The perfect gives way to the historic present (ll. 11–13), as the fateful incident begins to unfurl. However, it is quickly replaced by the past historic (ll. 14–17), as M. Grand, the teacher, begins the lesson – formal language is associated with him. The historic present returns (l. 28), as the personal hygiene lesson progresses, and continues until the past historic is reinstated when M. Grand's exposition is resumed, and then returns once again (l. 68) and persists until the end of the passage, as the drama unfolds.

Another contrasts exists in the use of relatively complicated sentence structures in the sections where Azouz is engaged in internal reflections (ll. 1–10, ll. 14–27, 123–8) and much more direct structures in the conversational and accompanying narrative. In ll. 1–10, there are three simple sentences, two compound-complex (with a large number of subordinate clauses) and one complex. In the conversational sections, short questions from M. Grand are followed by short answers from the pupils. Generally speaking, M. Grand uses standard French in his questions and comments, but when it comes to Moussaoui's outburst, a much lower register is employed. Moussaoui omits negative 'ne' on all but one occasion (ll. 89, 90, 91, 101, 106, 130, the exception being l. 134), whereas M. Grand never does. He indulges in much highlighting: in 'Mes chaussettes, je les enlève pas, moi' (l. 89), both object and subject are foregrounded; in 'Moi, tu me fais pas peur!' (l. 106), it is the indirect object. In 'Pourquoi que je les enlèverais, d'abord?' (l. 89), the question is formed with 'que' to avoid inversion. Ellipsis is apparent in his pronunciation ('pis' (l. 90), 't'es' (l. 101). 'Niquer', used twice (ll. 111, 112) by Moussaoui, is in fact of Arabic origin. The switch from 'vous' to 'tu' by M. Grand (l. 97) symbolizes his momentary loss of authority and control; for Moussaoui (l. 101) it symbolizes his rejection of authority. Whereas M. Grand retrieves his authority by returning to 'vous' (l. 113), Moussaoui stays in rebellious mode. Even Azouz, under the effect of consternation in being singled out by M. Grand in front of everyone for commendation and as his trump card, loses control of his language within the narrative itself: 'Quelle idée il a eue, là, le maître, de m'envoyer au front?' (l. 141), where 'front' acquires the meaning of battlefront.

Indeed the confrontation between M. Grand and Moussaoui, which takes the form of racial conflict as well as an uprising against authority, is expressed in strong, pusillanimous terms. (The expectation that Azouz might rebel (l. 6) comes to naught; Moussaoui acts.) At the first sign of insubordination, M. Grand 'vire au rouge', is 'paralysé' (l. 93). Moussaoui presses home his advantage, having taken the teacher by surprise: 'Moussaoui résiste, plus déterminé que jamais' (l. 95), 'Moussaoui . . . le foudroie d'un regard méprisant' (l. 99), 'Moussaoui s'enhardit' (l. 104) – the repetition of the boy's name adds extra power to his onslaught. The effect on the class is striking – 'Un froid givrant mortifie la classe' (l. 102), and M. Grand loses face, becomes speechless (l. 103). However, his counterattack (suggesting the cutting off of the Moussaoui family's state benefits) hits the mark: 'Ces derniers mots assomment Moussaoui' (l. 123), 'Le moribond' (l. 126); the fear he had rejected (l. 106) overwhelms him: 'La peur apparaît sur son visage et ses yeux retombent sur son bureau, vaincus' (l. 125). His counterattack (playing the racist card (l. 129)) is in turn repulsed (l. 131) and has a stunning impact not only on Moussaoui – 'Il agonise. Et cheikh au roi!' (l. 144) – but also on Azouz, the secret weapon – 'La réplique me cloue sur ma chaise' (l. 141). This conflictual language is supported by other devices – the description of Moussaoui's aggressive stance (ll. 99, 104), the comparison with Mohamed Ali (l. 117).

As a counterbalance to the tension caused by the battle between M. Grand and Moussaoui, there are touches of humour in the extract: the pupils twitter 'comme des nouveau-nés dans un nid d'oiseau' (l. 30); Azouz gingerly tests his socks – 'Je m'exécute, mets le nez dans mes chaussettes pour en tester le parfum. Hum! ça va' (l. 74) – and moderates his enthusiasm – 'Un chritte et une kaissa! dis-je trois fois moins fort que précédemment, persuadé que quelque chose d'anormal est en train de se passer' (l. 46); M. Grand is extremely cautious in inhaling the odour of their socks: 'M. Grand passe dans les rangs, cueille ici et là quelques échantillons; se garde bien de les renifler trop profondément' (l. 77); Nasser does not want to take risks with his family's benefits (l. 136). The description of the oral hygiene of the elders from the *chaâba*, expressed in a host of short clauses and an array of graphic verbs, is also executed in humorous, mock-heroic fashion (l. 19). In his description of racial tension in French schools, Begag highlights possible sources of conflict, but shows a dispassionate attitude towards both sides, the authority figures as well as those subordinated to them. The conflict is real and may be waged in strident terms, but the reader's sympathies are shared among the protagonists.

Chapter 8

Nina Bouraoui

La Voyeuse interdite (Paris: Gallimard, 1991), pp. 124–8.

La soirée des jours accumulés explosait en une formidable soustraction qui emplit la totalité de mon cadre sensible. Il n'en restait plus qu'un, ce jour précisément. Intermède entre l'ennui et l'ennui, je devais le vivre avec beaucoup d'attention afin de conserver quelques bribes de couleurs jusqu'au prochain. Une femme musulmane quitte sa maison deux fois: pour son mariage et pour son enterrement. Ainsi en a décidé la tradition! Concentrée sur les choses, sur mes gestes et sur toutes mes pensées, je devenais mon propre témoin, et par en effort réflexif, je me regardais étreindre l'aventure. Les objets avaient revêtu le voile de la mort, avant l'heure, j'assistais et participais à de joyeuses funérailles: les miennes. J'enterrais mon enfance pour aller vivre au-delà d'elle, de moi et du connu.

Le salon défiguré par un véritable cataclysme s'est transformé en salle de bal. La mutation du lieu-dit s'est opérée pendant la nuit. L'événement a marqué un autre «E» en travers du rideau protecteur. Poufs, coussins, tables, canapé retirés pour la cause ont laissé libre champ à la perspective qui jongle entre le trompe-l'œil et la réalité avec malice et habileté; dans ce grand espace, l'auteur de la tragédie n'a pas oublié les personnages appropriés, chacun est à son poste. Centre, coins, recoins, angles aveugles ou voyeurs, meubles mouvants, soie, paillettes, clochettes d'argent sur rythme de déhanchement, chaussures piquantes, bas de résille et bras de chair, volcans d'or sur décolletés moites, faces tricolores des yeux au menton, étincelles de la fête, bouches bavardes, grimaçantes ou figées, profil de singe et de déesses, brocards et satin brillant, formes grasses ou transparentes, du joufflu à l'anémiée, l'orfèvrerie est au complet!

Dépliant leurs roues émeraude, affichant pierreries et bracelets d'époque, effacées ou cancanières, les Mauresques occupent la totalité de mon salon. Je ne croyais pas ma famille si nombreuse! Nièces, tantes, cousines, grand-tantes, plus petites tantes, mères, belles-mères, grand-mères, habilleuses, maquilleuses, musiciennes, mangeuses, voyeuses, pleureuses, toute la palette féminine de l'est, de l'ouest, du nord et du sud d'Alger est réunie en mon honneur. Quel honneur! Lèvres timides et bouches gourmandes, ventres gras et cotelés, un orchestre désaccordé joue la symphonie bien connue de la basse-cour en folie! Les mâchoires claquent dans l'air trop parfumé tandis que les plus vieilles Sarrasines, accrochées aux murs comme des anciennes tentures ressorties pour la fête, tapent dans leurs mains pleines de corne et de souvenirs.

La tradition est une dame vengeresse contre qui je ne peux lutter. C'était ainsi pour elles, ce sera comme ça pour les autres. Mouvement répétitif qui ne s'enquiert ni du temps ni de mon refus et encore moins de notre jeunesse. Changement de décor, retour au semblable sur chant monocorde. A ton tour Fikria! Aujourd'hui c'est moi. Moi, moi, moi! Tout mon être porte et supporte l'aventure, je suis sa mère nourricière, l'épicentre, le dépliant touristique que des mains curieuses et interrogatives tripotent dans tous les sens. Froissent. La pierre sacrée que des bouches superstitieuses embrassent. La dernière nuit du condamné. Un porte-bonheur vivant, blanc et orangé dans les paumes avec deux cernes noirs sous les yeux qui rappellent l'ancienne couleur du sexe. Ne voyez-vous pas? Je porte le malheur!

Résignée, fatiguée, écœurée, lésée, blessée sous les aisselles, irritée entre les cuisses, je me laisse faire accueillant sans joie ni peine les compliments des anonymes et le son lourd de la derbouka qui gronde pour moi. Caissette à fond ouvert, décorée sur les côtés par des figurines kabyles, voilà la source du rythme ce soir.

Avide de savoir, je m'écarte de la ronde moite pour regarder la coupable. Ma mère valse fièrement entre ses amies, ses ennemies, et ses sœurs d'une nuit, elle a attaché ses cheveux en fines tresses confinées dans un lourd chignon, la crinière auburn se tient sagement au-dessus de sa tête comme la couronne d'une reine qui se fait sacrer. Poudrée de la tête aux pieds, ravigotée par la proche victoire, extasiée devant le buffet de la fête, l'«entre-fête» huileux de contentement, ma mère, ma très chère mère fuit mon regard; elle vole, elle virevolte, elle papillonne, elle compte, elle additionne, y aura-t-il assez de couverts, assez de place, assez de joie? elle étincelle commme une pépite au milieu d'une source vaseuse, gling gling gling, font les bracelets qui tinteront plus tard dans mes mains tremblantes.

La vieille Mauresque soufflée par les gâteaux trop gras et le désœuvrement a retrouvé sa jeunesse d'antan, ricanant, critiquant, veillant, jurant, elle tournoie comme une guêpe affolée autour du miel de la nouvelle histoire, renaissant, elle semble être la mariée d'un soir! tout le monde est là, oubliant ses formes inhumaines, à la féliciter. Moi je suis cachée derrière la porte entrouverte de la cuisine. Personne ne me voit sauf une petite main grassouillette qui joue avec les pans de la robe trop longue: peureuse Leyla! Projection de moi sur ma mère. Projection de ma mère sur moi. Je sens mon sexe se huiler. De peur. La sauterelle enceinte de l'événement sautille autour de ses hôtes en vantant les mérites de sa fille, seule féconde de la maison, «Elle m'aime, elle me respecte, jamais elle ne me décevra, elle embaume comme l'air du printemps» et je réponds «J'embaume comme la frustration embaume les pantalons des hommes de la rue, maman, je te déchiquette de baisers. Et de pensées meurtrières!».

Gling gling font les cymbales de ta cuisine. Roturière! te voilà unie pour la vie à une autre sœur: ma belle-mère! Grasse sœur! Toute vieille vêtue, elle a vingt ans de plus que ma mère, un fils adipeux et des chucots dorés qui flamboient dans l'obscurité du salon surchargé dans le Très sombre de mes pensées; l'arrière-train gondolé par une crinoline orientale, son paquet me semble plus gros, ses hanches plus larges que celles de ma génitrice, à moins que ce ne soit la forme évasive de sa robe qui lui donne une silhouette conique et peu séduisante. Noblesse apparente, cuissardes de cellulite, arriviste endiamantée, sexe verrouillé et œil de vautour, gling gling font les griffes rouges de ma belle-mère sur les assiettes de porcelaine. J'entends mon pouls. Dans toute la maison. Il s'affole. Je le cajole. Mes seins ont mal au cœur. La nuit gronde. La derbouka s'émoustille. Les notes s'accrochent aux rideaux. Le son bave des fenêtres. La fête commence!

Text and context

La Voyeuse interdite, her first published novel, won Nina Bouraoui the Prix Inter in 1991. Narrated in the first person, the novel is a young girl's subjective view of the world around her. Her field of vision is limited to the confines of her home where she remains alongside her mother and sisters. The only glimpse she has of the outside world is through the window of her room. The street, with its swarming people and traffic, is inaccessible to her. She can gaze at it but not be in it. But even this limited, vicarious participation in street life is achieved only by breaking the rules; even looking is forbidden, as the oxymoron of the book's title suggests.

The prison-like context in which women spend their daily life in the traditional Algerian society is the overall theme in *La Voyeuse interdite*. The tone of the narrative is frustrated, angry. The narrator's impatience stems from her observation of women around her. Their lack of action and their acceptance of their effective incarceration provoke both anger and judgement in her. Though the theme elaborated by Bouraoui in this novel is not necessarily new (a whole generation of women writers before her, including Assia Djebar, have pursued the theme), the style with which she approaches the subject lends it a freshness and a new profile.

The excesses with which Bouraoui characterizes the confinement of women in Arabo-Muslim society do not come across as an act of writing indulging in self-pity and martyrdom, but as an act which is deliberately meant to shock and awaken consciences. If Bouraoui makes her heroine gaze accusingly at her society and infuses her with hatred and anger, it is for the purpose of highlighting the inertia of Arabo-Muslim women in accepting and embracing patriarchal laws whose intent is to degrade and diminish them.

The time of publication of *La Voyeuse interdite* is relevant, falling within the period – the late 1980s and early 1990s – when Muslim fundamentalism was increasingly gaining ground in Algeria. The abuse of Islamic laws to justify women's enslavement is hinted at in the novel when the narrator deplores the attitude of 'les barbes brunes', who 'acide à la main, vitriolent les jeunes filles dénudées' (p. 73). Not only does Bouraoui cast a critical eye on the fundamentalists (recognized here by the wearing of beards) and their extremist acts in subjugating women in the name of an Islam-alibi, but also on the acquiescent women, who 'couvrent leurs chevilles et répudient leur sexe' (ibid.) without resistance.

So women, in the eyes of Bouraoui and her heroine, are just as guilty as men in depriving their own gender of its rights. The novel shows women as destined not only to live in confinement, but most importantly to turn against their own interest. It is a Hegelian situation whereby woman acknowledges man as her master and, by implication, accepts her relationship to him as a slave.

The passage analysed here is situated on the eve of the narrator's marriage. Fikria, the narrator, is a young girl who is about to be married to a man she has never met or even seen. The passage sums up her anguish, anger and resignation as she witnesses the marriage preparations. Fikria, like all girls and women around her, has no power over her destiny. It is planned and shaped for her by her father. The decision to put her in a marriage is sealed like a business transaction between the two interested parties: her father and the husband-to-be. As for her, she has no control over such decisions, nor is she consulted. In fact, through the predicament of Fikria, Bouraoui emphasizes the tragedy of young girls being forced into arranged marriages. While Islam does not prescribe such acts and situations, deeply entrenched traditions do – and they are the norm in some Islamic (and other) communities, though in reality patterns vary greatly. The narrator's words, 'La tradition est une dame vengeresse contre qui je ne peux lutter' (l. 34), not only stress the well-embedded norms but also carry an irony in referring to tradition as 'dame'. Though it is a well-understood fact that traditions are set by men and bear the mark of male ideology, they are implemented by women. Women are the gatekeepers and perpetuators of traditions which often work against their own interests.

The institution of marriage, silence and confinement are all means whereby women are kept under control. In Muslim societies, there is an assumption that women are aware of their sexuality and are sexually dynamic. The family unit in Muslim (and Mediterranean, in general) cultures is based on the notion of honour; and women, generally speaking, are considered the most likely to tamper with that honour and bring shame to the family. It is, therefore, with such assumptions in view that the reader learns that the father in *La Voyeuse interdite* beats up his daughter and stops talking to her when she menstruates for the first time (p. 33). In his eyes, she is no longer a child, for her menstruation is equated with fertility. Similarly, the mother seems to be less concerned with her daughter's happiness than with her virginity. Consequently, confinement, imposition of the veil and child marriages ensure that a girl's virginity and the family's honour are safe and intact.

The powerless narrator can only watch as her mother, 'la coupable', enthusiastically prepares for the celebration; which Fikria refers to with the oxymoron 'joyeuses funérailles'. Fikria casts an accusing gaze over her mother who, having gone through a similar experience herself as a child, allows traditions to inflict the same punishment on her own daughter. By deliberately using an Orientalist discourse, calling women 'Mauresques' (l. 24) and 'Sarrasines' (l. 31), she sarcastically underlines their own lack of action, their passivity, at a moment which resonates with older times when women were kept prisoner in harems as concubines.

Fear of the father and his wrath trigger the mother's obedience. Earlier in the novel, the hatred the narrator feels for her father is made explicit in defining him as 'Le complice de Satan' (p. 66). He is the source of her misery by imposing on her a life within closed walls. He is 'Le responsable qu'[elle] accuse!' (ibid.). Through her accusing eyes, the narrator simultaneously blames the father as a dictator and the mother as the executioner of his orders. Far from pitying her mother as a victim herself, whose role is to obey the father's rules, the narrator sharply judges her for her cowardice. Looking up to the mother in an ultimate cry for help to rescue her from her forced marriage, the narrator finds no compassion but a cowardly detachment: 'ma mère, ma très chère mère fuit mon regard' (l. 55). Left alone in her inner turmoil, the child-bride has no choice but to resign herself to her fate.

As the last day (which the narrator calls 'Intermède entre l'ennui et l'ennui' (l. 3)) in the paternal home comes to a close, the narrative voice takes on a faster rhythm. Fikria's feelings of despair and entrapment are expressed with staccato. Her mind becomes blurred by the sound of music and the whirling dancers. Simultaneously, the narrative builds to a crescendo which displays a powerful image of the narrator's state of mind summed up as 'La dernière nuit du condamné' (l. 41). Indeed, far from being a liberation, Fikria's marriage is nothing more than an exchange of authority between her father and her future husband, an exchange in which she is the object.

Marriage is here equated with death. Throughout the novel, death is contantly present as an obsessively deployed metaphor. The incarcerating paternal home is for the narrator a morbid space where a child is denied the innocence of childhood ('J'enterrais mon enfance' (l. 9)). She regards her marriage as death itself, comparing it to the funeral of a new-born baby (p. 141). The beginning of this passage highlights the deadly plight of the traditional Algerian woman whom Fikria characterizes in the following statement: 'Une femme musulmane quitte sa maison deux fois: pour son mariage et pour son enterrement' (l. 4). And as confirmation of this, the last paragraph in the novel shows Fikria being guided into the car, designated as 'le véhicule de la mort' (p. 143), that is going to take her to her marital home.

Overall, this extract shows the destructive effects that confinement and certain taboos have on women living in a traditional social context. It also stresses the excesses of patriarchal laws: not only are women subdued and silenced, but even their gaze is a 'voice' which needs to be veiled. Such is the fate of the 'voyeuse interdite' who, in the end, loses her only freedom – her gaze – to become 'borgne' (ibid.).

Further reading

Bouraoui, Nina, *Poing mort* (Paris: Gallimard, 1992).
—— *Le Bal des Murènes* (Paris: Fayard, 1996).
—— *L'Age blessé* (Paris: Fayard, 1998).

Abu-Haidar, Farida, 'Le chant morne d'une jeune fille cloîtrée: *La Voyeuse interdite* de Nina Bouraoui', *Bulletin of Francophone Africa* 3 (1993), pp. 56–60.
Bivona, Rosalia, 'L'interculturalité dans *La Voyeuse interdite* de Nina Bouraoui', in M. Bencheikh and C. Develotte (eds), *L'Interculturel: réflexion pluridisciplinaire* (Paris: L'Harmattan, 1995).
Bougharara, Nassima, 'Littérature algérienne au féminin', *Cahiers d'études maghrébines* 8 (1995).
Chikhi, Beida, *Littérature algérienne. Désir d'histoire et esthétique* (Paris: L'Harmattan, 1997).
Déjeux, Jean, *La Littérature féminine de langue française au Maghreb* (Paris: Karthala, 1994).

Language and style

The indictment of Arabo-Muslim arranged marriages mediated by this passage is expressed in a series of 'explosions', concentrations of powerfully evocative descriptions. Each scene contains an explosion: the family's living quarters in paragraph 2, the guests in paragraph 3, Fikria herself in the next two paragraphs, her mother in paragraphs 6 and 7, and her future mother-in-law in the last. The word itself occurs in the opening sentence – 'La soirée des jours accumulés explosait en une formidable soustraction qui emplit la totalité de mon cadre sensible' (l. 1) – accompanied by an oxymoron, a subtraction filling a totality. Fikria sees the prenuptial celebration in terms of another oxymoron – 'de joyeuses funérailles' (l. 9). The adjective preceding the noun suggests that it needs to be interpreted with caution, and the likening of a marriage to a funeral or death becomes a theme of the passage, continuing in the next sentence (l. 9).

The explosive effect which marriage is to have on her is foreshadowed in the transformation of the family's living quarters: 'Le salon défiguré par un véritable cataclysme s'est transformé en salle de bal. La mutation du lieu-dit s'est opérée pendant la nuit' (l. 11), where 'défiguré, cataclysme, mutation, nuit' all contribute to the fear that marriage will have irreparable consequences for her. Other explosions occur in the shape of events taking place and objects assembled for the celebration – overpowering concentrations of names of places, materials, accessories, parts of the body are spread over five lines (beginning l. 16) – twenty-one items in all. Immediately following that explosion of detail is another involving types of jewellery (l. 23). Then comes an explosion of family members (l. 25), fourteen types, 'toute la palette féminine de l'est, de l'ouest, du nord et du sud d'Alger' (l. 27) – even the points of the compass are enumerated. What these explosive enumerations have in common syntactically is that after a long list comes a very weak copula/passive verb – 'l'orfèvrerie est au complet!' (l. 22), 'toute la palette féminine . . . est réunie en mon honneur' (l. 27); Fikria to the right of the verb is powerless against the forces of tradition massed against her. Another enumeration consists of body parts and sounds, the audible combines with the visual (l.29). A grotesque impression, which was present but subdued in the earlier enumerations, comes to the fore in this one: the women, described derogatively as 'une palette' earlier (l. 27), now become 'une basse-cour' (l. 30), their jaws clack, they look 'comme des anciennes tentures ressorties pour la fête' and hung on walls (l. 32), their hands are horny – 'leurs mains pleines de corne et de souvenirs' (l. 33) (another example of syllepsis occurs towards the end of the passage – 'elle a vingt ans de plus que ma mère, un fils adipeux et des chucots dorés' (l. 74)).

Fikria describes herself in the fourth paragraph – 'je suis sa [l'aventure = *mariage*] mère nourricière, l'épicentre, le dépliant touristique que des mains curieuses et interrogatives tripotent dans tous les sens. Froissent. La pierre sacrée que des bouches superstitieuses embrassent. La dernière nuit du condamné. Un porte-bonheur vivant' (l. 38) – comparing herself to six very different objects, five inanimate, one animate. The images used are extremely evocative: for example, Fikria sees herself as a tourist brochure, turned this way and that by curious customers who then – and full focus is brought to bear since the verb constitutes a sentence by itself – 'Froissent' (= screw her up). But there is also the traditional, religious aspect, brought out in the reference to the holy stone revered by the superstitious. Those around her, those reading the brochure and kissing the stone, are seen as disembodied hands and mouths – not proper humans at all.

The enumerations become more grotesque with the description of her mother, the focus of twenty-three lines of disparaging remarks (from l. 50), and her future mother-in-law, who also undergoes severe negative appraisal (l. 74). An explosion of uncomplimentary details surrounds both figures. The triplet naming Fikria's mother's dancing partners suggests the hypocrisy of the event (l. 51); another triplet, consisting of exaggerated past participles – 'Poudrée de la tête aux pieds, ravigotée par la proche victoire, extasiée devant le buffet de la fête' (l. 54) – describes her appearance, followed by six identically constructed clauses – 'elle vole, elle virevolte, elle papillonne, elle compte, elle additionne . . . elle étincelle' (l. 56), displaying a mixture of enjoyment and materialistic concern. A series of present participles are even less complimentary – 'ricanant, critiquant, veillant, jurant' (l. 61). Five images are devoted to her, each presenting in increasing order of virulence a new angle on her grotesqueness. The first underlines her majesty and self-ascribed glory: her hair is 'comme la couronne d'une reine qui se fait sacrer' (l. 53), the second couples majesty and squalor: 'elle étincelle commme une pépite au milieu d'une source vaseuse' (l. 58). In the third she is compared to an over-excited wasp – 'elle tournoie comme une guêpe affolée autour du miel de la nouvelle histoire' (l. 61) – then to a newly-wed (l. 63) and in the fifth to a locust, about to give birth to the marriage – 'La sauterelle enceinte de l'événement sautille autour de ses hôtes' (l. 67). The antagonism between mother's and daughter's views of the event appears forcefully when the comments made by the mother – '«Elle m'aime, elle me respecte, jamais elle ne me décevra, elle embaume comme l'air du printemps»' (l. 69) – are weighed against Fikria's reaction – '«J'embaume comme la frustration embaume les pantalons des hommes de la rue, maman, je te déchiquette de baisers. Et de pensées meurtrières!»' (l. 70). In two further grotesque explosions the future mother-in-law is presented as even more repulsive: a triplet (l. 76) and five nouns constitute a savage character assassination – 'Noblesse apparente, cuissardes de cellulite, arriviste endiamantée, sexe verrouillé et œil de vautour' (l. 79).

Indeed, as this last quotation and also her reaction to her mother's unreal assessment of her (quoted above) show, sexual anxieties and fantasies assail Fikria. Apart from the general sickly, oppressive, sensual atmosphere of the passage, there are a number of other specific references to sexual organs and desires (ll. 44, 45, 67, 69, 71, 80). Noises also play a significant role in the passage. The dull noise of the derbouka associated with Fikria (ll. 47, 83) is eclipsed by the more metallic, strident 'gling gling gling' of her mother's bracelets (l. 58), which becomes louder as cymbals clash (l. 73) and more threatening still as her future mother-in-law taps the porcelain plates (l. 81). The two matriarchal figures are combined by this unnerving sound. The derbouka which 'gronde' at the first mention of the instrument (l. 47) becomes more frenzied at the climax of the passage – now it is the night which 'gronde' (l. 83) – and 'le son bave des fenêtres' (l. 84). Fikria, suffering a racing pulse and aching breasts (l. 82), cannot escape and must submit to her fate.

The scene/passage is like a minefield for Fikria: series of adjectives, nouns, participles, clauses, explode around her, as she describes the 'enemy'. The atmosphere is heavy with grotesque, garish descriptions of people and objects. Furthermore, a profusion of questions (ll. 43, 57), exclamations (e.g. ll. 28, 38, 84), repetitions (ll. 38, 66, 70), non-use of articles (ll. 29, 36, 47, 79), minor sentences, appeals to protagonists (ll. 71, 73), alliteration (ll. 74, 76), together with a verb-only sentence (l. 40), represent lesser explosions punctuating the desperate situation she finds herself in.

Part 2

Black Africa and the Indian Ocean

Chapter 9

Introduction

Having first arrived in West Africa in the sixteenth century, the French did not really begin to establish their African empire until the nineteenth century with the conquest of Senegal in the 1860s. In the meantime, however, they had gradually been establishing administrative bases and trading posts in strategic areas around the Gulf of Guinea. The growth of the slave trade during the previous three centuries culminated in the 1814 Treaty of Paris, which gave France the monopoly on all trading in the region around what became Senegal. Although slavery was officially abolished thirty-four years later, in practice the trade continued until the end of the nineteenth century. In spite of determined resistance from such famous African warrior kings as Lat Dior and Samori Touré, the French armies conquered over 3 million square kilometres of the African continent. In 1854 France drew up the constitution of what was to become known as Afrique Noire Française, a vast colonial bloc, *le pré carré*, which was eventually to extend from what is now Senegal in the west across to the Central African Congo basin. Throughout this century, the French seized more and more portions of the African continent, battling for imperial power with other European nations, in particular Germany and Great Britain. The European 'Scramble for Africa' culminated in the Berlin conference of 1884 when the colonizing powers divided up the continent to produce the arbitrary geographical spaces we recognize as African nations today.

Such was the size of the French colonial presence in Africa that, at the beginning of the twentieth century, France decided to split the colonies into two administrative blocs: Afrique Occidentale Française (AOF) and Afrique Equatoriale Française (AEF). The colonies themselves had already been divided into smaller administrative units known as *cercles*, each governed by a *commandant* such as we see in Ferdinand Oyono's *Une vie de boy* (see Chapter 10 below). In 1903 France established a French education system in the African colonies, through which it was to promote the policy of assimilation intended to create 'French Africans'. The concept of assimilation grew out of the *mission civilisatrice* with which the French constantly justified their colonial exploits. African pupils followed the same baccalaureate syllabus as those in metropolitan France, learning the geography and history of France rather than of their motherland. The most cited example of educational assimilation describes African pupils being taught that their ancestors, the Gauls, had blue eyes and blond hair. In the first instance, colonial education was only available to boys. All lessons were held in French, and punishments were dispensed to pupils speaking indigenous languages at school.

The black African writer therefore has an ambiguous relationship with French. On the one hand, particularly for the first generations of authors, French is the language of education and, according to French colonial policy, of social aspiration. On the other, French is the language of the former colonial oppressor; to write in French can thus be seen as an endorsement of the cultural superiority of France. This issue is further complicated by the question of audience: who is the African author writing for? To write in French is to exclude all those who have not been educated in a French-speaking school. On the other hand, to write in an African language is automatically to restrict one's readership to a single ethnic group, whereas French is a language spoken in fifty-two countries in the world. The African writer is thus faced with a difficult choice, particularly if he or she hopes to make a living from writing fiction. To publish in French also gives access to French publishing houses which are generally more prestigious and more financially secure than those based in Africa. For these reasons, all the authors in this section except Mariama Bâ have published their work in France. That is not say that they are not sensitive to the consequences of their decision to write in French. On the contrary, the texts themselves often demonstrate the authors' desire to resist the hegemony of the French language. This may be on a linguistic level through the subversion of standard French, on a formal level through the hybridization of traditional narrative forms, or on the level of content which reveals the hypocrisy and barbarity of colonialism and the brutality of the legacy it left behind.

African literature in French began to make its mark in the inter-war period when a group of black intellectuals, inspired by the Harlem Renaissance movement in the USA, produced the first and only issue of a journal entitled *Légitime défense* (published in 1932). This journal was followed by a second, *L'Etudiant noir* (1935), this one founded by Léopold Senghor, Aimé Césaire and Léon Damas to publish writings by fellow black students. Based in Paris, these journals formed the roots of the movement that was to be known as Negritude, a term first used by Césaire in his *Cahier d'un retour au pays natal* (1939). Negritude was a political movement as well as a literary and philosophical one; it has also been described as the expression of black consciousness or of being black in the world. The first generation of negritude writers (notably Césaire, Senghor and Birago Diop) produced poetry rather than prose. Indeed, Jean-Paul Sartre in his famous essay, 'Orphée noir', preface to Senghor's *Anthologie de la nouvelle poésie nègre et malgache* (1948), proclaimed that poetry was the most suitable genre for the expression of Negritude. However, subsequent generations of francophone African writers have tended to opt for the novel, as reflected in the choice of extracts in this *Companion*.

In spite of the commitment of the negritude poets, early novels from francophone Africa were often descriptive and lacking any strong sense of political agenda, the best-known example of this being Camara Laye's *L'Enfant noir* (1953), a novel condemned by the Cameroonian writer, Mongo Beti, as 'littérature rose'. The negritude writers saw literature as a political weapon with which to fight against colonialism as well as a means of reaffirming the humanity of the colonized black peoples of the world. Oyono's *Une vie de boy* (1956) demonstrates the influence of Negritude on the post-war African novel in the way that it simultaneously challenges colonial oppression and resists the dehumanization of the Blacks. This text is a good example of the anti-colonial novel, which flourished from the 1950s up to the independence of the black African French colonies in the early 1960s.

In 1958 France offered the African colonies a choice between self-government and independence. At this point, only one country – Guinea – opted for independence. One year later, however, the colonies themselves called for independence which was granted the following year. Therefore 1960 marks a turning point in the history of francophone Africa, a fact that is well reflected in Ousmane Sembène's *Les Bouts de bois de Dieu* (see Chapter 11 below). This novel combines a retrospective look at Senegal's colonial history (through the

1947 railway workers' strike) with an optimistic vision of an alternative post-colonial future that has unfortunately not yet been experienced in reality. Independence also led to the end of some writers' literary careers: Oyono, for example, stopped publishing when he became a Cameroonian diplomat in 1960. Others such as the new Senegalese president, Senghor, continued to combine writing with their political careers. The immediate post-independence years also gave rise to the creation of the first African publishing house: Editions CLE, based in the Cameroonian capital, Yaoundé, was founded in 1963. A decade later, Les Nouvelles Editions Africaines and CEDA were established, the former in Dakar (Senegal), Lomé (Togo) and Abidjan (Côte d'Ivoire), the latter in Abidjan.

For many Africans, however, independence was a grave disappointment and this is reflected in much of the writing published after 1960. The texts by Sony Labou Tansi and Ahmadou Kourouma illustrate the disillusionment felt by Africans with post-colonial leaders who are at best neo-colonial puppets and at worst brutal dictators. Both novels depict fictitious African nations that present striking similarities to the geographical realities of the authors' homelands. Censorship is still an important factor in many African writers' lives. Anyone found to be criticizing the government faces very severe penalties: Sony was held under house arrest; Mongo Beti spent thirty-two years in exile from Cameroon. In spite of fear of the censor, African writers continued to publish in the 1960s and 1970s, many of their novels highly critical of the failure of independence. Good examples of this are Alioum Fantouré, *Le Cercle des Tropiques* (1972), V. Y. Mudimbe, *Le Bel Immonde* (1976) and Tierno Monénembo, *Les Crapauds-brousse* (1979). The post-independence era was a time of much political instability south of the Sahara, marked by military coups and murders (notably of Patrice Lumumba, newly elected president of the former Belgian Congo, in 1961). In spite of their differences, the majority of the leaders of the independent African states soon revealed very similar approaches to government, establishing single-party states led by self-proclaimed *pères de la nation* or *Guides*, and characterized by nepotism and corruption. Development was never very high on the agenda and, by the 1970s, the economic health of the continent was in serious decline.

Towards the end of the 1970s and during the 1980s, African women begin to become more visible on the francophone literary scene, notably Mariama Bâ whose first novel, *Une si longue lettre* (1979) (see Chapter 13 below) won the first ever Noma prize for publishing in Africa. Before Bâ, very few women had attempted to get their works in print since to do so would involve surmounting a number of social and cultural obstacles. Education for African women had traditionally not been a high priority, so that the first generation of women writers, like Mariama Bâ, were very much part of the élite in their own society. Moreover, social, religious and family constraints have made it difficult for African women's voices to be heard. For these reasons, when they do decide to write, African women often focus on women's issues, challenging patriarchal practices like polygamy, the dowry and genital mutilation. More recently, women writers like Véronique Tadjo, Tanella Boni and Calixthe Beyala have produced more experimental works of fiction which, like the writings of Québécois feminists Nicole Brossard and Madeleine Gagnon, blur the boundaries between literary genres to produce new fictional forms.

Formal experimentation is not, of course, restricted to writing by women. In fact, *Les Soleils des Indépendances* by Ahmadou Kourouma (see Chapter 12 below) is generally recognized as marking a turning point in the evolution of the black African novel in French, its innovatory language skilfully fusing French with Malinke patterns of speech. Kourouma also draws on traditions of oral story-telling to structure his narrative, thereby creating a hybrid text which combines two literary traditions in a new and exciting way. More recent examples of non-realist, experimental writings include Boubacar Boris Diop, *Le Temps de Tamango* (1981) and Henri Lopès, *Le Chercheur d'Afriques* (1990).

The 1990s began with the Francophone Summit at La Baule at which the former French president, François Mitterrand, imposed as a condition of bilateral cooperation the transition to democracy in the dictatorships of francophone sub-Saharan Africa. This imposition of multi-party systems can be seen as another turning point in African literature in French. Whereas the 1970s and 1980s can be described as a period of disenchantment, the literature of the 1990s is characterized by more overt resistance to single-party rule. The novels of such writers as Achille Ngoye and Pius Ngandu Nkashama are marked by a political realism which makes overt reference to real events in Central Africa. It is not without significance that both these Zaïrean authors, writing under Mobutu, were (and still are) living in exile.

Such is the size of the continent and the diversity of the countries within it that it is impossible to make generalizations about black African literature in French. The extracts which follow have been selected to represent the evolution of this literature: from the anti-colonial novel in the 1950s (Oyono) to issues of immigration and exile (Beyala) at the end of the twentieth century. They have also been chosen to demonstrate a range of both formal and ideological concerns. It is hoped that this small sample will encourage readers to deepen their knowledge of francophone Africa and its literature.

Further reading

Blair, Dorothy, *African Literature in French* (Cambridge: Cambridge University Press, 1976).

Clark, John F. and Gardinier, David E., *Political Reform in Francophone Africa* (Boulder, Colo.: Westview, 1997).

Dabla, Séwana, *Nouvelles écritures africaines: romanciers de la seconde génération* (Paris: L'Harmattan, 1986).

Dumont, Pierre, *Le Français, langue africaine* (Paris: L'Harmattan, 1990).

Hitchcott, Nicki, *Women Writers in Francophone Africa* (Oxford: Berg, 2000).

Ibnlfassi, Laïla and Nicki Hitchcott, *African Francophone Writing: a Critical Introduction* (Oxford: Berg, 1996).

Manning, Patrick, *Francophone Sub-Saharan Africa, 1880–1995* (Cambridge: Cambridge University Press, 1999).

Mortimer, Mildred, *Journeys through the French African Novel* (London: James Currey, 1990).

Mouralis, Bernard, *Littérature et développement* (Paris: Silex/ACCT, 1984).

Ricard, Alain, *Littératures d'Afrique noire: des langues aux livres* (Paris: Karthala, 1995).

The Indian Ocean

The very diverse populations of the Indian Ocean islands – Madagascar, Mauritius, Réunion, Rodrigues, the Comoro Islands and the Seychelles – reflect the complexities and differences in the histories of these islands. Although geographically close to the African continent, these islands are in many ways historically and culturally closer to the French *départements d'outre-mer* of Martinique and Guadeloupe. For the purposes of this book, we shall focus on the Mascarene island of Réunion (formerly Bourbon), in order to situate Axel Gauvin's *L'Aimé* (Chapter 16 below) in its geographical and historical contexts.

Unlike the larger island of Madagascar, the Mascarenes had no indigenous population when Europeans first colonized them in the sixteenth century. When the French arrived in Réunion a century later, the island was inhabited by a small number of runaway slaves who had escaped the early settlers from the Netherlands and Portugal. France decided to use the island for the banishment of mutineers who were first sent there in 1643. Twenty years later the first colonial settlers arrived along with their Malagasy servants. Since Bourbon was in a strategic trade position on the route to India, Louis XIV granted it as a concession to the French East India Company. The Company bought in large numbers of slaves from Madagascar and East Africa to maintain the coffee plantations that they established on the island. Recorded sales of slaves in Réunion date back to 1672. Slavery is at the root of the contemporary population of Réunion since, from the beginnings of colonization, white masters had sex with their Malagasy, Indo-Portuguese or African slaves, producing mixed-race children. In 1764, Louis XV bought back Bourbon and Mauritius (formerly l'Ile de France) from the East India Company but France did not fully regain control of these islands until 1767 when the Company collapsed. The Company's coffee plantations were quickly replaced with sugar cane, a crop which made the island prosper during the nineteenth century. Unfortunately, as in the Caribbean, the abolition of slavery in 1848 did not extend to the sugar cane plantations; Indian and African workers were drafted in to work in conditions not very different from those of slaves. The plantations themselves were owned by a small number of aristocrats, mainly of European origin. After the Second World War, the crisis in the sugar industry called for alternative crops, notably 'Bourbon' vanilla.

Bourbon was first named Réunion in 1793 in celebration of the union between the people of Marseille and the National Guards of the Tuileries, a union that played an important role in the French Revolution. In 1806, however, the island was renamed Bonaparte Island, only to be occupied by the English four years later when it became Bourbon Island again. In 1815 the island was returned to the king of France, and in 1848 became Réunion once more. Almost one hundred years later, in 1946, the French Assembly granted Réunion the status of a *département d'outre-mer*, along with the three colonies of Martinique, Guadeloupe and Guyana.

The best-known Réunionese poet is Leconte de Lisle who was born on the island in the nineteenth century but spent much of his life in France. The earliest example of an anti-colonial novel also appeared in the nineteenth century: the story of four runaway slaves, *Les Marrons*, published by Louis Timagène Houat in 1844. The first specifically Réunionese text, however, is generally recognized to be Jean Albany's *Zamal* (1951) since it no longer assumes France to be the centre against which Réunionese reality is measured. Albany was also one of the first writers from Réunion to incorporate the Creole language into his writings. Towards the end of the 1970s, a group of Creole speakers and writers formed the 'Octobre 77 group', one of whose roles was to draw up a Réunionese Creole orthography which they named 'Lékritir 77'. This inspired the formation of the *Créolie* movement, a grouping, mainly of poets, whose aims are to safeguard the traditions of Réunion and to construct a Réunionese cultural identity. Since 1980, however, the *Créolie* movement has become depoliticized and therefore criticized by those who support a more fluid, hybridized notion of Réunionese identity which bears a close resemblance to the Caribbean concept of *Créolité* expounded by the Martinican writers Jean Bernabé, Raphaël Confiant and Patrick Chamoiseau (see Chapter 22 below).

The population of Réunion, like that of the other islands of the Indian Ocean, is the result of the arrival of settlers from many different ethnic groups and cultural backgrounds: Tamil, Malagasy, Muslim Indian, Chinese, Comorian, European, African and mixed race. For the supporters of *Créolité*, it is precisely this ethnic plurality and mixing that makes Réunionese identity unique, and it is the Creole language that binds the population together. Novels such as Axel Gauvin's *L'Aimé* demonstrate the political ideology of *Créolité* in the way in which they promote the specificity of life in Réunion. *L'Aimé* also exemplifies the aesthetic innovation encouraged by *Créolité* as it is a hybridized novel, whose form and content (both cultural and linguistic) are woven from the multiple strands inherited from the diverse peoples of the island.

Further reading

Armand, Alain, Marimoutou, J. C. C. and Séverin, Monique *Figures de la littérature réunionnaise contemporaine* (Saint-Denis: Comité de la Culture, de l'Éducation et de l'Environnement, 1988).

Baggioni, Daniel and Mathieu, Martine (eds), *Cultures(s) empirique(s) et identité(s) culturelle(s) à la Réunion* (Saint Denis: Université de la Réunion, 1985).

Carpanin Marimoutou, Jean-Claude, 'Créolie et créolité', *Notre librairie*, 104 (1991), 95–8.

Joubert, Jean-Louis, *Littératures de l'Océan Indien* (Vanves: EDICEF, 1991).

Lionnet, Françoise, '*Créolité* in the Indian Ocean: two models of cultural diversity', in Françoise Lionnet and Ronnie Scharfman (eds), *Post/Colonial Conditions* (*Yale French Studies*, 82) (1993), 101–11.

Notre librairie, 72 (1983).

Roche, Daniel-Rolland, *Lire la poésie réunionnaise contemporaine* (Saint Denis: UFOI, 1982).

Sam-Long, Jean-François, *Guide bibliographique du roman réunionnais d'expression française et créole* (Saint Denis: UDIR, 1989).

—— *De l'élégie à la créolie* (Saint Denis: UDIR, 1989).

Chapter 10

Ferdinand Oyono

Une vie de boy (Paris: Julliard, 1956), pp. 130–6.

Madame faisait son courrier. Elle levait de temps en temps la tête et ses yeux erraient, sans me voir, sur le réfrigérateur que j'étais en train d'astiquer. Elle repoussa la table sur laquelle elle était en train d'écrire et vint cueillir quelques pétales d'hibiscus dans le bouquet du salon. Elle les mit dans l'enveloppe, la mouilla avec sa petite langue rose et la colla. Elle se leva, prit ses papiers et disparut dans sa chambre.

– Boy! ma douche est-elle prête? me demanda-t-elle à travers la cloison.

– Oui, Madame, répondis-je.

Elle essaya de siffler mais comme elle semblait manquer de souffle, elle se tut. Le bruit d'un flacon se brisant sur le ciment lui arracha un «Zut!». Elle m'appela pour que j'enlève les débris. C'était l'un des flacons de produits qu'elle met sur son visage le soir. Des fragments de verre avaient pénétré sous le lit. Je m'agenouillai et sondai le dessous du lit d'un grand coup de balai qui ramena non seulement les débris de verre, mais aussi de petits sacs de caoutchouc. Il y en avait deux. Quand Madame n'entendit plus le frottement du balai, elle se retourna. En me voyant en train de tourner et de retourner les petits sacs avec mon balai, elle bondit sur moi et tenta de les repousser sous le lit d'un coup de pied. Elle ne réussit qu'à en piétiner un qui éjecta un liquide sur le sol.

– Fiche-moi le camp! rugit-elle, fiche-moi le camp! C'est ça! tu ne sais pas ce que c'est, hein? continua-t-elle, hors d'elle. Tu ne sais rien! Ce sont des préservatifs, m'entends-tu? Des préservatifs, oui, des préservatifs! Va le raconter partout! Cela te fera un sujet de conversation avec tous les boys de Dangan . . . Allez! Fiche-moi le camp!

Il y a des moments où les colères d'un Blanc vous laissent sans réaction. Vraiment, j'avoue que du coup je ne comprenais rien . . . absolument rien. Madame me poussa dehors et je me retrouvai abasourdi à la véranda.

Le cuisinier me guettait de la fenêtre de la cuisine. Il hocha tristement la tête, frappa sa main droite contre la gauche et appliqua la paume de cette dernière contre sa bouche. Cette façon qu'il avait de montrer son étonnement avait le don de m'exaspérer. Il détourna la tête et disparut. Je tenais encore stupidement mon balai.

Je descendis l'escalier et revins à la cuisine. Le cuisinier me tourna le dos et s'abstint pendant un bon moment de m'adresser la parole. Enfin, il parla:

– Toundi, tu ne connaîtras jamais ton métier de boy. Un de ces quatre matins, tu seras cause d'un malheur. Quand comprendras-tu donc que, pour le Blanc, tu ne vis que par tes services et non par autre chose ! Moi, je suis le cuisinier. Le Blanc ne me voit que grâce à son estomac . . . Vous, les enfants de nos jours, je ne sais pas ce que vous avez . . . Depuis les Allemands, le Blanc n'a pas changé, c'est moi qui te le dis. Il n'a fait que changer de langue . . . Ah ! vous, les enfants de nos jours, vous nous désolez . . .

Il fit une pause.

– Qu'est-ce que tu as encore fait à Madame ce matin? reprit-il.

– . . .

Il répéta sa question.

– . . .

– Ne me regarde pas avec ces yeux-là, reprit-il. Je suis plus vieux que toi, tu pourrais être mon fils. C'est la voix de la sagesse qui te parle . . . Hors de son trou, la souris ne défie pas le chat . . .

– Ce que tu dis est la vérité, lui répondis-je enfin, mais dis-moi . . . ces petits sacs de caoutchouc . . . le boy ne peut-il pas . . .

Il ne me laissa pas achever. Un rire énorme fendit latéralement son visage grave de l'instant d'avant. Il se laissa choir sur une caisse vide, secoué par les spasmes du rire. Il me regarda et se mit à rire de plus belle. Baklu accourut de la buanderie.

– Qu'est-ce qu'il y a? demanda-t-il, prêt déjà à s'esclaffer. Qu'est-ce qu'il y a?

Le cuisinier se tenait les côtes. Il leva le bras dans ma direction, une crise de rire le fit baisser aussitôt. Il haletait et s'essuya les yeux. Pendant ce temps, Baklu montrait ses dents de chèvre en se donnant une avance sur le rire que le cuisinier lui promettait en soufflant: «Attends . . . aaa . . . at . . . attends!» Il se calma enfin et remonta son pantalon avec ses avant-bras, puis il s'avança vers le buffet comme un gorille vers un arbre. Il se versa un petit verre de vin rouge. Il se racla la gorge et revint s'asseoir sur la caisse.

– Des occasions de rire comme ça, commença-t-il, on en trouve une fois par an!

Il s'essuya à nouveau les yeux.

– Ne sois pas égoiste! dit Baklu qui s'impatientait. Combien me vends-tu la nouvelle?

– Une femme! dit le cuisinier en éclatant de rire.

Cela signifiait que la nouvelle coûtait tellement cher qu'il préférait la lui annoncer pour rien.

– Eh bien, commença-t-il, Toundi et Madame se sont querellés pour des petits sacs . . .

– Lesquels? demanda Baklu, la lèvre pendante, faussement interloqué.

– Les petits sacs de caoutchouc, tu sais . . . que les Blancs . . .

Il termina sa phrase en empoignant ses parties. Baklu se plia en deux, fit marche arrière jusqu'à ce que son derrière cognât le buffet. Il se laissa glisser à terre et ses épaules se soulevèrent et s'affaissèrent successivement tandis qu'il laissait échapper de petits jappements de chien. Le cuisinier se leva et alla lui tapoter l'épaule.

– Ça fait longtemps que je n'ai pas ri comme ça! dit Baklu en époussetant le fond de son pantalon.

– Raconte-nous ça, petit! me dit le cuisinier en me donnant une bourrade.

Il ne me laissa pas commencer.

– Ces Blancs! s'exclama-t-il, avec leur manie d'habiller tout, même leurs ...

Ils se mirent encore à rire.

– Ça même, ça sert à quoi? demanda Baklu d'une manière faussement naïve.

– Paraît que c'est pour faire bien ... Ils mettent ça comme ils mettent le casque ou les gants ... disait le cuisinier avec de petits airs entendus qui narguaient ma naïveté.

– C'est très juste, repartait Baklu. C'est un petit vêtement pour ça ...

Ils rirent encore.

– Je me sauve, dit Baklu en s'en allant, j'ai deux paniers de linge sale ...

Le cuisinier renifla, s'essuyant le nez du revers de sa main.

– Petit, commença-t-il, tu sais bien qu'on rit partout, même quand on veille un mort. J'espère que tu ne m'en veux pas pour ce satané rire qui m'a pris tout à l'heure?

Il sourit encore puis redevint grave.

– Je comprends que tu aies exaspéré Madame, reprit-il, ton balai a été un peu loin. Vois-tu, c'est un peu comme si tu avais découvert la chose de M. Moreau à la Résidence ... Une femme ne pardonne pas ces choses-là. C'est plus grave que si tu avais regardé sous sa robe. Une femme blanche n'admettra jamais que son boy fasse de pareilles découvertes ...

Il faisait beaucoup d'efforts pour ne pas rire encore. Sa puissante mâchoire inférieure tremblait. Il me tourna le dos, un spasme secouait sa nuque.

Madame apparut sur le perron. Elle ouvrit la bouche mais aucun son ne sortit de sa gorge. Elle m'appela enfin pour que je lui donne le balai. Elle me l'arracha des mains et disparut. Un moment plus tard, j'entendis le petit bruit sec de la paille sur le ciment.

– Elle va balayer elle-même sa chambre à ce que je vois! dit le cuisinier. Si au moins elle pouvait venir faire elle-même la cuisine!

– Elle balaie elle-même sa chambre! nous cria Baklu dans notre langue. Si elle pouvait aussi laver son linge!

A onze heures, lorsque Madame eut fini de s'habiller, la femme du docteur vint la chercher en voiture.

– Je ne rentrerai pas déjeuner, nous dit-elle d'une voix un peu tremblante.

La voiture démarra. Elle avait à peine disparu que Baklu et la sentinelle nous rejoignirent. Ils commencèrent encore à rire.

– J'avais tout entendu! dit le garde. Je pensais que j'allais éclater avec cette maudite ceinture!

Il pinça sa cartouchière.

– Qu'est-ce que les Blancs n'iront pas inventer! dit le cuisinier. Ils sont déjà incirconcis comme ça et ils éprouvent encore le besoin de se fabriquer d'autres enveloppes!

– Celle qu'on achète à la pharmacie empêchent leurs femmes d'être enceintes, dit Baklu. Ils les emploient aussi quand ils couchent avec les femmes indigènes pour ne pas avoir de maladie. C'est l'infirmier qui m'a dit ça . . .

– Alors pourquoi font-ils la chose? demanda le garde. Ils sont fous, ces Blancs . . . Comment peuvent-ils dire qu'ils font la chose si c'est avec un peu de caoutchouc!

Ils discutèrent préservatifs tout l'après-midi. Madame revint à quatre heures. Elle traversa la cour, la tête à demi baissée. Elle s'engouffra dans sa chambre et ne reparut qu'au dîner. Elle toucha à peine au poulet, mangea une banane et but sa tasse de café habituelle. Elle avala des comprimés et nous dit de ne pas partir avant minuit.

Quand nous partîmes, elle ronflait déjà. La sentinelle m'aida à fermer les fenêtres et les portes de la Résidence.

Text and context

Ferdinand Oyono's *Une vie de boy* rewrites the traditional colonial text in which the colonized was presented as the exotic object of the colonizer's gaze. In this novel, the singular perspective of the first-person narrator/protagonist, Toundi, places the reader in the position of the colonized, forcing her/him to view people and events through the eyes of the black houseboy in the commandant's home. In this passage, the discovery of used condoms under Madame's bed is incomprehensible to Toundi. Yet the western reader is placed in the privileged position of understanding the significance of these 'petits sacs de caoutchouc' (l. 13). Much of the humour in the scene derives from the fact that the reader knows more than Toundi. However, ultimately it is the Whites and not the Blacks whom the text holds up to ridicule.

The physicality of this scene, in which Madame, attempting to sweep the evidence back under the bed, manages to stand on a condom which squirts its contents over the floor, has an element of farce. Madame's behaviour, which is described in minute detail, appears unnecessary and ridiculous to Toundi and reader alike. Throughout *Une vie de boy*, Oyono uses a behaviouristic technique to portray the colonizers' actions. The minutiae of Toundi's descriptions strip the Whites' behaviour of any signification so that, like the French to Montesquieu's Persians, the colonizers' antics become as meaningless and absurd as adorning a penis with a decorative 'enveloppe' (l. 119). The emphasis in this novel is on the mutual incomprehension with which the colonized and colonizer view one another: the Blacks cannot understand why the Whites would have sex if not to have children; the Whites do not even consider the fact that it might be demeaning for an African man – Baklu – to wash Madame's sanitary towels. Such incompatibility extends even to the two communities' use of the French language: Toundi's figurative description of the condoms as 'petits sacs de caoutchouc' contrasts with Madame's clinical 'préservatifs' (l. 20), showing how, even linguistically, the colonial *cercle* is irrevocably divided.

The antinomical nature of the two communities as well as the debauched behaviour of the Whites in Dangan point to the illegitimacy of the French colonial *mission civilisatrice.* Furthermore, there is a strong feeling in *Une vie de boy* that the colonial mission will soon be coming to an end. (The book was published in 1956, four years before the independence of Cameroon.) The Whites, desperate to cling on to the final vestiges of power, often behave irrationally and even violently, conveying both their frustration and their impotence. Here, Madame erupts into a fit of temper, swearing at Toundi and pushing him out onto the veranda. Paradoxically, while she is convinced that Toundi has never seen a condom before, Madame assumes that he will understand its significance, particularly as he has already seen his mistress with her lover. Knowledge of her infidelity gives Toundi a degree of power and it is this that the colonizer fears most. This fear also explains Madame's trembling voice when she leaves the house with the doctor's wife (l. 101).

The complex power relations between colonizer and colonized are represented in *Une vie de boy* through the metaphor of the gaze. This metaphor is a key to understanding the novel. It is through the gaze of the Other that the Self is defined: the colonizer only exists as colonizer while he is perceived and recognized as such by the Other (the colonized). Thus, in order to maintain his position of superiority within the colonial situation, the colonizer must constantly be recognized and legitimated by the colonized. The reverse is also true. The dialectical nature of colonial power relations requires both sides to recognize the other as colonizer and colonized respectively. Once either side begins to challenge the legitimacy of the other's position, the relationship destabilizes and will ultimately collapse. In the opening of this scene, Madame glances at the refrigerator Toundi is polishing without seeing him: 'sans me voir' (l. 2). Later, when she returns to the house, Madame's head is 'à demi baissée' (l. 126), allowing her to pass without looking Toundi in the eye. By refusing to acknowledge Toundi's gaze, Madame refuses to be judged by him. She also simultaneously denies Toundi the right to challenge the way she judges him. Moreover, by refusing to acknowledge Toundi's presence, Madame strips him of his humanity and sees him only as an object, indistinguishable from the fridge.

The dehumanization of the Blacks by the Whites is a major theme in *Une vie de boy* and was, Oyono's text suggests, the essence of the French colonial mission: only by denying the humanity of the Blacks and the value of their culture could the colonial Whites begin to justify their presence in sub-Saharan Africa. Other methods of dehumanization are demonstrated elsewhere in the novel. For example, when Janopoulos sets his dog on the Africans, Toundi notes that the European women are amused. This impartial observation causes the reader to reflect on the racism of the Whites who have reduced the Blacks to the status of animals to be tracked down for entertainment. It is during the dog chase that the commandant appears not to recognize Toundi, his own houseboy who, terrified by the dog, is forced to climb a tree. Realizing his master has not recognized him, the narrator simply comments, 'Comment aurait-il pu me reconnaître? Pour les Blancs, tous les nègres ont la même gueule' (p. 44). The racist myth that all Blacks look the same reduces the indigenous peoples of Africa to a faceless mass with no individuality and therefore no humanity.

Generalizations are also made by the Blacks about the Whites. Following Toundi's discovery of the condoms, the cook remarks that 'Depuis les Allemands, le Blanc n'a pas changé' (l. 37) and a number of references are made to 'typical' white behaviour. Whereas the cook's suggestion that the French are no different from the Germans could equally be perceived as racist, he is referring to the Whites in their specific role as colonizer (Cameroon was a German protectorate from 1884 to 1916). Whereas 'colonizer' is a role that the Whites themselves have created, the role of 'colonized' has been imposed on the people of Cameroon. Moreover, unlike the Europeans in Dangan's colonial *cercle*, the Africans question and try to understand why the Whites do the things they do. In this passage, Toundi is troubled when he cannot understand Madame's irrational behaviour. Later, all three servants spend the afternoon discussing why the Whites use condoms. The colonial policy of assimilation meant that the indigenous peoples of Africa were forced to adopt many aspects of French culture which were totally foreign to them. On the other hand, the racist mythology on which the colonial mission was based facilitated the ignorance and erosion of African culture, which the white characters in this book demonstrate.

What is interesting about Toundi is that, unlike the other African characters in the book, he has internalized the colonial mythology of racial difference and therefore has a negative image of the identity which has been prescribed for him. In other words, he is initially brainwashed into believing that Whites are superior to Blacks. For this reason, he aspires to become like the Whites, an ambition which, of course, he can never realize. In the first half of the novel, Toundi over-invests in his role as the commandant's houseboy. His telling remark, 'Je serai le boy du chef des Blancs: le chien du roi est le roi des chiens' (p. 32) reveals to what extent he has subscribed to the myth of White as master and Black as slave. Ultimately, Toundi finds himself too close to the Whites as he becomes embroiled in the affair between Madame and Moreau. It is a combination of this unacceptable proximity and the power that it creates, along with Toundi's own naïveté and 'gourmandise', which will lead to his tragic end. The inevitability of Toundi's downfall is punctuated in the novel by a number of warnings which the wiser Africans supply and Toundi fails to heed. This passage contains an example of such a warning when the cook declares: 'Toundi, tu ne connaîtras jamais ton métier de boy. Un de ces quatre matins, tu seras cause d'un malheur' (l. 33). What the cook does not realize at this point is that the misfortune will in fact be Toundi's arrest, torture and finally death at the hands of Madame's lover, Moreau.

The power which Toundi unwittingly acquires makes him a threat to the Whites' security and this is why Moreau engineers his arrest for a crime he did not commit. In fact, the reader learns that Toundi is not a threat at all since the commandant has known all along about his wife's infidelity. However, the very fact that Toundi finds himself in a position of judgement over the Whites means that the colonial balance of power is potentially reversed. This is why the commandant does not resist Toundi's arrest. The colonizer must ensure that the colonized has no weapon which might threaten the former's illegitimate situation. Stripped of power, the colonized therefore finds it very difficult to resist colonial oppression. What resistance there is in the novel tends to be limited to undetected acts such as Toundi spitting in the commandant's glass, or speaking about the Whites in indigenous languages which, it is assumed, Europeans do not understand. Although oppression cannot be resisted without some kind of revolution, the colonized can resist the dehumanization on which the colonial situation relies. Undoubtedly, the most important way in which the Africans resist dehumanization is through laughter since, in a world of violence and oppression, laughter becomes a symbol of humanity. Indeed, humour is a powerful source of solidarity and strength for the Blacks in *Une vie de boy*. The hilarity of the condom episode creates a positive shared experience for Toundi and the others, and provides an antidote to the bleak reality of colonial oppression. Laughter becomes a strategy for coping with despair. As the cook explains to Toundi, 'tu sais bien qu'on rit partout, même quand on veille un mort' (l. 90).

Further reading

Oyono, Ferdinand, *Le Vieux Nègre et la médaille* (Paris: Julliard, 1956).
—— *Chemin d'Europe* (1960; Paris: Christian Bourgeois, 1973).

Battestini, Monique and Simon, *Ferdinand Oyono: écrivain camerounais* (Paris: Nathan, 1964).
Britwum, Kwabena, 'Temps et fiction dans *Une Vie de boy* ', *Présence francophone* 21 (1980), 47–52.
Chevrier, Jacques, *Oyono, Une Vie de boy: profil d'une œuvre* (Paris: Hatier, 1977).
Flannigan, Arthur, '"The eye of the witch": non-verbal communication and the exercise of power in *Une Vie de boy*', *The French Review* 56, 1 (1982), 51–63.
Ogunsanwo, Olatubosum, 'The narrative voice in two novels of Ferdinand Oyono', *English Studies in Africa* 29, 2 (1986), 97–120.
Okolie, Maxwell, 'Le Regard et le drame de Toundi dans *Une vie de boy*', *Ethiopiques* 5, 1–2 (1988), 205–12.

Language and style

Having learnt to read and write, the young Toundi decides to follow the example of his late mentor, Père Gilbert, and keep a diary of his experiences among the Whites (p. 15). This episode, by introducing him to one of their seemingly bizarre habits, the use of contraceptives, brings him into conflict with Madame, the wife of the local commandant, and epitomizes the distance and alienation between the black and white communities. Furthermore Toundi is a victim of his age, and the episode also serves to illustrate the lack of comprehension that the young boy has of the adult world.

Toundi recounts events in the Whites' world exactly as he perceives them, without any attempt to interpret their significance or hint at their consequences. Oyono's presentation of Toundi's perception may be illustrated through an analysis of the sentence structure of the narrative sections of the text (ll. 1–32, 50–60, 109–30). Of the fifty-one sentences contained in these sections, twenty-one (41 per cent) are simple in structure, sixteen are compound (31 per cent), ten complex (20 per cent) and the rest compound-complex (8 per cent). Although this distribution is not particularly significant, what is significant is that the sentence structure itself is usually uncomplicated, as befits an apparently naïve narrator, with only fourteen subordinate clauses (eight relative, four temporal, one causal, the other final). The simple sentences are generally short; clauses in the compound sentences also tend to be short, with combinations of two (eleven cases) and three (five cases) clauses only. The complex and compound-complex sentences never involve more than one subordinate clause. The first element of all but six of the fifty-one sentences is the subject. In the compound sentences fourteen of the sixteen have the same subject for all clauses, and in one only case (l. 57) is the subject repeated. This tight cohesion of the text, together with the short simple sentences and short clauses in the other sentences, and an almost consistent occurrence of the subject as first element, propels the narrative along at a fairly rapid pace.

The narrow range of subjects also proves significant. 'Madame'/'elle' and the cook between them account for about two-thirds of the occurrences of subjects. The subordination of Toundi to Madame, the dominant authority figure, is emphasized, in that 'Madame' or 'elle' or 'ses yeux' is the subject of every one of the ten main clauses in the first paragraph, and Toundi is relegated to merely being subject of an embedded relative clause (l. 2). Toundi himself accounts for only a very small proportion of the subjects (about 7 per cent): this small role played by 'je', the 'hero', underlines his powerlessness in a colonial world.

Although the sentence structure evokes a naïve adolescent's narrative technique, the syntax making up the sentences is far from simple. The register is high – for example, the use of the past historic (no historic presents), past anterior (l. 109), imperfect subjunctive ('cognât', l. 73), use of 'non seulement . . . mais aussi' (l. 12). This tone is enhanced by the lexis that Toundi uses: it also is of a consistently high register throughout and would not normally be associated with an adolescent, e.g. 'éjecta' (l. 17), 'abasourdi' (l. 25), 'guettait' (l. 26), 'exaspérer' (l. 29), 's'abstint' (l. 32), 'latéralement' (l. 50), 'choir' (l. 51).

There is an important thematic contrast between Toundi's lack of competence in understanding the alien culture of the Whites and his competence in understanding his own. This is brought out in a number of ways: first, his ignorance of White cosmetic and contraceptive practices: 'C'était l'un des flacons de produits qu'elle met sur son visage le soir' (l. 10), 'de petits sacs de caoutchouc' (l. 13), but his ready understanding of the guard's equipment: 'Il pinça sa cartouchière' (l. 116); second, the fact that as narrator he can say: 'Ils discutèrent préservatifs tout l'après-midi' (l. 125); and third his ability to interpret remarks and actions made by his African companions: 'Cela signifiait que la nouvelle coûtait tellement cher qu'il préférait la lui annoncer pour rien' (l. 66, also ll. 28, 82). The noun-phrase 'de petits sacs de caoutchouc' becomes a leitmotiv in the passage and performs a number of functions according to its user: for Madame it is a source of deep embarrassment (e.g. l. 18); for Toundi as protagonist it highlights his ignorance; for the cook it becomes the source of a linguistic joke (l. 63), and for the other Africans it is repeatedly referred to to express scorn and mockery of western practices (ll. 68, 80, 118). Toundi's innocence and lack of understanding of the sexual behaviour of the Whites is exemplified explicitly in the lexical cluster 'abasourdi' (l. 25), 'stupidement' (l. 29) (also ll. 82, 85). In addition, 'je ne comprenais rien' (l. 24), 'tu ne connaîtras jamais ton métier de boy' (l. 33, also ll. 19, 34) and the fact that much of the conversation between the servants gently mocks Toundi confirms his alienation and confusion. Mockery is expressed in a number of ways – Baklu is 'faussement interloqué' (l. 70) and speaks 'd'une manière faussement naïve' (l. 82) – and in the exaggerated physical effects of laughter, e.g. 'Il se laissa choir sur une caisse vide, secoué par les spasmes du rire' (l. 51, also ll. 50, 72, 114). The lexical cluster associated with laughter is fully exploited: 's'esclaffer' (l. 53), '[il] se tenait les côtes' (l. 54), 'éclater' (ll. 65, 114); 'rire' itself (noun and verb) occurs thirteen times in the passage, proving the truth of the cook's statement (l. 90) about the importance of laughter for the colonized Africans.

In the representation of the speech of the two communities other contrasts are visible. On the one hand, the speech of both contrasts with Toundi's narrative style: where Toundi's sentence structure is fairly uniform and unemotional, that of both communities is vigorous and diverse. On the other hand, they contrast with each other, with Madame's mood swings, from the furious and peremptory (ll. 17–22), by way of the subdued and embarrassed (l. 111), to the speechless (l. 101), and the Africans': garrulous, witty, spiced with imagery, philosophical, physical even. In the sections devoted to the Africans' comments on the Whites' practices and their attitudes towards them, a greater variety of sentence structure is used than in the narrative, with exclamations, imperatives, questions as well as reasoned statements. The questions demonstrate a rich mixture, with inversions (e.g. ll. 34, 63), use of 'est-ce que' (l. 53), post-position of question word (l. 82), direct order and intonation (e.g. l. 91). There is a dignity about the speech of the 'wiser' older men, especially the cook, who regularly use complicated sentence-structure, certainly more complicated than Toundi's own narrative, but also, as already seen, a love of the humorous. Ante-position of direct object ('Des occasions de rire comme ça . . . on en trouve une fois par an!' (l. 61), complex sentences (e.g. ll. 34, 37, 76, 83), use of subjunctive after 'comprends' (l. 94) and 'n'admettra jamais' (l. 97)), all indicate a sophisticated sentence structure, far removed from Toundi's. The language put in the mouths of the older Africans is lively and dynamic, with seldom a spoken passage without an exclamation or rhetorical question, all of which is further enlivened by indigenous expressions. The author deliberately distinguishes between Toundi and the other Africans linguistically, although they would of course be speaking in their own language (but compare l. 107).

Imagery is used sparingly by the author in the text, but when it is, it informs on Toundi's relationship with the older Africans or relates directly to the themes of the passage. Of the seven examples, four involve animals – one an aphorism from the cook (l. 46), the others derogatory but humorous comments by the youthful Toundi on the behaviour of his African elders: e.g. 'puis [le cuisinier] s'avança vers le buffet comme un gorille vers un arbre' (l. 58, also ll. 56, 75). The other three keep to the major theme of the passage – condoms, as viewed by Whites and Blacks: one mocks their use: '[Les Blancs] mettent ça comme ils mettent le casque ou les gants' (l. 83); the other two are warnings to Toundi – e.g. the fact of finding the condoms 'est plus grave que si tu avais regardé sous sa [de Madame] robe' (l. 96, also l. 95): Toundi becomes a marked man.

Chapter 11

Ousmane Sembène

Les Bouts de bois de Dieu (Paris: Le Livre Contemporain, 1960), pp. 121–8).

La journée s'achevait et, venue des quatre coins du ciel, l'ombre peu à peu envahissait la ville. Dans la courette de N'Diayène, les femmes jetaient les morceaux de viande de mouton dans la grande marmite, celle des jours de réjouissance. Les flammes dansantes d'un feu bien nourri éclairaient les visages affamés des enfants. Parfois, quelqu'un de plus pressé activait le feu en enfonçant dans les braises une bûche qui faisait jaillir une explosion d'étincelles. Depuis un moment, la faim semblait avoir cessé de torturer les ventres car on savait que, dans quelques instants, la viande serait cuite.

C'est alors que les policiers firent irruption dans la grande cour. Cette soudaine apparition des hommes en armes jeta le trouble parmi les femmes. Dans leur affairement, elles n'avaient plus pensé, ou mieux pas cru, à la menace de l'intervention policière. Quelques-unes désorientées, effrayées, se précipitèrent dans la rue, mais, là aussi, il y avait des uniformes. Mame Sofi remonta son pagne et saisit les deux bouteilles pleines de sable bien tassé qu'elle avait préparées; Bineta, sa «rivale», Houdia M'Baye et plusieurs autres l'imitèrent.

L'agent qui servait d'interprète, s'avança et amorça sur un ton d'homme habitué à être obéi:

– Nous voulons voir Ramatoulaye et reprendre le mouton!

– Le mouton, le mouton ... répétèrent les femmes comme si elles ne comprenaient pas.

Celles qui étaient les plus proches de la chaudière éteignirent le feu, prirent des morceaux de viande qu'elles enveloppèrent dans des feuilles et les jetèrent pardessus la palissade, dans la courette des frères Sow. Des gosses les imitèrent avec force piaillements.

– *Macou!* (Silence!) reprit l'auxiliaire. Nous voulons voir Ramatoulaye.

– Pas habiter ici, Missié blanc, dit l'une des femmes en français, en s'adressant à l'Européen qui commandait le détachement.

– Elle ment, répliqua l'auxiliaire.

Mais, au même instant, l'on vit apparaître Ramatoulaye sur le perron. Visiblement encore éprouvée par son combat avec le bélier, elle descendit les marches à pas lents.

– C'est elle, chef, dit l'auxiliaire, et six policiers s'avancèrent à la rencontre de Ramatoulaye tandis que les yeux de l'assistance étaient fixés sur elle.

– Tu vas nous donner le mouton et nous suivre au poste de police, dit l'auxiliaire.

– Où est N'Deye Touti? demanda Ramatoulaye à ses voisines.

– Elle est partie téléphoner au syndicat, répondit Houdia M'Baye.

L'interprète avait entendu et compris ces paroles; il s'approcha de son supérieur et lui dit quelques mots en français. Celui-ci appela un agent, lui donna un ordre et l'on vit l'homme partir en courant.

– Nous voulons le mouton, répéta l'interprète.

– Dis à ton chef que le mouton ne sortira pas d'ici. Vous me voulez, moi, me voici, mais le mouton a dévoré notre riz . . .

– Il dit qu'il faut venir avec le mouton!

– Dis-lui que ce soir nous souperons avec le mouton!

L'intepréte ne rapportait à son supérieur qu'une partie des paroles de Ramatoulaye, encore ne le faisait-il qu'à sa manière. Il essaya de la persuasion:

– Viens avec le mouton. On ne te gardera pas; tu n'auras qu'à signer un papier. Je connais le chef, il est juste. Il n'est pas comme les autres toubabs . . .

– Moi, je ne connais aucun toubab! Ils sont tous pareils. Le seul qui était bon est mort en naissant. Le mouton ne sortira pas d'ici!

– Que dit-elle? demanda le Blanc qui s'était approché.

– C'est une mauvaise femme. Elle ne veut pas nous suivre. Faut-il appeler du renfort?

– Dis-lui que nous ne prendrons que le mouton et qu'elle pourra venir demain. Dis-lui que je ne suis pas méchant . . .

– Méçant, pas méçant? moi connaître pas, interrompit Ramatoulaye. Vendredi pas pâti . . . lui manzer riz, moi couper cou ! Enfants beaucoup faim, Vendredi manzer riz enfants. Moi venir avec toi. Vendredi pas venir, Vendredi pour manzer.

Puis, se tournant vers les femmes qui se massaient derrière elle:

– Taisez-vous. Qu'est-ce que tu as à pleurer, Houdia M'Baye, comme s'il y avait un mort dans la maison?

Le silence se rétablit. Seule, venant de la rue, une rumeur sourde. Chacun se demandait où Ramatoulaye avait bien pu puiser cette volonté nouvelle. L'officier de police voyant briller devant lui ces gros yeux blancs où flambait la colère, se sentant bravé, commençait, lui aussi, à s'échauffer. Les autres femmes étaient proches de la panique. Elles ne reconnaissaient pas leur compagne, habituées qu'elles étaient à la voir simple, sociable, douce avec les enfants. Jamais à la borne-fontaine elle ne prenait part aux discussions, jamais elle ne médisait comme les autres. D'où lui était donc venue cette force neuve, où était la source de cette force qui se déchaînait soudain? Ce n'était pas à la guerre, Ramatoulaye n'était pas un homme, n'avait pas été soldat, elle n'avait pas connu les longues marches sac au dos au cours desquels on amasse les rancœurs. Ce n'était pas à l'usine, Ramatoulaye n'avait jamais été soumise aux inhumaines cadences du travail ouvrier. Ce n'était pas dans de multiples étreintes d'hommes. Ramatoulaye n'était pas de celles qui dilapident leur tendresse. Où donc alors? La réponse était simple comme elle l'était elle-même: dans les cuisines aux foyers éteints.

Ramatoulaye avança encore d'un pas:

– Missé, toi pâti! Ici, maison pour nous, pas maison pour Blancs! Vendredi manzé riz enfants, moi coupé cou Vendredi, enfants gagné manzé, c'est quitte! . . .

Autour d'elle on commençait à brandir des bouteilles, des *taparquats*, des pilons, des morceaux de bois ramassés çà et là. Les policiers se virent rapidement encerclés.

L'auxiliaire voulut dire quelque chose. Ramatoulaye lui coupa la parole:

– Toi, je n'ai plus rien à te dire. Si tu es encore debout, c'est grâce à ce toubab!

Cependant, dans la rue, des renforts étaient arrivés, gendarmes et soldats, et c'est dans la rue que, sans que l'on sût trop comment, la bagarre commença entre les femmes et les forces de police.

– Pour un mouton! dit la femme au cure-dents, nous vendrons cher sa peau!

Mame Sofi qui avait repéré près de la cabane un policier de petite taille, l'assomma d'un seul coup de ses bouteilles de sable, puis, comme une furie, elle se rua sur l'auxiliaire et lui envoya la seconde bouteille en plein visage. Bineta se servait d'un pilon avec lequel elle faisait de grands moulinets au-dessus des têtes. Houdia M'Baye, elle, telle un petit fauve, s'était accrochée des bras et des jambes à un agent qui lui martelait le crâne avec une satisfaction visible.

La chatte elle-même avait sorti ses griffes et crachait des injures.

Au long des quelque quinze cents kilomètres de voies du Dakar–Niger qui desservaient plus de deux millions de kilomètres carrés à l'est du continent africain, les hommes commençaient à avoir assez de palabrer sur la grève. Ils étaient fermement décidés à ne pas reprendre le travail, mais il fallait tuer le temps, tromper la faim, remplir tous ces dimanches qui se succédaient semaine après semaine, cette oisiveté que l'on avait d'abord dégustée avec délice et dont maintenant on se saoulait jusqu'à la lie. Vêtus de ce qui restait de leurs meilleurs hardes – celles qu'avaient refusées les prêteurs sur gage – les hommes jouaient aux vacances. Dès le matin, on les voyait partout, ils envahissaient les marchés, les grandes places comme les plus petites placettes; en bandes joyeuses ils allaient butinant de boutique en boutique. Dieu lui-même s'était mis de la partie, il avait balayé ses parterres, son ciel n'avait plus un nuage; au-dessus des toits, des arbres, des montagnes, il n'y avait plus qu'un immense vide bleu, on ne voyait même plus onduler les minces fumées qui d'habitude encrassaient l'air.

On avait ressuscité des fastes des jours anciens, oubliés depuis des temps immémoriaux. Les femmes se teignaient les mains et les pieds au henné rehaussé de noir de caoutchouc brûlé, elles passaient leurs lèvres à la pierre de *djenné* (antimoine); elles arboraient, surtout les jeunes filles, les coiffures les plus compliquées, faites de tresses enchevêtrées ou curieusement séparées. Elles déambulaient dans les rues, s'abandonnant gracieusement au rythme des baras que l'on entendait à chaque carrefour. Des hommes armés de bâtons mimaient des combats au sabre dont les règles remontaient au temps du règne de El Mami Samori Touré.

Mais ces réjouissances ne durèrent pas très longtemps. L'ombre d'une absence pesait sur tous, l'absence de la machine. Au début, les hommes avaient proclamé avec orgueil qu'ils avaient tué la «Fumée de la savane». Maintenant, ils se souvenaient du temps où pas un jour ne se passait sans voir cette fumée rouler au-dessus des champs, des toits, des arbres de la brousse, où pas une nuit ne s'écoulait sans le bruit de ferraille, le heurt des tampons des wagons, le sifflet des locomotives, sans les lueurs rouges, vertes ou blanches des falots des équipes de manœuvre. Tout cela avait été leur vie. Ils y pensaient sans cesse, mais gardaient jalousement ces pensées comme un secret, tout en s'épiant l'un l'autre comme s'ils avaient peur de voir le secret échapper à quelqu'un d'entre eux. Pourtant, ils sentaient confusément que la machine était leur bien commun et que la frustration qu'ils éprouvaient tous en ces jours sombres leur était également commune.

Tels des amoureux éconduits, ils revenaient sans cesse aux alentours des gares. Ils restaient là, les yeux fixés sur l'horizon, immobiles, échangeant à peine quelques phrases banales. Parfois, un îlot de cinq ou six hommes se détachait du groupe compact et partait à la dérive en direction de la voie. Pendant quelques instants, ils longeaient les rails puis soudain, comme pris de panique, ils se hâtaient de revenir s'agglomérer à la masse. Alors ils restaient là, accroupis ou debout au pied d'une dune, les yeux fixés sur les deux parallèles qui s'allongeaient sans fin pour aller se fondre au loin dans la brousse. Quelque chose de nouveau germait en eux, comme si le passé et l'avenir étaient en train de s'étreindre pour féconder un nouveau type d'homme, et il leur semblait que le vent leur chuchotait une phrase de Bakayoko souvent entendue: «L'homme que nous étions est mort et notre seul salut pour une nouvelle vie est dans la machine, la machine qui, elle, n'a ni langage, ni race.» Mais eux restaient muets. Seule se voyait dans leurs yeux une lueur de mauvaise extase qui contenait à la fois l'horreur grandissante de la famine et la douloureuse attente de retour de la machine. Parfois, la tempête s'élevait. On voyait au loin les cimes des grands arbres s'agiter furieusement. Dans les gares dont les toitures de plaques de ciment s'étaient fendues sous l'action du soleil, des ruisselets d'eau se glissaient partout et les portes des vérandas, les portières de wagons de voyageurs ou de marchandises s'ouvraient soudain sous la poussée du vent comme des gueules béantes, puis se mettaient à battre et à grincer sur leurs gonds sans huile. Cette intrusion des forces de la nature contre la machine était un spectacle déchirant qui humiliait le cœur des hommes.

Une fois par semaine seulement la «Fumée de la savane» courait à travers la brousse, conduite par des Européens. Alors les grévistes tendaient leurs oreilles, tels des lièvres surpris par un bruit insolite. Pendant un instant, le passage de la locomotive apaisait le drame qui se jouait dans leur cœur, car leur communion avec la machine était profonde et forte, plus forte que les barrières qui les séparaient de leurs employeurs, plus forte que cet obstacle jusqu'alors infranchissable: la couleur de leur peau. Puis, la fumée disparue, le silence ou le vent s'installait de nouveau.

Text and context

Sembène's most famous novel, *Les Bouts de bois de Dieu*, is based on a real event: the 1947–8 strike by the workers on the Dakar–Niger railway. The main aims of the strike are equality of pay for the African workers and family allowance for all children of polygamous fathers. The strikers and their families suffer considerable hardship; the women, in particular, are forced to take desperate measures to ensure that their children are fed. This extract follows Ramatoulaye's killing of her brother Mabigué's ram, Vendredi. Mabigué, a shopowner, had previously refused to give the strikers' families rice on credit. Vendredi then made his way into N'Diayène's *concession* where he ate what little rice remained.

Unlike *Une vie de boy* (see Chapter 10 above), this is not a text that foregrounds racial oppression. Not all the Africans support the strike. Mabigué, for example, believes that the strikers should go back to work, telling his sister that 'les toubabs [blancs] sont là: c'est la volonté de Dieu' (p. 83). This remark is particularly ironic as El Hadji Mabigué, a devout Muslim, cites Allah as justification for colonial domination.[1] However, just as, like Mabigué, there are Blacks who support the white employers, so there are Whites, notably the symbolically named Leblanc, who support the striking workers. A self-proclaimed Marxist, Sembène presents the strike as a class struggle rather than a racial one. While, to a certain extent, the two are inseparable in the colonial context, in the final analysis the strike is one of workers against bosses rather than Blacks against Whites.

That is not to say that the novel does not critique the French colonial system. In this passage, the French judicial system, which demands Ramatoulaye's arrest for slaughtering a ram when her children are starving, is contrasted with the 'natural justice' carried out by the women. Moreover, the excessive violence of the police who, for example, batter Houdia M'Baye's skull, 'avec une satisfaction visible' (l. 95) reveals the apparent dispensability of indigenous human life from the colonizer's point of view. Most significantly, however, in this passage, the absurdity of colonization is revealed in the French police's attempts to communicate with the women. While the women, though uneducated, are able to converse on a basic level in pidgin French, the policemen evidently have no knowledge of Wolof at all. The colonized are thus presented as more linguistically competent than the representatives of the 'civilized' colonial power.

One of the most striking features of *Les Bouts de bois de Dieu* is the central role played by the women in the strike, particularly when, later in the novel, they march from Thiès

1 The appellation El Hadji denotes that Mabigué has made a pilgrimage to Mecca.

to Dakar to confront the employers. In this scene, the resourcefulness and courage of the strikers' wives are demonstrated in the way in which they fearlessly attack the policemen who have come to arrest Ramatoulaye. Indeed, the strike is presented as a transformative experience for both men and women, suggested here by the apparent 'masculinization' of Ramatoulaye: 'D'où lui était donc venue cette force neuve, où était la source de cette force qui se déchaînait soudain? Ce n'était pas à la guerre, Ramatoulaye n'était pas un homme . . .' (l. 70). The reader is told that Ramatoulaye's strength is drawn from 'les cuisines aux foyers éteints' (l. 77), and that the women use domestic utensils to attack the police. Here, the text exposes the arbitrary nature of gender roles in contemporary West Africa, and demonstrates the potential contribution of women in alternative societies in the future.

However, while Sembène's novel implicitly criticizes the way in which women's role in society is undervalued and underused, the text is careful not to condemn such traditional practices as polygamy. Whereas Mariama Bâ's *Une si longue lettre* (see Chapter 13) presents an unambiguous condemnation of the fact that many African men have more than one wife, *Les Bouts de bois de Dieu* offers a more equivocal view. For example, Mame Sofi's co-wife, Bineta, is simply presented as 'sa "rivale"' (l. 14) without further comment.[2] Polygamy is important for two reasons in this novel: first, because the strikers' demand for family allowances is generated by the colonial employers' refusal to recognize more than one wife; in this respect, polygamy symbolizes the French authorities' lack of respect for the cultural practices of the peoples of the colonies. Second, unlike the colonial authorities who aimed to eradicate African traditions in the name of so-called progress, Sembène's view of progress is that it is not incompatible with tradition. In this passage, the strikers' behaviour is informed by collective memories rooted both in tradition and modernity: the very modern concept of a strike forces the railway workers to celebrate long-forgotten festivals; and the traditional rules of sword fighting, which date back to the time of El Mami Samori Touré (l. 118),[3] briefly distract them from thoughts of the train, the modern machine, whose absence fills them with sadness.

The 'Fumée de la savane' (l. 122) functions as a polyvalent figure in the novel. Not only a symbol of technological progress, it is the central focus of the narrative as well as that of the characters' lives: 'Au long des quelque quinze cents kilomètres de voies du Dakar–Niger . . . les hommes commençaient à avoir assez de palabrer sur la grève' (l. 97). As this extract illustrates, all the characters live in one of three cities linked by the railway (Dakar, Thiès and Bamako), the events of the narrative taking place at different points along the line. Furthermore, the train unites the men who work on it since it does not recognize hierarchies of age, ethnic group or race: 'la machine qui, elle, n'a ni langage, ni race' (l. 144). Indeed, the importance of the train is such that it is described almost as a lover. The men have secret thoughts of how much they miss it; they are even presented as behaving like 'amoureux éconduits' (l. 133). Ultimately, the train, like the strike, points to the possibility of a better future: 'notre seul salut pour une nouvelle vie est dans la machine' (l. 143).

2 'Rivale' denotes 'co-wife', and does not connote antagonism between the two women.

3 Samori Touré was a Guinean national hero who resisted French rule in the 1880s until he was captured and deported in 1898. His descendant, the controversial Guinean leader, Ahmed Sekou Touré, was instrumental in the formation of the RDA (Rassemblement Démocratique Africain), a federation of African trade unions.

The driver of the train is Bakayoko who here seems to speak to the strikers through a whisper in the wind. As shop steward for the railway workers, Bakayoko is in many ways the leader of the strike. However, he does not actually appear until page 264 of the novel. Instead, he is the name on all the other characters' lips, his words recited like maxims to maintain the morale of the striking railwaymen. Through the character of Bakayoko, the text emphasizes the need for a strong leader in any revolution but, by keeping him absent for two-thirds of the novel, also suggests that such a leader is not enough and that all the people must be united for progress to be achieved. Bakayoko is the figurehead of the strike in the same way that, as driver, he is at the front of the train. However, the train needs all the workers in order to keep running. The text also suggests that the benefits of this new technology should be shared by the collective: 'la machine était leur bien commun' (l. 130). Thus, the novel promotes an alternative economy where wealth is distributed equally and is no longer controlled by the rich minority (in this case, the Whites).

However, as this extract suggests, the strikers and their families will not only have to endure great personal difficulties in order to achieve their goals; they will also be forced to overcome the natural obstacles presented by the African environment and landscape. Here the two go hand in hand as the description of the natural elements reflects the psychological and physical conditions of the striking men. 'Cette intrusion des forces de la nature contre la machine' (l. 153) predicts the way in which the progress of the strike will be tested by both man-made obstacles such as renegades and bribes, and natural obstacles like hunger and even death. On the other hand, the passage ends on an optimistic note, since the strikers' communion with the train and, by extension, their commitment to progress, are such that, as the narrator suggests, they will overcome the seemingly insurmountable barriers of race and class.

Further reading

Sembène, Ousmane, *Xala* (Paris: Présence Africaine, 1973).

—— *Guelwaar* (Paris: Présence Africaine, 1996).

Ahmad-Slavin, Fawzia, 'Ousmane Sembène's *Les Bouts de bois de Dieu*: the Mechanics of Change', *LittéRéalité* 7, 1–2 (1995), 49–61.

Harrow, Kenneth W., 'Art and ideology in *Les Bouts de bois de Dieu*: realism's artifices', *The French Review* 62, 3 (1989), 483–93.

Minyono-Nkodo, Mathieu François, *Comprendre les Bouts de bois de Dieu* (Paris: Les Classiques Africaines, 1979).

Ni Chreachain, Firinne, 'Sembène Ousmane incorporated?', in Peter Hawkins and Annette Lavers (eds), *Protée noir* (Paris: L'Harmattan, 1992), pp. 126–40.

Scharfman, Ronnie, 'Fonction romanesque féminine: rencontre de la culture et de la structure dans *Les Bouts de bois de Dieu*', *Ethiopiques* 1, 3–4 (1983), 134–44.

Smith, Craig, 'The stereography of class, race, and nation in *God's Bits of Wood*', *Research in African Literatures* 24, 1 (1993), 51–66.

Language and style

This passage is built on contrasts, united by a common theme – hunger. There are two scenes, two groups of Africans, two sexes; the aggressive activity of the scene with the women is in striking contrast to the more restrained disillusionment and dispirited inactivity of the men; the past and the present are conveyed, as the men view their lives before and during the strike. In addition two languages are presented, French, the language of the authority figures, and Wolof, the major indigenous language of Senegal.

Various strategies are employed in the linguistic exchanges between the women and the police. The police chief and his adjutant speak French to each other; the women speak in Wolof to each other and this is conveyed in French (apart from the single word '*Macou*' (l. 25 glossed in the text as 'Silence'), but they are not understood by the police chief; the adjutant and the women converse in their common language, again recorded in French, but excluding the police chief, and finally one or two women speak in pidgin French to the police. The characteristics of the pidgin French are as follows: phonologically, an inability to produce |ʃ| (l. 57), nasal *o* (l. 79), /r/ (ll. 57, 79, compensated for by *â*); syntactically, omission of all articles, use of infinitive to represent all persons and tenses of verbs, use of disjunctive pronouns as subject pronouns (e.g. ll. 57, 58, 59), use of 'pas' without *ne* to mark negation (ll. 57, 59), use of apposition to mark possession (ll. 59, 80), insertion of pronouns to underline an imperative (l. 80), the omission of *avoir* (l. 59) and the copula (ll. 59, 79).

The French of the narrative is of consistently high register: important issues are at stake. This may be illustrated from both lexical and syntactical perspectives. There is great variation in sentence length, from three words (l. 76), four words (l. 63), five words (l. 147) to sixty-three words (l. 122), sixty-five (l. 148) and seventy-one (l. 140), the longest. The most complicated sentence has five main clauses and one subordinate (l. 107); another has two main clauses and three subordinate (l. 99). Sentence structure is also highly varied, with two minor sentences (3 per cent), twenty-nine simple sentences (41 per cent), fifteen compound (21 per cent), thirteen complex (18 per cent) and eleven compound-complex (16 per cent). Compound-complex sentences constitute a distinctive feature of the passage; there are ten permutations of main and subordinate clauses displayed in eleven sentences. Twenty-eight of the thirty-four subordinate clauses (82 per cent) are relative clauses. This predominance of relative clauses emphasizes the linear, descriptive nature of the passage: there is no suggestion of a cause producing a particular effect, no evaluation of events – no causal, final, consecutive, concessive clauses. Indeed one sentence states 'c'est dans la rue que, sans que l'on sût trop comment, la bagarre commença' (l. 87) – the cause is unknown. A range of devices to link sentences is also used. Short sentences often occur in strategic places after long sentences and are used to provide a brief, succinct finale or summary (especially in the second half), e.g. 'Tout cela avait été leur vie' (l. 127; also ll. 63, 120, 145). There are series of sentences beginning in identical manner, e.g. 'Ce n'était pas à la guerre . . . Ce n'était pas à l'usine . . . Ce n'était pas dans de multiples étreintes . . .' (l. 71; also ll. 90–5); there is inversion, e.g. 'Seule se voyait dans leurs yeux une lueur de mauvaise extase' (l. 145, also ll. 47, 65, 104). Similarly, sentences beginning with complements of the subject indicate sophisticated writing, e.g. 'Tels des amoureux éconduits, ils revenaient' (l. 133, also ll. 29, 103, 145). The paragraph beginning l. 63 is particularly rhetorical, with questions formed in similar ways, symmetrical answers (l. 70), expressed in the negative and finally by anticlimax (bathos): 'La réponse était simple comme elle l'était elle-même: dans les cuisines aux foyers éteints' (l. 76). A multiplicity of subjects and/or adverbs of time in initial position gives a considerable pace to the passage. However, it is pace coupled with detail, details almost tripping over each other in their profusion. This is particularly noticeable in the scene when the women are struggling with the police. However, there is also a more reflective atmosphere, one of taking stock and counting the cost, in the scene featuring the men.

A variety of internal sentence patterns has the effect of introducing energy into the passage. There are sentences designed with symmetrical structures, often involving repetition of expressions, e.g. 'Jamais à la borne-fontaine elle ne prenait part aux discussions, jamais elle ne médisait comme les autres' (l. 68; also ll. 70, 100, 121, 159). There is above all the frequent use of present and past participles (nine and ten respectively), which avoid the use of relative or other clauses and accelerate the action, e.g. 'L'officier de police voyant briller devant lui ces gros yeux blancs où flambait la colère, se sentant bravé, commençait . . . à . . .' (l. 64, also ll. 116, 128). The use of past participles is particularly striking in this respect, e.g. 'La journée s'achevait et, venue des quatre coins du ciel, l'ombre . . .' (l. 1, also ll. 30, 67). A related feature which also contributes to the speed and economy of the narrative is the large number of complements in apposition, e.g. 'la grande marmite, celle des jours de réjouissance' (l. 3); 'tel' is often used in this way (ll. 94, 133, 157).

Imagery pervades the passage. A few extended images occur, e.g. 'Quelque chose de nouveau germait en eux, comme si le passé et l'avenir étaient en train de s'étreindre pour féconder un nouveau type d'homme' (l. 140, also l. 101). There is also an extended personification with somewhat incongruous details: 'Dieu lui-même s'était mis de la partie, il avait balayé ses parterres, son ciel n'avait plus un nuage' (l. 107) Normally, however, the images are much shorter: similes, e.g. 'comme une furie' (l. 91), 'telle un petit fauve' (l. 94), 'comme des gueules béantes' (l. 152, also ll. 133, 157), personifications, e.g. 'l'ombre peu à peu envahissait la ville' (l. 1), 'le vent . . . chuchotait' (l. 142; and especially 'la faim' (l. 6); metonymy, e.g. 'là aussi, il y avait des uniformes' (l. 13 = policemen), 'les deux parallèles' (l. 139 = railway tracks). Indeed much of the language is highly evocative, rich in detail and concise – the imagery selected for comment so far has been reasonably original, but there are other images which are less dramatic, sometimes verging on the cliché, e.g. 'un îlot de cinq ou six hommes' (l. 135, also l. 65). The style sometimes has an impressionistic flavour, using abstract nouns before defining the referent, e.g. 'qui faisait jaillir une explosion d'étincelles' (l. 6, also ll. 9, 153). There is an abundance of adjectives in the passage: the following sentence is a good example where three of the four nouns are qualified by an adjective, 'Les flammes dansantes d'un feu bien nourri éclairaient les visages affamés des enfants' (l. 3). Adjectives are used in striking ways: placed before the noun, e.g. 'soudaine apparition' (l. 9), 'inhumaines cadences' (l. 74, also l. 147); contrasted in chiasmus, 'une lueur de mauvaise extase qui contenait à la fois l'horreur grandissante de la famine et la douloureuse attente de retour de la machine' (l. 145). Abstract nouns, even to express speed and action, e.g. 'firent irruption . . . cette soudaine apparition' (l. 9), 'l'intervention policière' (l. 11, also ll. 9, 74), literary terms, e.g. 'déchaînait' (l. 71), 'rancœurs' (l. 73), 'délice' (l. 102), 'fastes' (l. 111), 'ressuscité' (l. 111 and many others), archaic expressions, e.g. 'avec force piaillements' (l. 23), all contribute to the drama of the events. Furthermore, sentences are often constituted from lexis composed of fine details which resonate with energy; even static scenes are described in active terms, e.g. the following sentence:

> Dans les gares dont les toitures de plaques de ciment s'étaient fendues sous l'action du soleil, des ruisselets d'eau se glissaient partout et les portes des vérandas, les portières de wagons de voyageurs ou de marchandises s'ouvraient soudain sous la poussée du vent comme des gueules béantes, puis se mettaient à battre et à grincer sur leurs gonds sans huile.
>
> (l. 148)

Likewise, the penultimate sentence, through repetition, a combination of abstract language and detailed description, culminates in a resounding crescendo:

> Pendant un instant, le passage de la locomotive apaisait le drame qui se jouait dans leur cœur, car leur communion avec la machine était profonde et forte, plus forte que les barrières qui les séparaient de leurs employeurs, plus forte que cet obstacle jusqu'alors infranchissable: la couleur de leur peau.
>
> (1. 157)

It is clear that the passage is shot through with highly charged vocabulary and that its syntax is constructed with extremely careful crafting. This language, just as evident in the section devoted to the women as in that devoted to the men, lends powerful, rhetorical support to them in their struggles for integrity and respect and shows how the two sexes contribute in equal measure to those struggles. However, it is also clear that Sembène's linguistic virtuosity goes beyond the portrayal of these struggles: he delights in creating artistic, almost poetic, prose for its own sake. Practically every sentence becomes a mini-sculpture in its own right, every word, every phrase and clause carved to produce maximum stylistic and aesthetic effect.

Chapter 12

Ahmadou Kourouma

Les Soleils des Indépendances (Paris: Seuil, 1970), pp. 18–24.

Dans la rue, Fama souffla, tempêta, grogna, la colère ne s'éteignit pas d'une petite braise. Il s'ordonna d'attendre le fils de chien de Bamba pour persuader tous les dégénérés de bâtards qu'encore sur cette terre vivait un homme viril et d'honneur, un sur lequel on ne pouvait pas porter importunément la main.

La rue, une des plus passantes du quartier nègre de la capitale, grouillait. A droite, du côté de la mer, les nuages poussaient et rapprochaient horizon et maisons. A gauche les cimes des gratte-ciel du quartier des Blancs provoquaient d'autres nuages qui s'assemblaient et gonflaient une partie du ciel. Encore un orage! Le pont étirait sa jetée sur une lagune latérite de terres charriées par les pluies de la semaine; et le soleil, déjà harcelé par les bouts de nuages de l'ouest, avait cessé de briller sur le quartier nègre pour se concentrer sur les blancs immeubles de la ville blanche. Damnation! bâtardise! le nègre est damnation! les immeubles, les ponts, les routes de là-bas, tous bâtis par des doigts nègres, étaient habités et appartenaient à des Toubabs. Les Indépendances n'y pouvaient rien! Partout, sous tous les soleils, sur tous les sols, les Noirs tiennent les pattes; les Blancs découpent et bouffent la viande et le gras. N'était-ce pas la damnation que d'ahaner dans l'ombre pour les autres, creuser comme un pangolin géant des terriers pour les autres? Donc, étaient dégoûtants de damnation tous ces Noirs descendant et montant la rue. Donc, vil de damnation, un damné abject, le bâtard de Bamba qui avait porté la main sur Fama. Alors pourquoi attendre sur un trottoir un damné? Quand un dément agite le grelot, toujours danse un autre dément, jamais un descendant des Doumbouya.

Fama se commanda de continuer et traversa la rue. Un bout de temps éloignait encore de l'heure de la quatrième prière, le temps de marcher vite et d'arriver à la mosquée. Il évita deux taxis, tourna à droite, contourna un carré, déboucha sur le trottoir droit de l'avenue centrale et se mêla à la foule coulant vers le marché. Là, entre les toits, apparaissaient divers cieux: le tourmenté par les vents qui arrachaient des nuages pour les jeter sur le soleil déjà couvert et éteint, le bas épais et indigo montant de la mer et avançant sur les maisons et les arbres inquiets et tremblotants. L'orage était proche. Ville sale et gluante de pluies! pourrie de pluies! Ah! nostalgie de la terre natale de Fama! Son ciel profond et lointain, son sol aride mais solide, les jours toujours secs. Oh! Horodougou! tu manquais à cette ville et tout ce qui avait permis à Fama de vivre une enfance heureuse de prince manquait aussi (le soleil, l'honneur et l'or), quand au lever les esclaves palefreniers présentaient le cheval rétif pour la cavalcade matinale, quand à la deuxième prière les griots et les griottes chantaient la pérennité et la puissance des Doumbouya, et qu'après, les marabouts récitaient et enseignaient le Coran, la pitié et l'aumône. Qui pouvait s'aviser alors d'apprendre à courir de sacrifice en sacrifice pour mendier?

Les souvenirs de l'enfance, du soleil, des jours, des harmattans, des matins et des odeurs du Horodougou balayèrent l'outrage et noyèrent la colère. Il fallait être sage. Allah a fabriqué une vie semblable à un tissu à bandes de diverses couleurs; bande de la couleur du bonheur et de la joie, bande de la couleur de la misère et de la maladie, bande de l'outrage et du déshonneur. D'ailleurs faisons bien le tour des choses: Fama pouvait-il prétendre avoir eu raison sur tous les bords? Le cœur n'avait pas été froid et la langue était allée trop vite. En tout, un fils de chef et un musulman conserve le cœur froid et demeure patient, car à vouloir tout mener au galop, on enterre les vivants, et la rapidité de la langue nous jette dans de mauvais pas d'où l'agilité des pieds ne peut nous retirer.

Maintenant naissaient dans les rues et les feuillages les vents appelant la pluie. Le coin du ciel où tantôt couraient et s'assemblaient les nuages était gonflé à crever. De brefs miroitements embrassaient et secouaient. Fama déboucha sur la place du marché derrière la mosquée des Sénégalais. Le marché était levé mais persistaient des odeurs malgré le vent. Odeurs de tous les grands marchés d'Afrique: Dakar, Bamako, Bobo, Bouaké; tous les grands marchés que Fama avait foulés en grand commerçant. Cette vie de grand commerçant n'était plus qu'un souvenir parce que tout le négoce avait fini avec l'embarquement des colonisateurs. Et des remords! Fama bouillait de remords pour avoir tant combattu et détesté les Français un peu comme la petite herbe qui a grogné parce que le fromager absorbait tout le soleil; le fromager abattu, elle a reçu tout son soleil mais aussi le grand vent qui l'a cassée. Surtout, qu'on n'aille pas toiser Fama comme un colonialiste! Car il avait vu la colonisation, connu les commandants français qui étaient beaucoup de choses, beaucoup de peines: travaux forcés, chantiers de coupe de bois, route, ponts, l'impôt et les impôts, et quatre-vingts autres réquisitions que tout conquérant peut mener, sans oublier la cravache du garde-cercle et du représentant et d'autres tortures.

Mais l'important pour le Malinké est la liberté du négoce. Et les Français étaient aussi et surtout la liberté du négoce qui fait le grand Dioula, le Malinké prospère. Le négoce et la guerre, c'est avec ou sur les deux que la race malinké comme un homme entendait, marchait, voyait, respirait, les deux étaient à la fois ses deux pieds, ses deux yeux, ses oreilles et ses reins. La colonisation a banni et tué la guerre mais favorisé le négoce, les Indépendances ont cassé le négoce et la guerre ne venait pas. Et l'espèce malinké, les tribus, la terre, la civilisation se meurent, percluses, sourdes et aveugles . . . et stériles.

C'est pourquoi, à tremper dans la sauce salée à son goût, Fama aurait choisi la colonisation et cela malgré que les Français l'aient spolié, mais avec la bénédiction de celui qui . . . Parlons-en rapidement plutôt. Son père mort, le légitime Fama aurait dû succéder comme chef de tout le Horodougou. Mais il buta sur intrigues, déshonneurs, maraboutages et mensonges. Parce que d'abord un garçonnet, un petit garnement européen d'administrateur, toujours en courte culotte sale, remuant et impoli comme la barbiche d'un bouc, commandait le Horodougou. Evidemment Fama ne pouvait pas le respecter; ses oreilles en ont rougi et le commandant préféra, vous savez qui? Le cousin Lacina, un cousin lointain qui pour réussir marabouta, tua sacrifices sur sacrifices, intrigua, mentit et se rabaissa à un tel point que . . . Mais, l'homme se presse, sinon la volonté et la justice divines arrivent toujours tôt ou tard. Savez-vous ce qui advint? Les Indépendances et le parti unique ont destitué, honni et réduit le cousin Lacina à quelque chose qui ne vaut pas plus que les chiures d'un charognard.

Après le marché, l'avenue centrale conduisait au cimetière et au-delà à la lagune qui apparaissait au bout chargée de pluies compactes. Cette avenue centrale, Fama la connaissait comme le corps de sa femme Salimata; cette avenue parlait et du négoce et de l'agitation anticolonialiste.

Mais au fond, qui se rappelait encore parmi les nantis les peines de Fama? Les soleils des Indépendances s'étaient annoncées comme un orage lointain et dès les premiers vents Fama s'était débarrassé de tout: négoces, amitiés, femmes pour user les nuits, les jours, l'argent et la colère à injurier la France, le père, la mère de la France. Il avait à venger cinquante ans de domination et une spoliation. Cette période d'agitation a été appelée les soleils de la politique. Comme une nuée de sauterelles les Indépendances tombèrent sur l'Afrique à la suite des soleils de la politique. Fama avait comme le petit rat de marigot creusé le trou pour le serpent avaleur de rats, ses efforts étaient devenus la cause de sa perte car comme la feuille avec laquelle on a fini de se torcher, les Indépendances une fois acquises, Fama fut oublié et jeté aux mouches. Passaient encore les postes de ministres, de députés, d'ambassadeurs, pour lesquels lire et écrire n'est pas aussi futile que des bagues pour un lépreux. On avait pour ceux-là des prétextes de l'écarter, Fama demeurant analphabète comme la queue d'un âne. Mais quand l'Afrique découvrit d'abord le parti unique (le parti unique, le savez-vous? ressemble à une société de sorcières, les grandes initiées dévorent les enfants des autres), puis les coopératives qui cassèrent le commerce, il y avait quatre-vingts occasions de contenter et de dédommager Fama qui voulait être secrétaire général d'une sous-section du parti ou directeur d'une coopérative. Que n'a-t-il pas fait pour être coopté? Prier Allah nuit et jour, tuer des sacrifices de toutes sortes, même un chat noir dans un puits; et ça se justifiait! Les deux plus viandés et gras morceaux des Indépendances sont sûrement le secrétariat général et la direction d'une coopérative . . . Le secrétaire général et le directeur, tant qu'ils savent dire les louanges du président, du chef unique et de son parti, le parti unique, peuvent bien engouffrer tout l'argent du monde sans qu'un seul œil ose ciller dans toute l'Afrique.

Mais alors, qu'apportèrent les Indépendances à Fama? Rien que la carte d'identité nationale et celle du parti unique. Elles sont les morceaux du pauvre dans le partage et ont la sécheresse et la dureté de la chair du taureau. Il peut tirer dessus avec les canines d'un molosse affamé, rien à en tirer, rien à sucer, c'est du nerf, ça ne se mâche pas. Alors comme il ne peut pas repartir à la terre parce que trop âgé (le sol du Horodougou est dur et ne se laisse tourner que par des bras solides et des reins souples), il ne lui reste qu'à attendre la poignée de riz de la providence d'Allah en priant le Bienfaiteur miséricordieux, parce que tant qu'Allah résidera dans le firmament, même tous conjurés, tous les fils d'esclaves, le parti unique, le chef unique, jamais ils ne réussiront à faire crever Fama de faim.

Text and context

First published in 1968, Kourouma's first novel, *Les Soleils des Indépendances*, moved francophone black African literature into a new arena. The novel tells the story of Fama, the pathetic antihero who represents disillusionment with independence in the fictitious African state, Côte des Ebènes (a fairly transparent allusion to Côte d'Ivoire). Fama, whose name is simply the Malinke word for chief, is a member of the fallen aristocracy, stripped of nobility by both the colonial and post-independence governments. Whereas, in the past, 'les griots et les griottes chantaient la pérennité et la puissance des Doumbouya' (l. 36), the disinherited Doumbouya prince is now reduced to singing praises at other people's funerals.[1]

Fama is very much a comic figure in the text, mocked by the narrator through the use of free indirect speech. The excessive use of exclamation marks demonstrates the exasperation of Fama at the fact that his nobility has become meaningless in modern African society. Moreover, the narrator's over-use of 'bâtard' and 'bâtardise' parodies the character's frustration at what he sees as the illegitimate nature of the post-independence hierarchy. Not only have people like Fama lost their ancestral inheritance but also the city remains divided along racial lines: the 'Toubabs' (Whites) live in 'les blancs immeubles de la ville blanche' (l. 11), enjoying 'la viande et le gras' (l. 16); the Blacks, despite independence, are still picking up the scraps: 'les Noirs tiennent les pattes' (l. 15). Fama is presented as completely alienated by the new regime. Despite fighting for independence during 'les soleils de la politique' (l. 98), Fama now finds himself obsolete, a fact symbolized by both his illiteracy and, more importantly, his sterility. In this extract, the narrator draws a parallel between Fama's own infertility and the future of the Malinke ethnic group: 'l'espèce malinké, les tribus, la terre, la civilisation se meurent, percluses, sourdes et aveugles . . . et stériles' (l. 73). The fact that Fama can produce no heirs signals the end of the already waning Doumbouya dynasty.

However, the novel is not calling for a return to traditional Malinke social structures since these are implicitly undermined by the narrator's free indirect mockery of Fama's nostalgic

1 *Griots* are story-tellers or praise-singers in sub-Saharan Africa.

lament: 'Ah! nostalgie . . . Oh! Horodougou!' (l. 32).[2] Rather, the text is criticizing both pre- and post-colonial societies for the arbitrary nature of their hierarchies. Fama's assumption that he is superior because of his lineage is as illogical as both colonialism and the single-party system that replaced it.

The 'parti unique' refers to the PDCI (Parti Démocratique de la Côte d'Ivoire) which came to power in the year of independence (1960) under the leadership of Félix Houphouët-Boigny and remained there until his death in 1993. Throughout his 33-year-long presidency, Houphouët maintained a close-knit totalitarian regime ('une société de sorcières' (l. 107)) which did not respond well to criticism. He was also keen to continue economic links with France, paralleled here in Fama's own ambiguous attitude towards the French: 'Surtout, qu'on n'aille pas toiser Fama comme un colonialiste! . . . Mais l'important pour le Malinké est la liberté du négoce. Et les Français étaient aussi et surtout la liberté du négoce' (l. 61). In the days of colonialism, Fama had witnessed the oppression of 'travaux forcés, chantiers de coupe de bois' (l. 63), etc. However, he, like Houphouët, recognized the importance of France for trade. Indeed, the mention of 'travaux forcés' makes a direct connection with Houphouët, whose first act, as people's deputy for the French colony of Côte d'Ivoire, was to ensure the abolition of forced labour in 1946.

In spite of the disclaimer at the outset of the novel, which states that 'toute ressemblance avec des noms de personnes ou de lieux déjà existants est purement fortuite', the reader is left in little doubt about the real geographical and political contexts which underlie this work of 'fiction'. Indeed, it was undoubtedly to escape the censor that Kourouma first published *Les Soleils des Indépendances* in Montreal. When this thinly veiled critique of Ivoirien post-independence politics was reluctantly allowed into Côte d'Ivoire, it was not surprisingly accompanied by a concerted attempt to discredit Kourouma as an author.[3]

However, Kourouma's novel is not only interesting as a political satire. It also experiments with form and language, drawing on the rich heritage of oral literature in sub-Saharan Africa. Questions are posed and then answered by the narrator, for example: 'le commandant préféra, vous savez qui? Le cousin Lacina' (l. 82). This quasi-dialogic technique invites readers to participate in the story and draws their attention to details which are shocking and/or surprising. It also represents a fictional reconstruction of the relationship between a griot and his audience, in which the audience's responses are, to a certain extent, controlled by the oral skills of the griot. Other narrative elements which are drawn from the African oral tradition include: free indirect speech (discussed above); repetition; and parenthetical explanations (for example, the reader is informed that Fama cannot work as a farmer in Horodougou because the soil is too hard for a man of his age (l. 122)). The novel also contains many examples of stories within stories. In this passage, the narrator begins to expand on Lacina's desperate attempts to inherit the chiefdom, but cuts the story short, mirroring the way in which traditional story-tellers sometimes digress (l. 85). Elsewhere in the novel, songs are transcribed (pp. 192 and 194), further emphasizing the link between written text and oral performance.

Kourouma also incorporates into the narrative a large number of Malinke proverbs and idioms which have been translated into French. The meaning of these proverbs is not always

2 Horodougou, home of the Doumbouya clan, means 'land of kola' in Malinke. Kola nuts are traditionally exchanged as symbols of friendship and/or respect. In the novel, the fictitious land of Horodougou has been split, by colonization, between Nikinai (Guinea) and Côte des Ebènes.

3 One rumour suggested that *Les Soleils des Indépendances* had in fact been written by Kourouma's French wife.

transparent to the uninitiated, e.g. 'N'était-ce pas la damnation que de . . . creuser comme un pangolin géant des terriers pour les autres?' (l. 16), and the reader may be forced to negotiate unfamiliar cultural references in order to understand the text. Kourouma thus creates a narrative which resists (neo-)colonial incorporation, simultaneously subverting the French language and reclaiming Malinke culture.

Even the title of the novel is a Malinke expression: *Les Soleils des Indépendances* are, of course, the days of independence. However, throughout the novel, Kourouma manipulates the double meaning of 'soleil' to emphasize further the disillusionment of the people of post-independence 'Côte des Ebènes'. In this passage, Fama regrets the 'soleil' of his childhood in Horodougou when the sun represented warmth, positivity and hope for the future. Now in the city, the sun is 'couvert et éteint', the 'quartier nègre' shadowed by clouds (l. 27). In other words, 'les Indépendances' have metaphorically extinguished 'les soleils'.

For Fama, then, the post-colonial city is a place without hope. Although he knows its streets 'comme le corps de sa femme Salimata' (l. 91), he has no future there. In many ways, the central avenue in this passage (Abidjan's boulevard de la République) is a metaphor for Fama's life. The reference to sex with Salimata (l. 91) recalls Fama's infertility which, for an African, is the equivalent of not having lived. The road also reminds Fama of his former life as a trader and anti-colonial protester, donating all his time and money to the pro-independence cause. Moreover, the central avenue leads to the cemetery and the lagoon, both of which are associated with stagnation and death. This emphasizes the inevitability of Fama's death which, at the end of the novel, takes the reader back to the funeral of Malinke Ibrahima Koné which opens the book. The circular nature of the text, like Fama's sterility, denies the possibility of a future. As such, *Les Soleils des Indépendances*, like Fama himself, presents a pessimistic vision of post-independence Africa.

Further reading

Kourouma, Ahmadou, *Monnè, outrages et défis* (Paris: Seuil, 1990).

—— *En attendant le vote des bêtes sauvages* (Paris: Seuil, 1998).

Borgomano, Madeleine, *Ahmadou Kourouma: le 'guerrier' griot* (Paris: L'Harmattan, 1998).

Gourdeau, Jean-Pierre, 'L'Islam dans *Les Soleils des Indépendances*', *Nouvelles du Sud* 6 (1986–7), 129–38.

Ireland, K. R., 'End of the line: time in Kourouma's *Les Soleils des Indépendances*', *Présence francophone* 23 (1981), 79–89.

Mortimer, Mildred, 'Independence acquired – hope or disillusionment?', *Research in African Literatures* 21, 2 (1990), 35–57.

Ni Chreachain, Firinne, 'Reading *Les Soleils des Indépendances* or: Kourouma and precolonial Africa', in Claude Bouygues (ed.), *Texte africain et voies/voix critiques* (Paris: L'Harmattan, 1992), pp. 91–108.

Okafor, R. C., 'Politics and literature in francophone Africa: the Ivory Coast experience', *Okike: an African Journal of New Writing* 23 (1983), 105–21.

Language and style

Narrative occupies only a small portion of the passage. The storyline is constantly disrupted by a stream of reflections, as Fama, the antihero of the novel, makes his way across town, almost talking aloud to himself, furious, smarting from the insults he has just received from Bamba and others concerning his performance as professional mourner at a funeral.

In the first narrative section (ll. 1–12), his fury is unabated – a triplet of dramatic verbs leaves the reader in no doubt about that. The strongest possible invective is used to condemn Bamba (ll. 2, 12, 16). This leads on to the first digression, a vitriolic denunciation of the Blacks in general for continuing to be content with an inferior position after independence (ll. 12, 15, 18), while the Whites succeed in maintaining their privileged positions – summarized in a concise chiasmus, 'les blancs immeubles de la ville blanche' (l. 11). Fama unleashes his scorn on his fellow Blacks, using a number of rhetorical devices. The 'talking aloud' aspect, reflecting the African tradition of oral story-telling, is evident in the minor sentences, exclamations (ll. 8, 12, 14), questions (ll. 16, 20) and the insertion of a proverb, e.g. 'Quand un dément agite le grelot, toujours danse un autre dément' (l. 21). Moreover, the inversion – 'Donc, étaient dégoûtants de damnation tous ces Noirs descendant et montant la rue' (l. 18) – followed by the parallel – 'Donc, vil de damnation, un damné abject, le bâtard de Bamba' (l. 19) – is powerfully impassioned and hard-hitting.

The second narrative section (ll. 23–30) sees Fama hurrying to the mosque; mirroring the triplet of verbs used in the first narrative section, a series of five verbs conveys his haste (l. 25). The filthy condition of the city (Abidjan) makes Fama reflect upon his homeland. His yearning for Horodougou is expressed, again in rhetorical manner, through a number of triplets – in a minor sentence, 'Son ciel profond et lointain, son sol aride mais solide, les jours toujours secs' (l. 31), in parentheses (l. 34), and in three temporal clauses describing the early morning rituals of his residence (l. 34), the last clause of which contains yet another triplet – 'marabouts récitaient et enseignaient le Coran, la pitié et l'aumône' (l. 37) – and through repetition, e.g. 'manquais/manquait' (l. 32), alliteration – in the same line (l. 36) 'griots et griottes', 'la pérennité et la puissance'. The power of memory and a reminder of the teaching of the Koran soothe Fama's mind (l. 42). More carefully constructed sentences follow: a series of six nouns (l. 40); parallel phrasing – 'Les souvenirs . . . balayèrent l'outrage et noyèrent la colère' (l. 40); and, almost inevitably, a triplet, formed from parallel expressions each consisting of two prepositional phrases – 'un tissu à bandes de diverses couleurs; bande de la couleur du bonheur et de la joie, bande de la couleur de la misère et de la maladie, bande de l'outrage et du déshonneur' (l. 42). Questions and exclamations also figure largely (ll. 30, 31, 32). Fama examines his own behaviour (l. 45), and in a series of balanced phrases and repetitions accepts his own responsibility:

> Le cœur n'avait pas été froid et la langue était allée trop vite. En tout, un fils de chef et un musulman conserve le cœur froid . . . et la rapidité de la langue nous jette dans de mauvais pas d'où l'agilité des pieds ne peut nous retirer.
>
> (l. 45)

The third narrative section (ll. 50–4) is located in the market and inspires a long reflection on trade and the effects of colonization (ll. 54–88). The same devices apparent in the earlier sections are employed again: inversion (l. 51), repetition (ll. 54, 67), series of verbs (ll. 70, 84, 87), series of nouns (ll. 55, 63, 70, 73, 78), series of adjectives (ll. 74, 80), minor sentences (ll. 57, 79), parallel constructions (ll. 62, 71). The symmetry of the following sentence – four subjects + verb + four complements of the subject – is particularly striking, 'Et l'espèce malinké, les tribus, la terre, la civilisation se meurent, percluses, sourdes et aveugles . . . et stériles' (l. 73). The fourth narrative section is very brief (ll. 89–90), evoking trade again and anti-colonial agitation (l. 92), and is expressed in the same deliberately rhetorical way as the previous ones.

Two main sets of imagery stand out, those relating to the natural world and those relating to the sun and other meteorological features. Animal images abound. How low Fama has fallen is illustrated by the fact that there is no reference here to his tribe's totem, the panther (see p. 9), let alone the despised vulture and hyena associated with his current profession, mourner (p. 9). Instead he is compared to a treacherous rat: 'Fama avait comme le petit rat de marigot creusé le trou pour le serpent avaleur de rats' (l. 100); his intellectual ability to a donkey's tail: 'Fama demeurant analphabète comme la queue d'un âne' (l. 105); his contribution to the cause of independence to 'la feuille avec laquelle on a fini de se torcher' (l. 101); his fate to flies on excrement: 'Fama fut oublié et jeté aux mouches' (l. 103). In his rage against Bamba he compares him to a dog (l. 2), in his annoyance with the European administrator he compares him to 'la barbiche d'un bouc' (l. 81), in his scorn for his fellow Blacks he compares their labours to those of a giant pangolin (l. 17), in his jealousy of his cousin Lacina he compares his present status to 'les chiures d'un charognard' (l. 88); independence despoiled the land like locusts (l. 99) and his own seemingly worthless benefits (an identity card and membership of the single political party) are like 'la chair du taureau. Il peut tirer dessus avec les canines d'un molosse affamé, rien à en tirer, rien à sucer, c'est du nerf, ça ne se mâche pas' (l. 120). His disillusionment as he is passed over for any significant government post is expressed in the following simile: 'Passaient encore les postes de ministres, de députés, d'ambassadeurs, pour lesquels lire et écrire n'est pas aussi futile que des bagues pour un lépreux' (l. 103). The irony of his attitude towards the French – striving for their departure and, having achieved it, regretting it – is well illustrated in the image of the weed and the silk-cotton tree: 'comme la petite herbe qui a grogné parce que le fromager absorbait tout le soleil; le fromager abattu, elle a reçu tout son soleil mais aussi le grand vent qui l'a cassée' (l. 59). This image forms a link with the second major series of images, those connected with the sun.

'Le soleil' is an ever-present but ambivalent factor in the passage, having a figurative meaning (ll. 94, 98, 99) as well as its literal one (ll. 60). Even when it is used literally, it may at times also be interpreted symbolically: it is 'harcelé' by clouds (l. 10), overcast (l. 28); for Fama it represents nostalgia for Horodougou (ll. 34, 40). At other times it seems to carry both values at once: 'Partout, sous tous les soleils, sur tous les sols, les Noirs tiennent les pattes; les Blancs découpent et bouffent la viande et le gras' (l. 15). Clouds (ll. 6, 8, 10, 28, 51, 98), storms (ll. 9, 30, 94, 95) and rain (ll. 10, 30, 50, 90) all have similar double values.

The passage portrays a disillusioned man, whose glorious past is for ever lost and whose future seems frighteningly bleak. As he casts his eye over his present situation, he is led to protest against the subordinate behaviour of his fellow Blacks, the disgusting condition of the town, his exclusion from any position of power or potential gain. All is expressed in a style which captures and exploits the techniques of traditional African story-telling and is spiced with graphic imagery. Although all Fama's ambitions have been dashed and he is humiliated, he is able to assert himself in his anguished outbursts, and his strident language provides the passion which spearheads a vigorous attack on post-colonial political and social conditions in Côte d'Ivoire.

Chapter 13

Mariama Bâ

Une si longue lettre (Dakar: Les Nouvelles Editions Africaines, 1979), pp. 47–53.

En me rendant ma valise, Tante Nabou me présenta la petite Nabou; elle la présenta également dans toutes les maisons amies.

La petite Nabou entra, par mes soins, à l'école française. Mûrissant à l'ombre protectrice de sa tante, elle apprenait le secret des sauces délicieuses, à manier fer à repasser et pilon. Sa tante ne manquait jamais l'occasion de lui souligner son origine royale et lui enseignait que la qualité première d'une femme est la docilité.

Après son certificat d'études et quelques années au lycée, la grande Nabou conseilla à sa nièce de passer le concours d'entrée à l'Ecole des Sages-Femmes d'Etat: «Cette école est bien. Là, on éduque. Nulle guirlande sur les têtes. Des jeunes filles sobres, sans boucles d'oreille, vêtues de blanc, couleur de la pureté. Le métier que tu y apprendras est beau; tu gagneras ta vie et tu conquerras des grâces pour ton paradis, en aidant à naître des serviteurs de Mohamed. En vérité, l'instruction d'une femme n'est pas à pousser. Et puis, je me demande comment une femme peut gagner sa vie en parlant matin et soir.»

La petite Nabou devint donc sage-femme. Un beau jour, Tante Nabou convoqua Mawdo et lui dit: « Mon frère Farba t'a donné la petite Nabou comme femme pour me remercier de la façon digne dont je l'ai élevée. Si tu ne la gardes pas comme épouse, je ne m'en relèverai jamais. La honte tue plus vite que la maladie.»

Je savais. Mawdo savait. La ville savait. Toi, Aïssatou, tu ne soupçonnais rien et rayonnais toujours.

Et parce que sa mère avait pris date pour la nuit nuptiale, Mawdo eut enfin le courage de te dire ce que chaque femme chuchotait: tu avais une co-épouse. « Ma mère est vieille. Les chocs de la vie et les déceptions ont rendu son cœur fragile. Si je méprise cette enfant, elle mourra. C'est le médecin qui parle, non le fils. Pense donc, la fille de son frère, enlevée par ses soins, rejetée par son fils. Quelle honte devant la société! »

C'est «*pour ne pas voir ma mère mourir de honte et de chagrin*» que Mawdo était décidé à se rendre au rendez-vous de la nuit nuptiale. Devant cette mère rigide, pétrie de morale ancienne, brûlée intérieurement par les féroces lois antiques, que pouvait Mawdo Bâ? Il vieillissait, usé par son pesant travail et puis, voulait-il seulement lutter, ébaucher un geste de résistance? La petite Nabou était si tentante . . .

Alors, tu ne comptas plus, Aïssatou. Le temps et l'amour investis dans un foyer? Des bagatelles vite oubliées. Tes fils? Ils ne pesèrent guère lourd dans cette réconciliation d'une mère et de son «seul homme» ; tu ne comptas plus, pas plus que tes quatre fils: ceux-ci ne seront jamais les égaux des fils de la petite Nabou.

Les enfants de la Nabou, les griots diront d'eux, en les exaltant: «Le sang est retourné à sa source.»

Tes fils ne comptèrent pas. La mère de Mawdo, princesse, ne pouvait se reconnaître dans le fils d'une bijoutière.

Et puis, une bijoutière, peut-elle avoir de la dignité, de l'honneur? C'est comme si l'on se demandait si tu avais un cœur et une chair. Ah! pour certains, l'honneur et le chagrin d'une bijoutière sont moindres, bien moindres que l'honneur et le chagrin d'une Guélewar [Princesse du Sine].

Mawdo ne te chassait pas. Il allait à son devoir et souhaitait que tu restes. La petite Nabou résiderait toujours chez sa mère; c'est toi qu'il aimait. Tous les deux jours, il se rendait, la nuit, chez sa mère, voir l'autre épouse, pour que sa mère «ne meure pas»; pour «accomplir un devoir».

Comme tu fus plus grande que ceux qui sapaient ton bonheur!

On te conseillait des compromis: «On ne brûle pas un arbre qui porte des fruits».

On te menaçait dans ta chair: «Des garçons ne peuvent réussir sans leur père.»

Tu passas outre.

Ces vérités, passe-partout, qui avaient jadis courbé la tête de bien des épouses révoltées, n'opérèrent pas le miracle souhaité; elles ne te détournèrent pas de ton option. Tu choisis la rupture, un aller sans retour avec tes quatre fils, en laissant bien en vue, sur le lit qui fut vôtre, cette lettre destinée à Mawdo et dont je me rappelle l'exact contenu:

Mawdo,

Les princes dominent leurs sentiments, pour honorer leurs devoirs. Les «autres» courbent leur nuque et acceptent en silence un sort qui les brime.

Voilà, schématiquement, le règlement intérieur de notre société avec ses clivages insensés. Je ne m'y soumettrai point. Au bonheur qui fut nôtre, je ne peux substituer celui que tu me proposes aujourd'hui. Tu veux dissocier l'Amour tout court et l'amour physique. Je te rétorque que la communion charnelle ne peut être sans l'acceptation du cœur, si minime soit-elle.

Si tu peux procréer sans aimer, rien que pour assouvir l'orgueil d'une mère déclinante, je te trouve vil. Dès lors, tu dégringoles de l'échelon supérieur, de la respectabilité où je t'ai toujours hissé. Ton raisonnement qui scinde est inadmissible: d'un côté, moi, «ta vie, ton amour, ton choix», de l'autre, «la petite Nabou, à supporter par devoir».

Mawdo, l'homme est un: grandeur et animalité confondues. Aucun geste de sa part n'est de pur idéal. Aucun geste de sa part n'est de pure bestialité.

Je me dépouille de ton amour, de ton nom. Vêtue du seul habit valable de la dignité, je poursuis ma route.

Adieu.

Aïssatou.

Et tu partis. Tu eus le surprenant courage de t'assumer. Tu louas une maison et t'y installas. Et, au lieu de regarder en arrière, tu fixas l'avenir obstinément. Tu t'assignas un but difficile; et plus que ma présence, mes encouragements, les livres te sauvèrent. Devenus ton refuge, ils te soutinrent.

Puissance des livres, invention merveilleuse de l'astucieuse intelligence humaine. Signes divers, associés en sons; sons différents qui moulent le mot. Agencement de mots d'où jaillit l'idée, la Pensée, l'Histoire, la Science, la Vie. Instrument unique de relation et de culture, moyen inégalé de donner et de recevoir. Les livres soudent des générations au même labeur continu qui fait progresser. Ils te permirent de te hisser. Ce que la société te refusait, ils te l'accordèrent: des examens passés avec succès te menèrent toi aussi, en France. L'Ecole d'Interprétariat, d'où tu sortis, permit ta nomination à l'Ambassade du Sénégal aux Etats-Unis. Tu gagnes largement ta vie. Tu évolues dans la quiétude, comme tes lettres me le disent, résolument détournée des chercheurs de joies éphémères et de liaisons faciles.

Mawdo? Il renoue avec sa famille. Ceux de Diakhao envahissent sa maison; ceux de Diakhao soutiennent la petite Nabou. Mais, et Mawdo le sait, il n'y a pas de comparaison possible entre toi et la petite Nabou, toi, si belle, si douce; toi, qui savais éponger le front de ton mari; toi, qui lui vouais une tendresse profonde, parce que désintéressée; toi, qui savais trouver des mots justes pour le délasser.

Mawdo? Que ne disait-il pas? «Je suis déboussolé. On ne change pas les habitudes d'un homme fait. Je cherche chemises et pantalons aux anciennes places et ne tâte que du vide».

Je ne plaignais pas Mawdo.

«Ma maison est une banlieue de Diakhao. Impossible de m'y reposer. Tout y est sale. La petite Nabou donne mes denrées et mes vêtements aux visiteurs.»

Je n'écoutais pas Mawdo.

«Quelqu'un m'a dit t'avoir vue en compagnie de Aïssatou, hier? Est-ce vrai? Est-elle là? Comment est-elle? Et mes fils?»

Je ne répondais pas à Mawdo.

Car Mawdo demeurait pour moi une énigme et à travers lui, tous les hommes. Ton départ l'avait bien ébranlé. Sa tristesse était bien évidente. Quand il parlait de toi, les inflexions de sa voix se durcissaient. Mais, ses allures de désabusé, les critiques acerbes de son foyer, sa verve qui houspillait tout, n'empêchaient point le gonflement périodique du ventre de la petite Nabou. Deux garçons étaient déjà nés.

Mis devant ce fait visible, preuve de ses communions intimes avec la petite Nabou, Mawdo se contractait avec fureur. Son regard me fustigeait: «Voyons, ne fais pas l'idiote. Comment veux-tu qu'un homme reste de pierre, au contact permanent de la femme qui évolue dans sa maison?» Il ajoutait, démonstratif:

«J'ai vu un film où les rescapés d'une catastrophe aérienne ont survécu en mangeant la chair des cadavres. Ce fait plaide la force des instincts enfouis dans l'homme, instincts qui le dominent, quelle que soit son intelligence. Débarrasse-toi de ton excès de sentimentalité rêveuse. Accepte la réalité dans sa brusque laideur.»

«On ne résiste pas aux lois impérieuses qui exigent de l'homme nourriture et vêtements. Ces mêmes lois poussent le «mâle» ailleurs. Je dis bien «mâle» pour marquer la bestialité des instincts . . . Tu comprends . . . Une femme doit comprendre une fois pour toutes et pardonner; elle ne doit pas souffrir en se souciant des «trahisons» charnelles. Ce qui importe, c'est ce qu'il y a là, dans le cœur; c'est ce qui lie deux êtres, au-dedans . . .» (Il frappait sa poitrine, à la place du cœur.)

«Acculé aux extrêmes limites de la résistance, je me repais de ce qui se trouve à ma portée. C'est vilain à dire. La vérité est laide quand on l'analyse. . .»

Ainsi, pour se justifier, il ravalait la petite Nabou au rang de «mets». Ainsi, pour changer de «saveur», les hommes trompent leurs épouses.

J'étais offusquée. Il me demandait compréhension. Mais comprendre quoi? La suprématie de l'instinct? Le droit à la trahison? La justification du désir de changement? Je ne pouvais être l'alliée des instincts polygamiques. Alors, comprendre quoi? . . .

Comme j'enviais ta tranquillité lors de ton dernier séjour! Tu étais là, débarrassée du masque de la souffrance. Tes fils poussaient bien, contrairement aux prédictions. Tu ne t'inquiétais pas de Mawdo. Oui, tu étais bien là, le passé écrasé sous ton talon. Tu étais là, victime innocente d'une injuste cause et pionnière hardie d'une nouvelle vie.

Text and context

Winner of the 1980 Prix Noma for her first novel, *Une si longue lettre*, the Senegalese novelist Mariama Bâ is one of the pioneers of women's writing in francophone sub-Saharan Africa. This novel confronts the African institution of polygamy through the parallel stories of two women friends, recounted in the form of a long letter from one (Ramatoulaye) to the other (Aïssatou).

Epistolary novels are extremely rare in francophone Africa. In this case, it could be argued that the novel resembles more a diary than a letter, particularly as, at the end, the reader infers that the letter will not be sent. The text also reads as an imagined conversation between Ramatoulaye and her absent friend, with contributions from other voices (Mawdo and Tante Nabou). However, the importance of letter writing is reinforced in this passage when Ramatoulaye recalls and recreates, apparently from memory, a letter sent by Aïssatou to her now ex-husband, Mawdo Bâ. This is one of only two examples of letters within the 'so long letter', and it is significant that both signal a woman's refusal to participate in a polygamous marriage. Here, Aïssatou announces her decision to leave her husband following his marriage to her co-wife, 'la petite Nabou'. Later in the novel, Ramatoulaye, having previously resigned herself to polygamy with her late husband, Modou Fall, now rejects Daouda Dieng's proposal, on the grounds that he is already married.

Both women, then, defy polygamy in writing, as does the novel itself. In contrast to the conforming 'docilité' (l. 6) of la petite Nabou, Ramatoulaye and Aïssatou openly criticize and reject a system which allows a man to take up to four wives. These decisions to challenge this patriarchal institution are now recorded for posterity and reflect the potentially subversive nature of women's writing in Africa.

The emphasis on written forms of communication also highlights the importance of education as a means of empowering women to resist oppressive social structures. Such a liberating effect of education is contrasted, in this passage, with the school of midwifery that la petite Nabou is advised to attend. Selected by Mawdo's mother who endorses the patriarchal view that 'l'instruction d'une femme n'est pas à pousser' (l. 13), this school is described as a production line for exemplary models of traditional feminine virtues: 'des jeunes filles sobres, sans boucles d'oreilles, vêtues de blanc, couleur de la pureté' (l. 9). Furthermore, la petite Nabou's formal preparation for the quintessentially feminine career of midwife is complemented by her training in the traditionally female domestic tasks of cooking, ironing and pounding grain, always under the guidance of her future mother-in-law.

La petite Nabou's traditional education stands in marked opposition to the schooling Ramatoulaye describes in an earlier chapter of the novel. Whereas la petite Nabou is taught not to question a woman's role in society, Ramatoulaye remembers school as a place where she became 'libérée des tabous qui frustrent' and 'apte à l'analyse' (p. 28). Indeed, the headteacher's aim was to encourage freedom of thought and a more global vision of the world. Ramatoulaye presents the pupils of this school as 'de véritables sœurs destinées à la même mission émancipatrice' (p. 27). Moreover, the fact that both women left school and entered into unconventional marriages (Aïssatou to a man of higher caste; Ramatoulaye without a dowry) reinforces the emancipatory role of education for women. In this passage we learn that it is through education that Aïssatou is able to resist the stigma attached to the divorced woman in Africa: 'ce que la société te refusait, ils [les livres] te l'accordèrent' (l. 87). Study provides both emotional and financial independence. Moreover, Aïssatou's low status as both goldsmith and divorcee becomes meaningless when she is nominated to a post at the Senegalese Embassy in the USA.

As well as exposing traditional gender inequality, *Une si longue lettre* addresses the hierarchy of the Senegalese caste system. Because Aïssatou's husband, Mawdo, was a Toucouleur of noble origin, his mother did not consider Aïssatou worthy of her son, refusing to recognize her grandchildren: 'La mère de Mawdo, princesse, ne pouvait se reconnaître dans le fils d'une bijoutière' (l. 39). As the daughter of a goldsmith, Aïssatou is associated with one of the lowest castes in Senegal. Indeed, her love marriage to Mawdo was the subject of much controversy, viewed by many as an insult to his mother, a princess of the Sine. La petite Nabou, on the other hand, is a Toucouleur like her husband. This explains Ramatoulaye's remark that the traditional praise singers – the *griots* – will exalt the continuation of the noble ancestral line since 'le sang est retourné à sa source' (l. 37).

Such is Tante Nabou's apparent concern with maintaining the social hierarchy that, as explained earlier in the novel, she offers la petite Nabou to her son as revenge for the social humilation she has suffered (p. 41). In this passage, she draws once more on the importance of maintaining appearances, claiming that she will literally die of shame if Mawdo refuses to marry la petite Nabou. Here Bâ's text is criticizing the way in which women unwittingly become collaborators in the perpetuation of gender inequality, maintaining rather than challenging patriarchal institutions. Tante Nabou uses the polygamous system to restore her identity and reputation in the eyes of the collective. In so doing, she manipulates la petite Nabou and humiliates Aïssatou, demonstrating the extent to which women like her have internalized social expectations, and the way in which female solidarity is consequently undermined.

The men in the novel reinforce gender inequality on rather spurious grounds. Although he is a medical doctor, Mawdo initially claims he cannot refuse marriage to la petite Nabou for fear that his mother will indeed die of grief. The narrator's incredulity is made implicit in the passage when she describes Mawdo visiting his second wife 'pour que sa mère «ne meure pas»' (l. 47). The use of quotation marks undermines Mawdo's claim and emphasizes its ridiculousness. Later, Ramatoulaye's dismay becomes explicit when she describes Mawdo as an 'énigme' (l. 109) who, in spite of his sadness at Aïssatou's departure, is now happily producing children with la petite Nabou. At this point in the passage, Mawdo rewrites his defence, arguing this time on the basis of men's uncontrollable desire or 'la bestialité des instincts' (l. 126). Again, the justification is invalidated by the male character's own words: Mawdo's bizarre analogy of plane crash survivors eating other dead passengers represents an unconvincing attempt at explaining a common African phenomenon – polygamy – through an extraordinary one. Moreover, the metaphor of cannibalism is extended by Ramatoulaye when she writes that 'Ainsi, pour se jusifier, il ravalait la petite Nabou au rang de «mets». Ainsi, pour changer de «saveur», les hommes trompent leurs épouses' (l. 132). Polygamy, like cannibalism, is thus portrayed as an unacceptable face of African society and one that cannot be excused or explained on the grounds of biological need.

The repeated use of questions in this passage conveys Ramatoulaye's attempts to come to terms with the gender inequality that she, like other women, has experienced. Her realization that this is, in fact, impossible is signalled by the repetition of 'comprendre quoi?'(ll. 134, 137): there is no 'natural' or biological explanation. The questions, like the exclamations in this passage, also point to the dialogic nature of this 'letter' in which Aïssatou's voice sometimes appears to be speaking inside the narrator's head. Ramatoulaye imagines her friend asking her about her husband when she writes 'Mawdo? Il renoue avec sa famille . . . Mawdo? Que ne disait-il pas?' (l. 93). Each imagined question is followed by an answer so that the 'letter' reads like a conversation with a close but absent friend. In these ways, as both imaginary dialogue and letter, the novel stresses the importance of communication, spoken and written, as a route to solidarity based on the shared experiences of women. Ultimately, the final line of this passage suggests a way forward for women in Senegal: by recognizing, like Aïssatou and Ramatoulaye, that they are 'victime[s] innocente[s] d'une injuste cause', women can become 'pionnière[s] hardie[s] d'une nouvelle vie' (l. 141).

Further reading

Bâ, Mariama, *Un chant écarlate* (Dakar: Les Nouvelles Editions Africaines, 1982).

D'Almeida, Irène Assiba, 'The concept of choice in Mariama Bâ's fiction', in Carole Boyce Davies and Anne Adams Graves (eds), *Ngambika: Studies of Women in African Literature* (Trenton, NJ: Africa World Press, 1986), pp. 161–71.

Grésillon, Marie, *'Une si longue lettre' de Mariama Bâ: étude* (Issy les Moulineaux: Editions Saint-Paul, 1986).

Irlam, Shaun, 'Mariama Bâ's *Une si longue lettre*: the vocation of memory and the space of writing', *Research in African Literatures*, 29, 2 (1998), 76–93.

Mortimer, Mildred, 'Enclosure/disclosure in Mariama Bâ's *Une si longue lettre*', *French Review* 64 (1990), 69–78.

Riesz, Janos, 'Mariama Bâ's *Une si longue lettre*: an Erziehungsroman', *Research in African Literatures* 22, 1 (1991), 27–42.

Rueschmann, Eva, 'Female self-definition and the African community in Mariama Bâ's epistolary novel, *So Long a Letter*', in Anne E. Brown and Marjanne E. Goozé (eds), *International Women's Writing: New Landscapes of Identity* (Westport, Conn.: Greenwood Press, 1995), pp. 3–18.

Language and style

In this letter, which is so much more than a letter, Mariama Bâ provides a catalogue and powerful critique of many aspects of post-colonial Senegalese life, all expressed in high-register French. This is done through a series of often irreconcilable contrasts and conflicts. The passage presented here concentrates particularly upon the conflict between the old, traditional values as represented by Tante Nabou and Mawdo and the new, liberating values espoused by Aïssatou and more or less supported by Ramatoulaye, the author of the 'letter'.

It is the linguistic expression of these contrasts which will form the basis of this study, in particular the use of balance, parallelisms and repetition. Repetition, the most obvious of these rhetorical devices, is found on a large number of occasions. The effect is sometimes to underline the concentrated, tightly packed argumentation of the passage, e.g. 'pour que/pour' (l. 47), 'On te' (ll. 50), 'amour' (l. 64), 'souffrir/souffrance' (ll. 127, 139), sometimes to express gentle irony, e.g. 'présenta' (l. 1), 'savais/savait' (l. 19), 'comptas/comptèrent' (ll. 33/39), 'honneur et . . . chagrin' (l. 41), 'moindres' (l. 43), 'passas/passe-partout' (ll. 53/54), 'Mawdo?' (l. 93/99), 'trahison' (ll. 128/135), and at others to illustrate the emotion expressed by the protagonists (through the narrator's voice, who claims to remember incidents in detail, cf. l. 57), e.g. 'Aucun geste' (l. 72), 'pur idéal/pure bestialité' (l. 73), in the panegyric about books, 'sons' (l. 83), 'mots' (l. 84), also 'ceux de' (l. 94), 'toi/toi qui' (five occasions (ll. 95–7). Dense argumentation and emotion combine in Mawdo's self-justification in ll. 119–31, where repetition is powerfully concentrated, suggesting his exasperation with his unconvincing stance – with 'instincts' occurring three times and repeated again (ironically) in l. 136, 'lois', 'mâle', 'comprends/comprendre' (taken up three times in ll. 134–7, as Ramatoulaye expresses her incomprehension at his attitude), 'doit', 'c'est ce qui', 'cœur'. 'Vérité' is used both by Tante Nabou – 'En vérité, l'instruction d'une femme n'est pas à pousser' (l. 12) – and Mawdo – 'La vérité est laide quand on l'analyse' (l. 131) – and on both occasions it is a travesty of truth that is presented. Conversely, Ramatoulaye's admiration for Aïssatou's present situation is emphasized by her triple use of 'tu étais là' in the final paragraph.

Ramatoulaye's admiration is further underlined by the perfect symmetrical structure of the final sentence of the passage: 'victime innocente d'une injuste cause et pionnière hardie d'une nouvelle vie' (noun + adjective + de + adjective + noun × 2). In a similar vein, Ramatoulaye, again full of admiration for her friend's courage in rejecting traditional values, uses parallel clauses/sentences to signal the phases in Aïssatou's emancipation: there are series of clauses beginning with 'tu' in ll. 78–80 and the last paragraph. Other such clauses occur at significant points in the narrative, depicting the obstacles that Aïssatou has had to overcome: e.g. 'On te conseillait des compromis . . . On te menaçait dans ta chair' (ll. 50/52), 'Je ne plaignais pas Mawdo . . . Je n'écoutais pas Mawdo . . . Je ne répondais pas à Mawdo' (ll. 102–8). Other balanced clauses occur in less pivotal parts of the text, e.g. 'tu gagneras ta vie et tu conquerras des grâces' (l. 11), 'la fille de son frère, enlevée par ses soins, rejetée par son fils' (l. 25, also ll. 33, 61, 65, 121). Short compound sentences are especially susceptible to this treatment, e.g. 'Il allait à son devoir et souhaitait que tu restes' (l. 45), 'Tu louas une maison et t'y installas' (l. 78). A triplet relating to Mawdo reinforces Ramatoulaye's low opinion of him: 'Mais, ses allures de désabusé, les critiques acerbes de son foyer, sa verve qui houspillait tout, n'empêchaient point le gonflement périodique du ventre de la petite Nabou' (l. 111). Focusing on individuals and encapsulating their characters is achieved through placing present and past participles in initial position on a number of occasions, e.g. 'Mûrissant à l'ombre protectrice de sa tante, elle apprenait le secret des sauces délicieuses' (l. 3, also l. 1), 'Vêtue du seul habit valable de la dignité, je poursuis ma route' (l. 74, also ll. 83, 115, 130).

Lexical balancing is also evident. A major lexical contrast is that between 'dignité et honneur', reflecting the traditional view of a woman's position in the family (ll. 17, 41, 42, 43, 60, 74) and 'honte' if that view is not adhered to (ll. 18, 25, 27). A number of others, less general but still significant, occur. Tante Nabou says, 'je me demande comment une femme peut gagner sa vie en parlant matin et soir' (l. 13): ironically the post which Aïssatou obtains is one involving speech *par excellence* – interpreting. While everyone 'savait' Tante Nabou's mission for la petite Nabou, Aïssatou was blissfully ignorant, 'tu ne soupçonnais rien' (l. 19). '[D]égringoles' and 'hissé' contrast (l. 68), as does 'd'un côté . . . de l'autre' in the same paragraph; also 'en arrière' and 'avenir' (l. 79), and 'refusait' and 'accordèrent' (l. 87). An amusing lexical contrast which has deeper significance is that involving clothes: Aïssatou declares herself to be 'Vêtue du seul habit valable de la dignité' (l. 74) whereas Mawdo is concerned about his 'chemises et pantalons' (l. 100).

Strong emotive language is used on a number of occasions. Contempt for Tante Nabou's espousal of traditional values leads Ramatoulaye to express herself thus: 'Devant cette mère rigide, pétrie de morale ancienne, brûlée intérieurement par les féroces lois antiques' (l. 28). Similar invective is reserved for Mawdo on a number of occasions (e.g. ll. 111–13, 134–7). The longest section of such emotive language occurs in Ramatoulaye's eulogy of books (ll. 82–92), where internal rhyme ('puissance'/'intelligence', 'merveilleuse'/'astucieuse'), repetition ('sons', 'mots') and alliteration ('Signes divers, associés en sons; sons différents qui moulent le mot. Agencement de mots') contribute to the effect.

Little attempt is made to vary the register of the different parts of the passage – the conversational sections are produced in as high-register French as the narrative. With the final outburst from Mawdo used as an exemplar (ll. 116–31), it is possible to discern a number of high-register features. Mawdo speaks 'avec fureur' with a look which 'fustigeait', in other words not necessarily in a tone which would normally be associated with the most careful of registers. From a lexical point of view items such as 'plaide', 'enfouis', 'dominent', 'ton excès de sentimentalité rêveuse', 'brusque laideur', 'lois impérieuses', 'acculé', 'je me repais' are not the stuff of normal emotional speech. From a syntactic point of view, a number of features are also present: the use of a concessive construction, anteposition of an adjective which normally follows the noun ('brusque laideur'), non-use of articles ('nourriture et vêtements'), past participle and phrase as first element of a sentence, transposition of direct object and prepositional object ('exigent de l'homme nourriture et vêtements'). Of high register stylistically is the symmetry of sentences such as 'Acculé aux extrêmes limites de la résistance, je me repais de ce qui se trouve à ma portée' ('extrêmes limites' versus 'à ma portée'). In addition, the structure of the outburst as a whole is coldly logical and abstract, not how one would expect the speech of an impassioned man to be.

In short, the passage is characterized and unified by high-register French. There is a steady rhythm of repetition, symmetrical balancing and parallelism throughout, which provide the powerful language required to support the challenging positions adopted by Aïssatou and Ramatoulaye as representatives of those fighting for women's rights in a traditional society.

Chapter 14

Sony Labou Tansi

La Vie et demie (Paris: Seuil, 1979), pp. 14–20.

Le Guide Providentiel quitta son air de supplication et ragea longuement, il se fit apporter son grand sabre aux reflets d'or et se mit à abattre la loque-père en jurant furieusement sur ses trois cent soixante-deux ancêtres, rappelant par sa hardiesse et sa fougue les jours lointains où ces mêmes ancêtres abattaient la forêt pour construire la toute première version d'un village qui devait devenir Yourma, la capitale; il enfonçait des bouts de phrase obscènes au fond de chaque geste. La loque-père fut bientôt coupée en deux à la hauteur du nombril, les tripes tombèrent avec le bas du corps, le haut du corps restait là, flottant dans l'air amer, avec la bouche saccagée qui répétait la phrase. Puis le Guide Providentiel se calma et retomba dans son air de supplication, épongeant la sueur qui mettait son visage en nage, il poussa des pieds le bas du corps, se fit apporter une chaise de salle à manger, la fit mettre devant le haut du corps, y prit place, fuma un cigare complet avant de se relever.

– Enfin, Martial, sois raisonnable.

Il se mordait fortement la lèvre inférieure, une violente rage lui gonflait la poitrine, faisant tournoyer ses petits yeux semés au hasard du visage. L'instant d'après, il parut plus calme, tourna longuement autour du haut du corps suspendu dans le vide, considéra avec un début de compassion cette boue de sang noire qui en goudronnait la base.

– Sois raisonnable, Martial, et dis-moi quelle mort tu veux mourir?

Aucune voix ne sortit de la loque-père; le Guide Providentiel pensa à une de ces gammes de poisons dont il se servait quand il avait eu pitié d'une loque et qu'il avait décidé de lui accorder la grâce d'une mort en vitesse.

– C'est parfait, dit-il. Tu as gagné, Martial: tu l'auras.

Il alla lui-même chercher la dose, la versa dans le verre qui lui avait servi à boire les vins vendus aux Quatre Saisons, il y ajouta du champagne jusqu'au bord.

– Une mort au champagne, maugréait le Guide Providentiel. Pour un chiffon d'homme qui a blessé la République d'une vingtaine de guerres civiles, la mort au champagne devient un hommage. Je te la donne à contrecœur, Martial.

Il versa le contenu du verre dans la bouche ouverte de la loque-père, le liquide traversa la gorge, sortit par le trou du couteau, coula le long du torse nu, vint se mêler aux torchons de viande déchiquetée avant de s'égoutter comme un faux sang sur le sol carrelé. Le Guide Providentiel attendit, il y eut un long silence, puis la voix sortit, moitié par la bouche, moitié par la blessure du couteau. Le Guide Providential se fâcha pour de bon, avec son sabre aux reflets d'or il se mit à tailler à coups aveugles le haut du corps de la loque-père, il démantela le thorax, puis les épaules, le cou, la tête; bientôt il ne restait plus qu'une folle touffe de cheveux flottant dans le vide amer, les morceaux taillés formaient au sol une sorte de termitière, le Guide Providentiel les dispersa à grands coups de pied désordonnés avant d'arracher la touffe de cheveux de son invisible suspension; il tira de toutes ses forces, d'une main d'abord, puis des deux, la touffe céda et, emporté par son propre élan, le Guide Providentiel se renversa sur le dos, se cogna la nuque contre les carreaux, il en serait mort sur le coup, mais ce n'était pas un homme fragile, il constata que ses mains étaient devenues noires, d'un noir d'encre de Chine; plus tard, le Guide Providentiel passa des journées à vouloir laver ce noir de Martial à tous les savons et à tous les dissolvants du monde, le noir ne disparut pas.

– Vous allez me bouffer ça, dit le Guide Providentiel aux autres loques. Je n'y ai pas enfoncé ma sueur pour rien.

Il ordonna qu'on vînt prendre la termitière et qu'on en fît moitié du pâté et moitié une daube bien cuisinée pour le repas du lendemain midi.

– Il y a huit ventres, précisa le Guide Providentiel à son cuisinier personnel.

Il jeta un coup d'œil triomphal au lieutenant. Le lieutenant se mit comme un i, prêt à recevoir les ordres.

– Remmène ces chiffons. Qu'ils viennent manger demain.

Le lieutenant poussa les huits loques devant lui, le cuisinier qui avait fini de déplacer la termitière enlevait ses gants pour laver la place.

Chaïdana se rappelait ces scènes-là tous les soirs, comme si elle les recommençait, comme si, dans la mer du temps, elle revenait à ce port où tant de cours étaient amarrés à tant de noms – elle était devenue cette loque humaine habitante de deux mondes: celui des morts et celui des «pas-tout-à-fait-vivants», comme elle disait elle-même.

Le lendemain, le lieutenant les ramena pour le repas de midi: c'était une table ronde. Cette part des événements, Chaïdana la revivait tous les midis, ce qui lui donnait l'amère impression de passer deux fois sur certaines séquences de son existence. On avait mis huit couverts en argent et en or. On avait placé Chaïdana et Providentiel, sa mère et ses trois frères directement en face. La cuvette de pâté présidait au milieu des champagnes, à côté d'une autre cuvette d'une daube bien assaisonnée et parfumée. Devant le couvert en or fumait l'éternelle viande venue aux Quatre Saisons, entre quatre mâts de champagne Providencia, la seule marque qui entrait dans le ventre du Guide Providentiel, et qui portait la mention «Cuvée de Son Excellence Matéla-Péné-Loanga».

Le Guide Providentiel commençait toujours ses repas par deux doses d'un alcool local fabriqué à l'intention des guides.

– Je suis carnassier, dit-il en tirant le plat de viande vers lui.

Le Guide Providentiel avait toujours son garde du corps à sa gauche, sans doute voulait-il observer la rigueur de la superstition selon laquelle la mort des grands vient toujours de la gauche.

– Vous avez ce soir et maintenant pour terminer vos deux plats.

Chaïdana se rappela comme ils avaient commencé par le pâté plus facile à avaler que la daube pleine de cheveux et dont les morceaux résistaient aux dents et à la langue, d'une résistance plus offensante. Le Guide Providentiel parla de sa vie, des vins, des femmes, du football, des Espagnols qui incitaient les voisins à d'outrageantes provocations, des Français qui se battaient pour le permis de prospection en mer: «Ils me font de vraies prières, ces gens, ils sont contraints de m'aimer, et c'est presque vrai qu'ils m'aiment.»

– N'en jetez rien, s'il vous plaît.

Jules, l'aîné ne mangeait pas. Le Guide Providentiel s'était levé, lui avait caressé le menton puis le front, il lui avait même souri gentiment.

– Alors, mon ange, tu le manges ton pâté?

– Je n'ai pas faim.

– Mange quand même.

– Non.

Le Guide Providentiel lui avait simplement planté son couteau de table dans la gorge. Pendant qu'ils mangeaient, le cadavre de Jules se vidait de son sang. Chaïdana se souvint qu'ensuite le sang avait mouillé ses pieds nus – elle s'en rappelait la tiédeur. Le soir, ils eurent mangé le pâté et la daube: le Guide Providentiel leur adressa les félicitations les plus cordiales avant de déclarer qu'il restait le pâté de l'autre, à la fin duquel leur serait rendue la liberté. Le lendemain, à midi, ce furent la loque-mère, Nelanda, Nala, Zarta, Assam et Ystéria qui refusèrent de manger. Le Guide Providentiel planta dix fois son couteau de table, Chaïdana et Tristansia mangèrent de la daube pendant sept jours. Le soir du septième jour de viande, elles remplirent la salle d'un tapis de vomi d'un noir d'encre de Chine où le Guide Providentiel glissa et tomba, il salit le côté gauche de son visage d'une tache indélébile, semblable à celle qu'il avait sur les mains, tache qu'il allait garder jusqu'au jour des obsèques nationales prévues par la Constitution, tache que les gens eurent raison d'appeler «noir de Martial».

Quand il voulut rejoindre son lit après ses quatre heures habituelles de table, le Guide Providentiel y trouva le haut du corps de la loque-père qui avait horriblement sali les draps «excellentiels» au noir de Martial. Le Guide entra dans une rage infernale, il tira huit chargeurs avec son PM sur le haut du corps, il fit un grand trou au milieu du lit, à l'endroit où il avait vu le haut du corps, il marcha longuement dans toute la pièce, beuglant, jurant, insultant, menaçant. Essoufflé il s'assit sur la table de chevet et retrouva son vieil air de supplication.

– Enfin, Martial! Combien de fois veux-tu que je te tue?

On avait changé le lit «excellentiel» seize fois en l'espace d'un mois, temps pendant lequel le Guide Providentiel n'avait pas fermé l'œil une seule nuit, le haut du corps de Martial venait toujours à côté de lui, noircissant les draps qu'on devait maintenant brûler et changer tous les jours, il demanda qu'on lui affectât les quarante plus courageux et plus charnus gorilles de l'armée – c'était pour la plupart des hommes grands comme deux, forts comme quatre et velus comme des ours. Le Guide dormait entre quatre d'entre eux collés à sa peau, tandis que le reste du contingent s'ajoutait à une cinquantaine de soldats ordinaires qui remplissaient les veillées de son Excellence du bruit ferré de leurs sinistres souliers; et quand les reins du Guide avaient posé leur problème, on remplaçait les peaux-collants directs par des êtres du sexe d'en face, les gardes assistaient alors aux vertigineuses élucubrations charnelles du Guide Providentiel exécutant sans cesse leur éternel va-et-vient en fond sonore aux clapotements fougueux des chairs dilatés. Le haut du corps de Martial venait toujours couper les appétits et le sommeil du Guide Providentiel jusqu'à ce jour où Kassar Pueblo, le cartomancien préféré du Guide Providentiel, établit cette chose:

– Son Excellence doit partager son lit avec la fille de Martial pour chasser l'image du revenant. Mais Son Excellence doit absolument éviter de faire la chose-là avec la fille de Martial.

Text and context

In this passage, taken from the opening section of Sony Labou Tansi's debut novel, Chaïdana recalls witnessing the death of her father, Martial, at the hands of Katamalanasie's leader, le Guide Providentiel. She, along with the rest of her family, is then forced to eat her father's corpse which is transformed into paté and stew by le Guide's personal chef. Those who refuse to eat have their throats cut. The horror of this scene immediately signals the brutality of Sony's fictional African state in which human life is dispensable and violence knows no bounds. Martial is executed because, as a revolutionary, he threatens the stability of le Guide's totalitarian regime. However, the fact that Martial initially refuses to die and then, when dead, returns to haunt le Guide demonstrates the impossibility of total control, even for the Hitlerite leader of Katamalanasie.[1]

The excessive terms in which Martial's execution is described give the passage a science fictional quality. Sony's depiction of first the torso, then the head of Martial floating in the air, repeating the same phrase over and over again ('Je ne veux pas mourir cette mort' (p. 13)) while le Guide tries various different methods of assassination pushes the narrative into the realms of the supernatural. The figure of the corpse returning from the dead – 'le revenant' (l. 131) – also features in many traditional African tales. Here, then, the text employs magic realist strategies to criticize and parody a political reality (neo-colonialism), and also to present a nightmarish image of a possible future. So horrific are the crimes of some contemporary African nations that any satire of them must, in order to be effective, be more horrific still. In other words, the fantastic events in the novel represent absurd, but

1 The name of the country makes a direct allusion to Hitler's Germany: read Katamalanasie as Katamalanazi.

nevertheless logical, exaggerations of real situations. The scene in which le Guide discusses women, wine and football while the prisoners are forced to eat a stew full of hair demonstrates the way in which *La Vie et demie*, like Gabriel García Márquez's novel, *One Hundred Years of Solitude*, weaves together the extraordinary and the banal. There are many other intertexts in Sony Labou Tansi's novel. This extract recalls two famous French figures of excess: François Rabelais's *Gargantua* and Alfred Jarry's immature tyrant, *Ubu roi*.

Like all his ministers and the long succession of *Guides* who follow him, le Guide is presented as very much a victim of his sexual urges. Later in the novel, Chaïdana uses her remarkable beauty to her own ends by luring politicians to the Hôtel la Vie et Demie where, following le Guide's treatment of her father, she murders them with a glass of poisoned champagne. Sex, like everything else in Katamalanasie, is presented as a means of control. Martial's ghost prevents le Guide from enjoying his 'vertigineuses élucubrations charnelles' (l. 125); as a consequence, le Guide is advised by his fortune teller to sleep with Chaïdana but not to 'faire la chose-là' (l. 131). When she eventually marries le Guide (in preparation for murdering him), Chaïdana is raped by her father, Martial. Chaïdana's body thus becomes a weapon of revenge but also a site of conflict which, like the fictional African nation she represents, is violated and dominated in the struggle for power.

Though disturbing, violence and the grotesque are the source of much of the humour in the novel. The horror of the family eating their father's dead body is turned into black humour when Chaïdana remembers that the stew full of hair was particularly difficult to swallow (l. 79). Earlier in this passage, le Guide's repeated attempts to kill Martial dissolve into the comic when, on grabbing his victim's floating tuft of hair, he slips and bangs his head on the tiles (l. 41). For a moment the brutal tyrant appears vulnerable and ridiculous, the hair a symbol of Martial's resistance. Later, he slips again, this time on Martial's regurgitated remains (l. 102). Generally, the absurd nature of le Guide's behaviour provokes amusement in the text: unable to kill Martial with his golden sword, le Guide pulls up a chair and smokes a cigar (l. 11). Having sliced in two the body of Martial who nevertheless refuses to die, le Guide pleads with his victim: 'Sois raisonnable, Martial, et dis-moi quelle mort tu veux mourir?' (l. 19). The irony of such an unreasonable man begging a dismembered body to be reasonable points to one of the key themes of *La Vie et demie*, that is the unreliability of neo-colonial discourse, and the way in which language loses its meaning under a totalitarian regime.

The use of repetition in the novel parallels attempts by neo-colonial leaders to standardize everything, including language and thought. Banal descriptions such as 'son grand sabre aux reflets d'or' (ll. 2, 34) are repeated in this passage – and throughout the novel – to reflect the repression of the imagination in such a controlled environment. Martial and his family, imprisoned in the presidential palace, are frequently described as 'loques' (ll. 2, 6, 20, 46, 54, 98, 107) and 'chiffons' (ll. 26, 53), in illustration of the extent to which they have been stripped of their humanity. Yet the frequent repetition of these words causes them to lose their original meaning so that they eventually become nothing more than synonyms for people. Le Guide thus creates a new system of signs – a new language – over which he hopes to maintain total control. Any new signs outside le Guide's control are treated with immediate suspicion as they are potentially subversive. Hence le Guide's subsequent attempts to ban the colour black when the mysterious stains he acquires are named by the people as 'le "noir de

2 The point here is also, of course, a racial one, indicating post-independence governments' failure to promote equality for their own people.

Martial"' (ll. 44, 108).[2] At the same time, however, Sony's text demonstrates the power of language to resist such control. Some of the characters' names are chosen either to reflect or contradict their roles within the novel, 'Martial' and 'le Guide Providentiel' being the most obvious examples of this. The irony of repeated neologisms such as 'excellentiel' makes a similar point, undermining the authority of 'Son Excellence' and highlighting the emptiness of le Guide's neo-colonial rhetoric.

The novel also presents a large number of factual details, the precision of which often makes them absurd. Here we learn that le Guide has 362 ancestors (l. 3), a fact that is both ridiculous in its apparent accuracy and completely unbelievable; the reader cannot accept that such an illegitimate tyrant can have such an impressive family tree. Such information causes the reader to doubt the reliability of the narrator, thereby mirroring the text's suggestion that the discourses of power are not to be trusted. On the other hand, information is included to ground the text in a recognizable context. In this extract, an overt reference to the duplicity of le Guide and, by extension, of many post-independence African leaders, is found in the comments he makes about the French wanting to dig for oil: 'Ils me font de vraies prières, ces gens, ils sont contraints de m'aimer, et c'est presque vrai qu'ils m'aiment' (l. 83). This is no doubt an oblique reference to the relationship between the French and the Congolese president, Marien Ngouabi, whom they initially supported on the understanding that he would join their struggle to defend oil-rich Cabinda from Angolan advances. In other words, *La Vie et demie*, like Kourouma's *Les Soleils des Indépendances* (see Chapter 12 above) presents a fictionalized critique of an identifiable African nation.

It is the blurring of the fantastic and the real which makes Sony's text so powerful, paralleling the way in which, as Chaïdana explains, the people of Katamalanasie find themselves living in two worlds, 'celui des morts et celui des "pas-tout-à-fait vivants"' (l. 59). This is a world of zombies, the living dead, symbolized by the omnipresent figure of the ghost of Martial who, like the conscience of le Guide, prevents him from sleeping. Humanity has been crushed by the totalitarian regime. However, Martial's refusal to disappear does offer a glimmer of hope, suggesting that political opposition can never be completely extinguished but will forever rebuild itself in places and in forms that dictators least expect.

Further reading

Sony Labou Tansi, *La Parenthèse de sang* (Paris: Hatier, 1981).
—— *L'Anté-peuple* (Paris: Seuil, 1983).
—— *Les Sept solitudes de Lorsa Lopez* (Paris: Seuil, 1985).

Anyinefa, Koffi, *Littérature et politique en Afrique noire: socialisme et dictature comme thème du roman congolais d'expression française* (Bayreuth: Eckhard Breitinger, 1990).

Devésa, Jean-Michel, *Sony Labou Tansi: écrivain de la honte et des rives magiques du Kongo* (Paris: L'Harmattan, 1996).

Julien, Eileen, 'Dominance and discourse in *La Vie et demie*: or how to do things with words', *Research in African Literatures* 20, 3 (1989), 371–84.

—— 'Rape, repression, and narrative form in *Le Devoir de violence* and *La Vie et demie*', in Lynn A. Higgins and Brenda R. Silver (eds), *Rape and Representation* (New York: Columbia University Press, 1991), pp. 160–81.

Moudileno, Lydie, '*La Vie et demie* or the tortuous path of the fable', *Research in African Literatures* 29, 3 (1998), 21–33.

Kadima-Nzuji, Mukala, Kouvouama, Abel and Kibangou, Paul (eds), *Sony Labou Tansi, ou, La quête permanente du sens: actes du colloque international tenu à Brazzaville les 13, 14 et 15 juin 1996* (Paris: L'Harmattan, 1997).

Language and style

This passage is a study in sadism. The sadism of le Guide Providentiel is reflected linguistically in a subversion of ordinary words. Words are used with unaccustomed values, and an atmosphere of unease and anxiety is induced in the reader. The very title of le Guide is a good example, but many other words are used in unfamiliar ways, e.g. 'raisonnable' (l. 13), 'compassion' (l. 17), 'grâce' (l. 22), 'hommage' (l. 28), 'souri' (l. 87), 'ange' (l. 88), 'félicitations . . . cordiales' (l. 96). Even the words used to describe his accomplishments have a hollow ring: 'sa hardiesse et sa fougue' (l. 3) square ill with his cruel treatment of his subjects. Whereas his so-called ancestors chopped down trees to create a village, he chops down his subjects with savagery to eliminate opposition. Humans are regularly referred to as 'loques' (see above, especially 'elle était devenue cette loque humaine habitante de deux mondes' (l. 58)), less often as 'chiffons' (see above). le Guide refers to Chaïdana and her family as 'ventres' (l. 50), simply anatomical parts. Another aspect of Le Guide's sadism and linguistic subversion is apparent in the use of euphemisms to describe murder. The effect is all the more disturbing because the references are so brief and elliptical, e.g. 'Le Guide Providentiel lui avait simplement planté son couteau de table dans la gorge' (l. 92), 'Le Guide Providentiel planta dix fois son couteau de table' (l. 99). A further group of euphemisms is used in a bizarre way to mask le Guide's bodily functions: 'quand les reins du Guide avaient posé leur problème' (l. 123), 'des êtres du sexe' (l. 124), '[les] vertigineuses élucubrations charnelles du Guide Providentiel exécutant sans cesse leur éternel va-et-vient en fond sonore aux clapotements fougueux des chairs dilatés' (l. 125), where additional attention is drawn to the chiasmus – 'vertigineuses élucubrations – éternel va-et-vient' (v / é // é / v) – through the ante-position of the two adjectives (also l. 118). The label on the champagne, 'Cuvée de Son Excellence Matéla-Péné-Loanga' (l. 69), evokes through slight linguistic distortion le Guide's self-proclaimed sexual prowess (= *matelas – pénis – long*).

The sinister atmosphere is exacerbated by the use of extremely long sentences. A nightmarish effect is created as the reader discovers that s/he cannot assimilate their meaning – clause after clause after clause prevents the reader from pausing to take a breathing space and assess the situation. The consequence is that s/he loses touch with reality and does not fully appreciate what is happening. Just as words are manipulated by le Guide and acquire disorientating connotations, so the sentences become sites of further disorientation: it is not possible to dwell on the individual details of le Guide's sadistic actions before another detail and then another force the pace, and the horrendous impact is dissipated. The first paragraph consists of twelve lines of text but contains only three sentences, the first of which, six lines long, consists of five main and two subordinate clauses, the second of three main and one subordinate, the third of seven main and one subordinate. The sentences (in the non-conversational sections) are distributed in the following proportions according to their structure: simple 25 per cent (ten examples), compound 23 per cent (nine), complex 18 per cent (seven), compound-complex 35 per cent (fourteen). Most unusually, compound-complex sentences dominate, and by a considerable amount. The most impressive sentence from the point of view of structure is thirteen lines long, beginning l. 33 with fifteen clauses; the internal structure of many of the clauses is also complicated. The first simple sentence does not occur until l. 48 and even that has two noun clause objects.

The horrific sadism of the despotic Guide is displayed in all its grotesqueness in the descriptions of his treatment of his victims. The narrator announces that 'il enfonçait des bouts de phrase obscènes au fond de chaque geste' (l. 6), and this obscene vocabulary is only too evident. A few examples must suffice: 'La loque-père fut bientôt coupée en deux à la hauteur du nombril, les tripes tombèrent avec le bas du corps' (l. 6); 'le liquide traversa la gorge, sortit par le trou du couteau, coula le long du torse nu, vint se mêler aux torchons de viande déchiquetée avant de s'égoutter comme un faux sang sur le sol carrelé' (l. 29), 'il se mit à tailler à coups aveugles le haut du corps de la loque-père, il démantela le thorax, puis les épaules, le cou, la tête; bientôt il ne restait plus qu'une folle touffe de cheveux flottant dans le vide amer' (l. 34), 'Le soir du septième jour de viande, elles remplirent la salle d'un tapis de vomi d'un noir d'encre de Chine où le Guide Providentiel glissa et tomba' (l. 100). The nauseating effect is on the one hand brought into relief by references to le Guide's burlesque accident (also l. 41) and on the other heightened by references immediately following a sadistic act to normal, civilized behaviour, e.g. '[il] se fit apporter une chaise de salle à manger, la fit mettre devant le haut du corps, y prit place, fuma un cigare complet' (l. 11), 'il y ajouta [au poison] du champagne jusqu'au bord' (l. 25), 'Le Guide Providentiel commençait toujours ses repas par deux doses d'un alcool local fabriqué à l'intention des guides' (l. 71). The contrast between this vocabulary and the subverted vocabulary and euphemisms used elsewhere could scarcely be greater – and adds to the Kafkaesque atmosphere of the passage. The despotism of le Guide is indirectly shown by the fact that of the twenty lines of speech reported, all but four come from him: 'Je n'ai pas faim' (l. 89) followed up by 'Non' (l. 91) express Jules's futile resistance. The other two lines are full of obsequious respect for le Guide: 'Son Excellence doit partager son lit avec la fille de Martial pour chasser l'image du revenant. Mais Son Excellence doit absolument éviter de faire la chose-là avec la fille de Martial' (l. 130).

The violent and horrific nature of the scene would normally be fertile terrain for the use of imagery – but instead direct description prevails. The narrative is starkly presented with very little figurative usage. Only eight images are found. Half of them add to the macabre nature of the scene: 'cette boue de sang noire qui en goudronnait la base [du corps]' (l. 17), 'les morceaux taillés formaient au sol une sorte de termitière' (l. 37, repeated ll. 48, 55); 'ses mains étaient devenues noires, d'un noir d'encre de Chine' (l. 43); 'elles remplirent la salle d'un tapis de vomi d'un noir d'encre de Chine' (l. 101). The description of the lieutenant – 'Le lieutenant se mit comme un i, prêt à recevoir les ordres' (l. 51) – and of the bodyguard – 'les quarante plus courageux et plus charnus gorilles de l'armée – c'était pour la plupart des hommes grands comme deux, forts comme quatre et velus comme des ours' (l. 117) – are banally unexceptional. It is Chaïdana's flashbacks that provide the most developed simile: 'Chaïdana se rappelait ces scènes-là tous les soirs, comme si elle les recommençait, comme si, dans la mer du temps, elle revenait à ce port où tant de cours étaient amarrés à tant de noms' (l. 56, also l. 59).

Similarly, very few of the stylistic features noted in other passages are in evidence here. Apart from a host of ante-posed adjectives (ll. 14, 31, 39, 67, 81, 118) and the repetition of 'amer' (ll. 8, 37, 63), triplets (only l. 119), series of items (only l. 80, 111 and the clauses discussed above), repetitions (only ll. 43, 79, 102), symmetry (none), alliteration (only 'sinistres souliers' (l. 122)), parallel phrasing (none) are rare. Nothing must be permitted to deflect attention from the horrendous nature of the scene. Subversion of language, subversion of text, subversion of traditional stylistic devices reflect the abuse of power wielded by le Guide.

Chapter 15

Calixthe Beyala

Le Petit Prince de Belleville (Paris: J'ai lu, 1992), pp. 89–94.

Ça pas été facile, le contrôle d'orthographe. C'était pas très dur non plus, sauf que le français a des mots compliqués et que j'écris pas vite. Le temps de terminer RANGER qu'on était déjà à MANGER. Ça me remontait pas l'enthousiasme. Enfin, j'ai fait comme j'ai pu. Pierre Pelletier, lui, il écrit facilement. Quand il a fini, il regarde ma copie, il m'envoie des sourires d'encouragement.

Après l'école, Mademoiselle Garnier m'a appelé, elle s'est penchée vers moi et elle a dit en me tendant la main:

– Félicitations, Mamadou! Tu t'en es bien tiré.

Elle a des mains merveilleuses, longues avec des ongles roses bien dessinés. C'est comme un manège quand on les regarde.

Faut continuer comme ça.

Inch Allah, je dis.

Elle a rigolé. Elle a tourné le dos et elle est partie.

Ça m'a fait un choc.

J'ai glandouillé un peu, histoire de calmer mes émotions. D'habitude je rentre avec Alex, mais il ne m'a pas attendu. Il se passe rien – j'aimerais bien qu'il se passe quelque chose.

Au lieu de rentrer directement, je prends la rue Ramponeau, j'atterris rue de Belleville. Je regarde partout autour de moi. Il y a des restaurants chinois avec des poulets grillés suspendus à la vitrine. Il y a des hors-d'œuvre que je connais pas. Alors, je marche et j'observe tout ça. Un jour, j'aimerais bien aller au restaurant. Mais M'am dit que c'est comme jeter de l'argent par la fenêtre d'un train.

C'est alors qu'il s'est passé quelque chose. J'ai vu Lolita. Elle est avec Johanne. Elles marchent de l'autre côté du trottoir. Je traverse la rue pour être reconnu. Mais elles sont peut-être occupées, alors, elles me voient pas. Je les suis. Elles bavardent. Lolita balance son sac comme ça comme une dame. Ça va, ça vient, ça va, ça vient, ça touche sa robe, et ça fait comme une sorte de vague dans sa robe. De toute façon, elle est sublime.

Lolita entre au n° 65 qui donne à l'intérieur sur une cour. La maison de Lolita est celle avec une baie vitrée et des rideaux blancs au deuxième étage. Je l'ai vue penchée au balcon et c'est comme ça que je l'ai su. Mais Lolita ne m'a pas vu. J'aimerais bien habiter une maison comme celle-ci. J'ai sorti une feuille et j'ai fait un dessin. Je voulais le glisser sous la porte de Lolita. Bof, finalement je m'ai dit: elle saurait même pas que c'est moi.

J'avais mon dessin dans la main et je regardais la fenêtre de Lolita. Pendant que j'attendais, deux flics de surveillance sont venus. J'ai eu la trouille mais j'ai pas bougé, vu que dès qu'on se met à courir, on est coupable sans procès. Alors, j'ai regardé la fenêtre de Lolita, l'air de rien. Le flic a vu mon dessin.

– Qu'est-ce que c'est, un crapaud?

– Non, c'est un chien.

Il me regarde. Il prend mon dessin, il le montre à son compagnon. Ils éclatent de rire.

– T'es dingue ou quoi? il me demande.

– Oui, Monsieur.

– Avec ces nègres, faut s'attendre à tout.

– Rendez-moi mon dessin, Monsieur.

– Ah! qu' c'est drôle, qu'il fait.

Mais je suis pas pour rire. Je saute en l'air et j'arrache mon dessin.

– On se calme, espèce de petit con!

– Fous-lui la paix, dit l'autre flic.

Je lève la tête et je vois Lolita. Elle me voyait et elle criait:

– Oh, la la! Quel brave garçon!

A la maison, les femmes parlent. Elles se lèvent, elles bavardent. Elles lavent par terre, elles bavardent, elles cuisinent, elles bavardent.

– J'en crois pas mes yeux qu'il soye là, fait Soumana.

– J' t' l'avais dit. Faut attendre.

– Mais moi, ça change pas que j'ai envie de partir.

– Pour aller où? Tu connais personne.

– J'me débrouillerai. J' suis pas plus mal que celles qui montrent leur derrière au cinéma.

M'am sourit. Et là, Soumana passe son cure-dent de l'autre côté de la joue et se fâche.

Elle sort, quand elle rentre de nouveau dans la cuisine, elle est comme je l'avais jamais vue. Elle porte un chapeau qui lui va pas parce que c'est pas possible. Elle a mis un pantalon gris prince-de-galles qui lui fait un cul indescriptible, vu que ça prend toute la place. Elle tient son sac peau de crocodile. Elle l'a de l'Afrique et elle le garde pour des raisons sentimentales que j' connais bien. Elle nous regarde avec élégance comme une étrangère, quelqu'un qui n'a jamais servi.

M'am la regarde des pieds à la tête et puis elle dit:

– Tu ferais mieux d'enlever ça avant qu'il arrive.

– Jamais! Abdou m'aime bien en pantalon. A l'époque, j'avais un rouge. Ça l'excitait drôlement. Comme un taureau, si tu vois de quoi j' veux parler.

Là, elle sourit. On dirait qu'on vient de lui annoncer une bonne nouvelle. Ses yeux vont loin, loin. Ça se voit qu'elle a des pensées roses, sans limites. Des pensées comme le ciel. M'am hausse les épaules et les laisse tomber.

– Moi, j' crois que j' peux devenir actrice de cinéma, dit Soumana en mettant une main sur ses hanches et en battant des cils.

– Et pourquoi pas la reine d'Angleterre?

– J'ai pas pensé. Mais c'est vrai que ça va ensemble.

Elle se tait. Elle jette la tête en arrière et elle continue:

– Après tout, c'est comme ça que Grace Kelly a connu le prince Rainier.

– C'est ça, qu'elle dit M'am en pouffant. N'oublie pas de m'envoyer une invitation.

– Et comment que tu vas faire pour devenir actrice? j'demande.

– J'irai à Cannes. Y a les producteurs là-bas. Y en a qui va tomber amoureux, alors . . .

Puis elle a continué à parler comme pour elle-même.

– A Cannes, il y a les mers, les lords anglais qui se promènent sur la plage, il y a les bateaux, les oiseaux, les clowns dans les rues et des ballons qui tombent du ciel, des princesses de Monaco qui s' battent en caleçon sur les plages. J'aurai des belles robes, des manteaux de fourrure, des voitures, des bijoux . . .

– Et une bonne trempe, M'am fait en rigolant. T'as bien entendu ce qu'a dit M'dame Saddock! Qu'il essaye de lever la main sur moi et je vais lui foutre toutes les femmes de la France au cul.

Elle n'a pas fini de dire ça que le père rentre. Il n'est pas seul. Mon oncle Kouam l'accompagne.

Quand ils voient la Soumana habillée comme ça, mon oncle met sa main sur sa bouche pour pas rigoler. Mon papa la regarde comme si elle était un tas de boue. Avec des yeux qui disent: «Qu'est-ce que c'est qu' ce monstre?»

– Va m'enlever ça! dit mon papa.

– I no be talking! qu'elle dit M'am.

La Soumana a baissé la tête. Elle est partie se changer. Mais avant de disparaître, j'ai vu ses yeux. C'était pas regardable. Il y avait là tous les démons d'Afrique.

Ils se sont assis et M'am leur a servi un thé à la menthe. Mon papa a cassé de la cola. Il a donné une lune à mon oncle Kouam.

– J'me demande quoi faire pour que Mathilda m'écoute, qu'il explique à mon papa. Elle n'en fait qu'à sa tête. Elle n'obéit jamais et en plus, elle me répond. Le soir, si elle veut sortir avec les amis, elle se tire. Je lui dis qu'on est mariés, et que bon, après tout, sa place est auprès de moi. Elle répond que ça n'empêche. Si tu veux venir, t'as qu'à venir. Fiche-moi la paix! Elle va se pomponner devant la glace, elle siffle. Je sais plus quoi faire . . .

– T'as qu'à lui foutre une! Il n'y a que ça qui marche avec les bonnes femmes. Tu la bats. Tu la b . . . Ensuite, tu peux mourir en paix.

Mon oncle Kouam regarde ses mains. Il est gêné.

– J'peux pas, il fait d'une petite voix.

– Alors, te plains pas . . .

– J'crois juste qu'il y a un autre moyen.

– Alors, cherche sans moi.

Puis il y a eu un gros silence. Mon papa a craché *floc-flac!*

La Soumana pleure assise sur une chaise dans la cuisine. Tous ses habits sont tombés. Pas pour vrai, bien sûr. Mais c'est une expression pour dire qu'elle n'en peut plus. Qu'elle est vraiment découragée. M'am prépare le dîner, des ignames avec de la poitrine. Elle la regarde pas. Personne pourrait lui réapprendre à vivre, même si on l'aime bien. C'est-à-dire marcher sans penser qu'elle marche, manger sans penser qu'elle mange et rire comme le bébé ému par les cliquetis d'un bracelet. Personne ne pourrait lui rendre sa jeunesse. Je lui prends la main. C'est tout c' que je peux faire pour elle.

Text and context

Written by a Cameroonian-born woman now living in Paris, *Le Petit Prince de Belleville* is a novel which describes the cultural clashes experienced by a family of Malian immigrants in the Parisian *arrondissement* of Belleville. The first-person narration switches between the family's ten-year-old son, Loukoum (Mamadou), and his father, Abdou Traoré, whose italicized musings interrupt the narrative and highlight the problems of integration which Loukoum describes. In this passage, reference is made to a number of the social and economic difficulties faced by immigrants in France: Loukoum finds the spelling test so taxing because he is only now learning to read and write; he has never eaten in a restaurant because the family cannot afford it. On a more sinister note, the suspicion with which immigrants are viewed by a sizeable proportion of the French public informs Loukoum's comment about the police that 'dès qu'on se met à courir, on est coupable sans procès' (l. 38).

As West African Muslims, the Traoré family are doubly marginalized – through religion as well as race. In this passage, the aspect of Islamic tradition which appears to be most incompatible with the culture of the majority ethnic population is that of polygamy. Here, Abdou has just returned home to his two wives, Soumana and M'am, who suspect that he has been with another woman. (We later learn that he has been having a relationship with a prostitute, M'amzelle Esther.) As in Mariama Bâ's *Une si longue lettre* (see Chapter 13), the text presents a pair of women who demonstrate opposing reactions to male infidelity. The first wife, M'am, appears resigned to the situation, remaining rational and calm in contrast to Soumana's outrage. Soumana's position is, however, less secure than M'am's in that she and Abdou are not actually married. This may partly explain the differing reactions. In fact, Soumana is an illegal immigrant, having had to borrow M'am's papers to claim *allocations familiales* for her children. This information is discovered and eventually manipulated by Madame Saddock who, at the end of the novel, reports Abdou to the French authorities, causing him to be arrested and then imprisoned for defrauding the social security system.

In this passage, Madame Saddock is quoted to support Soumana's view that husbands should not beat their wives (l. 93). Here she is referring to her first meeting with the white

French woman who has a significant effect on both co-wives, but on Soumana in particular. Madame Saddock teaches M'am and Soumana about women's rights, encouraging Soumana to leave Abdou. On one level, the character of Madame Saddock points to the apparent incompatibility of western feminist ideals and African women's lives, in this case because the feminist tries to erase cultural difference and also ignores the precarious economic and legal positions of African working-class immigrant women in France. This is not to say that the text endorses husbands beating their wives. Rather, Beyala's novel demonstrates the ways in which the infiltration of western ideologies – such as feminism – into the once closed communities of the immigrant population of France can have a disturbing, and sometimes destructive, effect. In this passage, Soumana suddenly appears foreign to Loukoum: 'Elle nous regarde avec élégance comme une étrangère, quelqu'un qui n'a jamais servi' (l. 68). Dressed differently, Soumana threatens the men's image of her as wife and mother. They therefore quickly dismiss her as ridiculous or grotesque: Loukoum describing her in trousers 'qui lui fait un cul indescriptible' (l. 66); Abdou looking at her as if she is a monster (l. 99); and uncle Kouam trying hard to stop himself from laughing (l. 97).

Soumana, of course, cannot leave her husband since, as an illegal immigrant woman, she literally has nowhere to go. While she dreams of becoming an actress, her only possible option would be to work illegally in the sex industry, as she unwittingly remarks: 'J' suis pas plus mal que celles qui montrent leur derrière au cinéma' (l. 60). Soumana's frustration at the lack of alternatives is epitomized by the final image of her weeping in the kitchen, traditionally the quintessentially feminine domestic space. Madame Saddock's feminist influence thus becomes a source of tension in the family as it rubs up against the traditional African view (voiced by Loukoum and Abdou) of how a wife should behave. Significantly, Abdou and Kouam respond to Soumana's behaviour by taking refuge in their traditional gender role – sharing a kola nut together while M'am brings them mint tea (l. 104) – thereby denying Soumana's dilemma and refusing to confront change. A similar tension emerges in this passage between uncle Kouam and his white French wife, Mathilda. Kouam's description of his wife echoes Madame Saddock's advice to Soumana and M'am: 'Elle n'en fait qu'à sa tête' (l. 107). Like Soumana, Kouam appears to be bewildered and frustrated by the seeming incommensurability of the two cultural spaces he inhabits (African on the one hand, French on the other), and emphasizes the problematic nature of integration for African immigrants in France. Whereas Abdou's response is that Kouam should regain control of his wife through violence, Kouam believes that there must be an alternative solution: 'J'crois juste qu'il y a un autre moyen' (l. 117).

Beneath this mention of another way, 'un autre moyen', lies the suggestion that a polarized world of 'them' and 'us', or France versus Africa, is not the most useful model for post-colonial identities. Indeed, there are two alternative models of post-colonial identity presented in this passage: the first in the figure of Loukoum, the child narrator; the second in the references to another space beyond the binary of France and Africa, here represented by Soumana's fantasies about becoming a film star. Drawing on images from magazines and television, Soumana does not dismiss M'am's sarcastic suggestion that she could become the Queen of England: 'Après tout,' she remarks, 'c'est comme ça que Grace Kelly a connu le prince Rainier' (l. 82). By making comparisons with cultural icons from Britain, Monaco and North America, the text points to the way in which post-colonial identities are formed by a complex mix of cultural influences, not just from the countries of birth and migration, but also from the international space which forms the francophone diaspora. Later in the novel,

Loukoum's biological mother Aminata refers to 'tous nos grands hommes, Mitterrand, De Gaulle, Senghor, Delon, Frank Sinatra, Martin Luther King' (p. 210).

Loukoum also identifies with cultural icons beyond France and Mali. Abdou laments that his son no longer wears a djellaba because he wants to wear the same suits as Sylvester Stallone (p. 198). As the child of a Malian Muslim family, growing up in France in the late 1980s–1990s, Loukoum is constantly subjected to a wealth of cultural influences from all over the globe. Although his mother tongue is Bambara, he has learnt Arabic in order to read the Koran and is now learning French at school. This multilingualism is reflected in the ironic opening scene to this passage when Loukoum, having been congratulated by his teacher for his performance in a French spelling test, replies with the Arabic formula, 'Inch Allah' (l. 12). Indeed, Loukoum's narrative voice is not the standard French he is taught in school; rather it is the vernacular French spoken by the immigrant population of Belleville. In creating a narrator who speaks in a French which is incorrect, slangy and often obscene, Beyala's text challenges the French colonial notions of *la mission civilisatrice* and *l'assimilation*, both of which are now incorporated under the label of *l'intégration*. The French language has always been seen as the route by which assimilation would be achieved. Loukoum's language subverts the French of the Académie Française and reworks it to his own ends.

Like Oyono's Toundi in *Une vie de boy* (see Chapter 10), Loukoum is a seemingly naïve narrator whose voice is never innocent. Through his often matter-of-fact observations, Loukoum exposes inequalities both in and outside his home. Although presented without comment, incidents such as the explicit racism of the police ('Avec ces nègres, faut s'attendre à tout' (l. 46)) along with the covert discrimination of his classmate, Lolita, who pretends not to see him when she is walking down the street (l. 26), invite the reader to consider the situation of African immigrants in France from their point of view. In other words, *Le Petit Prince de Belleville*, while decrying assimilation, encourages readers to overcome cultural barriers, to recognize cultural difference, and to think about identity in a more fluid, less polarized way.

Further reading

Beyala, Calixthe, *C'est le soleil qui m'a brûlée* (Paris: Stock, 1987).

—— *Maman a un amant* (Paris: J'ai lu, 1993).

—— *Lettre d'une Africaine à ses sœurs occidentales* (Paris: Spengler, 1995).

Baumgardt, Ursula, 'Les voix de l'amour: les romans de Calixthe Beyala', in Daniel Delas and Danielle Deltel (eds), *Voix nouvelles du roman africain* (Paris: RITM, 1994), pp. 31–47.

D'Almeida, Irène Assiba, *Francophone African Women Writers: Destroying the Emptiness of Silence* (Gainesville: University of Florida Press, 1994).

Gallimore, Rangira Béatrice, *L'Œuvre romanesque de Calixthe Beyala: le renouveau de l'écriture féminine en Afrique francophone sub-saharienne* (Paris: L'Harmattan, 1997).

Hitchcott, Nicki, 'Calixthe Beyala and the post-colonial woman', in Alec G. Hargreaves and Mark McKinney (eds), *Post-Colonial Cultures in France* (London: Routledge, 1997), pp. 211–25.

King, Adèle, 'Calixthe Beyala et le roman féministe africain', in Régis Antoine (ed.), *Carrefour de cultures: mélanges offerts à Jacqueline Leiner* (Tübingen: Gunter Narr Verlag, 1993), pp. 101–7.

Volet, Jean-Marie, 'Calixthe Beyala or the literary success of a Cameroonian woman living in Paris', *World Literature Today* 67, 2 (1993), 309–14.

Language and style

It should be remembered from the outset that, as with the majority of novels by black African writers using first-person narratives, French is not the mother tongue of the majority of the protagonists in this novel. Consequently the author, by making her narrator use it, has created an artificial linguistic scenario. Loukoum, the narrator, son of an immigrant family from Mali, has Bambara as his mother tongue and his knowledge of French is limited, although less so than that of his parents. He is trying to learn it and finding it difficult (l. 2). However, Beyala makes him recount his story in a particular variety of French, the urban vernacular of Paris, to which he would be exposed outside the school room and which is normally associated with the underprivileged and marginalized social groups of the capital, both native and immigrant, with whom he would normally identify.

As an example of a child narrative, *Le Petit Prince de Belleville* has connections, both thematically and stylistically, with a number of other child narratives in French. It shows the influence of Saint-Exupéry's *Le Petit Prince* not only in its title but more importantly from a thematic point of view, first by a reference to the book itself (p. 7) and subsequently in the way Loukoum tries to understand and comment on the complexities of the adult world around him. It also shows the influence of Sempé and Goscinny's *Le Petit Nicolas*, again through its title, but this time more importantly stylistically, as the ten-year-old narrator uses the French which he hears around him to relate his story. In contrast to the practice in *Le Petit Nicolas*, Loukoum applies the same quality of French without fear or favour throughout the text, whether he is reporting his own pronouncements, the speech of his parents, the police, his school teacher or the narrative itself. No stylistic distinctions, or only the slightest ones, seem to be made.

An examination of the narrative style reveals significant characteristics at the phonetic, lexical and especially syntactic levels. Phonetic markers are, inevitably, the least numerous and centre on the treatment of final mute – *e* in such words as 'ce', 'que' and above all the personal pronouns ('j'' for 'je' accounts for eleven of the eighteen occurrences). The spelling 'soye' for the present subjunctive of *être* is a way of underlining the linguistic insecurity of the narrator (l. 56).

As far as the lexis is concerned, a number of low-register items are scattered throughout the passage – 'cul' (ll. 66, 94), 'dingue' (l. 44), 'espèce de petit con' (l. 50), 'fiche-moi le paix' (l. 110), 'flic' (ll. 37 etc.), 'foutre' (ll. 51, 93, 112), 'glandouillé' (= loafed about, l. 15), 'se pomponner' (= to doll oneself up, l. 110), 'pouffant' (= tittering, l. 83), 'quoi' (ll. 106, 111), 'rigoler' (l. 98), 'trempe' (= thrashing, l. 92), 'trouille' (= fear, l. 27); 'b. . '. (l. 113) presumably represents 'baiser'; the exclamative 'Bof' occurs in the narrative itself (l. 34); 'ça' is used consistently for *cela* (twenty-four times). Elliptical expressions occur – 'l'air de rien' (l. 39), 'histoire de . . '. (l. 15), 'pas possible' (l. 65) – and some contorted English from M'am to disclaim any responsibility for Soumana's behaviour ('I no be talking', l.101), a further dislocation of the linguistic repertoire.

However, it is with the syntax that the distinctive nature of this variety of French is most in evidence. Among the most striking features is the deletion of negative 'ne' on twenty-six out of thirty-six occasions. The insertion of 'ne' seems to take place in circumstances which are particularly heightened emotionally, e.g. after 'mais' (ll. 16, 32), expressing disappointment for Loukoum, an emphatic imperative (l. 83), expressing uncle Kouam's distress (ll. 107–9) (although deletion also occurs (ll. 111–15)), expressing frustration for Soumana (ll. 121, 126). Deletion of impersonal 'il' occurs on five out of eleven occasions, twice involving 'il y a' and three times 'falloir' – once in the teacher's mouth (l. 10) and once by the police (l. 46) – again underlining the fact that the narrator draws little if any distinction between the characters. Four occurrences of 'il' occur in repetitions (ll. 19, 88), but in identical circumstances 'il'-deletion is also used (l. 85). This demonstrates that 'ne'- and 'il'-deletions are variables rather than constants in this variety of French.

Sentence structure is also affected – the use of 'avoir' as auxiliary with a reflexive verb (l. 34), the use of 'que' as an all-purpose conjunction (ll. 58, 95), non-inversion of pronoun and verb in clauses following a passage of speech, e.g. 'Inch Allah, je dis' (l. 12, also ll. 44, 84, 115), but normally not with nouns, e.g. '. . . dit l'autre flic' (l. 51, also ll. 56, 77), an exception occurring later – 'Et une bonne trempe, M'am fait en rigolant' (l. 92); on two other occasions 'que' is used to introduce the clause, e.g. 'C'est ça, qu'elle dit M'am en pouffant' (l. 83, also l. 101). Another low-register syntactic feature is highlighting of the subject: by anticipation, e.g. 'Mais moi, ça change pas que j'ai envie de partir' (l. 58); by post-position, e.g. 'Ça pas été facile, le contrôle d'orthographe' (l. 1); by repetition, e.g. 'Pierre Pelletier, lui, il écrit facilement' (l. 4). Minor sentences occur from time to time, e.g. 'Le temps de terminer RANGER qu'on était déjà à MANGER' (l. 2, also ll. 75, 99, 122, 124). The form of interrogatives also enhances the low-register tone of the passage: closed question – 'T'es dingue ou quoi?' (l. 44); open question – 'Pour aller où?' (l. 59), 'Et comment que tu vas faire . . .?' (l. 84, also ll. 79, 99).

In addition to features illustrating the low-register nature of this Parisian vernacular, other features point to the fact that the narrator's voice is that of a ten-year-old boy. This is at its most obvious in the sentence structure of the passage. Concentrating upon the fifty-four sentences of the passage (excluding speech) until Lolita shouts encouragement (l. 53) reveals the following tally: one minor sentence (see above), thirty-one simple, fifteen compound, five complex and two compound-complex. Clearly subordinate clauses are rare (nine in total): four temporal (ll. 4, 10, 36, 38), two relative (ll. 20, 30), two restrictive (l. 1), one causal (l. 38). What is most significant is the structure of the major sentences: the first element is a subject in forty-two cases (79 per cent), an adverbial expression in nine and a subordinate clause of time in two. If the analysis of the first elements is extended to the second and subsequent main clauses making up the compound sentences, it appears that every one is preceded by a pronoun, which often repeats the subject of the first clause, e.g. 'Mais elles sont peut-être occupées, alors, elles me voient pas' (l. 26), 'Je saute en l'air et j'arrache mon dessin' (l. 49). The effect of this regularity of structure is to convey the simplicity of Loukoum's narrative (specified subject immediately precedes verb), his sense of the dramatic (especially when he spots the girls and in his encounter with the police), the rapid pace at which the story is conducted (this is particularly apparent in ll. 24–9).

Imagery plays an important role in Loukoum's evaluation of character. Of the twelve instances in the passage, all have their brevity in common – the longest is '[Soumana] comme le bébé ému par les cliquetis d'un bracelet' (l. 125), and all but two are introduced by 'comme'. The imagery is mainly centred on the female protagonists – the teacher with her nails 'comme un manège' (l. 10), Lolita twice (ll. 27, 28), Soumana seven times (e.g. 'Mon papa la regarde comme si elle était un tas de boue' l. 98; also ll. 69, 74, 76, 103, 125). Abdou, Loukoum's father, is the focus of another, expressed by Soumana ('Ça [Soumana in red trousers] l'excitait drôlement. Comme un taureau' (l. 72). The remaining simile concerns wasting money (l. 22).

The unreal linguistic situation created by the author and the displacement to French from an African language allow an insight into the pressures, confusions and clashes facing immigrants in France.

Chapter 16

Axel Gauvin

L'Aimé (Paris: Seuil, 1990), pp. 69–75.

Grand-mère rit. Non par mauvaise plaisanterie où le poisson rouge – celui de la profondeur des mers, mets de vice-roi des Indes (s'il a son content d'épices et surtout de gingembre, dont moitié roussie à la tomate et moitié crue en finition s'opposent et s'allient, bref se renforcent) – tiendrait le rôle principal. Elle rit, non par cette succulence-là, qu'elle ne pourrait acheter même en guise de médicament, même avec ses feuilles bleues,[1] mais par un autre poisson rouge, minuscule celui-là. Oh! il faisait à peine une phalangette de long, ce monstre que Grand-gaby avait pêché dans le bassin de la cour, emmené à l'hôpital dans un pot à confiture – question d'aider Ptit-mé à tuer le temps, en attendant sa libération, la «quille», comme le grand disait.

Ce Grand-gaby, qui, du côté de Da Nang, avait joué – jeu inventé par le sergent-chef – au bilboquet-baïonnette à boule de petit Viet hurlant, accompagnait souvent Grand-mère à l'hôpital. Comme ça, sans raison apparente, du moins avouée. Car il tenait, en fait, à offrir lui-même à Ptit-mé quelque papillon vif aux ailes métallisées, quelque petit chien de terre dans son gazon, quelque bébête-Saint-Paul (Chrysalide-boussole se contorsionnant au bout des doigts, et trouvant à coup sûr, but du jeu, une ville à nom de saint). Et il était tout attendri – bouche bée, presque filet de bave – de la joie de Ptit-mé quand, de sa veste dure, il sortait, se cachant des blouses blanches, le bocal à merveilles vivantes.

Cette bête, cette herbe sèche, cette terre, Ptit-mé les voulait tout contre son oreiller, aussi près que pouvaient lui permettre ses jeunes yeux. Il restait ainsi, des heures durant, à observer de la taupe-grillon le remue-ménage dans sa motte brune et grasse, du criquet les élans cassés par le mur de sa prison transparente. Ou la lente métamorphose du Saint-Paul en sphinx effrayant – du moins pour la surveillante en chef.

La nuit, alors que Grand-mère avait dû «remonter» à la maison, les petits crissements des pattes contre le verre, les frottements des ailes l'une contre

1 De l'assistance médicale.

l'autre, la simple respiration de la poignée de terre étaient le meilleur barrage entre Ptit-mé et l'angoisse.

La surveillante en chef, que ces bêtes, cette terre, mettaient dans tous ses états, aurait bien voulu tout envoyer voltiger dehors sur la pelouse, si elle n'avait reçu d'ordres précis du directeur:

– Réglez les problèmes comme vous voulez. Mais pas de scandale, je vous prie! Pas de scandale!

– Pas de scandale! l'autre marmonnait. Pas de scandale. Mais il a été fait, le scandale! C'est sa chouchoute[2] à lui qui a fait le scandale! C'est elle qui est le vrai scandale! et il faut que les autres paient les pots cassés!

Elle laissait donc le bocal, mais, «pour qu'un minimum d'aspesie soit respecté», elle en frottait l'extérieur à l'alcool – plutôt dix fois qu'une – avant de le rendre à Ptit-mé.

Grand-mère, régulièrement, avant qu'ils meurent – pour éviter ce chagrin à Ptit-mé – remportait les bêtes. Elle les ramenait à la maison, car il lui semblait nécessaire de les libérer sur la terre même où elles avaient grandi, et non – comme le suggérait la surveillante en chef – dans la cour de l'hôpital, qu'en plus Grand-père disait «chargée de miasmes et de germes pathogènes».

Dès que Grand-gaby voyait le bocal vide, il se précipitait: vite une chevrette de terre,[3] une chipèk à antennes courtes,[4] un guerlet – ce guerlet que «Matante Margrite» ramena le jour même:

– Non, Gaby, non! Ça se met à jouer du violon, la nuit, ces bestioles-là! Celle-là va réveiller l'hôpital.

Toute sa ménagerie, Gaby la fourrait donc dans son bocal, le bocal dans la poche de sa veste, et il emboîtait le pas de Grand-mère jusqu'au lit de Ptit-mé.

Parmi tous ces petits compagnons de quelques jours: un minuscule poisson rouge, un monbrun à reflets dorés que Grand-gaby avait délogé du grand bassin à l'aide d'un vieux panier de bambou. Est-ce mythe du rouge des fonds marins – manger de grand seigneur? – mais à la vue du petit poisson Ptit-mé, cet alors boucard de Ptit-mé («anorexique», disait Grand-père) qui vous déclare vouloir le manger, et frit à l'huile, et avec du pain s'il vous plaît!

Ton petit qui se remet enfin à la nourriture des vivants, celle qui se prend par la bouche, par l'entrée du Bon Dieu au bas du visage, et non par des trous percés dans les tuyaux à sang! Ta joie! Le paradis sur terre existe, Margrite, voilà qu'il ouvre pour toi toutes grandes ses portes!

2 En créole, sexe de la femme.
3 Crevette de terre: puce d'eau.
4 Criquet.

Ça, tu n'as eu aucune pitié pour le requin-chagrin. Ptit-mé le voulait frit? Il termina sa carrière dans l'huile bouillante . . . Avant de se dessécher et raidir dans cette petite assiette à dessert que tu avais spécialement achetée pour. Car, évidemment, il n'avait pas pu le manger, son quart de bouchée de poisson rouge.

Par contre, il avait demandé que Grand-mère mette l'assiette tout près de son oreiller, à limite de netteté de ses yeux, comme elle le faisait pour ses courtilières et chrysalides. Et il s'était mis à le regarder, son monbrun, à le regarder, à lui parler par simples mouvements de lèvres, à froncer les sourcils comme pour mieux en saisir les réponses . . .

L'enfilement, gonflement, de ton cœur devant cette conversation muette entre le petit cadavre de poisson – si rouge, éclatant et doré, il y a peu – et celui de ton Ptit-mé! Car c'était bien d'égal à égal! D'inerte à inerte. De rigide à rigide. De sec à sec. Peau sur l'arête ou sur l'os: la mort devant son miroir.

Voilà ce que tu pensais, Margrite, jusqu'au moment où Ptit-mé avait fermé les yeux. Son visage était devenu d'un triste! comme s'il pleurait en dedans. C'est toi, en flots de pleurs, que le Dr S. avait trouvée dans le couloir. Il t'avait alors emmenée dans son bureau, avait fermé la porte, t'avait longtemps parlé, expliqué. Que, pour ce genre de maladie, les choses étaient lentes à se remettre. Que tout, tout était retrouvé: l'appétit, la course, les jeux, les rires, la gentillesse, l'insolence, le vice et la bonté. Ses paroles avaient fait naître en toi l'espoir, sans tuer son contraire. Car, si tu croyais en cet homme bien plus qu'en toi-même, t'aurait-il dit tout cela s'il t'avait trouvée riant aux larmes au sortir de la chambre du Ptit-mé?

Il avait, du moins, réussi à transformer le désespoir en doute. La cruauté du désespoir en le sadisme du doute . . .

C'est donc à ça que tu voulais venir, aujourd'hui, Grite Bellon! A ces pleurs, cette chialerie! Tu voulais en déverser à nouveau, et sur ton propre sort! T'es bien pareille aux autres: pleurnicharde et gniengien. Dé-ses-pé-rée au moindre petit bobo à ton cœur! Tu me fais pitié, tiens!

Mais pourquoi ne racontes-tu pas, plutôt, la tête de la vieille richarde qui, pour la préparation de ce repas gouverneur, t'avait prêté sa cuisine – et t'aurait même prêté sa bonne si tu avais voulu («Marie fera cela très bien pour vous»).

Tu te moques, Margrite, alors qu'elle a été si gentille! Mais ses billes d'yeux ont failli tomber de leur orbite, quand elle t'a vu sortir ton empereur[5] de ton sac à main! Ça, oui, ça mérite d'être conté. Mais toutes ces pleurnicheries, lamenteries ne peux-tu, définitivement, les mettre sous la grosse pierre?

Raconte et ris, même si tes larmes te voilent un peu les yeux! Raconte: toi, dans ta robe grise; toi, courbée – oui, courbée! qu'est-ce que tu crois: que soixante-treize années, en lui pesant sur la tête, ne font pas plier le bambou? Toi, le cœur battant,

5 Espadon.

le souffle court, trottant – battre le fer tant qu'il est chaud, préparer au plus vite (avant qu'Aimé ne change d'avis) ce premier repas d'après résurrection! Toi, galopant sur les trottoirs de cette immense rue de Paris.

Et tu ne t'arrêtes que devant les plus belles maisons, les plus riches: les blanches à colonnades; celles à jet d'eau; à varangues à dendrobium de pluie d'or; à immenses parterres de rosiers; à grand-mères n'ayant rien d'autre à faire qu'à tailler les rosiers.

Car pas question pour toi d'aller préparer le festin de monsieur Ptit-mé à la maison: les deux heures de remontée qu'il faudrait, celles de redescente, et retour à de l'hôpital: porte de bois dur – visites de 14 à 18 heures. Mais la vieille «Pour Cythère . . .» de Gaétan, car il a une voiture, Gaétan Bénard, qu'il a baptisée de ce drôle de nom. Elle mange la poussière du garage depuis bientôt dix ans, la «Pour Cythère . . .» La rouille a dû lui gangrener les tripes! Ote donc «Pour Cythère . . .» de ta pensée.

Hors de question aussi d'aller aux cuisines de l'hôpital. Pas à cause des miasmes et germes pathogènes (dont les seuls noms font blêmir Bénard). Mais de cuisine, ici, point: tu le sais pour avoir vu – toi qui arrives toujours bien trop trop tôt et qui attends l'heure de visite à l'ombre du pongame de l'entrée – le repas débarquer dans de grandes cuves carrées d'inoxydable qu'une camionnette apporte vers les onze heures et demie.

Alors, toi qui détestes fourrer ta cuiller sale dans le cari des autres, tu iras frapper aux cuisines des gens. Des riches. Pas pour des raisons de propreté – quoiqu'il soit tellement plus facile d'être propre par la serpillière et le torchon d'Ernestine! Pas pour des raisons directement prophylactiques, comme apprécierait Tino (le Tino du quartier: à peau noire, cheveux de grains de poivre, maigre, inconnu, et ne chantant même pas, qui descend en ville pour faire provision de mégots à bout filtre, celui des Craven: «Le riche ça peut pas te colloquer ses microbes: c'est jamais malade!»). Uniquement parce que la grand-mère aux rosiers devrait te comprendre, ne pas te faire perdre ton temps en d'interminables explications – avoir aussi de l'huile sous la main! et une poêle!

La première, que tu appelles à travers sa grille – qui donc t'a foutu une vieille de cet acabit! décidément tu n'es pas faite pour fréquenter vieillardise et sénilité –, la première est sourde comme un pot: tu peux t'égosiller comme tu veux, elle n'entend que la voix du dedans de sa tête, qui, en ce moment, lui demande à quelle hauteur elle va bien pouvoir couper ce vieux rameau tout sec qu'elle tient de sa main gantée.

La deuxième aussi a des gants. Elle est si cassée en deux, que le poids des années n'explique pas tout. C'est ce bricbrac d'or et de diamant qui l'attire vers le sol. Mais au moins, elle t'entend, te comprend, te répond – en créole, ce qui facilite. Elle aussi a des enfants, des petits-enfants, et qui ont leurs maladies: l'allergie de François, le rhume incoercible de Vincent. «Elle comprend très bien.» (Et assez vite, tout compte fait.) Elle ouvre toute grande sa cuisine, ses placards cirés, elle te propose un coup de main (celui de sa bonne), te fait tendre le poêlon.

Mais la tête, la tête de ce quatrième âge – d'au moins soixante-cinq ans! – quand tu as sorti de ton sac à main ton mouchoir, et de ton mouchoir cette civelle aplatie, ce quart de sardinelle, le tout petit kaniki monbrun de poisson rouge.

Et toi pour excuser le petit de ton petit:

– Ce n'est pas un caprice, vous savez. Cela fait un mois et demi qu'il est sous sérum et qu'il n'a rien mangé.

Text and context

Like the Caribbean islands of Martinique and Guadeloupe, Réunion in the Indian Ocean is a French *département d'outre-mer*. In fact, it is the most densely populated of the four DOM. However, unlike the islanders of Martinique and Guadeloupe, the peoples of Réunion do not have an established history of constructing their identity through oppositional ideologies such as Negritude and *Créolité*.[6] This lack of an identifiable cultural resistance movement, combined with high unemployment and illiteracy, has not surprisingly led to widespread disaffection among the creolophone Réunionese. There is, however, a minority group of individuals – mainly intellectuals – of whom Axel Gauvin is one, who, following in the footsteps of Jean Bernabé, Patrick Chamoiseau and Raphaël Confiant in the Caribbean, are committed to the promotion and the preservation of Creole language and culture.

In 1977, Gauvin published an essay, *Du créole opprimé au créole libéré: défense de la langue réunionnaise*, in which he stresses the importance of bilingualism in Réunion. His commitment to this bilingualism continues in his fictional writings which combine classical French with (often untranslated) Creole words. Moreover, the bilingualism of Gauvin's fiction extends beyond the lexical level, infusing both content and form: Creole proverbs and dictums are translated into French (for example, 'toi qui détestes fourrer ta cuiller sale dans le cari des autres' (l. 121)), and Creole patterns of oral story-telling are recreated in the written texts. This passage contains a large number of Réunionese Creole words, some of which are translated for the reader in footnotes, others of which are not, such as 'boucard' (l. 56) (a child who won't eat) and 'kaniki' (l. 146) (a small piece). Gauvin's decision to leave many words untranslated is not an attempt to titillate the non-Réunionese reader with 'local colour'; rather, it is an attempt to preserve the specificity of life on the island of Réunion. The fact that direct equivalents of these words often do not exist in French suggests that metropolitan French is an inadequate means of expressing Réunionese reality.

At times, Gauvin's novel reads as an itinerary of such details as the flora and fauna of the island.[7] In this extract, this is demonstrated by the large number of insects Grand-gaby brings to entertain Ptit-mé (Aimé) in his hospital bed. Whereas to the European reader, a 'bébête-Saint-Paul' (l. 15) may seem strangely exotic, to the Réunionese audience such creatures are part of everyday life. Indeed, the natural world has a profound influence on

6 See Chapters 9 and 17 for further discussion of Créolité and Negritude.

7 Gauvin is *professeur agrégé de sciences naturelles*.

the peoples of Réunion who are constantly at the mercy of its elements. For this reason, the novel opens with Margrite battling to protect her home against the cyclone. Moreover, the weather, flora and fauna often emulate the human characters in the text. In the previous chapter of *L'Aimé*, when he returns home from hospital, Ptit-mé describes himself as 'la grosse chenille . . . larve parmi les larves' (p. 64) since, suffering from ankylosis, he is unable to move his arms and legs. In the passage, which flashes back to Ptit-mé's stay in hospital, the reader is encouraged to make connections between the insects in the jam jar and the life of Ptit-mé. Like them, he is protected from the outside world by his grandparents and, in particular, his grandmother. Eventually he is described as metamorphosing into a butterfly (p. 94).

The influence of Creole continues on the formal level when, in this passage, the relationship between narrator and characters shifts from the seemingly impartial third-person narration to a kind of informal dialogue where the narrator addresses Margrite (Grand-mère) directly, chastising her emotional response, and suggesting that she recount a different episode in the story that the narrator has begun to tell for her: 'Tu me fais pitié, tiens! Mais pourquoi ne racontes-tu pas plutôt la tête de la vieille richarde. . .' (l. 90). Just as the traditional Creole story-teller would tell the same story many times in many different ways, so the narration offers alternatives to the characters it describes. This technique recurs throughout the novel, reminding the reader that there is no single version of any story, a point particularly resonant for the colonized peoples of the world. In the *départements d'outre-mer* there is only one official 'story', that of the French language and culture. Here, then, the text reveals its (and Gauvin's) political agenda: to retrieve the voices of the Creole peoples from beneath the hegemony of France.

Shifting points of view are accompanied by shifts in narrative time. The events described in this passage precede those described in the previous chapter. In fact, the entire novel is composed of a complex series of analepses and prolepses seamlessly woven together by Gauvin. Immediately before this extract, Margrite is thinking about how she will aid Ptit-mé's recovery by feeding him. She is pleased with the amount he has been eating so far and contemplates the possibility that he might even eat some red fish curry, a staple dish in Réunionese cuisine. This thought of red fish curry prompts her to remember the little red river fish that Ptit-mé claimed he wanted to eat and so inspires the remembrance of this entire episode. Throughout the text, narrative time is controlled by the characters' memories which themselves are often triggered by images or objects.

Margrite's initial reaction to this memory is to laugh. In *L'Aimé*, as in Oyono's *Une vie de boy* (see Chapter 10 above), the main protagonist is characterized by laughter in the face of adversity. Margrite's life is hard: her first husband died, followed by her son, Ptit-mé's father, from whom she was virtually estranged. Her current husband, Gaétan, is a hypochondriac (hence his horror at the thought of the germs and fumes in a hospital kitchen). The daughter of a plantation overseer, Margrite is now relatively poor, relying on *l'assistance médicale* rather than the usual French private medical insurance. Axel Gauvin is, like Margrite's husband, Gaétan, a former communist and deeply concerned with class division and social injustice in Réunion, particularly as, with unemployment affecting around 40 per cent of the population and the rate of inflation being the highest in France, the gap between rich and poor is quite considerable. At the end of this passage, the description of the rue de Paris houses in the Réunionese capital, Saint-Denis, illustrates this gap, particularly as the grandmother who allows Margrite use of her kitchen (and her maid) is bent over because of 'ce bricbac d'or et de diamant qui l'attire vers le sol' (l. 138). On the other hand, Margrite's seventy-three-year-old body is bent from cutting sugar cane. The class distinction is also apparent in the very French-sounding names of the rich woman's grandchildren – Vincent and François – compared to the Creole nickname, 'Ptit-mé', Margrite chose for her own beloved grandson. However, the two women can communicate about their love of their grandchildren. The fact that they do so in Creole further emphasizes Gauvin's commitment to promoting the use of Creole as a living language which bridges the economic and ethnic gaps between the different peoples of the island.

There is no direct reference in this passage to Réunion's relationship with France. However, Grand-gaby's obsession with his role as a French soldier in the Indochinese war reminds the reader of Réunion's departmental status. Indeed, the war itself is presented in brutal terms when Grand-gaby recalls playing a game of cup-and-ball with a bayonet 'cup' and a screaming Vietnamese 'ball' (l. 12). Later in the novel, when Gaétan wants to give Grand-gaby a nickname derived from the horrors of the war, Margrite and the text explicitly condemn France: 'Grand-mère, d'un regard sans appel, avait tué le sobriquet dans l'œuf: Gaby était-il donc responsable "des politiques" de la France?' (p. 84).

Gaétan's love of nicknames extends, as we see in this passage, to his car, 'Pour Cythère' ('For Aphrodite'). His decision to name his car after the goddess of love initially strikes the reader as strange since Gaétan's relationship with Margrite is largely a loveless marriage. However, later in the novel it is revealed that, before lying rusting in the garage, the car had been used to seduce young women, and, as Ptit-mé begins to recover, his rusty joints gradually loosening, the rusty car also returns to the road. Gaétan eventually dies in it, his heart unable to cope with his renewed libido as he mentally recreates the sexual relationships of his youth. Before his death, however, he is transformed, the car symbolizing his repressed masculinity and allowing him to retrieve his dormant libido.

For Margrite, on the other hand, desire is sublimated by her love for her grandson, Ptit-mé, so much so that they are described almost as lovers at several points in the text (e.g. pp. 196, 246). This is an uncomplicated story, the one truly remarkable event being the arrival of Ptit-mé in the middle of the cyclone; other events, like the story of the red fish, are remarkable to the individual characters but remain little more than anecdotal for the reader. Gauvin's decision to write a novel which simply traces the love of a grandmother for her grandchild emphasizes the importance of ordinary individuals in the history of a people and demonstrates his concern with human stories which convey the cultural particularities of life in Réunion. In this way, *L'Aimé* makes important connections with Caribbean writers like Maryse Condé and Patrick Chamoiseau (see Chapters 22 and 23) who subscribe to the view that Creole history is woven from the multiple, ordinary histories/stories (*histoires*) that official History chooses to ignore.

Further reading

Gauvin, Axel, *Du créole opprimé au créole libéré: défense de la langue réunionnaise* (Paris: L'Harmattan, 1977).
—— *Quartier Trois-Lettres* (Paris: L'Harmattan, 1980).
—— *Faims d'enfance* (Paris: Seuil, 1987).

Magnier, Bernard, 'La langue métisse d'Axel Gauvin', *Notre librairie* 104 (1991), 99–108.
Zalessky, Michele, 'Ce pied de fruit à pain, c'était mon pommier', *Carnets de l'exotisme* 7–8 (1991), 91–3.

Language and style

An interesting parallel may be drawn between the two red fish mentioned in the opening paragraph and Ptit-mé's physical condition. In no way does he resemble the deep-sea fish, the food of viceroys (l. 2); he is much more like the pathetic specimen that Grand-gaby fished from the pond in the yard (l. 8). The comparison is made even more explicit and poignant later on after the fish has been cooked: 'cette conversation muette entre le petit cadavre de poisson – si rouge, éclatant et doré, il y a peu – et celui de ton Ptit-mé! Car c'était bien d'égal à égal! . . . Peau sur l'arête ou sur l'os: la mort devant son miroir' (l. 72).

The relationship between the narrator and the main character changes as the passage progresses. Initially, Margrite, the grandmother, is referred to in the third person (ll. 1–55), then, after a brief appeal to 'vous' (ll. 56–8), she is referred to in the second person (l. 59), and this mode continues until the end, accompanied by a change in tone. Clearly borrowing from the oral tradition of story-telling of Réunion, the narrator becomes much more involved in the unravelling of the action, engaging personally and intimately with Margrite. Certain characteristics associated with an oral presentation are evident in both parts of the passage. Others figure more prominently in the later part. The major characteristic is the elliptical quality of many of the sentences, displaying a certain spoken spontaneity although produced by the narrator – for example in the use of such expressions as 'question d[e]' (l. 9), 'vite une chevrette de terre' (l. 46), 'et avec du pain s'il vous plaît!' (l. 58), 'Ça, tu n'as eu aucune pitié pour le requin-chagrin' (l. 63), but especially in the large number of minor sentences, some long (e.g. ll. 1, 24, 64, 80), others relatively brief (e.g. ll. 14, 74, 85, 89). Some paragraphs (e.g. ll. 72–5, 98–103) consist almost entirely of minor sentences. Other devices which mark the oral nature of the passage include extensive use of parentheses – used to express associations of ideas, through the use of dashes (e.g. ll. 11, 55, 73, 130) and brackets (e.g. ll. 16, 57, 93, 116, 125); in the following example both means of presentation are used:

> Non par mauvaise plaisanterie où le poisson rouge – celui de la profondeur des mers, mets de vice-roi des Indes (s'il a son content d'épices et surtout de gingembre, dont moitié roussie à la tomate et moitié crue en finition s'opposent et s'allient, bref se renforcent) – tiendrait le rôle principal.
>
> (l. 1)

Direct quotations from other characters, sometimes presented within brackets, are also used, this time to give direct authenticity to the account: Grand-gaby – 'la «quille», comme le grand disait' (l. 9, also l. 47); 'la surveillante en chef' – '«pour qu'un minimum d'aspesie soit respecté», elle en frottait l'extérieur à l'alcool' (l. 38); Grandfather – 'la cour de l'hôpital, qu'en plus Grand-père disait «chargée de miasmes et de germes pathogènes»' (l. 44, also l. 37); 'la vieille richarde' – '[elle] t'aurait même prêté sa bonne si tu avais voulu («Marie fera cela très bien pour vous»)' (l. 92, also l. 141). On other occasions more extensive quotations are recorded (e.g. ll. 33, 47, 148). Exclamations are used in both parts, but especially in the second – six in the first part (e.g. ll. 7, 35, 36, 37, 38), four of which occur in the commentary on the exchange of views between the director and the 'surveillante en chef' of the hospital, but nineteen in the second part. A similar situation applies to questions, only one in the first part (l. 55), four in the second (ll. 63, 83, 96, 99). Another device typical of oral delivery is *reprise*, where a part of speech is either anticipated or recalled by the use of a pronoun, suggesting hesitancy of construction or a desire to foreground on the part of the speaker, e.g. *reprise* of subject – 'Mais il a été fait, le scandale' (l. 35, also ll. 49, 87, 111), *reprise* of object – 'Cette bête, cette herbe sèche, cette terre, Ptit-mé les voulait tout contre son oreiller' (l. 20, also ll. 51, 69). On the other hand, demonstrating the fact that the narrator deliberately manipulates his material and is not being genuinely spontaneous, as it may seem, is the occurrence of sentences where climaxes and suspense are created and inversion of elements is used, e.g. 'il était tout attendri . . . de la joie de Ptit-mé quand, de sa veste dure, il sortait, se cachant des blouses blanches, le bocal à merveilles vivantes' (l. 17), 'Il restait ainsi . . . à observer de la taupe-grillon le remue-ménage dans sa motte brune et grasse, du criquet les élans cassés par le mur de sa prison transparente' (l. 21, also ll. 41, 59). Furthermore the narrator regularly corrects or qualifies what might be a false impression or conclusion drawn by his audience, through the use of 'non/pas', e.g. 'Grand-mère rit. Non par mauvaise plaisanterie . . . mais' (l. 1, also ll. 4, 43, 60), 'tu iras frapper aux cuisines des gens. Des riches. Pas pour des raisons de propreté' (l. 121, also ll. 108, 115, 124), or 'au/du moins', e.g. 'Ou la lente métamorphose du Saint-Paul en sphinx effrayant – du moins pour la surveillante en chef' (l. 24, also ll. 13, 85, 139). Gauvin's skill at manipulating the whole range of registers appears with the juxtaposition of fairly high-register vocabulary, treated ironically, with low-register syntactic constructions, e.g. 'Ptit-mé le voulait frit? Il termina sa carrière dans l'huile bouillante . . . Avant de se dessécher et raidir dans cette petite assiette à dessert que tu avais spécialement achetée pour' (l. 63). Similarly, the use of metonymy – e.g. '[les] blouses blanches' (l. 19) = hospital staff – betokens a desire to use language in a playful manner, as does the malapropism in Tino's speech – '«Le riche ça peut pas te colloquer ses microbes: c'est jamais malade!» (l. 127). Very frequent use of triplets, too, adds to this effect, e.g. '[red fish curry] dont moitié roussie à la tomate et moitié crue en finition s'opposent et s'allient, bref se renforcent' (l. 3, also ll. 14, 20, 22, 27, 47, 59).

The narrator's skill – and playfulness – is also evident in the thumb-nail sketches he provides of minor characters: in a very few words their idiosyncrasies are amusingly portrayed, e.g. Tino (l. 125) (his name is an allusion to the crooner, Tino Rossi), the old women whose cooking facilities Margrite tries to appropriate (ll. 133, 137), even Gaétan's car (l. 112). However, it is in his relationship with Margrite in the second part of the passage that the role of narrator is pushed to the limit. The narrator almost becomes a sort of mentor to Margrite, advising, cajoling, frightening and castigating her in turn, but always with a light touch – in the feeding of Ptit-mé (l. 59), in the cooking of the little fish (l. 63), in her dealings with the old women (ll. 91, 131, 137). Sarcasm, over-statement, irony, mock-heroic are all employed. Poor Margrite is ridiculed in the series of clauses beginning 'toi qui' (ll. 117, 121) or 'toi' + present/past participle (e.g. ll. 98, 99, 100, 102). The narrator's linguistic ability in manipulating different registers is again seen in the contrast between 'Il avait, du moins, réussi à transformer le désespoir en doute. La cruauté du désespoir en le sadisme du doute' (l. 85) and a little later 'T'es bien pareille aux autres: pleurnicharde et gniengien. Dé-ses-pé-rée au moindre petit bobo à ton cœur!' (l. 88).

The Creole influence and its political implications have already been referred to in the previous commentary. The use of Creole is particularly noticeable in the names of the insects gathered to encourage Ptit-mé's convalescence, but also in other terms and expressions distributed fairly thinly, it has to be said, throughout the text. The meanings of many of these are provided by Gauvin himself in footnotes. However, it has to be admitted that the Creole atmosphere is not so prominent as in some of the texts written in the Caribbean (compare Schwarz-Bart, Maximin and Chamoiseau (see Chapters 20, 21 and 22 below), to the last of whom he perhaps comes closest in his combination of humour and Creole sensitivity), but is a reminder that this novel is an effective demonstration that French writing with a Creole substratum is a worthy vehicle of literary fiction combined with a political agenda. This message is made all the more convincing and appealing by being reinforced through the constant use of humorous touches throughout the text.

Part 3

Caribbean

Chapter 17

Introduction

The Caribbean islands of Guadeloupe and Martinique are, as French overseas departments (*départements d'outre-mer* or DOM), among France's oldest surviving colonies. Haiti, meanwhile, gained independence from France in 1804, and was the first black republic in the western hemisphere. Each of these islands has a varied and ever-expanding corpus of literature in French, and despite the historical differences between the dependent DOM and the independent Haiti, the shared legacy of colonization and slavery has ensured that, at the level of intellectual activity at least, there has always been cross-fertilization and mutual influence.

All three of these islands were 'discovered' by Christopher Columbus at the time of his exploration of the Americas: Guadeloupe and Hispaniola (today divided into Haiti and the Dominican Republic) in 1492, and Martinique in 1502. None of them, however, was settled by the French until the early part of the seventeenth century and, soon, the indigenous populations – who refused to work the land for the Europeans – had been driven out or exterminated, and the system of importing indentured labourers from France failed. African slaves, mainly from the gulf of Guinea, began to be imported, and by the 1640s slavery and the sugar cane plantation – those distinctive features of Caribbean colonization – were beginning to be established.

In each of the new colonies, slaves soon outnumbered the white plantation owners, and in 1685 Louis XIV introduced the infamous *Code Noir*, a statute apparently intended to provide guidelines for plantation owners about the appropriate treatment of slaves, but which in fact reduced the slaves to 'des marchandises' or 'des choses mobiliaires', to be bought, sold and even bequeathed, like any other item of property. The threat of appalling punishment, even for the most minor of misdeeds, the promise of the rewards of the after-life through conversion to Catholicism and even the seeds of the infamous colonial policy of assimilation (to which we shall return later) were enshrined in the *Code Noir* as ways of ensuring the lasting subjugation of the growing slave population.

The plantation system continued throughout the rest of the seventeenth and eighteenth centuries, and on the eve of the French Revolution, Guadeloupe, Martinique and Saint Domingue (as the French half of Hispaniola was now known) were extremely prosperous islands, a fact which explains France's willingness, during the Seven Years War (1756–63), to trade the majority of its North American colonies with Britain in order to maintain its colonies in the Caribbean. The victory of the French Revolution in 1789, however, with its proclamation of 'liberté, égalité, fraternité', marked the beginning of a turning point in France's Caribbean colonies, and produced abolitionists in France (as elsewhere in Europe) and ever-more discontented slaves in the colonies. It was therefore perhaps unsurprising when, between 1793 and 1794, the abolition of slavery was announced. However, it was in this year, too, that Britain, taking advantage of France's disarray during the revolution, chose to invade its Caribbean colonies and attempt to take control of them. It was thus chiefly because large numbers of extra soldiers were needed at this time if France was to safeguard its empire that abolition occurred.

It is here, of course, that the history of the three islands diverges – with that of Saint-Domingue doing so dramatically and irrevocably. In Martinique, the larger and more powerful *béké* (white planter) class colluded with the British in order that the abolition of slavery could be prevented and the old balance of power maintained. Martinique therefore passed into British control until 1802, with slavery very much still in place. In Guadeloupe, however, with its much smaller *béké* population, abolition did take place and the ex-slaves joined the fight to defeat the British. However, with no slaves to work the plantations, the economy began to suffer and, in 1802, Bonaparte ordered the re-establishment of slavery. It was then that, led by the now legendary Martinican soldier Louis Delgrès, the black soldiers took up arms and opposed the reinstatement of slavery. Although they were defeated, the famous mass suicide of Delgrès and his army at Fort Matouba has come to constitute one of the most symbolic moments in Guadeloupean history, and a constant point of reference in both Guadeloupean and Martinican literature, as demonstrated in some of the extracts chosen here. Together with the maroons – those runaway slaves who established alternative, resistant communities in the hills and forests outside the plantations – Delgrès' name has become synonymous with heroism in these islands, islands which have been deprived of the national heroes that emerge from a history of revolution and independence.

Out of Saint-Domingue's own opposition to the reinstatement of slavery emerged just such a hero – Toussaint Louverture, the rebel leader who paved the way for the island's independence and who has frequently been adopted and celebrated by the dependent islands too. While he was himself exiled to France because of his part in the rebellions, and died there in 1803, the French were successfully expelled from the island in 1804 and, under General Dessalines, independence was proclaimed. The Spanish reclaimed the east of the island and, over the next few decades, the new Republic of Haiti emerged in the west, and the Dominican Republic in the east. The nineteenth century continued to see a series of power struggles and revolts, as well as an endless succession of emperors and leaders as, following the assassination or expulsion of the majority of Haiti's white population, the Catholic mulatto (mixed-race) bourgeoisie began to take over where the colonial élite had left off, exploiting and oppressing the majority poor, black population in a manner which has continued until the present day.

An even more layered version of this class-colour hierarchy was, by the nineteenth century, becoming a feature of Martinican and Guadeloupean society too, for there was by now an established 'intermediate class' made up predominantly of mulattos who had managed to free themselves from slavery. Positioned between the *békés* at the top of the social hierarchy and the black slaves at the bottom, these *gens de couleur libres* were beginning to realize that simply being freed from slavery did not guarantee access to French citizenship, despite implications to the contrary in the *Code Noir*. As the notorious French colonial policy of assimilation began to become more explicit, the conviction that it was possible, through hard work and education, to climb the social ladder towards 'Frenchness' meant that the free mulattos began to call for the right to full French citizenship, which they finally gained in 1833. With the abolition of slavery in 1848, and the extension of suffrage to all black men in 1870, black ex-slaves also began to aspire upwards, and both the *békés*' power and the mulattos' precarious position of upward mobility were felt to be under threat. Thus the class-colour hierarchy whose legacy is still evident in the Antilles today became firmly established, with each group defining itself in a relationship of superiority to the one below, and with the indentured workers brought over from India to work the plantations after abolition positioned at the very bottom.

And so the prosperous islands of Guadeloupe and Martinique continued under French rule through the nineteenth century, and well into the twentieth. Not until 1946, with the famous backing of the then communist mayor of Fort-de-France and Martinican *député* Aimé Césaire, did a change in status finally take place in the form of departmentalization. As France's other colonies throughout the world were beginning to call for independence, Martinique, Guadeloupe, Guyana and the Indian Ocean island of Réunion chose, along with Algeria until its independence in 1962, to become fully-fledged departments of France. For Césaire and his supporters, the only viable way out of poverty and underdevelopment for Martinique and Guadeloupe was to ensure that France finally kept its long promise of assimilation, and extended all the laws and rights of French citizens to the peoples of its oldest colonies.

In practice, the majority of laws and benefits were not extended to the Antilles until well into the 1950s and 1960s, with many not being extended until the 1970s and 1980s. Though certainly well off in relation to Caribbean islands which gained their independence from other European colonial powers, the French DOM are much worse off than France itself. Since the sugar industry began to decline in the 1950s, these once-prosperous islands have seen the virtual disappearance of viable economies, and have become increasingly dependent upon France instead. The cost of living is high, since most goods are imported from France and, despite the growth of the tourist industry, inadequate French government funding for the development of other industries means that high unemployment, and the mass emigration to France which began in the 1960s, will continue for the foreseeable future.

Although many older Guadeloupeans and Martinicans still see France as a benevolent *mère-patrie* without which the islands could not survive, pro-independence groups have been active since the 1960s. While the bombing campaigns of the 1970s and 1980s are now largely a thing of the past, there is still some support for the idea of independence, and in Martinique, traditionally the least militant of the Caribbean DOM, pro-independence parties like the Mouvement Indépendantiste Martiniquais have recently begun to win votes in regional and legislative elections. More popular than independence, however, and following Césaire's original stance upon departmentalization in 1946, is the idea of winning the right to more autonomy – that is, more local control for each island over its economic and social affairs – from France. The years 1999 and 2000 have seen the start of negotiations between political leaders of all persuasions in the DOM and the French government on what has come to be known as *le projet de loi d'orientation des DOM*, a law which, if passed, would give the DOM much more autonomy and would, at last, bring about a change in the relationship between France and *les quatre vieilles colonies* – Guadeloupe, Martinique, French Guyana and Réunion.

If the future of Guadeloupe and Martinique is uncertain, however, that of Haiti is doubly so. The early independence which gave the country iconic status in the eyes of the dependent islands has thus far failed to bring with it any sort of stability, and Haiti is now the poorest country in the western hemisphere, with overpopulation, illiteracy and unemployment endemic. This instability, and the violence which characterized the nineteenth and early twentieth centuries, led eventually to the first in a series of interventions, by the United

States, in the island's affairs, with the occupation of 1915–34. This occupation also failed to bring any lasting stability, and the refusal, on the part of the United States, to grant any further aid to Haiti when it left in 1934 in many ways made matters even worse. From 1934 until 1957, the island experienced more unrest and saw various governments come and go, until François (Papa Doc) Duvalier decided to use to his advantage the black majority's increasing anger at their endless history of exploitation and oppression – at the hands of the French, of the Americans and, particularly, of their own mulatto élite. He did this by exploiting the traditional link, which has existed since slavery, between politics and Voodoo, the religion of the black majority in Haiti. Inherited primarily from Africa, Voodoo has always been marginalized by the Catholic Church and the mulatto élite, who frequently organized campaigns to wipe it out. Indeed, it is for this reason that most Haitians declare themselves to be practitioners both of Catholicism and Voodoo, and that there are many parallels between the two religions at the level of iconography, liturgy and ritual. Although it has only been the official religion of Haiti since the new constitution of 1987, Voodoo was instrumental in the organization of the revolts which led to independence in 1804 and has continued to be an important means of mobilizing its adherents and participants against the agents of oppression. It was thus relatively easy for Duvalier, in the run-up to the 1957 elections, to use his links with the Voodoo priests to gain support from the black majority by convincing them that a vote for him was a vote against the Catholic Church and the mulatto élite. Then, upon election, he used Voodoo as a means of policing and controlling the masses through these same Voodoo priests, many of whom he turned into the notorious Tontons Macoutes.[1]

Thus Duvalier established and maintained his now legendary, violent dictatorship, which was taken over by his son Jean-Claude (Baby Doc) in 1971 and not overthrown until the intervention of the United States, once more, in 1986. The recent history of violence, poverty and instability in Haiti is, by now, familiar: after withholding aid from 1987 to 1989, the United States helped stage the first multi-party elections in 1990, in which the radical Catholic priest Jean-Bertrand Aristide was elected as president, only to be overthrown in 1991 after nine months in office. With Aristide forced to flee the country and a trade embargo imposed by the United States, thousands of Haitians fled to the USA only to be returned to Haiti. General Raoul Cédras's *de facto* military rule of Haiti then continued, characterized once again by violence and human rights abuses – some, according to Amnesty International, having possibly been backed by the US government via the CIA.[2] Aristide was returned to power in a US-led intervention in 1994, with the United States again effectively occupying the island until March 1995 and once more implicated in the human rights abuses that its presence was meant to curtail.

Nevertheless, during this time, and since René Préval took over the presidency from Aristide in 1996, a wide-ranging programme of institutional reform has been underway, with the judicial system a particular focus. The armed forces have been dismantled, paramilitary groups have been banned and a new police force, the PNH (Police Nationale d'Haïti) has

1 The Tontons Macoutes were the privately recruited presidential militia of the Duvaliers, father and son, and they were used to maintain the corrupt and oppressive Duvalier regimes through extortion, torture, 'disappearances' and murder.

2 This information has been taken from Amnesty International's 1997 report on Haiti, which is available on their website, http://www.amnesty.org. Other information included here on the political situation in Haiti since 1995 has also been taken from reports published on this website.

been established. A Commission Nationale de Vérité et de Justice was also set up to investigate human rights abuses during the military rule of 1991–4. Despite such progress, there has still been a general failure to implement institutional change sufficiently rapidly. The recommendations of the Truth and Justice Commission have not been rigorously acted upon, and the president has effectively been ruling without a parliament since the resignation of his prime minister in 1997 and the ensuing failure to appoint and ratify the new prime minister, Jacques Alexis, until 1999. Violence – revenge killings and lynchings, but also, since 1999 in particular, increased police and politically motivated violence in the run-up to the legislative and presidential elections of 2000 – has therefore continued to be part of Haitian life. The United Nations and the Organization of American States continue to be present on the island in a monitoring role, but Haiti's future, at the beginning of the twenty-first century, remains in many ways as uncertain as it has always been.

Such is the historical background to the literature from which extracts are taken and examined here. Despite the obvious historical differences between the dependent and independent islands, written literature in French has the same origins in Guadeloupe, Martinique and Haiti, for it began with the work of the priests and missionaries who were first sent to the new colonies in the seventeenth and eighteenth centuries. Such work, like Père du Tertre's *Histoire générale des Antilles habitées par les Français*, published between 1667 and 1671, and Père Labat's *Nouveaux voyages aux îles d'Amérique*, published in 1722, was not supplemented by that of Caribbean-born writers until well into the eighteenth century, when *békés* also began to write about the experience of living in the colonies. In the case of Guadeloupe and Martinique, it was not until the nineteenth and early twentieth centuries that the mulatto, and then black, populations began to write. Haiti was very different: it began to produce black, racially aware writers from its independence in 1804, well ahead of the dependent islands.

Anti-colonial pamphlets, literary journals and poetry by the newly established élite played a major role, throughout the nineteenth century, in establishing a literary scene in Haiti and, by the early twentieth century, the novel had also begun to emerge as an important Haitian genre. The twentieth century then saw the emergence of numerous movements, writers and theories in Haiti which would eventually have an enormous impact upon writers from the dependent islands. Led by Jacques Roumain and his journal, *La Revue indigène*, the *indigénistes* emerged in the 1920s. Inspired by nationalist opposition to the US occupation of 1915–34 and by the work of one of Haiti's greatest intellectuals, Jean Price-Mars, whose classic *roman paysan*, *Ainsi parla l'oncle* (1928), attacked the francophilia of the mulatto élite and celebrated the culture, Voodoo religion and Creole language of the black peasantry, the *indigénistes* called for an assertion and celebration of specifically Haitian culture and values. In the 1930s, *indigénisme* gave way to *noirisme*, formulated by a group named Les Griots,[3] of which François Duvalier was a member, and whose particular brand of black nationalism entailed an assertion of the 'essential Africanness' of Haitian culture and identity, and a celebration of Voodoo mysticism.

Although *noirisme* was to become the basis of the Duvalier regime, its perceived failure to challenge the political order at this stage meant that, intellectually, it gave way to the Marxism of writers such as Jacques Roumain (whose Marxist novel *Gouverneurs de la rosée* is examined in Chapter 18) and, then, to a combination of Marxism, surrealism and magical realism in

3 See Chapter 9 for an explanation of the word *griot*.

the work of Roumain, Jacques-Stéphen Alexis and René Depestre. With the Duvalier regime, however, came the repression of intellectual life: Depestre was, and has remained, exiled and Alexis was murdered; apart from Frankétienne's *spiralisme*, a late-1960s, anti-authoritarian call to literary experimentation, most Haitian literary and intellectual activity has now been exiled – to Montreal, Miami, New York, Paris and Dakar. The current climate of political instability means that the future of Haitian literature within Haiti is as uncertain as that of Haiti itself, while writers based outside Haiti, like the North American-based Dany Laferrière, included here (Chapter 24 below) are beginning to be seen not only as 'Haitian writers in exile', but also as a vital part of the literary traditions of their adopted country.

Progress towards racially aware black writing in the dependent territories was rather slower, and throughout the nineteenth century, *béké* texts continued to dominate the literary scene. Despite the acquisition by mulattos of the right to full French citizenship in 1833, the mulatto population – and still less the black population – produced hardly any writing until the late nineteenth century. The first volume of poetry attributed to a black Antillean was Eugène Agricole's *Fleurs des Antilles*, published in 1900, but it was not until the appearance of René Maran's novel *Batouala* (1921), Oruno Lara's *Questions de couleur* (1923), Suzanne Lacascade's *Claire-Solange, âme africaine* (1924) and Gilbert Gratiant's *Cris d'un jeune* (1926), that a racially aware writing really began to develop among the mulatto and black populations of the still dependent colonies.

It was in the work of the Martinican Aimé Césaire, however, that this black literary tradition began to emerge in earnest in the form of Negritude.[4] The ideals of Antillean Negritude were crystallized in Césaire's seminal text *Cahier d'un retour au pays natal*, first published in the Parisian journal *Volontés* in 1939. The journal *Tropiques*, founded in 1940 in Martinique by Suzanne Césaire, Aimé Césaire and René Ménil, then continued, until 1943, to develop and assert these ideas through essays and poems of a broadly surrealist nature. As if demonstrating the central importance of Negritude in the burgeoning Antillean literary scene, poetry remained the dominant genre throughout the 1940s and into the 1950s. Some novels, however, also began to appear around this time – most notably Joseph Zobel's *La Rue Cases-Nègres* (1950) – a novel characterized, as shown in the extract chosen here (Chapter 19), by the optimism of the newly departmentalized Antilles. Another key figure of this time, although a writer of theoretical rather than literary texts, was the Martinican Frantz Fanon, whose critique of assimilation and its psychological effects, *Peau noire masques blancs* (1952), influenced subsequent writers and intellectuals at least as much as Césaire's Negritude.

By 1960, poetry had ceased to be the dominant literary genre in the Antilles, and it is the novel which, during the four subsequent decades, emerged to take its place. Fiction of the 1960s largely followed the realist and broadly optimistic tone of that of the 1950s, but as the promises of departmentalization appeared increasingly hollow, the emergence of more experimental writers like Edouard Glissant, whose work spans poetry, theatre, theory and fiction, focused attention once more on literature as a means of interrogating the continuing colonial relationship between France and the DOM. It was during the 1970s that two other important changes occurred to the literary scene. First, much more significant numbers of women writers than ever before began to emerge, notably Simone Schwarz-Bart and

4 Negritude was a literary, philosophical and political movement common to students, intellectuals and activists from across France's empire. For a more detailed examination of it, see Chapter 9 above.

Maryse Condé, extracts from whose work are included here (Chapters 20 and 23). Second, and at the same time that pro-independence activity began to gain ground, the number of theatrical works being produced increased. Although writers like Césaire had been producing plays during the 1960s, and even before, it was only now that theatre emerged as an important means of reaching relatively large, and not necessarily book-reading, audiences, often drawing upon African and Caribbean traditions of oral story-telling and using Creole – the predominantly oral, local language which developed out of French and African languages during slavery – as well as French as a language of expression.

Theatre has never become the predominant literary genre in the Caribbean DOM, and it will certainly never overtake the popularity of the novel among a readership outside the islands. However, its use of Creole and the oral traditions of folk tale and story-telling have increasingly become a feature of Guadeloupean and Martinican novels, especially from the 1990s. Examples of written Creole literature can be found in Haiti as early as the mid-eighteenth century, but apart from the famous nineteenth-century Creole translations of La Fontaine's *Fables*,[5] it was not until the mid-twentieth century, with the work of Gilbert Gratiant (*Fab'Compè Zicaque*, 1958), that there was significant interest in producing texts in Creole in the dependent islands. Even in Haiti, where French is much less widely spoken, Creole has always had the secondary status of an oral *patois* in relation to French, the dominant language of education, administration and social mobility.

In Martinique and Guadeloupe, the difference in status between the two languages has been reinforced by the French education system's ban on the use of Creole in schools. Creole has certainly never been taught as a fully fledged language. This has produced a society in which, as in France, almost everyone is literate in French, but in which almost no one is literate in Creole, even though the vast majority of the population is bilingual in French and Creole. It is only recently that Martinican and Guadeloupean linguists have attempted to develop, and gain wide acceptance for, a standard written version of Creole, and it is only since the pro-independence groups began promoting Creole as a national language that a significant, literary interest in it has developed. Now, writers are faced with a situation in which writing entirely in Creole would not only limit the potential of a French and foreign readership, but would prevent the majority of Creole-speaking, but non-Creole-literate, Martinicans and Guadeloupeans from gaining access to their work. In Haiti, where literacy levels in any language are extremely low,[6] a local readership is necessarily limited, although for those writers living and working in exile a non-Haitian readership is increasingly accessible, while others, such as Anthony Phelps, are well known in Haiti because they have made recordings of their work.

In Martinique and Guadeloupe, the current trend – as is evident in the extracts here from the work of Maryse Condé, Simone Schwarz-Bart, Daniel Maximin (Chapter 21) and, especially, Patrick Chamoiseau (Chapter 22) – is to write in French, but to inflect that French with the words, rhythms and speech patterns of oral Creole, thus producing a hybridized language which remains accessible, if at times opaque, to non-creolophones and recognizably Creole to a bilingual French Caribbean readership. Indeed it is this hybridization, or

5 François Marbot, *Les Bambous, Fables de La Fontaine travesties en patois martiniquais par un vieux commandeur* (Paris: Casterman, 1976; originally published in 1846).

6 The exact figures for the rate of illiteracy in Haiti vary, but a recent study puts it at 60 per cent (Charles Arthur and Michael Dash (eds), *Libète: a Haitian Anthology* (London: Latin America Bureau, 1999), p. 260).

creolization, which is now a proud characteristic not only of the literature and language but also of the general culture of the francophone Caribbean. This is a culture which has been produced from the long, and particular, colonial history of the region. As ever more migrant groups – Chinese, Syrian, Lebanese – have gone to live in the DOM, as more and more Martinicans and Guadeloupeans are born in Paris or elsewhere, and as increasing numbers of Haitians spend their lives outside Haiti, it is a culture which is set to undergo ever more enriching hybridization and renewal.

Further reading

Abenon, Lucien-René, *Les Français en Amérique* (Paris: L'Harmattan, 1993).

Aldrich, Robert, *Greater France: A History of French Overseas Expansion* (Basingstoke: Macmillan, 1996).

Antoine, Régis, *La Littérature franco-antillaise: Haïti, Guadeloupe et Martinique* (Paris: Karthala, 1992).

Arnold, A. James (ed.), *A History of Literature in the Caribbean: Hispanic and Francophone Regions* (Amsterdam and Philadelphia: John Benjamins, 1995).

Arthur, Charles and Dash, Michael (eds), *Libète: a Haitian Anthology* (London: Latin America Bureau, 1999).

Burton, Richard and Reno, Frank (eds), *French and West Indian: Martinique, Guadeloupe and French Guyana Today* (Basingstoke: Macmillan, 1995).

Chamoiseau, Patrick and Confiant, Raphael, *Lettres créoles: tracées antillaises et continentales de la littérature 1635–1975* (Paris: Hatier, 1991).

Dash, J. Michael, *Haiti and the United States: National Stereotypes and the Literary Imagination*, 2nd edn (Basingstoke: Macmillan, 1997).

Dayan, Joan, *Haiti, History and the Gods* (London, Berkeley and Los Angeles: University of California Press, 1995).

Toumson, Roger, *La Transgression des couleurs: littérature et langage des Antilles, 18e, 19e, 20e siècles*, 2 vols (Paris: Editions Caribéennes, 1989).

Chapter 18

Jacques Roumain

Gouverneurs de la rosée (Fort-de-France: Editions Désormeaux, 1977 [1944]), pp. 93–7.

La vie recommençait, mais elle ne changeait pas: elle suivait le même parcours, le même sillon, avec une indifférence cruelle. On était debout dès l'avant-jour: par les craquelures du ciel obscur passaient et se répandaient les premières et confuses clartés. Plus tard, la ligne du morne se dessinait, frangée d'une pâle lumière. Aussitôt que le soleil touchait le bois, assez pour éclairer à travers les bayahondes les sentiers entrecroisés, Manuel partait. Il abattait les arbres, dressait dans la clairière la meule sous laquelle le bois brûlerait à feu lent. Puis, il prenait le chemin du morne. Il revenait de sa course, trempé de sueur et les mains pleines de terre. Délira lui demandait où il avait été. Il répondait avec des mots qui prenaient le détour. Il avait ce pli têtu au coin de la bouche.

Chaque samedi, Délira chargeait le charbon sur deux bourriques et s'en allait à la ville. Elle revenait à la nuit tombée, avec quelques misérables provisions et un peu de monnaie. Elle s'asseyait dans la case, toute cassée, sous le poids d'une immense fatigue. Bienaimé réclamait son tabac et ne le trouvait jamais assez fort.

Parfois la vieille contait ses déboires. Les inspecteurs des marchés, postés aux abords de la ville, s'abattaient sur les paysannes et les volaient sans pitié.

– Il vient et il me demande de payer. Je lui montre que j'avais déjà payé. Il se met en colère et commence à jurer. Regarde, si tu n'as pas honte, je lui dis, regarde mes cheveux blancs. Tu n'as donc pas de maman pour me traiter comme ça? Ferme ta gueule, il crie – voilà ce qu'il crie, ou bien je te traîne en prison pour rébellion et scandale public. J'ai été obligée de lui donner l'argent. Non, il n'y a pas de considération pour nous autres malheureux.

Manuel serrait les poings à les faire craquer.

– Le bandit, le nègre sans aveu, grondait Bienaimé.

Un moment plus tard, il disait:

– Va dormir, ma vieille femme. Tes yeux se ferment. Tu as fait une longue route.

Délira déroulait sa natte, l'étendait sur le sol. Malgré les protestations de Manuel, elle exigeait qu'il occupât, dans l'autre pièce, le lit d'acajou.

. . . Quelquefois, Antoine venait dans le courant de la journée.

Il s'accroupissait auprès de Bienaimé.

– Ah, Simidor, Simidor, disait le vieux, quelle est cette misère?

Le Simidor secouait la tête.

– Ça ne s'est jamais vu.

Et il ajoutait d'une voix étouffée, regardant tristement les champs brûlés:

– Ne m'appelle pas Simidor. Appelle-moi Antoine: c'est mon nom. Vois-tu, compère, quand tu dis: Simidor, ça me fait songer au temps longtemps. C'est amer ces souvenances-là, c'est amer comme le fiel.

... Les après-midi, Manuel tressait sur la galerie des chapeaux de paille de latanier. On les vendrait bien trente centimes pièce au bourg voisin. La cérémonie vodou avait dévoré le peu d'argent qu'il avait rapporté de Cuba. Dorméus à lui seul avait coûté quarante piastres.

Souvent, Laurélien venait le voir. Il s'asseyait sur le banc; ses grandes mains tordues faites pour manier la houe reposaient sur ses genoux; il disait à voix basse:

– Et cette eau?

– Pas encore, pas encore, répondait Manuel. Mais je suis sur sa trace.

Ses doigts habiles allaient et venaient tandis que ses pensées voyageaient vers Annaïse. A plusieurs reprises, il l'avait aperçue dans le village. Chaque fois, elle s'était détournée; elle s'était éloignée de ce long pas nonchalant et balancé.

Laurélien demandait à nouveau:

– Parle-moi de Cuba.

– C'est un pays, cinq fois, non dix, non vingt fois peut-être plus grand qu'Haïti. Mais, tu sais, moi je suis fait avec ça, moi-même.

Il touchait le sol, il en caressait le grain:

– Je suis ça: cette terre-là, et je l'ai dans le sang. Regarde ma couleur: on dirait que la terre a déteint sur moi et sur toi aussi. Ce pays est le partage des hommes noirs et toutes les fois qu'on a essayé de nous l'enlever, nous avons sarclé l'injustice à coup de machette.

– Oui, mais à Cuba, il y a plus de richesse, on vit plus à l'aise. Icitte, il faut se gourmer dur avec l'existence et à quoi ça sert? On n'a même pas de quoi remplir son ventre et on est sans droit contre la malfaisance des autorités. Le juge de paix, la police rurale, les arpenteurs, les spéculateurs en denrées, ils vivent sur nous comme des puces. J'ai passé un mois de prison, avec toute la bande des voleurs et des assassins, parce que j'étais descendu en ville sans souliers. Et où est-ce que j'aurais pris l'argent, je te demande, mon compère? Alors qu'est-ce que nous sommes, nous autres, les habitants, les nègres-pieds-à-terre, méprisés et maltraités?

– Ce que nous sommes? Si c'est une question, je vais te répondre: eh bien, nous sommes ce pays et il n'est rien sans nous, rien du tout. Qui est-ce qui plante, qui est-ce qui arrose, qui est-ce qui récolte? Le café, le coton, le riz, la canne, le cacao, le maïs, les bananes, les vivres et tous les fruits, si ce n'est pas nous, qui les fera pousser? Et avec ça nous sommes pauvres, c'est vrai, nous sommes malheureux, c'est vrai, nous sommes misérables, c'est vrai. Mais sais-tu pourquoi, frère? à cause de notre ignorance: nous ne savons pas encore que nous sommes une force, une seule force: tous les habitants, tous les nègres des plaines et des mornes réunis. Un jour, quand nous aurons compris cette vérité, nous nous lèverons d'un point à l'autre du pays et nous ferons l'assemblée générale des gouverneurs de la rosée, le grand coumbite des travailleurs de la terre pour défricher la misère et planter la vie nouvelle.

– Tu dis des paroles conséquentes, oui, fit Laurélien.

Il s'était comme essoufflé à suivre Manuel. Une ride marquait sur son front l'effort de la méditation. Dans le retrait le plus inarticulé de son esprit accoutumé à la lenteur et à la patience, là où les idées de résignation et de soumission s'étaient formées avec une rigidité traditionnelle et fatale, un rideau de lumière commençait à se lever. Il éclairait un espoir soudain, obscur encore et lointain, mais rude, certain et véridique comme la fraternité.

Il cracha un jet de salive entre les dents.

– Ce que tu dis là est clair comme l'eau courante au soleil!

Il était debout et ses mains se fermaient comme pour essayer de retenir le fuyant des mots.

Text and context

Widely regarded as one of Haiti's most important and influential writers, Jacques Roumain was also a political activist who rose to prominence during the nationalist opposition to the 1915–34 US occupation of Haiti, and founded the Haitian Communist Party in 1934. *Gouverneurs de la rosée* is his most famous novel and is at once an example of the *roman paysan* popularized by Jean Price-Mars and the *indigénistes*, and a testament to the author's Marxism and nationalism.[1] In it, we follow the fortunes of Manuel, who has returned from fifteen years in Cuba to find that his parents and the wider peasant community of Fonds-Rouge are faced with destitution following a long drought and the failure of their crops. This extract comes immediately after a full, and expensive, Voodoo ceremony has been performed in order to welcome Manuel home, and here we see the monotony of life in Fonds-Rouge resumed after the brief respite provided by the celebrations. We also see Manuel's increased determination to discover a source of water which, following methods of irrigation that he observed in Cuba, he can channel to serve each family's plot of land and therefore allow the community to re-establish the harmonious relationship with the land that was depicted at the beginning of the novel.

This earlier, almost utopic period in the history of Fonds-Rouge is referred to here with the visit of Antoine, a friend of Bienaimé, Manuel's father. Bienaimé initially calls Antoine 'Simidor', a name which is associated with the pre-drought period, when he was 'le Simidor' – the worker who beat time with a drum in order to provide a rhythm for the others to work to as they planted and harvested the land together. The memories of this period are

1 For a more detailed discussion of *indigénisme*, *noirisme* and the influence of Price-Mars, see Chapter 17 above.

now too painful, and Antoine thus prefers to return to his real name. The atmosphere is one of desperation and despair. Like Manuel's old friend Laurélien, whose 'grandes mains tordues faites pour manier la houe reposaient sur ses genoux' (l. 42), the workers have been deprived of the only means of livelihood that they know, and are portrayed as being at a loss without it.

Although the majority of the inhabitants of Fonds-Rouge are seen simply to be waiting either for the rains to come or for the crops to fail, some of them do also attempt to find other sources of income – notably the hat weaving undertaken here by Manuel and the charcoal taken by his mother Délira to the market each Saturday (l. 38). Délira's earnings are severely limited, however, by the unscrupulous activities of the local authorities, in this case the market inspectors who use the threat of prison to extract as much money as possible from peasants who set up stalls in the market (l. 15). '[L]a malfaisance des autorités' (l. 61) is a constant theme in the novel, and is rooted in historical reality. Later in this extract, Laurélien tells Manuel of the occasion when he was thrown into prison for failing to wear shoes while in town (l. 64), and the opportunity for political comment is taken here, as we are told: 'Le juge de paix, la police rurale, les arpenteurs, les spéculateurs en denrées, ils vivent sur nous comme des puces' (l. 61). Later in the novel, we will see how the local police officer, Hilarion, actively works to prevent Manuel from finding water, in the hope that the inhabitants of Fonds-Rouge will eventually be forced to leave their land, which he can then appropriate for himself.

Manuel is apparently the only member of the community who is unwilling simply to resign himself to 'fate', and here we see his daily departure in search of water, a secret from everyone but Laurélien. Despite her weekly trips to the market, Délira, in particular, is presented as extremely fatalistic, and puts her faith in the Voodoo priest, Dorméus, who conducted the previous evening's ceremony. Although it is made clear, during the ceremony, that Manuel sees Voodoo as an important part of Haitian culture, his disapproval of the resignation and submission entailed by his mother's religious faith is made very evident. This depiction of the submission and fatalism of peasant life is familiar from Roumain's previous novel, *La Montagne ensorcelée*, published in 1931. This intensely pessimistic novel, in which the passivity of the peasantry is heavily criticized, is in many ways the negative counterpart of *Gouverneurs de la rosée*. In the latter, however, Manuel's status as an insider who has nevertheless experienced life outside Haiti provides Roumain with the means to examine the reasons behind such passivity, and to articulate an alternative version of peasant life. Thus, according to Manuel, the greatest enemy of the Haitian peasantry is ignorance – an ignorance in which, it is implied, they have been wilfully kept. Historically, it has certainly been in the interests of the Haitian élite that the mass of black peasants be kept ignorant and submissive – and in Roumain's work, in a manner which seems almost to foresee the misuses of Voodoo under the Duvalier regime, Voodoo is implicated in this. As Manuel speaks to Laurélien, the reference to 'le retrait le plus inarticulé de son esprit' (l. 82) also reminds us of the lack of education available to peasants such as he and this, coupled with the daily struggle of life as a subsistence farmer, makes it entirely understandable that, now, Laurélien has to make a huge effort to understand Manuel's words, for 'son esprit [est] accoutumé à la lenteur et à la patience' (l. 82). It is made quite clear here that 'les idées de résignation et de soumission' engendered by such conditions are both self-perpetuating ('traditionnelle') and, potentially, 'fatale' (l. 84).

This speech by Manuel to Laurélien is central to *Gouverneurs de la rosée* as a whole, and it is here that the novel's *indigénisme* and Marxism both become evident. First, Manuel's *indigénisme* – although it is never named as such – is shown as he proclaims his pride in both his blackness and his 'haïtienneté', which he has held onto throughout his years in Cuba. He compares the blackness of the earth to that of his skin (l. 55) in order to reinforce the relationship between Haiti and the people who have fought for the country and worked on its land before and since independence in 1804. Like that of Roumain himself, however, Manuel's *indigénisme* is informed and tempered by what is evidently a Marxist discourse. He makes it clear that, in a country in which the black majority has always been exploited by the predominantly lighter-skinned, middle-class minority, it is specifically the black peasantry – 'les nègres-pieds-à-terre' (l. 66) – and not simply Haitians in general, which is connected to Haiti and the land. For him, it is only if 'les nègres des plaines et des mornes' (l. 75) are made aware of their potential strength in numbers, and then shown how to unite, that the present situation in Fonds-Rouge may be solved, and that a more positive future for the whole country may be built.

Laurélien finds Manuel's words important, and just as his consciousness begins to be awakened here – 'un rideau de lumière commençait à se lever' (l. 84) – so the consciousnesses of the other inhabitants of the village will be awakened as the novel continues. Immediately following this extract, Laurélien calls Manuel 'chef' and, indeed, Manuel does eventually become a leader, occupying a position somewhere between a Christ-like figure (he must die for the redemption of his people) and a Marxist hero, who teaches his community how to work together for the collective good. Manuel's role as someone who teaches others how to act for themselves, rather than simply acting on their behalf, begins here, for it is clear that, at this moment, Laurélien begins to pull himself from his customary passivity. By the end of this extract, he is shown standing, as if defiant, and is now putting his work-worn hands to another use, to try and 'retenir le fuyant des mots' (l. 89).

The importance of collective action and solidarity is emphasized here and throughout the novel, as is the positive potential of what they may achieve. The workers have always called themselves 'les gouverneurs de la rosée' because, as agricultural labourers, they start work before dawn and see the dew evaporate as the sun comes up. This has given them a sense of themselves as 'masters' of something, despite their poverty and dispossession. Here, Manuel takes this a step further and suggests that, through the collective action that he proposes, they have the potential to become ' l'assemblée générale des gouverneurs de la rosée' (l. 77). The political connotations of his choice of words are obvious, and the eventual, triumphant conclusion of the novel, in which 'le grand coumbite [= collective] des travailleurs de la terre' (l. 77) is formed and the land is irrigated, is clearly meant to be seen only as the beginning of the workers' wider mission to 'planter la vie nouvelle' both for themselves and for their country. While *Gouverneurs de la rosée* as a whole is certainly rather utopic, it is easy to see how the radicality of its views has earned it a reputation as one of the most important Haitian novels to date.

Further reading

Roumain, Jacques, *La Montagne ensorcelée, La Proie et l'ombre, Griefs de l'homme noir* (Paris: Les Editeurs français réunis, 1972).

—— *Les Fantoches* (Port-au-Prince, 1977).

Gilroy, James P., 'The theme of Christ in francophone Caribbean literature: Jacques Roumain's *Gouverneurs de la rosée*', in James P. Gilroy, *Francophone Literatures of the New World* (Denver, Colo.: University of Denver, 1982), pp. 137–47.

Hoffman, Léon-François, *Littérature d'Haïti* (Vanves: EDICEF, 1995).
Laroche, Maximilien, 'La diglossie littéraire dans *Gouverneurs de la rosée*: termes de couleur et conflit de langues', *Etudes littéraires* 13, 2 (1980), 263–88.
Ormerod, Beverley, *An Introduction to the French Caribbean Novel* (London: Heinemann, 1985), Chapter 1.
Prat, Michel, *Gouverneurs de la rosée, Jacques Roumain* (Paris: Hatier, 1986).
Sellin, Eric, 'Pastoralism and nostalgia in Jacques Roumain's *Gouverneurs de la rosée*', in Régis Antoine (ed.), *Carrefour de cultures: mélanges offerts à Jacqueline Leiner* (Tübingen: Gunter Narr Verlag, 1993), pp. 450–73.

Language and style

The opening paragraph, describing the first glimmer of sunrise, forms an allegorical precursor to the last section of the passage, when light begins to dawn in Laurélien's mind, bringing an awareness of the possibility of a brighter future. To be specific, the 'craquelures' in the sky prefigure the 'ride' on his brow – 'Une ride marquait sur son front l'effort de la méditation' (l. 81) – 'obscur' occurs in both sections (ll. 3, 85), as do 'clarté/clair' (ll. 4, 88), 'lumière' (ll. 4, 84), 'éclairer/éclairait' (ll. 5, 85); 'frangée' (l. 4) links up with 'rideau' (l. 84). As if to make the connection even more obvious, the author puts the following words into Laurélien's mouth – 'Ce que tu dis là est clair comme l'eau courante au soleil!' (l. 88). Another parallel lies in the comparison of Manuel at the beginning of the passage and Laurélien at the end: whereas Manuel sweats and his hands are covered in soil (l. 8), Laurélien spits and it is as if his hands are trying to retain Manuel's elusive words (l. 89).

What has caused this spark to develop in Laurélien's mind is Manuel's persuasive message, expressing his aspirations for the Blacks of Haiti. Although begged by Laurélien to speak of what he had witnessed in Cuba (l. 51), Manuel refuses and proclaims his identity with Haiti – 'Je suis ça: cette terre-là' (l. 55). Combining words with actions (caressing the texture of the soil (l. 54)) – a gesture bound to impress the peasant, Laurélien – he begins his political statement. The land belongs to the Blacks, the proof being that they are of the same colour; not only that, it is in their blood, it has permeated them. Manuel's determination to use violence if necessary to obtain their rights is hinted at when he says, 'toutes les fois qu'on a essayé de nous l'enlever, nous avons sarclé l'injustice à coup de machette' (l. 57). Laurélien is still thinking of the good life available in Cuba (l. 59) and produces a litany of grievances concerning the condition of Haitians (l. 60): despite enormous effort they cannot provide enough food for themselves, they are exploited by the authorities and can be imprisoned simply for not wearing shoes in town (l. 63). He finishes his lamentation with two fundamental questions – how do we get money and what are we? – concluded by an alliterative couplet, 'méprisés et maltraités' (l. 66).

It is the latter question to which Manuel responds first, and his language rises to the occasion; he becomes eloquent, oratorical and above all convincing. He repeats the fact of the identity of the Blacks and the land, each deriving its essence from the other (l. 69). A triplet of questions follows (l. 69), then a series of nouns plus another question (l. 70). Then Laurélien's second question receives a reply, in a sentence consisting of a triplet of synonymic expressions, interspersed with a chorus: 'Et avec ça nous sommes pauvres, c'est vrai, nous sommes malheureux, c'est vrai, nous sommes misérables, c'est vrai' (l. 72). It is ignorance that has created their wretched state, but it can be overcome. Through repetition, through a combination of nouns without a coordinating conjunction, through a movement from negative to positive – 'nous ne savons pas' (l. 74) / 'nous aurons compris' (l. 76) – through three sets of doublets, through imagery taken from the land – 'nous nous lèverons d'un point à l'autre du pays et nous ferons l'assemblée générale des gouverneurs de la rosée, le grand coumbite des travailleurs de la terre pour défricher la misère et planter la vie nouvelle' (l. 76), Manuel sculpts his speech to obtain maximum persuasiveness.

Earlier in the passage, the energetic but secret activities of Manuel in the woods contrast with the sketch of Délira's desperate attempts to earn money: both return worn out (ll. 8, 13); linguistically, the two portraits are structured in a similar manner, the use of subject pronouns preceding verbs in the imperfect tense being especially noticeable. Hands (fingers, fists) play a significant role in the passage, and in particular those of Manuel, the most active character in the novel. His fingers are nimble at plaiting – 'Ses doigts habiles allaient et venaient' (l. 47). When he returns from his daily labours, Manuel's hands, as mentioned above, are covered in soil (l. 8) and later it is recorded that he touches the ground lovingly (l. 54) – symbolic of his identification with the land. His hands react angrily at the news of the inspectors' treatment of Délira and her friends: 'Manuel serrait les poings à les faire craquer' (l. 23). His hands are shown, therefore, as skilful, caring, devoted to his land, powerful and ready to fight for his cause.

The sentences are generally short and uncomplicated. Excluding the passages of speech, the proportion of simple sentences is 60 per cent (twenty-four), compound 25 per cent (ten), complex 13 per cent (five), compound-complex 3 per cent (one); there are only six subordinate clauses. Syntactically, therefore, the passage is perfectly straightforward. Speech is expressed in fairly standard French: no effort is made to represent the language, Haitian Creole, actually used. Very little ornamentation is introduced into the passage: emotion is added by the very occasional use of ante-posed adjectives, e.g. 'les premières et confuses clartés' (l. 3), 'quelques misérables provisions' (l. 12), 'une immense fatigue' (l. 13). Imagery is kept to a minimum, mainly drawn from the daily life of the people – 'le . . . sillon [de la vie]' (l. 1), 'c'est amer comme fiel' (l. 37), 'ils vivent sur nous comme des puces' (l. 62), 'pour défricher la misère et planter la vie nouvelle' (l. 78), 'véridique comme la fraternité' (l. 86), 'clair comme l'eau courante au soleil' (l. 88, also l. 57 quoted above). The plight of the peasants is portrayed unequivocally in its stark reality. Their way of life follows the same course every day (l. 1), no variation, no luxuries, only 'indifférence cruelle' (l. 2), 'misère' (ll. 31, 78). The message is to be clear, unadulterated, and the language used faithfully reflects this.

Chapter 19

Joseph Zobel

La Rue Cases-Nègres (Paris: Présence Africaine, 1950), pp. 169–74.

Je restai sur le seuil de la porte et n'eus même pas l'idée d'aller voir dans quelle direction on emportait ma grand-mère.

Elle était donc morte. Pourtant, M. Médouze . . . Peut-être y avait-il plusieurs façons d'être mort . . . Allait-elle revenir? Ne la reverrais-je plus? Mam'zelle Délice avait dit qu'elle allait guérir. Ah! . . .

Mam'zelle Mézélie, qui était peut-être la seule personne à rester à la cour, me voyant là, vint à moi et, passant la main sur ma tête, me dit:

– José, pauvre petit!

Alors, je me blottis contre elle et commençai à sangloter.

Elle m'emmena chez elle, me fit boire un verre d'eau froide et me donna du pain.

– La semaine prochaine, ta maman va revenir, on l'a amenée à l'hôpital pour être soignée. Elle va revenir guérie.

Lorsque Mam'zelle Délice revint, avec son pied qu'elle pouvait à peine traîner et qui semblait la tirer à partir de ses tempes, elle m'expliqua que m'man Tine était à l'hôpital de Saint-Esprit.

Mam'zelle Délice lava tout, rangea tout dans la case, me donna à manger, et le soir me demanda si je voulais venir coucher chez elle ou dormir seul chez m'man Tine. J'optai pour la seconde proposition.

– T'auras pas peur? me demanda-t-elle.

Non, ma peur que m'man Tine fût morte étant passée, je ne craignais plus rien, et ce fut avec le cœur plein de tendresse que j'allai me blottir sur le grabat, à sa place.

Mam'zelle Délice s'occupait de moi, me donnait mes repas, me faisait changer de vêtements, lavait mon linge, me cajolait de temps en temps – me grondait aussi quand je m'étais sali ou qu'elle ne m'avait pas trouvé dans la cour à son retour du travail. Dès le lendemain du départ de m'man Tine, elle m'avait fait retourner à l'école.

Ce fut à Jojo seulement que je racontai mon chagrin, et je ne sais si je n'éprouvai pas quelque fierté d'être son égal par le malheur dont j'étais ainsi frappé.

Mais je ne tardai pas à sentir que l'absence de m'man Tine durait.

Je commençai même à souffrir, car je ne sais comment j'eus brusquement l'impression que les gens, dans la cour, me regardaient comme si j'étais une chose désagréable. Aucun d'eux ne pouvait me voir passer sans m'envoyer faire des courses; même, ils abusaient de mon obligeance, et il me semblait que plus il en était ainsi, moins ils avaient d'estime pour moi.

Je ne changeais plus de vêtements le vendredi et, avant la fin de la semaine, j'étais crasseux, dégoûtant, honteux de moi-même. Et puis, j'avais toujours faim. Une faim qui ne passait jamais. Le soir, après dîner, j'aurais mangé encore deux ou trois fois ce que je venais d'avaler. Heureusement, le sommeil venait me dérober à la faim. Mais le matin je me réveillais avec une faim plus revendicative encore. Je n'avais plus mon grand pot de café clair bien sucré, avec de la farine de manioc, mais un peu de café au fond d'un pot en fer-blanc, un morceau de légume cuit de la veille et grillé dans la braise le matin. Or, le matin surtout, je n'avais pas le temps de parcourir le Haut-Morne en quête de fruits.

A peine étais-je entré en classe que s'emparait de moi une immense envie de manger, de me régaler d'énormes pots de café sucré de grosses poignées de farine de manioc.

Et c'était justement alors que la maîtresse venait prendre son petit déjeuner.

Car, après l'exercice de lecture, elle nous donnait un devoir écrit et, pendant que nous étions ainsi occupés, elle passait dans son appartement et revenait avec, dans un plateau, un grand bol de porcelaine et un gros morceau de pain.

La maîtresse casse le pain en petits morceaux dans le bol. Le pain est doré et crisse sous ses doigts, en laissant tomber de petits éclats de croûte que je ramasserais avec avidité pour les manger. Puis, plongeant une petite cuiller en argent dans le bol, la maîtresse porte à sa bouche des morceaux de pain enrobés d'un liquide onctueux, brun et laiteux, et qui sent la vanille, et qui doit être sucré, délicieux.

Je n'écris pas. Je regarde la maîtresse. La main dont elle tient la belle cuiller est fine et propre. Ses cheveux sont bien coiffés. Son visage est clair, velouté par un nuage de poudre, ses yeux brillent d'un éclat pur et tranquille, et sa bouche qu'elle entrouvre au passage de la cuiller est la chose à la fois la plus jolie et la plus cruelle.

Et puis, ce bol de porcelaine blanche à fleurs roses et bleues, cette cuiller en argent, ce plateau en acajou verni, comme tout cela doit parfaire la saveur de ce déjeuner! Combien tout cela ajoute à mon supplice!

Ai-je réellement envie de goûter à ce chocolat au lait? Je n'en ai jamais mangé, mais c'est à peine si j'en désire. Peut-être ne suis-je pas encore bon pour un tel déjeuner? Des fois, m'man Tine fait du chocolat à l'eau avec du cacao brut, et l'épaissit de fécule toloman, ou bien en mouille mon pot de farine de manioc.

Mais mon estomac, toute ma poitrine m'en fait mal et ma main tremble, incapable d'écrire. J'ai le vertige.

La vue du chocolat au lait de la maîtresse me torture si odieusement que je n'éprouve que souffrance, sans désir. A tel point, en vérité, que j'ai la nette sensation d'être moins affamé une fois que, son déjeuner terminé, elle emporte le plateau chez elle, puis revient sur sa chaise en criant: «Apportez vos cahiers pour la correction.»

Mais lorsque, un peu plus tard, l'accès de faim me reprenait, c'était sous l'apparence d'un grand bol de chocolat au lait, fleurant la vanille, avec du pain doré, que se présentait le mirage du soulagement suprême.

Je ne pouvais en vouloir aucunement à Mam'zelle Délice. J'avais bien compris qu'elle n'avait pas les moyens de m'en donner davantage. Je l'aimais beaucoup. Je lui étais devenu si attaché que je ne remarquais même plus son pied monstrueux.

A cette même époque, un gros malheur s'abattit sur Jojo, qui me fit oublier pendant plusieurs jours mon triste sort. Mam'zelle Gracieuse avait quitté le bourg, partie avec un homme qui avait de grands jardins d'ignames et de patates douces à Chassin, de l'autre côté de Petit-Bourg.

Sa belle-mère lui défendait de pleurer.

Un après-midi, il s'était caché dans un petit coin de la maison pour sangloter, et Mam'zelle Mélie, l'ayant surpris, s'était écriée:

– Mais, qu'est-ce qui lui arrive, qu'il pleure, ce Jojo?

Et là-dessus, Mme Justin Roc l'avait mis en pénitence jusqu'à l'arrivée de son père.

La maman de Jojo était donc partie loin aussi, comme une personne morte ou qui est allée à l'hôpital . . .

Et dire que, malgré notre chagrin, nous nous délections certains soirs à rêver tout haut!

– Quand je serai grand, me disait Jojo, mon papa et maman Yaya seront morts. Je serai contremaître à l'usine. Je vais acheter une auto plus belle que celle de mon papa, et j'irai chercher m'man Gracieuse, et je ferai une belle maison pour habiter avec elle. Mais je n'épouserai pas une femme méchante comme m'man Yaya. Je préfère rester avec maman.

Moi j'aurais une grande propriété, grande comme toute la campagne alentour. Je ne planterais pas de canne à sucre, sauf quelques pieds pour mon dessert – car c'est bon à sucer, la canne à sucre. J'aurais beaucoup de gens qui cultiveraient avec moi des légumes, des fruits, qui élèveraient des poules, des lapins, mais qui s'habilleraient, même pour travailler, de culottes et de blouses non déchirées, et qui mettraient de beaux costumes le dimanche, et dont les enfants iraient tous à l'école. M'man Tine ne serait pas morte; elle soignerait les poules, assemblerait les œufs. M'man Délia s'occuperait du ménage.

Je rêvais pour de vrai, puisque Jojo, me rappelant à la réalité des faits, me disait, sans malice pourtant:

– Mais tu ne pourras pas avoir tout ça; tu n'es pas blanc, tu n'es pas un béké.

– N'empêche.

– Mais tes travailleurs, alors, ils seront presque aussi bien nourris et logés que les békés! Alors n'y aura plus de nègres; et les békés, qu'est-ce qu'ils vont faire?

Je restais dérouté, honteux, un peu triste.

Text and context

In 1983, Euzhan Palcy's film adaptation of *La Rue Cases-Nègres* won the Lion d'Argent at the Venice film festival, and since then it has become one of the best-known Antillean novels within and outside the Antilles. When this semi-autobiographical, realist novel was first published, however, Zobel's portrayal of the hardships of life on the Martinican plantation in the 1930s, and the poverty in which the majority black population was forced to live, over eighty years after the abolition of slavery, caused controversy. Indeed, a coalition of *békés* opposed its importation and distribution in both Martinique and Guadeloupe. The present extract is taken from the second of the novel's three parts, in which we have followed José from 'la Rue Cases-Nègres' (the shacks formerly inhabited by slaves) of the plantation on which his grandmother, m'man Tine, still works, to Petit-Bourg, where he has begun attending school. He is, at this point, seven years old, and thus the first-person narrative is still that of a child, but is beginning to show a level of social awareness which will grow steadily as the novel progresses (and reach its peak in the more sophisticated narrative style of part three), as well as being characterized by the occasional intervention of a more mature narrator, writing with hindsight.

The extract begins with the apparent realization of José's greatest fear: that his grandmother's life of unremitting work and self-sacrifice on his behalf has killed her before he has been able to rescue her from it. Although it soon becomes obvious that m'man Tine has simply been taken to hospital, we are made aware here of how precarious José's life of extreme poverty is, and of the extraordinary level of material provision achieved by m'man Tine for her grandson. Despite the best efforts of the neighbouring women, the material preoccupations which characterized part one of the novel reappear here in m'man Tine's absence. Clothing and food, in particular, were a constant concern for José and the other children of 'la Rue Cases-Nègres'. While other children on the plantation frequently had little or no clothing to protect them from the sun, m'man Tine always ensured that José was clothed and clean: from the beginning, her determination that he should escape a life in the canefields has entailed ensuring that he presents himself and behaves 'comme un enfant bien élevé' (p. 15). It is for this reason that José, here, is ashamed of himself when he fails to wash or change his clothes (l. 36).

More pressing, however, is the issue of hunger. This, too, was a constant preoccupation on the plantation, for very few workers could afford to provide sufficient food for themselves and their children, and m'man Tine often went without food in order that José should eat. Even so, this is neither the first time nor the last that he has experienced hunger so extreme that he has been unable to work adequately at school: 'mon estomac, toute ma poitrine m'en fait mal et ma main tremble, incapable d'écrire' (l. 71). It is for this reason that the narrative slows down when José recounts the daily ritual of his teacher's breakfast. Unable to write, he is transfixed by the sight of her eating bread and hot chocolate. He describes the food itself, the teacher's facial features and the action of her eating in precise detail, and with such clarity that the scene comes back to him later in the day as a quasi-hallucination when he is hungry again (l. 78).

His portrayal of this scene draws attention to one of the book's constant themes: the link between material deprivation and the ability to benefit from education. This, in turn, is important because of the novel's overriding faith in the power of education. A French education, and therefore at least some degree of assimilation, is consistently depicted as the sole means of achieving the social advancement necessary to escape from poverty and the apparently fixed social hierarchy of the Caribbean. Such a conviction is unsurprising, given that the novel was written only four years after the law of departmentalization, at a time when assimilation and the benefits of becoming part of France were seen as the only way forward by the majority of the population, and especially by those who, like m'man Tine and her fellow plantation workers here, had seen little or no improvement in their living conditions since the time of slavery.

The minute description of the school teacher and her breakfast thus takes on a wider significance. The teacher herself is described as 'propre', 'clair[e]', 'pur[e] et tranquille', 'bien coiffé[e]' (l. 59), and the utensils with which she eats her breakfast – 'ce bol de porcelaine blanche. . . cette cuiller en argent, ce plateau en acajou verni' (l. 63) – are luxurious: she is clearly part of the world to which m'man Tine has been teaching José to aspire. The food itself is, of course, also quintessentially French: 'le pain est doré et crisse sous ses doigts' (l. 52), and the hot chocolate is 'onctueux, brun et laiteux . . . sucré, délicieux' (l. 56). When these descriptions are compared to those, in this extract and elsewhere, of the food that José eats – the local foods eaten by the black workers' slave ancestors, fruit, cassava flour, sweet potatoes, salt cod – it becomes clear just how alien it is to him. Fresh French bread, milk, hot chocolate and even, somewhat ironically, refined sugar are not yet part of the everyday diet of a poor black Martinican like himself and, in this period, were emblematic of the better lifestyle to which Antilleans aspired through a closer relationship with France. Even José, however dimly, is aware that there is a link between the Frenchness of the food to which he here aspires and the future assimilation that he can expect after gaining a French education. As he asks: 'Peut-être ne suis-je pas *encore bon* pour un tel déjeuner?' (l. 67, emphasis added).

He does not, however, dwell on such preoccupations long: he is well aware, even at this age, that it is not Mam'zelle Délice's fault that she cannot provide him with more food, and he is even more aware that his problems are minor in comparison with those of his friend Georges Roc or Jojo. One of the important things to emerge out of his new life in Petit-Bourg and at school is that he comes into contact with Martinicans who occupy different positions in the class-colour social hierarchy of which he had thus far been largely unaware. Jojo is one of his best friends, and is the illegitimate son of a mulatto (himself the illegitimate son of a *béké*) who has rejected Jojo's *câpresse* mother, a plantation worker, and married a paler-skinned mulatto woman with whom he has taken his son to live. If José has now embarked upon the path of social advancement, Jojo is a victim of his father's own precarious social position as a member of the mulatto middle class, a position he must hold on to and aspire beyond. Unhappy and mistreated because darker-skinned than his father and stepmother, and discouraged from associating with 'des nègres' such as José, Jojo is nonetheless 'fortunate' to have been recognized by his father, and can be certain of his future position in the social hierarchy. He knows that, like his father, '[il] serai[t] contremaître à l'usine' (l. 99).

José, on the other hand, is confused about what his future will hold, for he knows that his education will save him from the canefields, but is as yet unable to envisage a realistic alternative. His vision of the future is thus rather like a socialist utopia, in which he, his grandmother and his mother will work alongside his employees, who will grow what food they need, have proper clothes and, most importantly, all go to school (l. 103). Childlike and naïve as such a vision seems, it is in keeping with the faith in the power of education as enabler of social change that has so far characterized José's life, and in fact demonstrates an extraordinary level of social awareness for a young child. Jojo, however, soon reminds him of reality, with the simple yet self-evident remark: 'tu ne pourras pas avoir tout ça; tu n'es pas blanc, tu n'es pas un béké' (l. 113). Unlike José, he is acutely aware of the link between class and colour, and realizes that, were José's dream to come true, the whole social order would crumble: 'Mais tes travailleurs, alors, ils seront presque aussi bien nourris et logés que les békés! Alors, n'y aura plus de nègres; et les békés, qu'est-ce qu'ils vont faire?' (l. 115). Jojo, however, runs away from home soon after this incident, never to return to school, and when José next encounters him, he has become a gardener, thus apparently proving that the social hierarchy is not necessarily as fixed as he had believed it to be. However, when we remember that Jojo is illegitimate, it is in fact unsurprising that, as has been the case from slave times on, he should have followed the condition of his *mother* and ended up working the *békés'* land, thus in fact confirming the established order of things. What is significant, however, both in the eventual fate of Jojo and in the boys' visions of the future here, is that education is confirmed as the only way in which the established social order may be changed. José, in his eventual educational success and elevated level of social awareness, is at this stage in Martinique's history an exceptional example of what in the 1950s could only be hoped would become a more generalized, post-departmentalization phenomenon.

Further reading

Zobel, Joseph, *Diab'là* (Paris: Nouvelles Editions Latines, 1940).
—— *La Fête à Paris* (Paris: La Table ronde, 1953) (sequel to *La Rue Cases-Nègres*).
—— *Et si la mer n'était pas bleue* (Paris: Editions Caribéennes, 1982).

César, Sylvie, *La Rue cases-nègres: du roman au film* (Paris: L'Harmattan, 1994).
Kande, Sylvie, 'Renunciation and victory in *Black Shack Alley*', *Research in African Literatures* 25, 2 (1994), 33–50.
Minot, Leslie Anne, 'Questions of narrative mastery: Joseph Zobel and Simone Schwarz-Bart', in Maryse Condé (ed.), *L'Héritage de Caliban* (Paris: Editions Jasor, 1992), pp. 165–74.
Ormerod, Beverley, *An Introduction to the French Caribbean Novel* (London: Heinemann, 1985), Chapter 3.
Warner, Keith Q., 'Emasculation on the plantation: a reading of Joseph Zobel's *La Rue Cases-Nègres*', *College Language Association Journal* 32, 1 (1988), 38–44.
Wylie, Hal, 'Joseph Zobel's use of Negritude and social realism', *World Literature Today* 56, 1 (1982), 61–4.

Language and style

Following the departure of his grandmother for hospital, life for José becomes extremely harsh. The details of his existence are described in this passage, which may be divided into three sub-sections, two of which shed light on a different aspect of the privations the young boy suffers, and the third of which illustrates his dreams of prosperity. Lines 1–35 describe the immediate consequences of m'man Tine's absence, his being cared for by Mam'zelle Délice. Lines 36–83 deal with the terrible sense of hunger that overwhelms him, lines 84–117 with his relationship with Jojo and his ambitions.

Different linguistic features characterize each of these sub-sections. In the first it is the good-natured activity of the women that is focused on, especially of Mam'zelle Délice who, despite her infirmity, does her best to provide for José's physical needs. This activity is conveyed via the verb-dominated sentences which sprinkle the section: first of all l. 10 – Mam'zelle Mézélie's provision of food and shelter until the return of Mam'zelle Délice – with three verbs; then l. 16 – similar provision of food and shelter for José – with four verbs, then l. 23 – Mam'zelle Délice's daily routine caring for José – with six main verbs. These verbs of action, set in very concise clauses, aptly underscore the busyness of the womenfolk. The emphasis upon food in the first sub-section (ll. 10, 16, 23) forms a link with the second sub-section, where food, or the lack of it, becomes the main topic.

The most notable linguistic feature of this second sub-section is the use of an exceptionally rich vocabulary to describe the alluring food eaten by the school teacher. This is achieved mainly through the use of adjectives. Since attributive adjectives are extremely rare in the first sub-section, the stylistic contrast between the two episodes is striking. Moreover, when decorative adjectives are opposed to functional ones, this paucity of occurrence in the first sub-section becomes even more apparent. The only decorative adjectives in ll. 1–35 are 'pauvre' (l. 8), 'froide' (l. 10), 'désagréable' (l. 33). By contrast, the second sub-section is full of such adjectives, not only applying to food but also to the protagonists. In l. 37, José uses three decorative adjectives to describe his own appearance: 'j'étais crasseux, dégoûtant, honteux de moi-même'; and later on the school teacher is subject to José's descriptive powers:

> La main dont elle tient la belle cuiller est fine et propre. Ses cheveux sont bien coiffés. Son visage est clair, velouté par un nuage de poudre, ses yeux brillent d'un éclat pur et tranquille, et sa bouche qu'elle entrouvre au passage de la cuiller est la chose à la fois la plus jolie et la plus cruelle.
>
> (l. 58)

However, it is the topic of food which receives the most detailed treatment, combining adjectives with adjectival expressions, beginning with his nostalgia for the meals which used to be prepared by m'man Tine and are no more:

> Je n'avais plus mon grand pot de café clair bien sucré, avec de la farine de manioc, mais un peu de café au fond d'un pot en fer-blanc, un morceau de légume cuit de la veille et grillé dans la braise le matin.
>
> (l. 40, also l. 68)

This is followed by his yearning for enormous quantities of sweet coffee: he has 'une immense envie de manger, de me régaler d'énormes pots de café sucré de grosses poignées de farine de manioc' (l. 45). His description of the school teacher's breakfast (ll. 52–7) is impressive by its descriptive power but disturbing because it is not for him (also ll. 66, 78). The switch from imperfect tense (l. 50) to historic present (l. 52), making the event seem to be happening in the here and now, serves to underline the acute feeling of deprivation that assails José. An atmosphere of abundance, opulence and gracious living is created which is all the more poignant because José is excluded from it.

Dreams of vanilla-flavoured hot chocolate and crusty bread lead on to dreams of a future of prosperity, fine clothes and education for all in the third sub-section. Jojo's projects are announced in direct speech, with the first-person pronoun featuring as subject of seven of the eight clauses, and always in first position (or after a conjunction). On the other hand, José chooses to report his own projects as free indirect discourse, thereby making them appear even more dreamlike (compare l. 103). The dreams have in common the fact that the two boys wish to live with the adults who have been kind to them (ll. 100, 109), but differ in that the former desires the death of the parents who raised him, whereas José does not – the use of 'mort' both unites and separates the two boys' dreams. José is able to demonstrate his descriptive powers again in his presentation of this dream with a wealth of detail concerning the crops, animals and management of the estate. Sadly, this dream bubble is burst by Jojo's superior knowledge of the political and social realities of the island, and poor José is left 'dérouté, honteux, un peu triste' (l. 117). The use of three adjectives here parallels the three which occurred at the beginning of the second sub-section (l. 37).

The text is expressed in the first person, telling the story of young José. However, there is rarely a match between the language used in the text and the linguistic expectations that a seven-year-old arouses. It is tempting to assume that the story is told at some years' distance from the events, but at times, especially ll. 103–10, through the use of conditional tenses, and ll. 52–77, with the use of the historic present and perfect tenses (rather than the past historic with which the extract commences and continues for the first sub-section), it is clear that the events are being reported as if they were happening contemporaneously. There are many lexical items, especially abstract ones, which are unlikely to form part of a seven-year old's vocabulary. A few examples will suffice: 'J'optai pour la seconde proposition' (l. 18), 'je ne sais si je n'éprouvai pas quelque fierté d'être son égal par le malheur dont j'étais ainsi frappé' (l. 28), 'ils abusaient de mon obligeance' (l. 34), 'le mirage du soulagement suprême' (l. 80); adjectives used in the descriptions of the school teacher's food and appearance also have an 'adult' flavour. Similarly, certain syntactic constructions seem inappropriate, for example: 'Ne la reverrais-je plus?' (l. 4), 'A peine étais-je entré en classe que s'emparait de moi une immense envie de manger' (l. 45); and many other occasions where the structure of the sentence betokens careful planning, for example: 'sa bouche qu'elle entrouvre au passage de la cuiller est la chose à la fois la plus jolie et la plus cruelle' (l. 60), 'Mais lorsque, un peu plus tard, l'accès de faim me reprenait, c'était sous l'apparence d'un grand bol de chocolat au lait, fleurant la vanille, avec du pain doré, que se présentait le mirage du soulagement suprême' (l. 78). Zobel thus succeeds in creating a tension between the mature author and the child autobiographical narrator, as well as emphasizing the exceptional linguistic abilities that will eventually provide José with a way out of his position at the bottom of the Martinican social hierarchy.

Chapter 20

Simone Schwarz-Bart

Pluie et vent sur Télumée Miracle (Paris: Seuil, 1972), pp. 58–63.

Se tournant vers moi, man Cia m'aperçut enfin, me dévisagea longuement et se mit à m'embrasser, un premier baiser sur le front, pour elle-même, dit-elle, pour la faveur de son plaisir; puis un deuxième sur la joue gauche, puisque j'étais de celles dont on ne tire pas la ficelle pour les faire danser, un troisième pour que la joue droite ne soit pas jalouse, et un dernier parce que, elle le voyait déjà, j'étais une vaillante petite négresse. Elle ajouta, me couvrant de son beau regard tranquille: tu seras sur terre comme une cathédrale.

Les deux vieilles commencèrent à parler, sous le grand manguier, tandis que je regardais avidement man Cia, à la recherche de ce qui en elle différait des autres humains. J'examinais ses doigts aux ongles courbes striés dans la longueur, comme des griffes, ses pieds grisâtres à talons larges et proéminents, ce petit corps tout en os, presque d'enfant, ce visage patiné, écaillé par endroits et plus je la voyais, plus je la trouvais pareille à tout le monde, une quelconque petite vieille de Fond-Zombi. Cependant elle avait tout de même quelque chose, l'amie de Reine Sans Nom, et ce qu'elle avait, man Cia? elle avait ces yeux-là . . . immenses, transparents, de ces yeux dont on dit qu'ils peuvent tout voir, tout supporter, car ils ne se ferment pas même en sommeil.

Comme je l'étudiais ainsi, la dévisageant à mon aise, soudain elle braqua sur moi son œil transparent de sorcière et dit:

Enfant, pourquoi me regardes-tu ainsi? . . . veux-tu que je t'apprenne à te transformer en chien, en crabe, en fourmi? . . . veux-tu prendre tes distances avec les humains, dès aujourd'hui, les tenir à longueur de gaffe?

J'aurais aimé soutenir l'action de ce regard si clair, tranquille, rieur par en dessous, qui semblait démentir le sérieux des paroles prononcées. Mais une grande peur me retint et je courbai honteusement la tête, murmurai d'une voix entrecoupée:

Vous le voyez bien que je ne suis pas une cathédrale . . . et si vous cherchez la vaillante négresse, elle n'est pas là.

Grand-mère fronça les sourcils:

Ah, c'est tout ce que vous avez à vous dire, par un si beau dimanche, quel gaspillage de lumière . . .

Maintenant, grand-mère était penchée sur son amie et lui racontait un rêve, voici . . . elle se baigne dans une rivière, des dizaines de sangsues courent autour de sa tête et l'une d'elles se fixant à son front, grand-mère se dit: à cet endroit, j'ai du mauvais sang que la bête est en train de pomper . . . mais n'était-ce pas sa vie que la sangsue aspirait, n'était-ce pas signe de sa mort prochaine? . . . conclut-elle avec un sourire inquiet.

Quelle mort? . . . s'écria man Cia d'un ton alerte, la bête a pompé ton mauvais sang et voilà tout. Quand ton heure sera venue, tu verras tes dents tomber en songe, tu verras ton corps et ton linge filer dans la rivière et tu te retrouveras dans un pays inconnu, avec des arbres et des fleurs que tu n'as jamais vus: ne te fie à aucun autre rêve que celui-là. En attendant, ma chère, caprice de mort ou caprice de vivant, l'odeur de cette daube qui mijote au feu m'enivre, et je sens déjà la viande qui fond dans ma bouche, allons . . .

Nous nous levâmes en riant, et quand nous revînmes un peu plus tard, chacune son écuelle de daube fumante à la main, Reine Sans Nom soupira:

Ah, ah, maudite, comme tu t'entends à parler, avec toi deux mots quatre paroles,x et il n'y a pas plus de mort que de banjo!

Et ce disant elle s'assit un peu brusquement, secouée d'un rire aigrelet, l'écuelle déversant un peu de sauce à ses pieds.

Ah, dit man Cia, les morts se servent en premier, maintenant?

Tu le sais, répondit grand-mère en souriant, Jérémie a toujours eu une faiblesse pour la daube de cochon planche.

Et comment va-t-il? s'enquit gravement man Cia.

Il ne m'a pas oubliée, dit grand-mère heureuse, il vient me voir toutes les nuits, sans faute. Il n'a pas changé, il est pareil que de son vivant . . .

Mais il va bien? reprit son amie.

Il va très bien, assura gravement grand-mère.

La clarté du jour nous pénétrait, la lumière arrivait par ondes à travers le feuillage que le vent secouait et nous nous regardions, étonnées de nous trouver là, toutes les trois, au milieu du courant de la vie, et tout à coup man Cia éclata de rire:

Crois-tu, Toussine, que si nous étions encore esclaves, nous mangerions cette bonne daube de cochon, le cœur si content? . . .

Ses yeux se firent tristes, ironiques, ils parurent tout à coup délavés par le soleil, la pluie et les larmes, toutes les choses qu'ils avaient vues et qui s'étaient incrustées jusqu'au fond même de sa cervelle. Surprise, je me risquai à l'interroger:

Man Cia chère, à quoi peut bien ressembler un esclave, et à quoi peut ressembler un maître?

Si tu veux voir un esclave, dit-elle froidement, tu n'as qu'à descendre au marché de la Pointe et regarder les volailles ficelées dans les cages, avec leurs yeux d'épouvante. Et si tu veux savoir à quoi ressemble un maître, tu n'as qu'à aller à

Galba, à l'habitation Belle-Feuille, chez les Desaragne. Ce ne sont que leurs descendants, mais tu pourras te faire une idée.

Que veux-tu qu'elle voie maintenant, à l'heure actuelle, man Cia? dit Reine Sans Nom. Elle ne verra rien, trois fois rien. Ces blancs-là sourient et on les salue, dans leur maison à colonnade qui n'a pas sa pareille de par ici. Mais qui dirait à les voir aujourd'hui si souriants, que leur ancêtre le Blanc des blancs vous encerclait un nègre dans ses deux bras, et lui faisait éclater la rate, comme ça? . . .

Et pourquoi faisait-il ça? dis-je effrayée.

Man Cia réfléchit longuement:

Autrefois, dit-elle, un nid de fourmis mordantes avait peuplé la terre et voilà, elles s'étaient elles-mêmes appelées hommes . . . pas plus que ça . . .

Reine Sans Nom s'appuyait contre man Cia, et s'efforçant de lui arracher un peu de son amertume, elle dit:

Qui peut reprocher au chien d'être attaché, et s'il est attaché, comment lui éviter le fouet?

S'il est attaché, dit man Cia, il lui faut se résigner, car on le fouettera. C'est depuis longtemps que pour nous libérer Dieu habite le ciel, et que pour nous cravacher il habite la maison des blancs, à Belle-Feuille.

C'est une bien belle parole en ce jour, dit grand-mère, et après cette tristesse en voici une autre: voir s'éteindre le feu et les petits chiens s'amuser dans la cendre.

Avec ta permission, mon amie, je dirai que c'est là un morceau de tristesse, pas une tristesse entière. La tristesse entière était le feu. Or le feu est éteint et cela fait bien longtemps que le Blanc des blancs est sous terre, viande avariée qui ne repoussera plus. D'ailleurs, la cendre elle-même n'est pas éternelle.

Les yeux brillants d'une fièvre étrange, Reine Sans Nom me regarda longuement et dit:

En vérité, la cendre n'est pas éternelle.

Les deux vieilles s'étaient tues, l'après-midi glissait, tout était clair, serein, au ciel et sur la terre. Reine Sans Nom et son amie Cia se tenaient appuyées l'une contre l'autre, les traits paisibles, assurés. Dans ce silence, je les regardais et je me demandais d'où venaient tous les feux, tous les éclats qu'elles tiraient de leurs vieilles carcasses rafistolées.

Un peu plus tard, nous fîmes un petit tour dans les bois, glanant des feuilles, des fruits sauvages, et man Cia semblait soudain toute pensive. Comme grand-mère et moi l'observions sans arrêt, attentives à toutes les ombres, toutes les lumières de son visage, nous vîmes que ça la gênait de penser devant nous, sans que nous sachions quelles idées se cachaient derrière son front. Alors grand-mère poussa un profond soupir, signifiant que notre visite s'achevait, et, se tournant vers l'enfant que j'étais, man Cia déclara . . . sois une vaillante petite négresse, un vrai tambour à deux faces, laisse la vie frapper, cogner, mais conserve toujours intacte la face du dessous. Grand-mère opina du chef et nous redescendîmes la pente aux herbes folles, agrippées l'une à l'autre. Le ciel était déjà tout bas, violet, et c'était l'heure où l'on sentait le vol exténué des phales et des phalènes dans l'air lourd. Aussitôt arrivée, je gagnai gravement le fond de la cour, me glissai sous une touffe de bambou en écartant les branches basses, jusqu'à me perdre dans la petite cage de feuillage. Pour la première fois de ma vie, je sentais que l'esclavage n'était pas un pays étranger, une région lointaine d'où venaient certaines personnes très anciennes, comme il en existait encore deux ou trois, à Fond-Zombi. Tout cela s'était déroulé ici même, dans nos mornes et nos vallons, et peut-être à côté de cette touffe de bambou, peut-être dans l'air que je respirais. Et je songeai aux rires de certains hommes, de certaines femmes, leurs petites quintes de toux résonnaient en moi, cependant qu'une musique déchirante s'élevait dans ma poitrine. Et j'écoutais encore les rires, je me demandais, je croyais entendre certaines choses, j'écartais les feuilles pour voir le monde du dehors, les lignes qui s'assombrissaient, le soir montant comme une exhalaison, effaçant toutes choses, la case d'abord, les arbres, les collines au loin, les pentes de la montagne dont le sommet flamboyait dans le ciel, bien que toute la terre fût plongée dans l'obscurité, déjà, sous les étoiles au scintillement tremblant, inquiet, irréel, qui semblaient posées là par erreur, comme tout le reste.

Text and context

A testament, primarily, to the strength of Guadeloupean women, *Pluie et vent sur Télumée Miracle* was inspired by the life of a woman named Fanotte, whom Schwarz-Bart knew as a child in Guadeloupe, and who represented for her a traditional, Antillean way of life which was beginning to disappear. This novel, for Schwarz-Bart, was a way of documenting the life of this woman, and paying homage to her and countless women like her who knew the same daily struggle for survival. Spanning the same years as did Fanotte's life – from around the turn of the twentieth century to the 1960s – the novel also represents a way of preserving a lifestyle for future generations of increasingly assimilated Antilleans.

This extract is taken from quite near the beginning of the novel, when Télumée is still a child, and has recently been sent by her mother to live with her grandmother Toussine, or Reine Sans Nom as she has been named by her community because of her incredible ability to survive trauma and hardship. In this episode, Reine Sans Nom takes her granddaughter to meet her closest friend, man Cia, 'une sorcière' – a healer respected for both her age and her wisdom, as the name 'man' (madame) signifies. Télumée has heard much about man Cia from the villagers who fear her magical powers, and is fascinated by her. What begins here is a relationship which will last throughout Télumée's life, and in which man Cia, alongside Reine Sans Nom, will nurture and encourage Télumée, and teach her how to take her place in the matrifocal lineage of Lougandor women – women who have always known how to survive the vicissitudes of life against all the odds. Thus, here, man Cia begins implanting in Télumée a self-confidence and will to survival, telling her that she is 'de celles dont on ne tire pas la ficelle pour les faire danser' (l. 3), 'une vaillante petite négresse' (l. 5), 'comme une cathédrale' (l. 7) and 'un vrai tambour à deux faces, [qui] laisse la vie frapper, cogner, mais conserve toujours intacte la face de dessous' (l. 112). Man Cia's predictions about

Télumée's future strength of character will, by the end of the novel, have been entirely fulfilled.

These predictions are significant for another reason, for they are part of the consistent oral, Creole quality of the novel. Here, as throughout her novel, Schwarz-Bart almost never includes any actual Creole words, but, rather – and somewhat ahead of her time[1] – she ensures that, though written in French, the narrative is shot through with Creole. Creole sayings, idioms and expressions, like man Cia's 'sois. . . un vrai tambour à deux faces' are in constant evidence, and all work to lend an oral quality to the narrative which may be unfamiliar to French readers but was highly familiar to the ordinary, Creole-speaking Antillean readers with whom this novel was so popular when it was first published.

A further way in which man Cia's advice to Télumée is significant is in the attitude that it displays towards life itself ('laisse la vie frapper, cogner', l. 113). Throughout the novel, 'la vie' is seen as a somewhat abstract, malevolent force, a constant cycle of good fortune and bad. Criticisms have been levelled at Schwarz-Bart because of this, and she has been accused of failing to pay sufficient attention to the historical reasons why life was hard for poor Blacks in this period. Yet here, as sporadically elsewhere, we are shown precisely the colonial past whose legacy now conditions the lives of ex-slaves and their descendants. The mention of the Desaragne family, in particular, is significant here, for man Cia uses these local *békés* to try to explain to Télumée the meaning of the word 'maître'. Reine Sans Nom objects that the present-day descendants of former slave owners have nothing to teach the younger descendants of slaves about the master–slave relationship: 'Ces blancs-là sourient et on les salue. . . qui dirait, à les voir aujourd'hui si souriants, que leur ancêtre le Blanc des blancs vous encerclait un nègre dans ses deux bras, et lui faisait éclater la rate, comme ça?' (l. 76). Despite the presence of a ten-year-old child, Reine Sans Nom does not hesitate in depicting the violence of slavery, a violence which terrifies Télumée but which will serve as an important lesson for her, especially since, when she is older, she will go to work as a servant in the Desaragne's house, and will be confronted by their continued contempt and condescension, as well as by M. Desaragne's attempt to rape her.

Slavery and the continuing colonial character of the relationship between ex-slaves and *békés* is also the subject of the somewhat allegorical conversation between man Cia and Reine Sans Nom which ensues here. This conversation – 'une bien belle parole' (l. 91) – is another example of the novel's oral, Creole quality, for in an attempt to explain Télumée's past to her in terms with which she might be familiar, it proceeds like a Creole *conte*, with animals taking the place of people, and natural disasters (here, fire) taking the place of historical events. There is a vast array of Antillean *contes* which, dating back from slavery or even from Africa, use this type of figurative language in order to tell stories about survival, rebellion, escape or the outwitting of the plantation owner, in language which would not have immediately aroused the suspicion of the Whites, convinced as they were of the Blacks' childlike inability to conceive of anything in complex terms. In this tale, and recalling the way in which Whites and Blacks were represented in colonial discourse itself, the Whites – 'un nid de fourmis' (l. 82) – have named themselves 'men', while slaves are figured as dogs (l. 92). Here, the two women use this figurative language to discuss something which, to them, is still too painful,

1 For a fuller discussion of the use of Creole in contemporary Guadeloupean and Martinican novels, see Chapter 17 and also the commentaries on the extract from Patrick Chamoiseau's *Chronique des sept misères* (Chapter 22).

and evokes too much bitterness, to be discussed directly and non-figuratively. In their tale, once a slave has been enslaved, there is little that he or she can do to prevent being mistreated by the Whites. Instead, 'il lui faut se résigner, car on le fouettera' (l. 88). And even after slavery has been abolished, all is not solved: 'après cette tristesse en voici une autre: voir s'éteindre le feu et les petits chiens s'amuser dans la cendre' (l. 91). The 'fire' that is slavery has not been extinguished sufficiently – its legacy, 'la cendre', continues to make life difficult for the freed slaves and their descendants. Their tale is not entirely pessimistic, however, for they are hopeful that 'la cendre n'est pas éternelle' (l. 97). Unfortunately, as we discover in the rest of the novel, the legacy of slavery is something which continues to exert its influence not only throughout the old women's lives, but also throughout that of Télumée.

The spirit of resignation which characterizes this conversation also characterizes the approach towards survival that Reine Sans Nom hands down to Télumée, and it is something for which Schwarz-Bart has again been criticized. This apparent representation of the black inhabitants of the Caribbean as able, and willing, to survive anything that they are faced with, has been seen by some as a worrying repetition of colonial myths about Blacks as 'beasts of burden' ideally suited to slavery. Moreover, the passivity of the 'chiens' in the women's tale could be seen to concur rather uncomfortably with the view that Guadeloupean history itself – the failure to prevent the reinstatement of slavery in 1802, as did Haiti; the preference for departmentalization rather than independence in 1946 – has been marked by passivity rather than resistance. Because of this, much historiographical and literary energy has gone into resuscitating heroic, rebellious figures – like Louis Delgrès[2] – who preferred to sacrifice their lives rather than resign themselves to simply surviving. Resignation and survival, in this tradition, become almost synonymous with cowardice, but for Schwarz-Bart this is too simplistic – and gendered – a reading. Throughout her novel, she portrays the pointlessness of grandiose, heroic (and usually male) acts of resistance, and consistently holds up an alternative model of resistance which is based on the ability to survive at all costs. This, of course, is a form of resistance, both in this novel and in reality, which has most usually been practised by women, who have historically been obliged to ensure the day-to-day survival not only of themselves but also of their children.

This is the model of resistance into which Télumée is here beginning to be initiated, and upon returning home, she takes time to think about what she has learnt from man Cia. As she begins to connect herself with the slave past that she has heard about, she seeks shelter 'dans la petite cage de feuillage' (l. 118) of a bamboo tree, thus putting herself in the position of the 'les volailles ficelées dans les cages' (l. 71) to which man Cia had initially compared slaves. It is a revelation to Télumée that slavery happened within the familiar surroundings of what has until now been a happy and contented life, that it occurred 'ici même, dans *nos* mornes et *nos* vallons' (l. 122, emphasis added). She suddenly feels a deeper connection not only with her surroundings, in which she has always felt entirely at home, but with her past, and with the links between the two. When darkness falls, suddenly, as it does in the Caribbean, it seems as if it is 'effaçant toutes choses' (l. 128), wiping away the relatively harmonious world that she has known until this point, and directing her eyes beyond it, up at the stars, forcing her to look further than her own experience and her own small village now that her horizons have begun to be broadened.

2 For a fuller discussion of the historical figure Louis Delgrès, see Chapter 17.

Further reading

Schwarz-Bart, Simone, *Ti Jean l'horizon* (Paris: Seuil, 1979).
—— *Ton beau capitaine* (Paris: Seuil, 1987).
Schwarz-Bart, Simone and Schwarz-Bart, André, *Un plat de porc aux bananes vertes* (Paris: Seuil, 1967).

Bernabé, Jean, 'Le travail de l'écriture chez Simone Schwarz-Bart: contribution à l'étude de la diglossie littéraire créole-français', *Présence africaine* 121–2 (1982), 166–79.
Condé, Maryse (ed.), *L'Héritage de Caliban* (Paris: Editions Jasor, 1992). See in particular the chapters by Priska Degras and Leslie Anne Minot.
McKinney, Kitzie, 'Memory, voice and metaphor in the works of Simone Schwarz-Bart', in Mary-Jean Green, Karen Gould, Micheline Rice-Maximin, Keith Walker and Jack Yeager (eds), *Postcolonial Subjects: Francophone Women Writers* (Minneapolis: Minneapolis University Press, 1996), pp. 22–41.
Ormerod, Beverley, *An Introduction to the French Caribbean Novel* (London: Heinemann, 1985), Chapter 5.
Proulx, Patrice, 'Situer le "moi" féminin dans *Pluie et vent sur Télumée Miracle*', in Suzanne Rinne, Joëlle Vitiello and Ginette Adamson (eds), *Elles écrivent des Antilles (Haïti, Guadeloupe, Martinique)* (Paris: L'Harmattan, 1997), pp. 135–43.
Rosello, Mireille, *Littérature et identité créole aux Antilles* (Paris: Karthala, 1992), Chapter 3.

Language and style

This passage, like the rest of the novel, is narrated from the perspective of the eponymous character, Télumée. However, here, the only actual passages of speech that Télumée records of herself involve (highly pertinent) questions – 'Man Cia chère, à quoi peut bien ressembler un esclave, et à quoi peut ressembler un maître?' (l. 68, also l. 80); there is also an indirect question – 'je me demandais d'où venaient tous les feux, tous les éclats qu'elles tiraient de leurs vieilles carcasses rafistolées' (l. 103). Otherwise she observes, and her extremely keen sense of observation is represented by a multitude of verbs and occasional nouns relating to sight: in the first nineteen lines eleven such expressions occur: 'aperçut' (l. 1), 'dévisagea' (l. 1), 'regard' (l. 6), 'regardais' (l. 9), 'examinais' (l. 10), 'voyais' (l. 12), 'trouvais' (l. 13), 'voir' (l. 16), 'étudiais' (l. 18), 'dévisageant' (l. 18), 'braqua . . . son œil' (l. 18). It may be that for a child external appearance is all-important in giving insights into an understanding of adults' behaviour and values. Indeed, an obvious characteristic of Télumée is her fascination with the older women, with man Cia in particular, and in the first part of the passage, on a number of occasions, she submits certain of man Cia's actions or physical details to microscopic examination – the four kisses (l. 2), her appearance, especially her hands and feet (l. 10), her eyes (l. 15, also later, l. 64), her look (l. 23). An evocative concentration of adjectives is marshalled to describe her appearance. The same detailed analysis is also deployed for Reine Sans Nom's dream.

Télumée is beginning to discover her destiny as the older women take her under their wing. There is a progression from introduction to man Cia, approval by a kiss, observation from the outside as the older women enjoy some complicity together, then inclusion (l. 59, 'nous nous regardions') and induction (answers to her questions). The complicity of the older women is brought out through verbs suggesting touching, e.g. 'grand-mère était penchée sur son amie' (l. 31), 'Reine Sans Nom s'appuya contre man Cia' (l. 84, also l. 102); Télumée is included when they all cling to each other: 'nous redescendîmes la pente aux herbes folles, agrippées l'une à l'autre' (l. 114). In addition to the physical description of the relationship between the protagonists, its spontaneity and open expression is evident. This is displayed through expressions of seriousness on the one hand and of happiness on the other. In the passage 'gravement' occurs three times (ll. 53, 57, 117), 'sérieux' once (l. 24) and 'froidement' once (l. 70). However, such expressions are more than counterbalanced by others evoking happiness and laughter. 'Rieur/rire' (both noun and verb) occur six times (ll. 23, 44, 48, 61, 123, 126), 'sourire' twice (ll. 36, 51). The disturbing effect of man Cia's witch's look is belied by the twinkle in her eye (l. 23). Humour is an integral part of the relationship of the older women: e.g. 'Et ce disant elle s'assit un peu brusquement, secouée d'un rire aigrelet, l'écuelle déversant un peu de sauce à ses pieds. – Ah, dit man Cia, les morts se servent en premier, maintenant?' (l. 48, also l. 63). Spontaneous switching between moods, from seriousness to laughter, is also apparent, for example: 'Il va très bien, assura gravement grand-mère' (l. 57); 'man Cia éclata de rire' (l. 60).

There is evidence in the passage of oral prototypes or at least of oral patterns underlying the rhythms and structures of the French, what might be called concealed Creole in the text. Expressions such as 'Quand ton heure sera venue, tu verras tes dents tomber en songe, tu verras ton corps et ton linge filer dans la rivière et tu te retrouveras dans un pays inconnu, avec des arbres et des fleurs que tu n'as jamais vus' (l. 38) and 'Elle ne verra rien, trois fois rien' (l. 76) evoke an atmosphere of Creole story-telling: all the examples occur in spoken sections. Yet another example is supplied by the tale of the dogs (l. 86). A Creole original is sometimes suggested by unorthodox French syntax, e.g. 'caprice de mort ou caprice de vivant' (l. 41), 'avec toi deux mots quatre paroles, et il n'y a pas plus de mort que de banjo!' (l. 46). Occasionally an expression in French is a reworking and refocusing of an originally Creole expression.'[S]ois . . . un vrai tambour à deux faces' (l. 112), for example, normally has a derogatory connotation, but has been manipulated here so that it becomes endued with a powerful positive force. This practice serves the three-fold purpose of preserving and highlighting the Creole setting, both linguistic and cultural, of the narrative; of allowing non-Creole speakers to get a glimpse of the allusive, inventive nature of Creole and of ensuring that the novel seems authentically Creole to a Creole-speaking readership.[3]

A number of other linguistic and stylistic features not necessarily linked to the use of Creole are also apparent in this text. There is the frequent use of doublets, often juxtaposed without a conjunction, focusing attention upon the point being described, for example: 'je me demandais d'où venaient tous les feux, tous les éclats qu'elles tiraient de leurs vieilles carcasses' (l. 104), 'attentives à toutes les ombres, toutes les lumières de son visage' (l. 108, also ll. 16, 25, 55, 65, 102, 106, 112, 113, 116, 120). Words with particular significance reappear at some distance from each other, giving the text strong internal cohesion: 'dévisager', used of man Cia staring at Télumée (l. 1) and later Télumée reciprocating (l. 18); Fond-Zombi (ll. 13, 121), 'feuilles/feuillage', as Télumée takes refuge among the leaves (l. 119); then, as her awareness of her destiny increases, she peeps out from among them (l. 127), and light (understanding) filters through them (l. 58), 'cage', holding fowls/slaves (l. 71); and imprisoning Télumée (l. 119). The spontaneous nature of a young person's narrative bursts through on a number of occasions, e.g. 'Cependant elle avait tout de même quelque chose, l'amie de Reine Sans Nom, et ce qu'elle avait, man Cia?' (l. 14, also l. 104). It is the final sentence which provides a fitting climax to the passage. Télumée's initiation into her vocation and her tentative adoption of it are seen in terms of the familiar, the homely, as the earthly disappears from view and is replaced by more distant signals, 'tremblant, inquiet, irréel', (l. 131).

3 For a discussion of the issue of readership and Creole/French bilingualism in the Caribbean DOM, see Chapter 17.

Chapter 21

Daniel Maximin

L'Isolé Soleil (Paris: Seuil, 1981), pp. 15–18.

Le pied de letchis

Depuis la mort du mille-pattes et de l'avion, tu n'es plus remontée dans le manguier, ton oreiller de verdure entre les draps du ciel et de la mer.

C'est sur le pied de letchis, planté il y a deux siècles, juste derrière la terrasse de l'habitation, seul à côté du prunier de Cythère, que tu t'es embusquée depuis lors contre la conspiration des femmes de la maison qui t'encerclent dans leur giron pour te réduire à leur condition.

Elles te croient toujours fourrée dans un livre comme avant, satisfaites que tu aies renoncé aux jupes et corsages pour y grimper en blue-jean et blouse de coton blanc, car elles savent les taches de letchis encore plus tenaces que celle des mangues et des cannes.

Seul ton grand-père Gabriel connaît ton secret: le pied de letchis est devenu ton arbre d'écriture, et tu caches dans le couvre-lit de ta mère deux gros carnets: *Le Cahier de J . . .*, et *l'Aire de la mer* dans lesquels tu notes en douce des idées et des images pour le roman que tu as décidé d'écrire pour faire revivre les pères disparus de notre histoire, depuis l'éruption de Delgrès jusqu'à celle du Boeing.

Tu as appris que ce n'est pas la crainte de la folie qui nous forcera à mettre en berne le drapeau de l'imagination: car tu as découvert dans le dernier numéro de *Tropiques*, annoté par ta mère, ce poème écrit par Suzanne Césaire, le mois même de ta naissance, dans lequel elle décrit, des années avant l'heure, la double chute de ton arbre et de l'avion:

«La consternation a saisi les objets et les êtres épargnés à la limite du vent. Au cœur du volcan tout a craqué, tout s'est écroulé dans le bruit de déchirure des grandes manifestations. Puis les radios se sont tues. La grande queue de palme de vent frais s'est déroulée quelque part dans la stratosphère, là où personne n'ira suivre les folles irisations et les ondes de lumière violette.

La mer de nuages n'est plus vierge depuis qu'y est passé l'avion.

Tu as depuis ce jour-là un vêtement d'étincelles, chacun de tes muscles exprime de manière personnelle une parcelle du désir éparpillé sur le manguier en fleur.»

En vérité, tels les fruits du sablier qui éclatent comme une grenade à leur maturité, ton père est mort dans l'accident d'avion: 22 juin 62, en compagnie de deux combattants de notre autonomie: Niger et Catayé.

Tu as failli te laisser mourir, sans boire ni manger. Mais tes yeux ont su voir les désirs préservés sous le grand camouflage des larmes inassouvies, la pluie a rafraîchi ta fièvre, le vent a ramené ton cœur à son logis, et ton grand-père t'a retenue dans la chaleur de sa main.

Ton père a explosé tout seul, sans son orchestre ni son piano, mais avec le journal secret qu'il apportait pour le faire lire à toi seule d'abord: *(«Tu as les yeux les plus sévères du monde devant le mensonge et les plus indulgents devant le jour, aussi je t'apporte sans trop de crainte mon journal de voyage: Désirades, quelques notes retenues sur la portée de ma vie. Je ne resterai pas longtemps au pays, car j'ai un grand projet sur l'histoire des Antilles à travers notre musique. Pour l'histoire, d'ailleurs, je compte bien sur l'aide de Mademoiselle-je-sais-tout-ce-qu'il-y-a-dans-les-livres! Il faudra aussi que j'aille dans les Grands-Fonds rafraîchir mes oreilles de gros-ka et de quadrille marie-galantais. Mais nous aurons bien du temps pour nos promenades et nos boléros. Ton père prodigue. Paris, le 12 juin.»)*

Il était musicien, saxophoniste, jazz, biguines et afro-cubain, selon les soirs et les pays. Il partit en dissidence clandestine en 1943, par la Dominique et les Etats-Unis, pour fuir l'air vicié des îles pétainisées; il resta à New York au Service d'accueil des volontaires antillais de la France libre, et parcourut depuis toutes les îles et les villes où il trouva à jouer la musique de son cœur: Cuba, Harlem, Londres, Paris, Haïti où ta mère et lui se rencontrèrent une dernière fois pour te donner la vie.

Tout ce qui reste de lui, c'est ce bracelet – une tortue à tête de bélier – envoyé de Harlem à ton grand-père pour célébrer ta naissance orpheline.

Ton père musicien est mort accidentellement. Mais tu crois que ton père poète, lui, s'est suicidé, car il portait dans l'étui de son saxophone les trois uniques cahiers du journal de sa vie. Comment peut-on confier toute sa vie rêvée à l'avion qui transporte déjà sa vie réelle? Il n'y a que le vent qui vole sans jamais se poser. La vie est sans pitié: la mort la punira un jour.

Il devait tout te réapprendre: danser le gros-ka et parler le créole, tout ce qui t'est refusé par la conspiration bienveillante de ceux qui veulent te bâtir un bonheur aliéné dans le bon-français et les désirs d'espace à jamais refoulés sur les plages dos à la mer. Tu recevais une nouvelle photo à chaque anniversaire, et cette année, pour la première fois depuis tes treize ans fêtés au club La Habana en compagnie de ses amis musiciens de Paris, il devait être présent. Mais voilà que ton soleil est parti loin vers les étoiles, imaginant que tu rêves à la folie de ce roman d'outre-amour pour ton désir en rade.

Alors, il le faudra: tu seras sans pays natal, comme les fruits et les oiseaux, dont tu prendras les couleurs et les chants pour refaire l'histoire de ton pays. Tu caresseras la vie comme les fougères, chanteras comme les palmistes sous le vent, lutteras seule dressée sur tes racines comme le figuier-maudit, tes lianes seront le rideau protecteur des révoltes, le poison de tes mancenilliers attirera la soif des chiens de garde.

Tu noirciras toutes les pages blanchies de ses cendres avec les couleurs naturelles à ta portée. Tu te méfieras hautement des nuages. Les nuages sont nos ennemis, les bisons blancs de nos prairies, le coton de notre esclavage. Tu te souviendras que les oiseaux sans mémoire qui plongent le bec dans les capsules de coton deviennent aveugles et condamnés au sol, car le coton est le manteau de Dieu, et Dieu a ainsi voulu punir les oiseaux et les Nègres qui l'ont voulu déraciner avec la complicité des vers, de la lune, du soleil et du vent.

Tu enfonceras tes racines jusqu'à trouver la source des feux de joie: un conte, un poème, une danse, une chanson. Tu ouvriras tes yeux, tes oreilles, ta bouche et tes mains à l'histoire de tes pères, et tu n'omettras pas de faire parler les mères, car elles ont des racines puisqu'elles portent des fruits.

Tu ouvriras les tiroirs de notre histoire confisquée, ceux d'héroïsme et de lâcheté, ceux de la faim, de la peur et de l'amour; tu rafraîchiras la mémoire des témoignages et des récits, tu mettras la vérité au service de l'imaginaire et non pas le contraire.

Tu écriras loin de tout désespoir, qui est le luxe des peuples saturés. A ton âge, tu sais déjà que c'est le désesepoir qui agrandit les déserts.

Chaque fois que tu oublieras de décrire la nature tropicale non pas comme un décor, mais comme un personnage de ton histoire, qui a aussi ses révoltes et ses lâchetés, qui offre trop de fleurs aux jardiniers, et trop d'anses aux caravelles, alors tu te souviendras que les pays où il fait trop beau sont comme des ventres maternels hostiles aux renaissances.

Text and context

L'Isolé Soleil is a complex and difficult novel, full of literary and historical references and written in an experimental mosaic of styles. Extracts from actual newspapers, poems, history books and folk tales, as well as from the letters, diary entries and novels of the various narrators, all make up its six very different parts. This extract is taken from the beginning of the novel, in which Marie-Gabriel, the main narrator, sets out her plans for a novel which she is about to embark upon, extracts from which we will later read as part of *L'Isolé Soleil*. As eventually becomes clear, Marie-Gabriel's novel mirrors that of Maximin both in content and in structure, and this extract introduces the key issues with which both Marie-Gabriel and the novel as a whole will be concerned: history and historiography; Guadeloupean and diaspora culture; the natural environment of the Caribbean.

As this second chapter opens, Marie-Gabriel is recovering from the news that her father has just died in a plane crash on his way to visit her on her seventeenth birthday. The plane crash alluded to here is one which actually took place, in June 1962. It was Guadeloupe's first major air disaster, and killed, among others, two pro-autonomy activists, Paul Niger and Justin Catayé, to whom Marie-Gabriel alludes here (l. 31). Here, as in reality, the plane burst into flames when flying over Guadeloupe's volcano, Soufrière, and the accident was initially taken to be a volcanic eruption. Within the context of the Guadeloupean history which is eventually rewritten both by Marie-Gabriel and throughout *L'Isolé Soleil* as a whole, this link between the 'eruption' of the plane and that of the volcano is highly significant. The volcano has come to be associated with the maroons who set up their illicit, and inaccessible, communities in that part of the island. More particularly, Soufrière has come to be associated with Louis Delgrès, mentioned here by Marie-Gabriel, and the blaze of gunfire as he and his followers jumped from the cliffs at nearby Fort Matouba.[1]

Marie-Gabriel learns of her paternal ancestors' involvement with Delgrès's revolt from the *Cahier de J. . .* sent to her by her friend Adrien. Unearthing it as she does, here, from her 'arbre d'écriture', she will use it as the basis of the first part of her novel, which we will read as part two of *L'Isolé Soleil*. Her novel as a whole, as she points out here, will span the years from the first explosion at Matouba to that of the plane over Soufrière, and she will write it 'pour faire revivre les pères disparus de notre histoire' (l. 14). Her own most immediate 'père disparu' is obviously her father, who died carrying the journal of his life, *Désirades*, and with unfulfilled plans for his own '*histoire des Antilles à travers notre musique*' (l. 42). Recalling the title of her father's journal, and the island of Désirade, just off Guadeloupe, from which his ancestors came, Marie-Gabriel proposes in her own novel to make up, in part, for her father's 'désir en rade' (l. 68). Her novel will therefore be a rehabilitation both of Guadeloupe's wider history and of her own family history, via the story of her paternal ancestors. For us, as readers of Maximin's novel, fact – real, historical details about Guadeloupe's past – will thus be supplemented by fiction. As with the treatment of the plane crash here, the story of Marie-Gabriel and her ancestors fills those gaps left by colonial history.

As Marie-Gabriel points out here, however, the particular history that she wants to write 'n'omettr[a] pas de faire parler les mères' (l. 84), and this is certainly what occurs both in the other extract from her novel which we read as part five of Maximin's novel, and throughout *L'Isolé Soleil*. Part five is based on the other journal which Marie-Gabriel keeps hidden in the lychee tree, '*L'Aire de la mer*' (l. 13). This becomes 'L'Air de la mère', and tells of her mother's life, her meeting with Marie-Gabriel's father, and her death giving birth to Marie-Gabriel. It is only through the telling of her mother's story that Marie-Gabriel is finally able to address herself as 'je', as she symbolically gives birth to herself through retracing her maternal history and situating it, once again, within the wider history of Guadeloupe.

History is not the only element of Guadeloupe's past – and present – to be rehabilitated: Guadeloupean culture, too, becomes a vital part of Marie-Gabriel's novel and *L'Isolé Soleil* as a whole. As we learn here, Marie-Gabriel herself is culturally assimilated: her grandfather has been careful to build for her 'un bonheur aliéné dans le bon-français' (l. 62). It is only through her parents' journals and stories that she is able to reconnect with her own culture – with its music and literature, and, later, folk tales – as well as begin to see the links between it and the cultures of the wider diaspora. As we see here, she learns of her father's life as a musician, travelling the black world yet always returning to immerse himself in the Creole

1 For a fuller discussion of the maroons and Delgrès, see Chapter 17.

culture and its music – the 'gros-ka', the 'biguine' and the 'quadrille' (ll. 44, 47)[2] – into which he was to initiate his daughter. Through her mother's story, she gains an insight into the literary history of the Caribbean and the black diaspora, an aspect of Antillean culture that this highly intertextual novel is generally intent on exploring. As with the history that is reimagined in *L'Isolé Soleil*, the literary past which is explored is one into which excluded women, like Suzanne Césaire, are reintegrated. As we learn here, Marie-Gabriel discovers this poet's work through the annotated copy of the wartime journal *Tropiques* that she inherited from her mother. Although a poet and co-founder of *Tropiques*, Suzanne Césaire's work has always been overshadowed by that of her more famous husband, Aimé. Here, Marie-Gabriel's constant references to it mirror Maximin's own frequently voiced admiration for her work.

These cultural elements, inherited by Marie-Gabriel from her dead parents, will all prove central to her exploration of Guadeloupe's past – as, indeed, will the other key element of *L'Isolé Soleil*'s historiographical project to be introduced here: the re-evaluation of the Antillean's relationship with the natural environment of the Caribbean. In order, quite literally, to make colonial history more 'black', she resolves to make use of the natural environment which surrounds her – 'tu noirciras toutes les pages blanchies des ses cendres avec les couleurs naturelles à ta portée' (l. 75) – and explores the possibility of developing a new, 'post-colonial' relationship to the landscape of the Caribbean. For the French settlers, *békés*, and even assimilated Antilleans, the landscape – especially when portrayed in literature – was frequently exoticized, or else was seen solely as something from which profit could be made. For the slaves, the natural environment – the sun and the canefields – was something to be battled against, and the land was something to be worked on someone else's behalf. It was only the maroons who developed a relationship with the land which was more harmonious, forced as they were to live off it and survive on it. They learned the significance of the different plants and trees, and learnt to make 'la nature tropicale' (l. 92) theirs, an integral part of their lives.

In a move familiar from the work of other contemporary writers, such as Edouard Glissant and Patrick Chamoiseau (see Chapter 22 below), it is this type of relationship with the land that Marie-Gabriel wishes to develop, and here she pledges to make it into more than just a setting, 'un décor' (l. 92), for her story. While remaining vigilant against simply idealizing her native land, thus reversing rather than revolutionizing colonial representations of it, she will attempt to make it into something like 'un personnage'. That is, she will attempt to allow the Caribbean landscape's place, and even role, in past events to be articulated. Thus, in this extract, she resolves actually to take on the characteristics, or at least to draw on the traditional significance, of local plants and trees (l. 69). In order to tell her forthcoming story about the heroism of slaves and maroons, she reconnects herself here with the solitary, yet deeply rooted, fig tree; with the protective cover of the lianas and with the

2 These are traditional Antillean forms of music and dance. The *gros-ka* (*gwo-ka* in Creole) is a Guadeloupean, drum-based dance, named after the principal drum itself, which is accompanied by a singer and call-and-response-type dancing. The rough equivalent in Martinique is the *bel air*, or *bèlè*. Both date back to slavery and are predominantly associated with the countryside. The *biguine* and the *quadrille*, along with another dance called the *mazurka*, are associated primarily with urban areas and, dating back to the early colonial period, are creolized versions of set, ballroom-type dances which arrived in the islands with the European settlers. All of these traditional dance forms began to wane in popularity during the 1950s and 1960s, but their legacy is still to be seen in more contemporary forms of music such as *zouk*.

poison, which she here imagines using against the dogs sent to recapture runaway slaves, of the 'mancenillier' tree (l. 73) ('mèdsigné' in Creole), which grows by the sea and whose sap burns until its antidote, sea water, is applied. Crucially, by 'rooting' herself in the landscape in this way, 'jusqu'à trouver la source des feux de joie: un conte, un poème, une danse, une chanson' (l. 82), she will also link herself to Creole culture. The natural environment of the Caribbean is intimately bound up with Creole culture, and both are means of rediscovering the 'histoire confisquée' (l. 86) of Guadeloupe and, ultimately, of leading to the 'renaissance' that she here feels is necessary. At the same time, the natural environment – like music and literature – is another means of connecting the slave past of Guadeloupe with that of other parts of the diaspora community whose peoples have undergone a similar history. Here, with the mention of 'les bisons blancs de nos prairies, le coton de notre esclavage' (l. 77), she particularly makes a link, which will be repeated throughout *L'Isolé Soleil*, with African Americans. The undoing of the false divisions and differences imposed by colonialism on the black diaspora as a whole, will prove to be yet another vital aspect of this novel's efforts to (re)write Guadeloupean history.

Further reading

Maximin, Daniel, *Soufrières* (Paris: Seuil, 1987).
—— *L'Île et une nuit* (Paris: Seuil, 1995).

Nesbitt, Nick, 'Jazz et mémoire dans *L'Isolé Soleil*: techniques vernaculaires d'historiographie dans la littérature antillaise', *LittéRéalité* 10, 1 (1998), 69–79.
Scharfman, Ronnie, 'Daniel Maximin's Caribbean discourse', in Maryse Condé (ed.), *L'Héritage de Caliban* (Paris: Editions Jasor, 1992), pp. 233–46.
Taleb-Khyar, Mohammed, '*L'Isolé Soleil* de Daniel Maximin: une écriture d'histoires, une histoire d'écritures', *Francofonia* 22 (1992), 131–41.
Zimra, Clarisse, 'The present always invents itself a past out of its own desire', Interview with Daniel Maximin and Introduction to Daniel Maximin, *Lone Sun*, trans. Clarisse Zimra *et al.* (Charlottesville and London: Virginia University Press, 1989).
—— 'Je(ux) d'histoire chez Daniel Maximin et Vincent Placoly', in Maryse Condé (ed.), *L'Héritage de Caliban* (Paris: Editions Jasor, 1992), pp. 265–87.
—— 'Daughters of Mayotte, sons of Frantz: the unrequited self in Caribbean literature', in Sam Haigh (ed.), *An Introduction to Caribbean Francophone Writing: Guadeloupe and Martinique* (Oxford: Berg, 1999), pp. 177–94.

Language and style

Throughout *L'Isolé Soleil*, the practice of writing is frequently alluded to by the various narrators, and each of these allusions is instructive as a marker of the way in which the novel itself may be read. For example, early on in the novel, the narrator states: 'Les mots ne sont pas du vent. Les mots sont des feuilles envolées au risque de leurs racines, vers les récoltes camouflées au fond du silence et de la mer' (p. 9). Here, words are to be understood as elusive and allusive, and this is true throughout, as well as in this extract, where, indeed, the word 'camouflage' is used once again (l. 34). Later, in one of Adrien's communications to Marie-Gabriel, he says: 'les écrivains . . . conseillent d'écrire d'une manière impure, parodique, mythique, et documentaire tout à la fois' (p. 89), and he claims that Marie-Gabriel herself utilizes three of these styles. As the novel progresses, it becomes clear that it, like Marie-Gabriel's own novel that she is planning here, is a mixture of styles and narrative techniques. In this extract, for example, the documentary style is clearly present, not only in the quotations from Suzanne Césaire (ll. 22–9) and from her father's private diary (ll. 38–46) in the sense that they are 'documents', but also in the biographical details that she provides of her father (ll. 47–53). These are presented in conventional narrative mode, but, as will be claimed later, also in very compact sections.

Of the other three narrative styles mentioned by Adrien, it is the 'mythique' which is the most obvious here – and which is by far the most difficult to penetrate. An enigmatic, mysterious atmosphere is created by the use of highly poetic language. Some of this involves what might be termed decorative images; in other words, images that are used to focus upon a point and clarify it by a picturesque but incidental illustration. Examples include the comparison of the mango tree to a pillow – 'le manguier, ton oreiller de verdure entre les draps du ciel et de la mer' (l. 1) – that of the abandonment of imagination to a lowered flag – 'ce n'est pas la crainte de la folie qui nous forcera à mettre en berne le drapeau de l'imagination' (l. 17) – and the metonymy of the womenfolk's lap – 'la conspiration des femmes de la maison qui t'encerclent dans leur giron pour te réduire à leur condition' (l. 5). There is a two-tier image (the original simile provokes another) when the plane deaths are compared to the way that the fruit of the sand-box tree burst, which in turn is compared to the explosion of a hand-grenade: 'tels les fruits du sablier qui éclatent comme une grenade à leur maturité, ton père est mort' (l. 30). On other occasions the image becomes extended: tenors may have two or more vehicles attached to them, e.g.

> Les nuages sont nos ennemis, les bisons blancs de nos prairies, le coton de notre esclavage.
>
> (l. 76)

> Tu caresseras la vie comme les fougères, chanteras comme les palmistes sous le vent, lutteras seule dressée sur tes racines comme le figuier-maudit, tes lianes seront le rideau protecteur des révoltes, le poison de tes mancenilliers attirera la soif des chiens de garde.
>
> (l. 70)

Or the image itself may extend over a number of lines, as in the case of cotton, which is first mentioned l. 77 but which is then taken up again l. 79, turned from a vehicle into a tenor and developed in a number of directions. In these cases the imagery becomes more functional and becomes integrated into the very fabric of the text. Interpreting every aspect of the image at times presents considerable difficulties, as associations of ideas intervene and interweave, one thought leading to another, one picture conjuring up another, sometimes rationally but often, it seems, arbitrarily. When Marie-Gabriel, describing her mission as author, compares herself to many local plants, it is possible to discern connections between the plant and the role she sees herself called upon to play. On the other hand, the comparisons generated by the clouds are partly inspired by legend, partly by history and partly by pure imagination:

> Tu te méfieras hautement des nuages. Les nuages sont nos ennemis, les bisons blancs de nos prairies, le coton de notre esclavage. Tu te souviendras que les oiseaux sans mémoire qui plongent le bec dans les capsules de coton deviennent aveugles et condamnés au sol, car le coton est le manteau de Dieu, et Dieu a ainsi voulu punir les oiseaux et les

> Nègres qui l'ont voulu déraciner avec la complicité des vers, de la lune, du soleil et du vent.
>
> (l. 76)

Here some of the allusions are transparent, others much less so. Images drawn from meteorology, sky, sun, clouds are in fact a regular feature of the novel. In addition to the reference to clouds just given (which is foreshadowed by another reference in the quotation from Suzanne Césaire, l. 27), Marie-Gabriel's father's death prompts her to compare him to a sun travelling towards the stars, an inspiration and incentive to her to write, and the first mention of 'soleil' as an image which will continue until the very last page. Poetic language is also to the fore in the paragraph devoted to reflections on his death: repetition, symmetry and alliteration in 'sa vie rêvée . . . sa vie réelle' (l. 58); more alliteration and onomatopoeia in 'Il n'y a que le vent qui vole sans jamais se poser' (l. 59); symmetry and unexpected climax in 'La vie est sans pitié: la mort la punira un jour' (l. 60).

There is an evangelical fervour about the 'mission statement' which Marie-Gabriel presents in the second part of the passage – she becomes the Elisha of her father's Elijah, picking up the mantle of his project. Sentence after sentence, clause after clause begins with 'tu' plus a future tense, as she outlines the grandiose programme that she is setting herself. Imagery inspired by the natural world permeates this section, as Marie-Gabriel takes on the task of using nature as a way of exploring alternative versions of Guadeloupe and its history (l. 93).

The complexity and density of the imagery have as a syntactic support complicated and intricate sentence structures. Single complex and compound-complex sentences constitute complete paragraphs (ll. 3, 7, 11, 17). These sentences, composed of many adjectival and adverbial expressions, are compact, using past participles instead of relative clauses to produce an impression of many thoughts being telescoped together, of condensed links between nouns and adjectival elements. This conveys the vigour and at the same time the discipline of the narrative. The density of the text is also enhanced through sentences consisting of a number of parallel clauses: evidence is accumulated in ll. 33–6:

> Mais tes yeux ont su voir les désirs préservés sous le grand camouflage des larmes inassouvies, la pluie a rafraîchi ta fièvre, le vent a ramené ton cœur à son logis, et ton grand-père t'a retenue dans la chaleur de sa main.

The poetic effect is present throughout, culminating in the use of the abstract 'chaleur de sa main' (rather than *sa main chaude*). Density is also present in the 'documentary' section, ll. 47–53, where the details of her father's career are piled up, tersely yet powerfully, reflecting the frenetic nature of his professional life.

Although 'le bon-français' may be alienating (l. 63), it provides the vehicle for the poetry and imagination associated with Creole, the climate, the dances, the atmosphere of the island. Together the French language and its expression of Guadeloupean culture combine to form a text which is challenging linguistically and original stylistically.

Chapter 22

Patrick Chamoiseau

Chronique des sept misères (Paris: Folio, 1986), pp. 176–81.

La rumeur disait que Pipi parlait à la terre de sa clairière maudite, buvait l'eau des pluies, s'alimentait de merles grillés sans sel et sans piments. Son chapeau touchait maintenant ses yeux. Les poils de son menton demeuraient au garde-à-vous. Il était devenu maigre comme un jour sans pain, et son regard conservait la fixité de celui d'un fils de Colson. Il ne quitta plus la clairière durant une charge de temps qu'Elmire nous chiffrait avec plusieurs calendriers. Quand les pluies et les coups de soleil dispersèrent ses vêtements, il se couvrit de feuilles de cocotier tressées. Bientôt, il ne demeura du Pipi que nous connaissions que le bakoua, indestructible et noirâtre, déformé par des poussées de cheveux libres. Ses jours étaient consacrés à parler au zombi et à l'écouter. Refusant de se mettre debout, il rampait pour piéger ses merles à la colle fruit-à-pain, ou au nœud coulant, et ne s'accroupissait que pour ses besoins derrière un mur de cabouyas. Sous pluies et rosées, il se désaltérait renversé sur le dos, bras et jambes écartés. Le reste du temps, à plat ventre, son corps dialoguait avec le zombi. Une tribu de rastas qui réinventait notre vie à quelques pas de là lui amenait des carreaux de fruit-à-pain, des bis de patates, des morceaux de poissons. Les rastafariens ne lui adressaient jamais la parole, mais s'asseyaient souvent en cercle autour de lui pour fumer de leur herbe divine dans une tentative de communion respectueuse. Cette chair qui les surpassait dans le rapprochement avec la terre, mère universelle, les impressionnait. Traquée par la police pour ses plantations de cannabis, la tribu s'enfonça dans les bois, sans laisser de traces sur les feuilles, mais en ayant pris soin d'abandonner dans la clairière plusieurs calebasses de fruits, quelques patates douces et trois plats d'igname sauvage.

Parfois, en compagnie de Man Elo, nous le visitions. Son accueil était d'une froide indifférence. Sans un regard à nos victuailles, il nous dévisageait avec une intensité insupportable, avant de clamer ses: Aaah voilà un Congo . . . Lui c'est un Bambara, dis donc . . . Roye roye mais c'est un Mandingue, qu'est-ce que tu dis de ça? . . . Ses propos délirants, sa triste indifférence, sa manière d'avaler nos vivres sans le merci et sans le travail des dents, et surtout son inexplicable dédain pour les bouteilles de rhum offertes qui s'entassaient au soleil jusqu'à l'explosion, nous précipitaient dans une senne de tristesse comme un banc de titiris travaillé par la lune, piégé par le courant.

Quand les merles désertèrent l'endroit et que nous perdîmes le goût des visites, Pipi se nourrit, dit-on, d'herbes grasses mâchées avec une placidité de ruminant. Cette nourriture insolite l'affligea des tremblades de la faim et il dut se rabattre sur les abeilles, les anolis, les punaises, les libellules, un peuple d'insectes et de bestioles qu'au début il grillait légèrement mais qu'il finit par avaler glouque! d'une manière soubaroue inusitée des bêtes, même des chiens. Les moustiques lui parlèrent de la vie. Sa peau se couvrit de boutons. Puis de squames. Enfin, elle se mua en une couenne indéfinissable, répugnante à la lumière mais moelleusement luisante dans le noir. Bien entendu, le phénomène déclencha le vocal à son propos. La parole en fit un papa-quimboiseur, et là même des foules furtives quittèrent cases et villages pour le consulter à la nuit tombée, sur les divagations de notre vie. Cette audience quasi religieuse sembla l'amuser. Les gens s'arrêtaient à une centaine de mètres de la clairière et se désignaient pour approcher à tour de rôle le papa-bête-à-feu et lui quémander une séance:

– L'ingrate est partie, elle m'a laissé trois petites personnes, oui! Tu peux la faire dévirer, han?

– Papa ho, tu sais le bon numéro pour la loterie des gueules cassées?

– J'ai une misère qui a pris pied sur moi et je ne me sens plus vaillant comme avant, est-ce que tu peux m'enlever cette malédiction-là, papa? . . .

Malgré les réponses insensées de Pipi, la clairière ne désemplissait pas. Les consultants, travaillés d'une générosité nullement gratuite, arrivaient chargés des offrandes-à-sorciers: coqs noirs et poules blanches, bougies Saint-Antoine, jambons de cochons-planches albinos, canaris de pois puants, eau bénite et médailles de Sainte Vierge, tibia gauche d'un couillon calciné à Saint-Pierre, cheveux de jeunes filles vierges, gouttes de la sueur nocturne d'une négritte en cauchemar. Cela se mélangeait aux simples victuailles dans des entassements qui encerclaient le corps luisant de Pipi. La clairière ressembla bientôt à l'entrepôt d'une épicerie chinoise, et le vent y souleva des effluves d'égouts qu'exhalait le manger délaissé, pourrissant. Car Pipi continuait à mâcher ses herbes grasses, affairé dans l'osmose entre son corps lumineux et la terre battue qui reproduisait fidèlement la topographie de ses reptations. Quand la procession de ses fidèles troubla sa quiétude au point de ne plus l'amuser, il accueillit toute intrusion dans la clairière avec un chapelet de malédictions, de Manman par-ci, de Manman par-là. L'endroit fut vite déserté des gens normaux. Seuls quelques têbês, fils de Colson en dérade, engagés déraillés par leur contrat avec le diable, affrontaient encore ses vociférations haineuses pour lui soumettre une douleur de la vie. Les autres stoppaient à quelques dizaines de mètres, derrière un rideau de fougères, et tentaient à l'aide de prières spéciales cher payées auprès d'un séancier de seconde zone d'obtenir une guérison à distance. Les autorités s'émurent de ce mouvement nocturne de foule quand le quotidien *France-Antilles* titra à la une: *Quimbois dans la forêt de Tivoli.*

Un substitut de procureur de la République, amateur de sorcellerie, se déplaça personnellement afin de lonviyer l'événement à la faveur d'une pleine lune. Autre fait extraordinaire, FR3 délaissa au cours d'un journal télévisé ses dossiers sur la neige des Alpes et le bouleversement des saisons dans le Bassin parisien, pour retransmettre durant sept secondes l'image du sorcier dans sa fabuleuse clairière. Pipi fut transporté trois fois de suite à l'hôtel de police, et dut à chaque fois être ramené dans les bois car ses arrestations rameutaient toutes qualités de politiciens autonomistes, indépendantistes, et autres modèles de nègres exaltés, qui en avaient fait, disaient-ils, *un symbole de la dégradation de l'homme antillais sous le régime colonial.* Ils avaient d'ailleurs investi la clairière en grande pompe, drapeau et tambours gwo-ka, pour rallier de manière patente le symbole à leur cause. Mais le symbole les avait accueillis par un tir de débris innommables et tant d'et caetera manman, et caetera manman, qu'il leur parut préférable de le laisser symboliser à son insu, sauvagement, mais en toute liberté. Depuis, Pipi connut dans sa clairière l'absolu des solitudes.

Les lueurs de sa peau attiraient des papillons nocturnes. Ils voletaient autour de lui avant de s'agripper à son boubou de feuilles tressées qu'ils ne quittaient plus, même quand émergeait l'aube mouillée. Couverte de ces écailles ternes aux dessins géométriques, frémissantes avec la nuit et le curieux réveil de l'épiderme luisant, la silhouette de Pipi se faisait monstrueuse. Il fournissait de moins en moins d'efforts et, pour manger, se contentait d'avaler des poignées de papillons. Ce régime lui infligea des douleurs abdominales, des fièvres, et un dérèglement nerveux qui l'agitait comme une épilepsie. Une vieille faiblesse vint l'habiter et il s'étala dans la clairière comme une tache. La lumière de sa peau et les papillons s'en allèrent. Soleil. Pluies froides. Sa respiration devint sifflante. Un étau emprisonna sa poitrine. Des courbatures naviguaient dans son corps. Il épuisa toutes les espèces de toux avant d'être secoué de quintes douloureusement silencieuses. Seules les extrémités du délire lui arrachent parfois des sons rauques de chiens ferrés. Sa vie chancelait comme une bougie de cimetière aux ultimes heures de la Toussaint, quand surgit Marguerite Jupiter, grosse chabine propriétaire d'une case des environs. Elle cherchait dans les sous-bois la sauvageonne igname nommée Sasa, en vue d'améliorer un canari, et s'était fourvoyée à son grand désespoir dans la clairière maudite. La découverte du corps délabré libéra toute sa miséricorde. Elle le chargea sur ses épaules pour le ramener là même dans sa case, d'où elle dépêcha deux de ses seize garçons à la recherche d'un papa-feuilles. En attendant, elle lui infiltra entre les dents des tisanes d'herbes-à-tous-maux recueillies derrière la maison, et frictionna sa peau boursouflée de rhum camphré, malgré ses hurlements d'agonie. Affolée par l'irritation qui en résulta, Marguerite Jupiter le massa longuement avec l'huile d'avocat qu'elle utilisait d'habitude pour assouplir ses épaisses nattes. Cet enduit apaisa l'écorché qui plongea soudainement dans l'abîme des rêves, la respiration sifflante et oppressée.

Text and context

Written in a similar style to his Prix Goncourt-winning novel *Texaco* (1992), Patrick Chamoiseau's first novel, *Chronique des sept misères*, tells the story of a group of *djobeurs*, men who set up stalls for the *marchandes* of Fort-de-France's market and carry their produce for them on their home-made barrows. Pipi, who is the focus of this extract, is a *maître-djobeur* and it is his story which is central throughout. The novel begins just before the Second World War, and it traces the rise and then fall of the *djobeurs*' way of life in post-war, post-departmentalization Fort-de-France. Having developed with the increasing, post-abolition urbanization of Martinique, *le djob* is a precarious and insecure living practised by those who have no real skills appropriate to the modern town.

When the events of this extract take place, the traditional, agricultural economy of the island is in decline and Fort-de-France is becoming increasingly *francisé*. The market is subject to more and more regulation and sanitization by the French authorities and the roles of the *marchandes* and *djobeurs* are changing so rapidly as to be under threat. In this extract, Pipi temporarily abandons the difficulties of his present life and, neglecting both his barrow and his friends, he becomes entirely immersed in the stories about the past told to him by Afoukal, 'l'esclave-zombi' (l. 10). Having learned that Africa was the land of his ancestors, he here becomes prey to the very Antillean temptation of seeing a 'return' to Africa as an answer to the present problems of life in the Antilles. Thus, when the other *djobeurs* come to see him in the forest, he seems not to recognize them and, instead, recites the African peoples from which he believes they come: 'Aaah voilà un Congo. . . Lui c'est un Bambara, dis donc. . . mais c'est un Mandingue' (l. 26). And later in the extract, as if to emphasize the connection that he has made with Africa, even the narrator describes Pipi's makeshift clothing as a 'boubou' (l. 89).

The refuge that Pipi takes both in the forest and in an imaginary past could, initially, be seen as reminiscent of the similar refuge sought by the maroons during slavery.[1] However, although the Rastafarians who come and give food to Pipi respect his 'rapprochement avec la terre, mère universelle' (l. 19), he is as yet too fixated on Afoukal and the past to be able to make anything of his relationship with the land. The Rastafarians themselves – growers of fruit and vegetables, able to wander the forests 'sans laisser de traces', and 'Traqué[s] par la police' (l. 20) – are much more reminiscent of the maroons, while Pipi merely sinks deeper and deeper into physical and mental collapse. Eventually, he begins to become animal-like, and is driven to stalking his prey in order to eat: 'Refusant de se mettre debout, il rampait pour piéger ses merles à la colle fruit-à-pain' (l. 10). Once the blackbirds have disappeared, he is forced to become a herbivore, and eat 'd'herbes grasses mâchées avec une placidité de ruminant' (l. 34). Later, in what by now appears to be a move of inverse evolution, a return to human origins, he becomes scaly, reptilian, and finally his skin 'se mua en une couenne indéfinissable' (l. 39). By the end of the extract, he has sunk so low that he is unable to feed himself at all.

Despite the desperate situation in which he finds himself, and once he has rejected the help of the *djobeurs*, his mother Man Elo and the Rastafarians, he becomes an object of interest to different sections of the surrounding community. First of all, he is taken for a 'quimboiseur', a traditional witch or healer with semi-magical powers. People bring him

1 For a more detailed explanation of the phenomenon of *marronnage*, see Chapter 17.

'offrandes-à-sorciers' in return for his advice or help, both of the traditional kind – 'Tu peux la faire dévirer, han?' (l. 47) or 'tu peux m'enlever cette malédiction-là, papa?' (l. 51) – and of the more modern kind – 'Papa ho, tu sais le bon numéro pour la loterie des gueules cassées?' (l. 49). Even the local newspaper, *France-Antilles*, runs a story about the 'quimboiseur' in the forest, and the state prosecutor's Martinican representative, 'amateur de sorcellerie' (l. 73), goes to investigate the phenomenon. Most surprising of all, however, are the seven seconds given over to Pipi by FR3 (l. 75), one of the French television channels received in Martinique and Guadeloupe, which normally pays little attention to events talking place in the DOM. There is much humour here, which is characteristic of Chamoiseau's work, but there are also serious points to be made. Not only do we see how, among some sections of the Martinican community, traditional beliefs have survived – even to the extent of adapting themselves to more contemporary Antillean needs, such as the lottery numbers – but we also see how for others, like the state prosecutor, they have been reduced to the level of 'hobbies'. This is something which happens throughout the novel: as life in Martinique becomes increasingly French, elements of Creole culture become little more than tourist attractions. And for the French media, Pipi is simply an interesting example of the harmless and exotic 'difference' of life in the DOM; it is this that they choose to report, not everyday life there. Even those Martinicans – 'politiciens autonomistes, indépendantistes' (l. 79) – who seem to take Pipi's plight more seriously, simply use him for their own selfish purposes. Their declaration that he is '*un symbole de la dégradation de l'homme antillais sous le régime colonial*!' (l. 81) is treated with irony here, and they are described, in the voice of the French authorities, as 'nègres exaltés' (l. 80). This is largely because, despite the fact that their evaluation of Pipi's situation is closest to his actual predicament, it remains little more than a 'sound-bite' used to score political points, and is far too simplistic.

From the beginning, Pipi has been described as 'un errant' and his desperate attempts here to find some sort of 'home' and certainty in the stories of Afoukal are in many ways the logical outcome of a life spent struggling to find a way to survive. He is, in fact, an example of one of Chamoiseau's key *figures de créolité*, a figure that he elsewhere names *le driveur*. *Le driveur*, according to Chamoiseau, has existed since slavery: maroons and freed slaves (*les affranchis*), as well as the ex-slaves of the post-abolition period, were all *driveurs*, condemned to wander aimlessly from place to place with no fixed role in society. After abolition, and particularly in the twentieth century, the majority of *driveurs* were to be found, like Pipi, in the emerging towns. Some were able to make a living out of their urge to wander, and *djobeurs* are a prime example of this. While the maroon is usually seen as the archetypal Creole figure of resistance, for Chamoiseau the *driveur* – who includes the maroon and the *djobeur* – is a more convincing example. Even if he is unaware of it himself, the *driveur*'s constant wandering can be seen as a radical refusal to put down roots in the French culture and the French language imposed from the time of the plantation on.

Unfortunately, however, the *driveur*'s resistance is never personally positive or successful. One likely outcome of his constant lack of a clearly defined social role is madness. This is why, here, Pipi, is compared to the 'fils de Colson' (ll. 5, 66) who, towards the end of his stay in the zombie's clearing, are among the only people to keep him company.[2] Although Pipi

2 Colson is the name of a psychiatric hospital in Martinique, and in this novel another *djobeur*, Bidjoule, is sent there. So close is the threat of a similar fate to the other *djobeurs* that none of them can bring themselves to visit him there.

does not succumb to madness, and is rescued by Marguerite Jupiter, he will only temporarily find a place in her family. Eventually, as is always the case for the *driveur* – and as is also true throughout Schwarz-Bart's *Pluie et vent sur Télumée Miracle* (see Chapter 20 above) – misfortune strikes again, and in Pipi's case he is brought down by the interference of the French authorities. By the end of the novel, this interference means that all the *djobeurs* have disappeared, and their barrows are thrown on a rubbish heap.

It is in the preservation of the memory of these disappearing elements of Creole culture that Chamoiseau sees the role of his fiction. For him, the Antillean writer is a *marqueur de paroles*, a scribe who writes down the stories of the Creole *conteur*, and thus helps to save them from extinction. It is therefore unsurprising that this novel, like his others, is very oral in style, and is concerned with showing the importance of the oral tradition in the French Caribbean. As we can see in this extract, the novel is narrated by a collective voice, the 'nous' of Pipi's fellow *djobeurs* who frequently, though not here, address their 'audience' directly. Here, as throughout, the orality of the text is also evident in the presence of Creole which, more explicitly than in Schwarz-Bart's novel and in a more sustained manner than in that of Maryse Condé (see Chapter 23 below), is evident at the level of both vocabulary and syntax. The importance of the oral tradition is manifest here both in the oral history of Martinique recounted to Pipi by Afoukal and then written down for posterity in the novel that we are reading, and in the way in which Pipi himself is shown to be passing into a continuing oral history as a semi-legendary figure, created by 'la rumeur' (l. 41), 'le vocal' and '[l]a parole' (l. 41) of the community around him. The oral tradition is thus shown to be still vibrant and still developing, and it is this Creole vitality to which writers such as Chamoiseau are determined to contribute in their written fiction.

Further reading

Chamoiseau, Patrick, *Solibo magnifique* (Paris: Gallimard, 1988).
—— *Antan d'enfance* (Paris: Hatier, 1990).
—— *Texaco* (Paris: Gallimard, 1992).

Bernabé, Jean, Chamoiseau, Patrick and Confiant, Raphaël, *Eloge de la créolité* (Paris: Gallimard, 1993).
Burton, Richard D. E, *Le Roman marron: études sur la littérature martiniquaise contemporaine* (Paris: L'Harmattan, 1997.)
Dash, J. Michael, *The Other America: Caribbean Literature in a New World Context* (Charlottesville: Virginia University Press 1998), Chapter 6.
Hazaël-Massieux, Marie-Christine, 'Chamoiseau, écrit-il en créole ou en français?', *Etudes créoles* XXI, 2 (1998), 111–26.
McCusker, Maeve, 'De la problématique du territoire à la problématique du lieu: un entretien avec Patrick Chamoiseau', *The French Review* 73, 4 (2000), 724–33.
Perret, Delphine, 'Lire Chamoiseau', in Maryse Condé and Madeleine Cottenet-Hage, *Penser la créolité* (Paris: Karthala, 1995), pp. 153–72.

Language and style

In this novel, and more than any of the other authors in this section, Chamoiseau makes extensive use of Creole, sometimes in single words, sometimes in longer expressions; these may or may not be accompanied by a translation, which is at times in the text, at others in a footnote; the translation may occur without the original and is sometimes signalled as such, sometimes not. This combination of Creole, whether in its authentic form or through translation, and French creates a very distinctive atmosphere in the text. The novel is clearly not a conventional French one. The author has deliberately set out to produce a text that will be associated with the Antilles, and that, although it exploits its French infrastructure, is independent of metropolitan norms. Writing entirely in Creole is scarcely an option, if a wide local, as well as French and foreign, readership is required.[3] By using a linguistic patchwork, French flecked with Creole, Chamoiseau is able to ensure that his message is accessible to a wide French-speaking public, to emphasize the Antillean character of his novel, to make points of a political, cultural or social nature relevant to the Antilles and to proclaim his allegiance to the island.

The world of Martinique is presented in various linguistic tiers: through specific references to flora and fauna with their Creole names, through proverbs and expressions often translated into French, and through descriptions of events and people made entirely in French. In this passage, Creole is used to name a plant, 'cabouyas' (l. 12), clothing, 'bakoua' = Martinican peasant's hat (l. 8), persons, 'têbês' = madmen (l. 66), 'quimbois' = witch doctor (l. 72), a type of drum, 'tambour gwo-ka' (l. 83); to express interjections, 'roye' = help (l. 27), 'han' = a grunting sound (l. 48), 'manman' = mamma mia (ll. 65, 85), 'avaler glouque' = to gulp down (l. 37); there is a verb, 'lonviyer' = to scrutinize (l. 74) and an adjective, 'soubaroue' = vulgar (l. 38). 'Papa-quimboiseur' = witch doctor (l. 42) is a hybrid of (Antillean) French and Creole. 'Zombi' (l. 10) is a Creole word which has gained currency in standard French; this is less the case for 'chabine' (l. 102) and 'négritte' (l. 57), types of mixed-race Martinican women. 'Boubou', a type of clothing (l. 89), is a word from Africa. More often a translation (calque) is used: a plant, 'herbes-à-tous maux' (l. 108), a cooking pot, 'canaris de pois puants' (l. 55), persons, 'papa-bête-à-feu' (l. 46), 'papa-feuilles' (l. 107), both of which mean traditional healers; local practices, 'offrandes-à-sorcier' (l. 54); 'une douleur de la vie' (l. 68); food, 'cochons-planches' (l. 55); an affliction, 'tremblades' (l. 35); a chorus, 'le vocal' (l. 41); even an adverb, 'là même' (ll. 42, 106); idioms, 'une charge de temps' (l. 5), 'une misère qui a pris pied sur moi' (l. 50); a proverb, 'maigre comme un jour sans pain' (l. 4). Still other words, orthodox French words, describe Afro-Caribbean phenomena, e.g. plants, 'igname' (ll. 23, 103), utensils, 'calebasse' (l. 22); others are less common, e.g. 'titiris' young fish (l. 31), 'anolis' lizard (l. 36).

The passage is transfused with a humorous, gently mocking tone, whether it is a question of the descriptions on numerous occasions of Pipi's appearance, or the visit of the Rastafarians or the 'consultants', or the reactions of the media to the witch doctor in the woods, or his elevation to symbolic status, or simply casual remarks sprinkled through the text. One characteristic is the use of mock heroic, antiphrasis or elevated language to convey a humble, insignificant matter, inflating it beyond its actual importance. Of numerous examples, among the most effective are: 'elle [sa peau] se mua en une couenne indéfinissable, répugnante à la lumière mais moelleusement luisante dans le noir' (l. 39) – enhanced by symmetry; 'Pipi continuait à mâcher ses herbes grasses, affairé dans l'osmose entre son corps lumineux et la terre battue qui reproduisait fidèlement la topographie de ses reptations' (l. 61); 'à l'aide de prières spéciales cher payées auprès d'un séancier de seconde zone' (l. 69); and perhaps the most ironic of all, the failure of the autonomists and

3 For a discussion of the issue of readership and Creole/French bilingualism in the Caribbean DOM, see Chapter 17.

pro-independence activists to secure Pipi as a symbol for their cause – 'le symbole les avait accueillis par un tir de débris innommables et tant d'et caetera manman, et caetera manman, qu'il leur parut préférable de le laisser symboliser à son insu, sauvagement, mais en toute liberté' (l. 84). There are also many cases of flippant remarks, some aimed at political groups, e.g. 'toutes qualités de politiciens autonomistes' (l. 79), 'autres modèles de nègres exaltés' (l. 80), some at Pipi's lifestyle, e.g. 'merles grillés sans sel et sans piments' (l. 2, also ll. 34, 36)), one at the gifts brought to Pipi, 'gouttes de la sueur nocturne d'une négritte en cauchemar' (l. 57).

The general style of the text is a combination of oral conventions, a mixture of sophisticated and standard constructions and rich vocabulary. The orality comes through in the first-person plural pronoun guise adopted by the narrator (*les djobeurs*, Pipi's erstwhile companions, e.g. ll. 6, 8, 15, 24), in the reference to 'la rumeur' (l. 1), in the parenthetical 'dit-on' (l. 34) and 'disaient-ils' (l. 81), in the interjection 'glouque' mid-sentence (l. 37) and in the familiar expression, 'Autre fait extraordinaire' (l. 74).

The text's sophisticated nature is illustrated in the varied sentence structure: in the passage from l. 88 to the end, of the twenty-one sentences, two are minor, nine simple, four compound, six complex (none are compound-complex). However, there are only six subordinate clauses (one per complex sentence), five of which are relative, the other temporal. As far as initial elements are concerned, the subject occurs in first position sixteen times and a complement of the subject twice (ll. 90, 110); the only other initial element is an adverb (l. 107). This somewhat unremarkable sentence structure contrasts with the fact that no two sentences begin with the same subject; each sentence introduces a new angle on Pipi's predicament. There is a concentration of six short minor and simple sentences between l. 96 and l. 101, which seem to imitate the effect of tightening the pressure on Pipi's chest. Initial participles are a distinctive feature of Chamoiseau's style, e.g. 'Refusant de se mettre debout, il rampait . . .' (l. 10), 'Traquée par la police . . '. (l. 20, also ll. 90, 107, 110).

As far as the vocabulary is concerned, it is especially in the use of adjectives that Chamoiseau's lexical skill may be seen. Significant items are richly described – e.g. 'le bakoua, indestructible et noirâtre, déformé par des poussées de cheveux libres' (l. 8), butterflies 'ces écailles ternes aux dessins géométriques, frémissantes avec la nuit' (l. 90). Lexical richness also appears in lists of items (reminiscent of Condé): food from the Rastas (ll. 15, 22), Pipi's behaviour (l. 28), insects devoured (l. 36), his appearance (l. 39), gifts offered to him (the longest) (l. 53), politicians (l. 79), illnesses (l. 94).

Again, rich vocabulary is apparent in the exploitation of imagery to enhance the Antillean atmosphere, the *Créolité* of the novel. This ranges from a fairly extended example relating to fishing – '[a number of inexplicable matters] nous précipitaient dans une senne de tristesse comme un banc de titiris travaillé par la lune, piégé par le courant' (l. 30) – to images based on dogs, e.g. 'qu'il finit par avaler glouque! d'une manière soubaroue inusitée des bêtes, même des chiens' (l. 37), 'chiens ferrés' (l. 100), to a more modern allusion, 'une épicerie chinoise' (l. 59), as well as the figurative use of single words e.g. 'effluves d'égouts' (l. 60, also ll. 90, 113) and mystical language, e.g. 'un chapelet de malédictions' (l. 64, cf. ll. 18, 44, 63). It is of course Pipi who attracts the most complex imagery with two images in a single sentence early on, using a Creole idiom and a local allusion – 'Il était devenu maigre comme un jour sans pain, et son regard conservait la fixité de celui d'un fils de Colson' (l. 3), and reaching its peak in an impressive concatenation of images to describe his plight, e.g. 'un dérèglement nerveux . . . l'agitait comme une épilepsie . . . il s'étala dans la clairière comme une tache' (l. 94, also ll. 97, 98), followed by another extended image

– 'Sa vie chancelait comme une bougie de cimetière aux ultimes heures de la Toussaint' (l. 101).

In his highly individualistic style, which involves manipulating both French and Creole linguistic resources to create a detailed and vivid tapestry of Martinican life, values and tensions, Chamoiseau becomes an extremely articulate spokesman for the Antilles; much more so, perhaps, than the political figures he caricatures in this novel.

Chapter 23

Maryse Condé

Traversée de la mangrove (Paris: Mercure de France, 1989), pp. 255–9.

Xantippe

J'ai nommé tous les arbres de ce pays. Je suis monté à la tête du morne, et j'ai crié leur nom et ils ont répondu à mon appel.

Gommier blanc. Acomat-boucan. Bois pilori. Bois rada. Bois trompette. Bois guépois. Bois d'encens. Bois pin. Bois la soie. Bois bandé. Résolu. Kaïmitier. Mahot cochon. Prune café. Mapou lélé. Arbre à lait. Malimbé.

Les arbres sont nos seuls amis. Depuis l'Afrique, ils soignent nos corps et nos âmes. Leur odeur est magie, vertu du grand temps reconquis. Quand j'étais petit, ma maman me couchait sous l'ombrage de leurs feuilles et le soleil jouait à cache-cache au-dessus de ma figure. Quand je suis devenu nèg mawon, leurs troncs me barraient.

C'est moi aussi qui ai nommé les lianes. Siguine rouge. Siguine grand bois. Jasmin bois. Liane à chique. Liane à barrique. Liane blanche des hauts. Les lianes aussi sont des amies depuis le temps longtemps. Elles amarrent corps à corps. Igname à igname.

J'ai nommé les ravines, sexes grands ouverts, dans le fin fond de la terre. J'ai nommé les roches au fond de l'eau et les poissons, gris comme les roches. En un mot, j'ai nommé ce pays. Il est sorti de mes reins dans une giclée de foutre. Longtemps, j'ai vécu ma vie, au creux des ananas bois, remplissant mon ventre de la sève des arbres. Parfois, j'étais fatigué de planer sur ces perchoirs et je descendais dans les savanes parmi les cannes en fleur. Je donnais mon dos aux hauteurs et je poussais vers la mer, recherchant les côtes basses, vaseuses que ronge l'eau braque des culs-de-sac marins. Je n'aimais que le sable noir, noir comme ma peau et le deuil de mon cœur.

Dans le temps d'autrefois, j'ai vécu avec Gracieuse. Gracieuse. Négresse noire. Canne Kongo juteuse. Malavois à écorce brodée. Tu fondais sous le palais de ma bouche.

Un jour, je lavais mes hardes à la rivière quand elle est venue devant moi, un tray en équilibre sur la tête. Elle a eu un rire de gorge et m'a dit:

– Est-ce que c'est un travail pour un homme celui que tu fais là?

J'ai répondu:

– Effectivement non. Mais je n'ai pas de femme. Veux-tu être celle-là?

Elle a ri aux éclats pour saluer la vie qui s'annonçait. Combien d'années passèrent, les unes derrière les autres, poussant devant elles leurs douze mois?

La journée, je plantais comme avant moi mon père et mon grand-père et la terre me donnait tous les trésors de son ventre. Le soir, je me couchais sur l'oreiller de satin des seins de Gracieuse, je me noyais dans l'eau salée de ses cuisses et nos enfants naissaient, parfois deux à la fois, solides et parés pour demain. Mais le bonheur n'est jamais qu'une parenthèse dans l'océan sans mesure du malheur.

Un matin, je m'éveillai dans la clameur des porcs qu'on égorge. C'était le jour de Noël et les bouchers assassins essuyaient leurs mains rouges aux feuilles de bois d'Inde. Les femmes lavaient les boyaux à la rivière. J'en avais le cœur retourné et, pour ne pas voir ce spectacle, je pris ma serfouette et descendis dans la savane tandis que Gracieuse se moquait:

– Es-tu bête? Est-ce que ce n'est pas ainsi que nos parents ont toujours fêté Noël? Préfères-tu les dindes surgelées dans les magasins?

Je ne répondis rien.

Sur le coup de trois heures, l'odeur de la fumée remplit mes narines. En même temps, un bruit sourd s'élevait pareil à celui que fait la ravine quand elle découche de son lit en saison d'hivernage. Je relevai la tête, essuyant la sueur de mon front, et je vis flamber le morne. Le temps de réaliser, de jeter mes outils et de courir de toute la vitesse de mes deux jambes, ma case flambait et tout mon bel avoir était réduit en cendres.

Les gendarmes métros firent ce qu'ils avaient à faire. Ils posèrent des questions. Comme ils avaient trouvé dans les parages un bidon de kérosène, ils en conclurent que j'avais des ennemis. D'après eux, tout le village me haïssait pour ma trop grande réussite et mon trop grand bonheur. Depuis ce jour, j'ai traîné mon corps sur les chemins défoncés de l'existence. J'ai vu ce pays changer.

J'ai vu les Blancs s'enfuir en grand désordre dans les tourbillons de fumée des plantations. J'ai vu les Nègres en joie donner dos à la gratelle de la canne et se presser dans les chemins menant aux villes. Les femmes les regardaient partir, essuyant l'eau de leurs yeux et berçant les bâtards, sachant quand même dans le secret de leurs cœurs que cette liesse ne durerait pas et que, sous peu, la misère les ramènerait au bercail. J'ai vu s'ouvrir les écoles et, n'en croyant pas mes oreilles, j'ai entendu les enfants chantonner: «Nos ancêtres les Gaulois . . .»

J'ai vu arriver la lumière et les poteaux électriques, les routes goudronnées, le béton, les voitures roulant sur quatre roues. A la Pointe, les golomines mouraient de soif au fond des dalots tandis que le cœur des hommes devenaient de plus en plus dur et mauvais, tout occupé de postes de radio et de télévision en couleurs. Quand je m'approchais des villages habités, les hommes prenaient des roches dans leurs mains pour me chasser et les femmes me criaient comme à un chien:

– Mache! Mache!

Alors je ne circulais plus qu'à la faveur de la nuit quand la lune me signifiait que la voie était libre.

Année après année, j'ai vu les bananiers partir à l'assaut des immortels. Les tracteurs remplacer les machettes et les gaïacs tomber raides sur la pelade de la terre. Où me cacher? Où me cacher? Je courais partout et le soleil blessait mes yeux.

Un jour j'ai débouché d'un chemin et des arbres m'ont hélé pour me donner de l'ombrage. J'ai obéi et je me suis rencogné dans la touffeur retrouvée de leurs aisselles. Je me suis garrotté avec les lianes. J'ai suffoqué de bonheur. Dès que le soleil avait commencé son voyage de l'autre côté du monde et que la noirceur pesait de son poids sur toute chose, je descendais au fin fond de la Ravine. Caché sous les roches, je devenais cheval à diable pour écouter la chanson de l'eau.

Rivière au Sel, j'ai nommé ce lieu.

Je connais toute son histoire. C'est sur les racines en béquilles de ses mapous lélé que la flaque de mon sang a séché. Car un crime s'est commis ici, ici même, dans les temps très anciens. Crime horrible dont l'odeur a empuanti les narines du Bon Dieu. Je sais où sont enterrés les corps des suppliciés. J'ai découvert leurs tombes sous la mousse et le lichen. J'ai gratté la terre, blanchi des conques de lambi et chaque soir dans le serein je viens là m'agenouiller à deux genoux. Personne n'a percé ce secret, enseveli dans l'oubli. Même pas lui qui court comme un cheval fou, flairant le vent, humant l'air. A chaque fois que je le rencontre, le regard de mes yeux brûle les siens et il baisse la tête, car ce crime est le sien. Le sien. Il peut dormir tranquille cependant, engrosser ses femmes, planter des fils, je ne lui ferai rien, le temps de la vengeance est passé.

Text and context

Set in contemporary Guadeloupe, *Traversée de la mangrove* is made up of a series of narratives, each one of them by or about a key inhabitant of the village of Rivière au Sel, a racially and culturally mixed community split apart by inherited rivalries and obsessed with the class-colour hierarchy characteristic of the Caribbean. The villagers are assembled at the wake of Francis Sancher, a mysterious stranger who had arrived among them a year previously and in this, the final narrative, the equally mysterious figure of Xantippe tells his story. Through it, we learn both why he has appeared, shadow-like, in all of the other villagers' narratives and why, for Sancher in particular, he has been a terrifying figure.

What is immediately obvious is that this narrative is something like an origin myth in which Xantippe emerges as a creator-figure who has named the flora and fauna (l. 1), 'planted' the earth and made it fertile (l. 11), and whose wife has had children two by two (l. 37). The necessity of inventing satisfactory explanations of origins is of central concern in much Caribbean literature, as is to be expected of a people born out of the experience of transplantation and slavery. Negritude, of course, with its focus on the African origin of Caribbean peoples, is the prime example, and it is from this that Xantippe's narrative at first appears to have taken its inspiration. The direct reference to Africa (l. 6) is followed a little later by a quotation – 'sexes grands ouverts' (l. 15) – from that seminal Negritude text, Aimé Césaire's *Cahier d'un retour au pays natal.* Xantippe himself has many of the qualities of a Negritude hero: he is black (blacker than most of the other characters in the novel) and he is virile, with a female companion whose role it is to bear his children, to help him in his heroic role (it is she who reminds him of their ancestors' way of celebrating Christmas) and, as 'authentic' Guadeloupean woman – 'Négresse noire. Canne Kongo juteuse' (l. 24) – to signify his pro-black, anti-assimilation politics.

Apart from the one mention of Africa, however, there is little here of the nostalgic preoccupation with African origins that characterizes Negritude. Rather, Xantippe's narrative focuses on the Caribbean as 'native land' and, as if expanding upon the section of Césaire's *Cahier* which deals with the hero's return from Africa to the Caribbean, is primarily concerned with describing the sense of rootedness that he feels there, the intimate relationship that he has with the land on which he lives. Xantippe can remember Africa, but is not fixated with it: he is a 'nèg mawon' (l. 9) who, like the original maroons, lives in 'les mornes' and the forests of the Basse-Terre region of the island. These maroons, too, carried with them knowledge remembered from Africa but, at the same time, knew intimately the Caribbean land that they had worked as slaves yet never owned and now relied upon for survival. Popularly contructed as a bogeyman, the maroon was, like Xantippe, long reviled and feared but, first in Creole *contes* and now in more recent fiction, has been enjoying a period of revival and celebration.

This link with the *conte* perhaps explains the timeless, mythical quality of the first part of Xantippe's narrative, which certainly reads like a Caribbean folk tale. However, as if to draw our attention to the links between the folk tale and the reality that it often allegorized,[1] the second part of the narrative rapidly becomes more realist and more specifically situated in time. We are first aware of this switch when Gracieuse mentions 'les dindes surgelées' (l. 45), and once reference has been made, immediately after the fire, to '[l]es gendarmes métros' (l. 53), the narrative begins to focus much more on the changing pace of life in post-departmentalization Guadeloupe. Thus we are shown by Xantippe how, as the plantations begin to close, other aspects of the traditional economy and culture are also neglected. '[L]es golomines' (l. 66), a type of fish, are washed up, unfished, in Pointe-à-Pitre and, as people are obliged to leave the country and migrate to the towns, the social fabric begins to break down. With the arrival of the positive aspects of modernization – electricity and concrete, roads and cars (l. 65) – comes a change for the worse in the behaviour of the people. Women are left in the countryside with their children, 'le cœur des hommes devenait de plus en plus dur et mauvais' (l. 67) and, like Chamoiseau's *driveur* (see Chapter 22 above), Xantippe himself is chased away from the rural villages that do remain as community-based life begins to fail (l. 68). Departmentalization and urbanization mean assimilation and gallicization, as evidenced by the newly opened schools which, now infamously, teach Antillean children about '[leurs] ancêtres les Gaulois' (l. 64) and strip them of their Creole culture.

It is this assimilation that Xantippe resists. Like Pipi and the other *djobeurs* in Chamoiseau's novel, he refuses to settle, and instead of migrating to the new towns he continues his endless

1 For an example of the allegorical character of folk tales, see the 'Text and context' commentary on Simone Schwarz-Bart's *Pluie et vent sur Télumée Miracle* (Chapter 20).

wandering. Just as the maroons avoided those areas too touched by the 'civilization' of the plantation, so Xantippe avoids those areas too touched by modernization, and seeks shelter in the natural environment. Although we are told at the beginning of the novel that Xantippe had arrived in Rivière au Sel shortly after Sancher, for Xantippe himself it is a place that he has always known intimately – and towards the end of this extract we return to the mythic discourse of the beginning, as Xantippe once more proclaims himself to be the founding ancestor of the village. And it is here that we are reminded that the importance of his role as 'nèg mawon' is that the maroon is a figure from slavery: if Africa is not dwelt upon as the origin of Caribbean peoples, it is slavery which is presented as that origin – an origin denied until recently and, like the maroon, currently being reclaimed in Antillean fiction and historiography. If the role of Sancher in *Traversée de la mangrove* is to bring together a disparate and divided community around his body at his wake, then the role of Xantippe is as repository of communal memory and, specifically, the lost memory of slavery.

It is for this reason that Xantippe is so feared by the villagers, for they do not want to remember that their origins are in slavery. It is also the reason why Sancher, in particular, finds Xantippe so terrifying, for Xantippe's chief memory is of a 'crime' (l. 86), and it is the curse entailed by an ancestral crime – the sudden death, in middle age, of all the male members of his family – that Sancher, throughout the novel, has been fleeing. We are never told the details of this crime but here we learn that Xantippe is the only villager who is able to remember it, and that this is why, 'A chaque fois que je le rencontre, le regard de mes yeux brûle les siens et il baisse la tête, car ce crime est le sien. Le sien' (l. 92). This crime, it is to be assumed, has to do with, or perhaps is, the larger crime of slavery: it took place 'dans les temps très anciens' (l. 87); it involves 'les corps des suppliciés' (l. 88) – slaves and maroons – and is associated with 'des conques de lambi' (l. 89) – *kòn a lanbi* in Creole, the conch shells used by slaves to communicate, especially during a rebellion.

Of course, within the context of slavery and the colour hierarchy which is its legacy, the very fact that the black Xantippe should look Sancher, a mulatto of *béké* ancestry, directly in the eyes, is of great significance, since it points to a major shift in power relations. Even if his fellow mulatto Loulou Lameaulnes believes the old hierarchy to be unchangeable, Sancher is no longer able to inspire fear or respect in Xantippe. Rather, it is the black 'nèg mawon' who is in the position of power, and who is able to imagine a future for his community in a way that Sancher cannot, fixed as he is by his personal, ancestral past. Xantippe's is a refusal to forget that slavery is the origin of his people, but it is also a refusal to become fixed and limited by the desire for vengeance. For him, 'le temps de la vengeance est passé' (l. 95), and this is in keeping with the general tone of the other villagers' narratives and the novel as a whole. While Condé's novel is by no means idealistic about the future of communities such as Rivière au Sel, which we may take as a microcosm of Guadeloupean society as a whole, it is optimistic. As each villager tells his or her story, and links it to the community's past, we see the first tentative steps being taken towards building relationships between those community members who have previously felt separated from one another. In the women's narratives in particular – all of which, like Xantippe's, are told in the first person – the resolve to change the future and to make a fresh start is strong. The other men's narratives, with the exception of that of the child Joby, are all written in the third person and are in general less committed to change and reconciliation. What thus emerges from the novel as a whole is a vision of the future in which the most socially disadvantaged, especially women, are beginning to find a voice in a community which has previously denied them agency. What emerges in Xantippe's narrative here is the voice of someone who has been marginalized by the larger community, as it rushes towards modernization and assimilation, but who is able, because he has remained vitally connected to his people's past, to learn from it and to see a way for his community to begin to move forward.

Further reading

Condé, Maryse, *Moi, Tituba, sorcière . . . noire de Salem* (Paris: Mercure de France, 1986).
—— *Les Derniers Rois Mages* (Paris: Mercure de France, 1992).
—— *Desirada* (Paris: Robert Laffont, 1997).

Balutansky, Kathleen, 'Créolité in question: Caliban in Maryse Condé's *Traversée de la mangrove*', in Maryse Condé and Madeleine Cottenet-Hage, *Penser la créolité* (Paris: Karthala, 1995).
Chamoiseau, Patrick, 'Reflections on Maryse Condé's *Traversée de la mangrove*', *Callaloo* 14 (1991), 389–95.
Condé, Maryse (ed.), *L'Héritage de Caliban* (Paris: Editions Jasor, 1992). See, in particular, the chapters by Danielle Kormos, Michel Lucey and Delphine Perret.
Haigh, Sam, *Mapping a Tradition: Francophone Women's Writing from Guadeloupe*, MHRA Texts and dissertations Series (Leeds: Maney, 2000), Chapter 4.
Lionnet, Françoise, '*Traversée de la mangrove* de Maryse Condé: vers un nouvel humanisme antillais?', *The French Review* 66 (1993), 475–86.
Pfaff, Françoise, *Entretiens avec Maryse Condé* (Paris: Karthala, 1993).

Language and style

In Xantippe's contribution at the wake for Francis Sancher, we are presented with a discourse that is a mixture of conventional story-telling and a mythico-mystical account of the origin of Xantippe's people. The legend that he constructs occurs principally in ll. 1–26 and is resumed at l. 78. The conventional story intervenes occasionally in the early part of the creation story (ll. 7–9, 22), before coming into its own at l. 27. That story is expressed in the main in a language that is factual, descriptive, typical of an autobiographical account – for example ll. 27–33, 34, 39–57. However, interspersed within it are sentences, clauses, expressions of quite different inspiration which form the link with the creation story. These include personification: of time, 'Combien d'années passèrent, les unes derrière les autres, poussant devant elles leurs douze mois?' (l. 32, see end); of the ravine, 'un bruit sourd s'élevait pareil à celui que fait la ravine quand elle découche de son lit en saison d'hivernage' (l. 48); and sensual imagery to describe his life with Gracieuse, 'Le soir, je me couchais sur l'oreiller de satin des seins de Gracieuse, je me noyais dans l'eau salée de ses cuisses' (l. 35).

However, it is the creation story that captures the attention of the reader. The shadowy figure of Xantippe takes on a significance which belies the earlier impressions he had evoked. His opening statement, with its short, measured clauses, produces a powerful effect, the declaration of the creator: 'J'ai nommé tous les arbres de ce pays. Je suis monté à la tête du morne, et j'ai crié leur nom et ils ont répondu à mon appel' (l. 1). 'J'ai nommé' occurs six times, five times in the opening section, and again in l. 84, when he declares that it is he who has brought Rivière au Sel into being. 'J'ai nommé', announcing creation, is later paralleled by the six instances of 'j'ai vu', announcing the impact of modernity on the area (from l. 57). The positive, pounding repetition of these verbs together with the stark lists of trees (ll. 3–5) and plants (ll. 11–12) marks Xantippe's act of creation: the act is described in language that is categorical, absolute, unequivocal in meaning, permitting no argument. Like the God of the

Old Testament, he 'plan[ait] sur ces perchoirs' (l. 19), and like that God 'j'étais fatigué' (l. 19) (God rested on the seventh day). It is at this point that Xantippe's language takes on a lyrical, pantheistic tone, as he descends from the heights to find repose in nature (ll. 19–22). In l. 21 the inversion of subject and verb produces a skilfully constructed symmetrical expression, which in a sense matches his creative act – 'recherchant les côtes basses, vaseuses que ronge l'eau braque des culs-de-sac marins'. Although nature is 'en fleurs' (l. 20), there is a regular undercurrent of discomfort, potential disaster, not only seen in 'vaseuse . . . ronge . . . braque', but also in the associated imagery – 'Je n'aimais que le sable noir, noir comme ma peau et le deuil de mon cœur' (l. 22), the first simile reinforcing Xantippe the maroon's identification with nature but the second his personal tragedy (see below). This tension between the flowers of nature and the brackish water of the inlets contains an impending premonition which is encapsulated in the two values of 'noir' (literally the colour of his skin and figuratively despair). This tension is specifically referred to later on when Xantippe asserts, 'le bonheur n'est jamais qu'une parenthèse dans l'océan sans mesure du malheur' (l. 37); this may be interpreted thematically on two levels, one personally with the destruction of his home and loved ones (l. 51) and the other with the socially destructive effects of modernity (ll. 58–64).

The pantheism of Xantippe's world is powerfully emphasized throughout by the use of imagery. By means of anthropomorphic metaphors, the natural world is compared to the human and reflects an important theme relating to the maroons, who, like Xantippe, lived in the 'mornes' and forests, in harmony with nature. Early on he says that the lianas are 'amies' with their bodies intertwined (l. 13), he likens the ravines to 'sexes grands ouverts' (l. 15), and describes the earth producing crops from its stomach (l. 34); later he is embraced by the arms of the trees. Conversely Xantippe and his wife are described in terms of the natural world – Gracieuse's breasts are compared to satin and her thighs to salt water (l. 36), and at the end he himself becomes an insect (l. 83). The mysterious person who had committed the crime, known only to Xantippe but not to himself, is seen as 'lui qui court comme un cheval fou, flairant le vent, humant l'air' (l. 91), with the alliterative quality of the *f/v* sounds emphasizing the secrecy of the matter. Another theme which was suggested near the beginning of the extract is also revived at the end: the black sand, black skin, the black of grieving (l. 22) are echoed when under cover of darkness he is able to commune with nature – 'Dès que le soleil avait commencé son voyage de l'autre côté du monde et que la noirceur pesait de son poids sur toute chose . . . je devenais cheval à diable pour écouter la chanson de l'eau' (l. 80).

Xantippe's omniscience concerning the crime is demonstrated in the repetition of 'je connais/sais', 'j'ai . . .' in initial sentence position in the last paragraph, and this also provides a linguistic echo of the 'j'ai nommé', 'j'ai vu' episodes. This omniscience, but refusal to act, is also conveyed through robust language, the use of 'le regard de mes yeux brûle' (l. 92) contrasted with 'il baisse la tête' (l. 93), the key words both introduced by a *b* sound, the use of the minor sentence 'Le sien' and the statement that he who could avenge the crime relents, allowing the criminal to continue with his existence. This is expressed in a triplet, again with the nature/human boundaries merging – 'Il peut dormir tranquille cependant, engrosser ses femmes, planter des fils, je ne lui ferai rien, le temps de la vengeance est passé' (l. 93).

As in Chamoiseau's text, but to a much lesser extent, Creole words and expressions are scattered throughout this extract, and the novel as a whole. Many of these are not immediately transparent to the non-Creole speaker though translated into French, whereas others are transcribed in their original form, but all combine to enhance the Guadeloupean atmosphere of the novel. Many of the names of trees (ll. 3–5) and creepers (ll. 11–12, 85) contain genuine Creole elements, others are translations into French, and the same applies to the comparisons of Gracieuse to sugar cane (l. 25), the reference to 'golomines' (fish) and 'dalots' (bays) (l. 67), to 'gaïacs' (type of tree) (l. 75), 'cheval à diable' (stick insect) (l. 83), 'conques de lambi' (conch shells) (l. 89). Other expressions are less botanical – 'nèg mawon', maroon (runaway slave) (l. 9), 'Mache, Mache', get moving (l. 71), and the personification of passing years (l. 33 already quoted). The inclusion of Creole in a French text encapsulates in linguistic form the problems of assimilation and *métissage* experienced by Antillean writers in general and shows the dilemmas facing them. Is it possible to produce and preserve Creole authenticity in a novel destined to a wide audience? What concessions should be made to a non-creolophone audience? The various strategies adopted, the decisions at times to translate and at others to transcribe, show the different directions that the authors may be led in. A comparison with the practices of Patrick Chamoiseau and Simone Schwarz-Bart is very instructive in this respect.

Chapter 24

Dany Laferrière

Pays sans chapeau (Quebec: Lanctôt Editeur, 1996), pp. 44– 8.

Un petit vent tapeur a emporté mes feuillets. Je les ramasse précipitamment, en fais une pile et pose une pierre dessus. J'écris torse nu, à Carrefour-Feuilles, en plein territoire bizango. J'entends ma mère raconter à la voisine avoir vu un bizango, il y a à peine un mois, qui descendait la pente du morne Nelhio tout en buvant du sang et en gueulant des chants obscènes. Le corps couvert de cendres, nu, indécent, le sexe à l'air, les yeux rouges, la bouche crachant le feu, à la recherche d'une nouvelle victime dans la nuit opaque. Ma mère s'est précipitée à l'intérieur de la maison, a vite refermé les portes et éteint toutes les lumières avant de s'étendre à plat ventre au milieu de son salon. Elle affirme n'avoir parlé de ça à personne jusqu'à aujourd'hui. Ma mère se retourne et remarque que je m'intéresse à son récit. Pas pour les raisons qu'elle croit. Moi, ce qui me touche, c'est sa capacité pratiquement illimitée à revivre ses peurs nocturnes. La nuit existe dans ce pays. Une nuit mystérieuse. Moi qui viens de passer près de vingt ans dans le nord, j'avais presque oublié cet aspect de la nuit. La nuit noire. Nuit mystique. Et il n'y a que le jour qu'on puisse parler de ce qui s'est passé la nuit. Me revient à l'esprit la fameuse interrogation de Thalès. Qui vient d'abord: la nuit ou le jour? Et Thalès tranche: la nuit est en avance d'un jour. On dirait que deux pays cheminent côte à côte, sans jamais se rencontrer. Un petit peuple se débat le jour pour survivre. Et ce même pays n'est habité, la nuit, que de dieux, de diables, d'hommes changés en bêtes. Le pays réel: la lutte pour la survie. Et le pays rêvé: tous les phantasmes du peuple le plus mégalomane de la planète.

– Tu sais, Vieux Os, ce pays a changé.

– Ça, j'ai bien vu, maman.

– Pas comme tu crois. Ce pays a vraiment changé. Nous avons atteint le fond. Ce ne sont plus des humains. Ils en ont peut-être l'apparence, et là encore . . .

Je remarque que ma mère parle comme si elle craignait que quelqu'un d'autre ne l'entende. Mais il n'y a personne autour de nous. La voisine est partie vaquer à ses occupations.

– En tout cas, conclut-elle, méfie-toi. Ils circulent le jour comme la nuit.

– Le jour aussi?

– Oui. La nuit, ce sont des bizangos. Et le jour, des zenglendos. Des fois, on ne sait plus si on est le jour ou la nuit.

– Et que fait-on?

– On ferme les portes à midi.

– Ah! c'est pour ça que vous gardez toujours les volets fermés. J'en ai parlé à tante Renée, et elle a fait celle qui n'a rien entendu.

– Je sais que tu n'écoutes personne . . . (Un temps) . . . Ecoute-moi bien pour une fois: je n'ai pas quitté ce pays, même pour une minute, alors je sais de quoi je parle. Méfie-toi d'eux. Méfie-toi d'eux de jour comme de nuit.

– Et comment les reconnaîtrai-je? dis-je, légèrement agacé de voir que ma mère a vieilli.

Elle semble avoir peur de son ombre maintenant.

– Tu les reconnaîtras . . . Ils n'ont pas d'âme.

– Et comment le saurai-je?

– Tu as une âme, toi.

Un moment de silence vaguement gênant. Je sens que ma mère est en train de réfléchir.

– Qu'est-ce qui ne va pas, maman?

– Non, rien, dit-elle tout en jetant à droite et à gauche de brefs coups d'œil inquiets.

– Je sens que quelque chose te tracasse, maman.

– Oui, finit-elle par avouer, ils sont tellement malins qu'ils seront capables de te faire croire qu'ils sont des êtres vivants.

– Je ne comprends pas. Tu ne parles pas sérieusement, maman? Tu ne crois pas dans ces trucs?

Ma mère a ce vif mouvement, comme si une décharge électrique venait de lui traverser le corps.

– Je crois dans l'Eternel, dit-elle fièrement.

– Alors, qui sont ces gens?

Une ombre passe lentement sur le visage de ma mère. Je vois sa main se refermer vivement sur le morceau de tissu qu'elle n'arrêtait pas de triturer. Du satin bleu. Bleu de Marie.

– L'armée des zombis, finit-elle par murmurer. Ils sont des dizaines de milliers. Les prêtres vaudous ont ratissé le pays du nord au sud, de l'est à l'ouest. Ils ont ratissé tous les cimetières du pays. Ils ont réveillé tous les morts qui dormaient du sommeil du juste. Partout – ma mère fait le geste en ouvrant ses bras largement et en pointant dans toutes les directions. Au Borgne, à Port-Margot, Dondon, Jérémie, Cayes, Limonade, Petit-Trou, Baradères, Jean-Rabel, Petit-Goâve, oui, Petit-Goâve aussi . . . Ils sont même allés chercher des morts jusqu'au pic Brigand dans le massif du nord.

Ma mère s'arrête un moment pour reprendre son souffle. Elle me jette de vifs regards pour tenter de voir l'effet de ses paroles sur moi. Je dois avoir l'air fasciné puisqu'elle poursuit avec un léger sourire au coin des lèvres.

– Ils sont vraiment allés partout. On les entendait la nuit quand ils entraient dans Port-au-Prince.

– Qui ça?

– Tu ne m'écoutais pas! Des files de gens qui marchaient la tête baissée, tout en marmonnant dans un sabir incompréhensible des histoires épouvantables.

– Donc, il ne reste plus un seul mort dans les cimetières d'Haïti à l'heure qu'il est, je lance sur un ton légèrement sceptique.

– Non . . . Oui . . . Oui, il doit y avoir encore quelques défunts dans ce pays, me dit-elle avec une telle candeur que je regrette tout de suite mon ton persifleur.

– Heureusement . . .

– Oui, paraît-il, poursuit ma mère, on ne peut pas faire revenir sur Terre quelqu'un qui est occupé . . . Les gens mettent dans les mains du mort, quand ils soupçonnent que cette mort n'est pas naturelle, une bobine de fil et une aiguille sans chas en lui demandant de filer l'aiguille. C'est comme ça qu'on occupe un mort. On a toujours fait ça dans notre famille. Je suis tranquille à leur sujet. On n'a sûrement pas pu les déranger.

Je visualise tous ces morts occupés à filer des aiguilles sans chas pour l'éternité.

– Donc, mon grand-père est occupé à essayer de filer cette aiguille sans chas – un frisson me parcourt l'échine – jusqu'à la fin des temps.

– Jusqu'à la résurrection, lance-t-elle fièrement. Seul Dieu peut le réveiller . . . Moi, je n'ai pas de mort à donner à ces assoiffés de sang pour qu'ils accomplisssent leur diabolique besogne.

Ma mère me regarde, cette fois-ci, droit dans les yeux.

– Tu ne peux pas savoir ce qu'on a vécu. On ne pouvait même plus aller au cimetière. C'était gardé par les militaires. Zone réservée. Bien sûr, le gouvernement ne voulait pas qu'on sache que les cimetières étaient pratiquement vides.

– Ils gardaient quoi? je finis par demander.

– C'était pour faire diversion . . . Pour qu'on ne découvre pas le pot aux roses. En réalité, ils gardaient le vide. Le néant. Un cimetière sans mort. Madame Lucien, tu te souviens d'elle? Eh bien! elle avait un mort au cimetière de Léogâne, un de ses oncles, homme tranquille, bienveillant, qu'elle consultait de temps en temps.

– Du temps qu'il était vivant?

– Non, je parle du mort. Ce mort avait l'habitude de lui faire gagner de bonnes sommes d'argent à la loterie, pas le gros lot, mais assez pour survivre par ce temps de disette. Eh bien! Mme Lucien a pu pénétrer dans le cimetière, une nuit, et elle a trouvé dans le cercueil, à la place du mort, devine quoi?

– Je ne vois pas, maman.

– Un tronc de bananier. Un tronc de bananier dans le cercueil. Elle est restée sans voix pendant une semaine. Tu te rends compte: un tronc de bananier! Et on ne sait pas depuis combien de temps elle priait devant ce tronc de bananier. La pauvre, elle était complètement déboussolée.

Une mangue tombe, presque aux pieds de ma mère. Elle ne cille même pas. Complètement ailleurs.

– Les gens sont morts, conclut-elle, et on refuse de les laisser se reposer en paix. Avant, le cimetière était le seul endroit sûr en Haïti. Maintenant, on se demande si on fait une bonne affaire en mourant dans ce pays.

Text and context

Dany Laferrière is a Haitian-born writer who now lives and writes in Montreal and Miami. In common with the strongly autobiographical – but also extremely playful – element of Laferrière's other novels, *Pays sans chapeau* has at its centre a narrator (at one stage referred to as 'Laferrière') who is also a writer. In this case, he is a writer who has been living in Montreal and Miami and has just returned to Haiti for the first time since leaving twenty years ago as a journalist exiled by the regime of Jean-Claude Duvalier. The novel charts the narrator's rediscovery of family members, old friends and acquaintances, and a way of life which appears to have changed little during his absence. We therefore see the difficulties encountered by the Haitian emigrant who returns to the native land, and also those of the Haitian writer, diasporic or otherwise, who writes in a country in which freedom of speech has been so dangerous for so long, and in which a large proportion of the population is illiterate. In this extract, the narrator has set up a table on which to write his novel, under a mango tree outside his mother's house in Port-au-Prince, the densely populated capital of this vastly overcrowded country.

Until this point in the novel, we have largely seen evidence of the Catholicism of the narrator's mother and her sister – and, here, references to 'l'Eternel' (l. 58), to her piece of cloth which is '[b]leu de Marie' (l. 62) and to 'la résurrection' (l. 92), all demonstrate her familiarity with the Catholic religion. As for most Haitians, however, for her Catholicism is only one of two religions in her life. Here it is Voodoo that emerges as the most important, and she is resentful of her son's implication – 'Tu ne crois pas dans ces trucs?' (l. 54) – that such beliefs are not to be taken seriously. Here, the narrator's own interest in Voodoo is awakened when he refers to the Carrefour-Feuilles area of the town, in which his mother lives, as being 'en plein territoire bizango' (l. 2). This reference to the best known of the Voodoo secret societies sparks off a conversation with his mother which will prove extremely significant as the novel progresses.

The bizango secret society is made up of people who have been chosen, by other members, to join them in following the warrior-spirit Bizango, who protects his followers from having their land stolen and ensures that their spirits return to Africa after their death. Like other secret societies – of which zenglendo, mentioned here by the narrator's mother, is also one – it is usually headed by the local Voodoo priest, who acts as a mediator between the secret society and the wider community that he serves. Such secret societies have their origin in the maroon communities of colonial Haiti, and the element of secrecy has survived since these times. Non-members know of their existence, but know little of their exact membership or of their secret rituals. It is for this reason that the narrator's mother, here, reports her alleged sighting of a bizango member in a rather sensationalized manner. In fact, her description is very reminiscent of the stereotyped descriptions of Voodoo practices which have been popularized in the West. However, the fear with which the narrator's mother speaks about the bizango runs much deeper, and is much more rooted in Haiti's recent history than that of a Westerner (to some extent like her son) looking into, and misunderstanding, Haitian religious practices. As becomes clear later in this extract, the hushed tones that she uses when discussing the phenomena she describes, the fear of being overheard and the general fear of night-time, can all be seen as legacies of life under the Duvalier dictatorship when people constantly risked being reported by neighbours, when violence and disappearances, especially at night, were part of everyday life, and when it was never safe to trust anyone, even within one's own community.

This fear of the night is something that the narrator, here, now recalls, as well as the respect for the night as the domain of the spirits, the ancestors and the dead – the *loa* of Voodoo. What he has more difficulty in coming to terms with are his mother's stories of the mass emptying of the country's cemeteries and her assertion that a large proportion of the people he sees walking about are actually the soulless bodies of the dead – what she eventually allows herself to name as zombies. Although the narrator has travelled and is educated, it is his mother, here, who is able to claim superior knowledge for, as she reminds him, 'je n'ai pas quitté ce pays, même pour une minute, alors je sais de quoi je parle' (l. 38), and he is in the position of cultural observer in his own country. The problem, according to his mother, is that the dead have been let out of their graves against their will, and have been prevented from '[dormir] du sommeil du juste' (l. 65), as is their right. The spirits of the dead are normally benign and, like the narrator's grandmother, exist peacefully alongside the living. It is only if the living relatives have failed to carry out the necessary funeral rituals, or if the dead person was killed by the vengeance of a spirit, that they return to harass the living. Zombies, on the other hand, are those who have been dug up and had their spirit captured and forced to do the bidding of the *bòkò*, a type of Voodoo priest. Traditionally, zombies were said to have been put to work on the sugar plantations, a phenomenon which is evoked in this extract when the narrator's mother refers to the 'files de gens qui marchaient la tête baissée, tout en marmonnant dans un sabir incompréhensibe des histoires épouvantables' (l. 76).[1] This is an 'armée de zombis' (l. 63) which, as she points out, has indeed been awakened by '[l]es prêtres vaudous' (l. 63). There are now so many of them that it is feared that hardly any graves in the entire country are occupied, and that, as the narrator also hears from other sources later, the majority of the inhabitants of Haiti are in fact dead, even while they wander the land of the living.

It is, however, his mother's simple phrase – 'Tu ne peux pas savoir ce qu'on a vécu' (l. 96) – which reveals most to the narrator, and to us, about the stories that she is now telling, for it is here that she hints once again at a more practical explanation for the grave-emptying phenomenon. She explains to her son how, during his absence, ordinary Haitians like herself were prevented from visiting the cemeteries, which are so central a part of their lives because of the importance of venerating and caring for the dead. As she explains: 'Avant, le cimetière était le seul endroit sûr en Haïti' (l. 118); now it has become as insecure as everywhere else. Although she never explicitly refers to the dictatorship years here, what she describes is clearly part of the general way in which, under the Duvaliers, every aspect of the daily life of ordinary Haitians was penetrated and regulated. Worse, that Voodoo, the religion which

1 This bears certain similarities to the phenomenon of the *angajé* in Martinique and Guadeloupe, who swaps labour for the white plantation owner for labour for the devil – see the extract in Chapter 22 above from Patrick Chamoiseau's *Chronique de sept misères*, and the commentaries on it.

until then had been a means of social support and cohesion, was turned against the people whom it had previously served. The chronic insecurity of the Duvalier years has left a huge legacy, and former certainties have been swept away. As becomes clearer later in the novel, there is some truth in the rumours that the majority of Haitians are the 'living dead', bodies without souls, for at the level of historical reality this is the state to which they have been reduced through centuries of oppression, exploitation, poverty and insecurity.

As the narrator explains in this extract, even now, during the second US 'occupation' of Haiti (1994–5), when *Pays sans chapeau* is set, stories of spirits and zombies provide a means of verbalizing, explaining, resisting and surviving the hardships of everyday life in Haiti. They are part of what the narrator calls the 'pays rêvé' (l. 20) of Haitian culture – the land of the dead, or 'pays sans chapeau' – as opposed to 'le pays réel' (l. 20) of the daily struggle for survival. For the narrator, as a writer, 'le pays rêvé' is also the world of his writing, both because he begins researching the phenomenon of the 'zombification' of Haiti for his current novel, and because – as in others of Laferrière's novels – writing itself is also a means of escaping the everyday struggle for survival. On another level, *Pays sans chapeau* itself alternates between 'chapters' entitled 'Pays rêvé', in which the narrator undertakes research for his novel or, as here, is seen at his desk engaged in writing it, and those entitled 'Pays réel', in which he recounts everyday sights and events, meetings with friends and strangers. In this extract, the narrator feels confident that these two worlds 'cheminent côte à côte, sans jamais se rencontrer' (l. 18). However, just as his mother feels unable here to be sure whether it is day or night, or whether people are living or dead, so the narrator finds it increasingly difficult, as the novel progresses, to separate the 'pays rêvé' and the 'pays réel': they are inextricably linked, and equally vital to Haitian life. For the reader, it becomes increasingly difficult to discern the difference between the 'pays réel' of the narrator's experiences in Haiti and the 'pays rêvé' of the material included in his novel. At another level, it also becomes difficult to distinguish between the 'pays réel' of Laferrière's own life and writing, and the 'pays rêvé' of the life and writing of his narrator in *Pays sans chapeau*. Indeed, this is a phenomenon which is familiar from the rest of Laferrière's *œuvre*, in which it is always impossible either simply to conflate author and narrator, autobiography and fiction, or to distinguish readily between them.

Further reading

Laferrière, Dany, *Comment faire l'amour avec un nègre sans se fatiguer* (Montreal: VLB Editeur, 1985).

—— *L'Odeur du café* (Montreal: VLB Editeur, 1991).

—— *Cette grenade dans la main du jeune Nègre est-elle une arme ou un fruit?* (Montreal: VLB Editeur, 1993).

Callaloo 22, 4 (1999) (special issue on Dany Laferrière).

Dash, J. Michael, *The Other America: Caribbean Literature in a New World Context* (Charlottesville: Virginia University Press, 1998).

Jonassaint, Jean, 'Des récits haïtiens au Québec (1937–95): repères pour une histoire', *Neue Romania* 18 (1997), 81–104.

Lahens, Yanick, *L'Exil entre l'ancrage et la fuite: l'écrivain haïtien* (Port-au-Prince: Deschamps, 1990).

Laroche, Maximilien, *L'Avènement de la littérature haïtienne* (Quebec: GRELCA, 1987).

Viticllo, Joëlle, 'Poétiques haïtiennes-québécoises', in Pierre Laurette and Hans-Georges Ruprecht (eds), *Poétiques et imaginaires: franco-polyphonie littéraire des Amériques* (Paris: L'Harmattan, 1995), pp. 349–59.

Language and style

In terms of its structure, this passage consists of one major narrative section (ll. 1–21) supplemented by other incidental comments throughout, and a longer conversational section involving mother and son. An atmosphere of tension is created by the opening sentences, with a string of dramatic expressions – 'Un . . . vent tapeur a emporté' (l. 1), 'Je les ramasse précipitamment' (l. 1), 'pose une pierre dessus' (l. 2), 'torse nu' (l. 2). The two simple and single compound sentences used to set the scene contribute by their direct structure (subject + verb + complement) to the abrupt and eventually ominous nature of the first paragraph (prefigured by 'en plein territoire bizango' (l. 2)). The tension and disturbing atmosphere is significantly increased in the next two sentences by the gruesome description of the bizango,

> qui descendait la pente du morne Nelhio tout en buvant du sang et en gueulant des chants obscènes. Le corps couvert de cendres, nu, indécent, le sexe à l'air, les yeux rouges, la bouche crachant le feu, à la recherche d'une nouvelle victime dans la nuit opaque
>
> (l. 4)

and by the overwhelming effect on the mother (l. 7). As for the narrator, he is much more detached emotionally and is more concerned about his mother. He analyses her tale as a cultural phenomenon rather than becoming personally involved. However, even he cannot resist the effect of the atmosphere. He also finds night in Haiti a frightening experience – expressed through repetition of the word itself (six times in three lines), the use of three minor sentences to focus attention on it (ll. 12, 14) and the use of evocative adjectives to describe it, e.g. night is 'mystérieuse', 'mystique'. Night precedes and therefore is more powerful than the day (l. 17). The contrast between night and day leads on to the contrast between 'Le pays réel: la lutte pour la survie. Et le pays rêvé: tous les phantasmes du peuple le plus mégalomane de la planète' (l. 20) and the implicit allegorical allusion, developed in the rest of the passage, that the people of Haiti have become zombies, creatures of the night, with no soul, no power. This climate of fear pervades the whole passage – 'peur' (ll. 12, 42) and its synonyms ('craindre' (l. 26), 'inquiet' (l. 50), 'tracasser' (l. 51), 'vif mouvement' (l. 56)), together with implicit allusions to fear (e.g. ll. 7, 34, 112, 124) occur throughout the passage. Linked to it is the concern as to how to cope with the omnipresent threat of death. The syncretism of Catholicism and Voodoo, alluded to by references to the soul (ll. 42, 45), 'l'Eternel' (l. 58), 'Bleu de Marie' (l. 62) and the resurrection (l. 92) on the one hand and burial customs (l. 84) and consulting the dead (l. 106) on the other, provides a partial solution for the mother in particular and the population in general.

The conversational section allows this thesis to be expanded and gives insights into the terror governing the lives of the ordinary people of the island. The conversation between mother and son is conducted in rational tones from a linguistic point of view, a series of comments, questions from son and answers from mother. However, a number of comments from the narrator (e.g. ll. 26, 42, 49, 56) suggest the anxiety and fearfulness experienced by his mother. Towards the end of the conversation, the mother declares that she is 'tranquille' (l. 87), that she has done all in her power to protect the dead, whereas the narrator begins to succumb to the eeriness of the situation – 'un frisson me parcourt l'échine' (l. 91). The mother's language becomes more impassioned – the short answers she had given earlier on in the conversation become longer and more detailed – and more rhetorical. In the speech devoted to Madame Lucien, there are minor sentences to attract attention, highlighting of Madame Lucien's name (l. 102), two appositions in the description of her uncle, two adjectives linked without *et*, a relative clause separated from its antecedent. The next two speeches are more emotional still, with exclamations (ll. 108, 112), a question (l. 109), repetition of 'tronc de bananier' (four times, ll. 111, 112, 113), suspense – 'elle a trouvé dans le cercueil, à la place du mort, devine quoi?' (l. 108) – twice switching attention from the banana tree trunk to Madame Lucien, and highlighting (l. 113). In this there seems to be a disjunction between content and speaker. Indeed, the words attributed to the narrator's mother are far from authentic – no creolisms are used, although both mother and narrator would of course have conversed in Creole; furthermore there is not even an attempt to use a correspondingly familiar French. Sentences like 'Moi, je n'ai pas de mort à donner à ces assoiffés de sang pour qu'ils accomplisssent leur diabolique besogne' (l. 93, also l. 76 quoted above on p. 207, and ll. 97, 103), and the use of words like 'défunts' (l. 80) and 'déboussolée' (l. 104) suggest a sanitization of language and are equivalent to what Laferrière, the narrator – or author – would say himself. Although the passage is presented as if it is a conversation between mother and son, it is more importantly a vehicle to describe the situation of fear and superstition that prevails in Haiti, to give insights into the forms of beings, both supernatural and governmental, which terrorize the population. The message takes priority over the medium.

However, the seriousness of the subject matter does not prevent the narrator from occasionally inserting light-hearted comments into his narrative. Some are typical of a mother–son relationship, e.g. 'Je sais que tu n'écoutes personne' (l. 37, also l. 76), 'Tu as une âme, toi' (l. 45). Others reflect his somewhat condescending, sceptical attitude towards life in Haiti, sometimes expressed aloud to his mother, e.g. 'Donc, il ne reste plus un seul mort dans les cimetières d'Haïti à l'heure qu'il est' (l. 78), sometimes conveyed in the words the author puts in the mother's mouth, e.g. the use of 'ratissé' in l. 64, the anecdote concerning Mme Lucien consulting her dead uncle, her lottery wins and the banana tree (l. 102), and sometimes given in asides made by the narrator in the text, e.g. 'Je visualise tous ces morts occupés à filer des aiguilles sans chas pour l'éternité' (l. 89).

Part 4

North America

Chapter 25

Introduction

The dream of *une Amérique française* died in 1759 with the defeat of the French by the British at the brief battle of the Plains of Abraham and the signing in 1763 of the Traité de Paris. When French territorial possessions were handed over to George III, the French settlers, the colonizers, became the colonized. France retained possession of Louisiana, but in 1803 Napoleon sold this last foothold on the continent to the United States. Because France's colonial enterprise on the North American continent was relatively short-lived, the position of francophones there is not like that of any of the other French-speaking populations treated elsewhere in this book. Yet throughout North America today traces of the French colonial past are be found, particularly in place names and family names. Minority francophone communities are scattered throughout Canada and the United States. Indeed, two of the writers to be introduced in this section come from these minority communities, Gabrielle Roy (Chapter 27) being a Franco-Manitoban and Antonine Maillet (Chapter 30) an Acadian from New Brunswick. But despite the existence of pockets of francophone culture across the North American continent, only Quebec has the readership, the publishing houses and sufficient state funding to ensure the vitality of a distinctive North American tradition of writing in French. The province of Quebec is the only North American region with a majority of francophones: about 80 per cent of the 6.5 million population are French speakers, though not necessarily of French extraction.

French settlement in North America began in 1604 when the first permanent residents arrived in present-day Nova Scotia. They survived a harsh winter before founding their settlement of Port Royal. The areas colonized by this population became known as Acadie and have included at different periods parts of modern-day New Brunswick, Nova Scotia, Prince Edward Island and Maine. Because of the geography of North America, these Acadian settlements on the Atlantic coastline of North America were cut off from the main thrust of French colonization that centred on the St Lawrence River, the route that opened up the heart of the continent to explorers, traders and missionaries. The French peasant settlers lived by farming and fishing, and cultivated a position of neutrality in the ongoing conflicts between French and British interests, an attitude which they sustained after the 1713 Treaty of Utrecht that handed Acadie over to British control. At the outset of the Seven Years War between France and Britain in 1755, the Acadian population refused to swear allegiance to the Crown, wishing to maintain their neutral stance. In response, the British army deported the community *en masse* out of the region and deposited them in various other colonies on the eastern seaboard of North America. Some returned to Europe, others travelled on to settle in Louisiana, where their descendants became known as the Cajuns, a community whose distinctive heritage still forms an important part of popular culture in the area, notably in terms of music and cuisine. Many of the deportees made their way back from exile and resettled in the Maritime Provinces. Displaced by British landowners, they were forced to cultivate the less fertile soil on the west of the Bay of Fundy and elsewhere in the Maritimes. This destruction of a community was known as *le grand dérangement* and it forms the historical background to Pélagie's epic journey north in Maillet's *Pélagie-la-Charrette*. The geographical and political separation of Acadie from Quebec, as well as the Acadian people's history as a dispersed minority in a majority anglophone province, has resulted in the preservation of a distinctive Acadian form of the French language, as will be illustrated in the extract from Maillet's novel. Modern-day Acadians in the area around Moncton speak a form of French known as *chiac*, which differs from, but is comparable to, the *joual* of working-class eastern Montreal.

The settlement of modern-day Quebec also dates back to the early seventeenth century. The St Lawrence valley was first explored by Jacques Cartier in the 1530s–40s and by Roberval in the 1540s, both having been sent by the French Crown in search of a shorter trade route to south-east Asia. However, it was only in the seventeenth century that French settlers began to colonize the St Lawrence valley. A permanent fur-trading post was established in 1599 at Tadoussac where the Saguenay River flows into the St Lawrence. The first settlers founded Quebec City in 1608 on a rocky promontory overlooking the St Lawrence, and Montreal was founded in 1642. At this time the Amerindian population of the modern-day province of Quebec was about 25,000, just over 10 per cent of the estimated Amerindian population of North America. Through their contacts with the aboriginal peoples, the French were able to explore the continent (thirty-one of the states of the USA were initially explored or colonized by francophones), and to organize a flourishing fur trade. In return, the European presence created divisions between the different Amerindian nations, undermined their culture, reduced their numbers (through warfare, disease and environmental factors) and redefined their place on the continent by confining them to a series of reserves. It was only in the last decades of the twentieth century that the First Nations[1] began to reclaim their territorial rights in a series of land claims in the federal courts. As a disadvantaged minority, working with other aboriginal peoples across Canada to assert their rights and gain greater autonomy, the aboriginal population of Quebec is hostile to the separatist cause.

From the period of exploration and colonization during the French regime there emerged the distinctive figures of the *coureurs des bois* (traditionally freedom-loving, nomadic francophone males, with a close knowledge of the territory gained through contact with the aboriginal population) and the *voyageurs* (paid employees of, for example, fur-trading companies, who acted as guides, interpreters, liaising with the Amerindian population). These figures have come to represent the archetypal image of the adventurous, independent, nomadic male of North America, a figure drawn on in texts across the span of the corpus selected for this book, particularly those by Félix-Antoine Savard and Jacques Poulin (see Chapters 26 and 32 below). Under French rule New France, as the colony was called, grew slowly. Its population was united by the French language and the institutions of the Catholic church and the family, features which became crucial to the identity of the francophone population once French rule came to an end. If France was relatively unconcerned by the

1 This term includes the Amerindians, the Métis (mixed-race population, usually of French-Canadian/Cree origin) and the Inuit people of Arctic Canada.

loss of its North American colony, the 1759 Conquest has proved to be as traumatic to Quebeckers as was the *grand dérangement* of 1755 to Acadians. What was perceived as an abandonment by France, the mother country, has become a frequent motif in Quebec literature. Since the signing of the Traité de Paris in 1763, the French-speaking population of Canada has been concerned with survival, demographically, linguistically and culturally.[2] Under the terms of the Quebec Act of 1774 Quebec was granted the right to practice Catholicism, retain its version of French civil law and the social system in place (under which, for example, local *seigneurs* or landlords held considerable administrative powers).[3] Nevertheless, francophones in Canada have experienced considerable pressure to assimilate. Historically they have suffered from a position of economic inferiority in relation to anglophones, despite their official position as one of the two 'founding peoples' of Canada. Culturally they have been under threat not only from anglophone Canadians, but perhaps more importantly from the United States (and most Canadians live within 200 miles of the border with the USA). In order to survive as a distinct society, the population long maintained a particularly inward-looking attitude. This was characterized by a reliance on their traditionally high birth rate (*la revanche du berceau*) and by harking back to the traditional values of New France. Yet there were some signs of active opposition to British rule, notably during the period of the Patriots' Rebellion (1837–8), a series of uprisings in favour of greater democratization and critical both of British rule and of the conservatism of the Catholic clergy.

In 1867 the British North America Act established the federal system that separated provincial and federal government. As a separate province Quebec gained certain areas of legislative autonomy, including that of education. But francophones in other provinces saw their access to French-language education diminishing as provinces protected the interests of their English-speaking majority. The second half of the nineteenth century saw repeated waves of emigration of francophone workers from Quebec, where fertile lands were becoming scarce and urban industrialized life seemed to offer better prospects. Between 1851 and 1900 about half a million French Canadians left for New England. Despite the best intentions of the *émigrés*, and the efforts of the Catholic priests who accompanied them to the States, it was difficult for these communities to resist assimilation. Jack Kerouac, famous as a beat generation writer, is one example of those children of French-speaking Canadian parents for whom English was the second language but became the language of their written expression.

In the twentieth century, Quebec, like the rest of Canada, was quickly becoming an urbanized, industrialized society. Yet because of the domination of the province by anglophone capital and by a largely conservative church (which was the provider of much of the educational, health and social services in the province) its francophone population was relatively oppressed. The effects of the Depression of the 1930s were particularly long-lasting in Quebec. In the post-war years, the rising economic expectations of the post-war western world, together with the growing politicization of the labour force, helped to bring about real change in Quebec, culminating in the period of rapid modernization and secularization known as the *révolution tranquille*. This ten-year period, 1960–70, saw the transformation of the social, economic, political and cultural life of Quebec. Much of the change was

2 It is significant that Margaret Atwood also adopts the notion of survival as a key to her interpretation of (predominantly English) Canadian literature in *Survival* (Toronto: Anansi, 1972).

3 The seigneurial system was eventually abolished in 1854.

achieved by reforms which took power away from the church and anglophone interests and gave it to a secular, francophone state. The gap between the revolutionary ideology of some and the reformist practice of the government led to a brief period of terrorist violence in 1970. Since the 1960s there has been a growth of nationalist sentiment in Quebec particularly in the wake of Le Parti Québécois coming to power in 1976 under René Lévesque. His was a modernizing, social democratic party that took as its slogan the phrase 'Maîtres chez nous'. There have been two referenda on the question of sovereignty, the first in 1980, when 60 per cent voted against the proposed model of sovereignty-association, and the second in 1995 when the nationalist campaign led by Jacques Parizeau was defeated by less than 1 per cent of voters. Quebec's position within Canada is now anomalous, not only because of the ongoing uncertainty about its eventual independence, but also because it refused as a province to accept the terms of the new Canadian constitution agreed by the other provinces in 1982. A number of attempts to accommodate Quebec's insistence on the recognition of its status as a distinct society have failed. Quebec's future within Canada remains unresolved at the beginning of the twenty-first century, but in many ways its cultural life has never been stronger.

Writing in French in North America dates from the period of colonization in the form of letters, *récits de voyage*, sermons. Two notable products of the early years of New France are the *Relations* of the Jesuit brothers, a series of reports on life in Canada between 1632 and 1673 that encompass politics, religion and anthropology, and the correspondence of Marie de l'Incarnation, the founder of the Ursuline convent in Quebec City. Her letters, which span a similar period (1639–72), concern spiritual matters, but also the geography and history of the new colony. But French-Canadian literature as a distinct literature developed relatively late, the first novel to be published in French Canada being *L'Influence d'un livre*, by Philippe Aubert de Gaspé, *fils*, in 1837. The atmosphere in French Canada from the 1840s onwards was hardly conducive to a flourishing new literature. After the quashing of the Patriots' Rebellion of 1837–8 by British soldiers, French-Canadian morale was low. In 1839 the Durham Report on the situation of the francophone population within Canada famously declared the French-Canadians to be a people without a history and without a literature of their own. The 1840 Act of Union, that united Upper and Lower Canada, pursued assimilationist policies, French Canada apparently having no distinctive culture worthy of preservation. Yet, from the mid-nineteenth century onwards, the French-Canadian population began to create their own tradition of writing. History and the agricultural way of life were the focus of many works. François-Xavier Garneau's *Histoire du Canada depuis sa découverte* (1845–8), which pays tribute to the role of the francophone population in the history of Canada, can be seen as a vigorous response to Lord Durham's findings. The rural novel, or *roman de la terre* (of which Savard's 1937 novel, *Menaud, maître-draveur*, is a late example), similarly looks to the past, and to the traditional bonds between the French-Canadian family, their Catholic faith, and the land. The popular myth of a rural, morally superior way of life is exemplified in the ideology underpinning much of the genre. However, it would be wrong to assume that all rural novels were nostalgic and idealistic. Some give a much more hard-hitting account of the economic realities of rural life and its injustices. This strand of social critique is developed more strongly in works of the 1940s and 1950s, when the settings selected tend to be industrialized urban communities, as is the case in Roy's *Bonheur d'occasion* (1945) (see Chapter 27 below).

As Quebec moved into the period of radical social transformation, the decade of the *révolution tranquille*, so a new generation of writers produced a rich variety of texts. Indeed it was the 1960s that saw the flowering of what writers now refer to as *la littérature québécoise*. Many, like Marie-Claire Blais (see Chapter 28 below), Roch Carrier and Jacques Godbout, blended social critique with the fantastic or the grotesque. Others, like Hubert Aquin and Réjean Ducharme, experimented with form and with language. The target of such writers was a society which had stifled free thinking and creativity. Michel Tremblay's work has also incorporated the fantastic in a variety of ways (see Chapter 29 below). But in the late 1960s it was the staging of his play *Les Belles Sœurs*, written in *joual*, the dialect of working-class eastern Montreal, that sent shockwaves through the artistic establishment. For here was a writer not only portraying the everyday life of ordinary Quebeckers, but unashamedly using their language to do so. He was thereby undermining the hold of standard French as a linguistic and cultural norm, that had been serving to uphold a subtle but undeniable form of cultural imperialism. In the 1960s and 1970s Quebec writers played a key role in raising awareness of the deep-seated effects of Canada's colonial past. The 1970s also saw the development of a feminist movement that drew inspiration both from the USA and from France. Writers such as Nicole Brossard, Madeleine Gagnon and France Théoret have been among the most innovative in Quebec, crossing the boundary between the genres of essay, poetry and fiction. Since the 1980s Quebec's literature has been less politicized, less national in focus and more interested in, on the one hand, alternative communities and minority groups, and on the other, the exploration of subjectivity and individual identity. The texts by Poulin and Régine Robin (see Chapter 31 below) illustrate this combination of intimacy and pluralism. The contribution of new Quebeckers, exiles or, like Robin, migrants from Asia, Haiti, Europe or South America, has added to the diversity of contemporary writing in Quebec. In a number of cases such writers who move between cultures cannot simply be categorized as belonging to a national literature. Dany Laferrière, the author of one of the texts included in the Caribbean section of this *Companion* (see Chapter 24 above), might equally have been included in the North American selection, as Quebec has been his home for many years and many of his texts relate to the experience of exile in Quebec.

North-American writing in French outside Quebec has a complex history, some non-Québécois writers having been absorbed into Quebec literary life, some remaining determinedly regional in focus, whether in New England or Western Canada. The two non-Québécois Canadian writers included in this volume have achieved considerable international recognition, while keeping some identification with their place of origin and raising the profile of their own minority francophone community. Antonine Maillet's name is synonymous with Acadie, her writing having played a key role in giving Acadians a voice and a place in history. Gabrielle Roy, though Manitoban-born, settled in Quebec once she had become a writer. While many of her works have drawn on her Manitoban roots, others, like *Bonheur d'occasion*, seem to be part of Quebec's literary tradition.

The passages chosen for this part of the *Companion* are intended to give some sense of the breadth of the novel genre in French in North America. The works range from a late *roman de la terre* (Savard) to an example of *l'écriture migrante* (Robin). Of the chosen extracts, all were originally published in Quebec, even though subsequent editions might have appeared in France, or in the form of joint France/Quebec publications. This slightly distorts the overall picture as a number of the better-known writers from Quebec (Jacques Godbout and Anne Hébert, for example) have had Paris-based publishers (Editions du Seuil in both cases). The reasons for this are various and views in Quebec are divided over the decision of writers to publish in France. The choice of a publisher has clear implications for distribution and hence for readership. Church control of publishing in the past meant that much more rigorous censorship applied in Quebec than in France. Because of Quebec's late modernization writers, as recently as the 1950s, who felt stifled by the cultural, political and moral establishment, might have looked to France for publication. While France-based publishers tend to distribute widely in francophone areas of Canada, Canadian/Quebec publishers have found it difficult to penetrate the French market and Quebec-published writers have been much slower to make their name in Europe, although there are now two specialist Canadian/Quebec bookshops in Paris. The distinctive situation of francophone writing in Canada means that translations in Canada are fairly common but by no means automatic and writers in French are still relatively little known despite the official bilingualism of Canada. The selection of extracts which follows does not claim to do any more than open up a literature which is very little known among readers of French outside Canada, but which is exciting and distinctive.

Further reading

Behiels, Michael D., *Quebec since 1945: Selected Readings* (Toronto: Copp Clark Pitman, 1987).

Brown, Craig (ed.), *Histoire générale du Canada* (Montreal: Boréal,1990).

Collectif Clio (Micheline Dumont, Michèle Jean, Marie Lavigne and Jennifer Stoddart), *L'Histoire des femmes au Québec depuis quatre siècles* (Montreal: Le Jour, 1992).

Dickinson, John A. and Young, Brian, *Brève Histoire socio-économique du Québec*, (Sillery (Quebec): Septentrion, 1995).

Griffiths, Naomi, *The Contexts of Acadian History* (Kingston and Montreal: McGill-Queen's University Press, 1992).

Hamelin, Jean and Provencher, Jean, *Brève Histoire du Québec* (Montreal: Boréal, 1997).

Mandel, Eli and Taras, David (eds), *A Passion for Identity: an Introduction to Canadian* Studies (Scarborough (Ontario): Nelson Canada, 1988).

Linteau, P.-A., Durocher, R. and Robert, J.-C., *Histoire du Québec contemporain, I: De la Confédération à la Crise* (Montreal: Boréal Express, 1978).

Linteau, P.-A., Durocher, R., Robert, J.-C. and Ricard, F. *Histoire du Québec contemporain, II: Le Québec depuis 1930* (Montreal: Boréal Express, 1986).

McRoberts, Kenneth, *Quebec: Social Change and Political Crisis* (Toronto: McClelland & Stewart, 1988).

Trofimenkoff, Susan Mann, *The Dream of Nation: a Social and Intellectual History of Quebec* (Toronto: Gage Publishing, 1983).

Chapter 26

Félix-Antoine Savard

Menaud, maître-draveur (Montreal: Bibliothèque Québécoise, 1992), pp. 34–9. First published Quebec: Librairie Garneau, 1937.

Une race qui ne sait pas mourir!

Voilà maintenant que cette parole flambait dans l'humble maison comme un feu d'abatis dans la clairière du printemps.

Avec ferveur, Menaud répéta: «Une race qui ne sait pas mourir!»

Il se tenait là, fixé sur ces mots d'où jaillissaient une force, une jeunesse, quelque chose de comparable au printemps miraculeux de Mainsal avec ses explosions de vie après le froid, la neige, les six longs mois d'hiver.

Une race qui ne sait pas mourir!

Il se fit un long silence.

Puis, il ouvrit la porte toute grande; et, dans le soir immobile, il contempla longtemps la campagne endormie, laissant ses regards voler jusqu'aux horizons lointains, et revenir ainsi que des engoulevents au nid de ses pensées.

L'homme était beau à voir. Droit et fort malgré la soixantaine. La vie dure avait décharné à fond son visage, y creusant des rigoles et des rides de misère, et le colorant des mêmes ocres et des mêmes gris que les maisons, les rochers et les terres de Mainsal.

La vie dure! Elle lui avait fait une âme sage, donné le goût des choses calmes, profondes d'où sa pensée sortait peu. On sentait, chez lui, cette force grave, patiente que donnent le travail et la nature austère. Il racontait ses souvenirs sur un ton simple, en long, triste souvent. Mais parfois, aussi, sous la surface tranquille, on devinait une passion sauvage pour la liberté; et, tel un fleuve de printemps, à pleine mesure d'âme, l'amour de son pays.

Veuf depuis quelques années, Menaud vivait seul avec sa fille et son fils.

Sa femme avait tout fait pour enraciner au sol ce fier coureur de bois. Et lui, par amour pour elle, il avait défriché cette âpre terre de Mainsal, toujours prêt, cependant, à s'évader du regard vers le bleu des monts dès que le vent du Nord venait lui verser au cœur les paroles magiques et les philtres embaumés.

Mais depuis la mort de sa femme, par un froid matin de novembre, tous ses instincts de chasseur s'étaient réveillés en lui.

Il avait retrouvé ses ailes, repris ses élans de jeunesse, et, avec Joson, son fils, il passait le printemps, l'automne et les premiers mois des longs hivers dans la montagne dont il était roi.

Or, comme on était à la fin d'avril, les cloches du printemps s'étaient mises à sonner là-bas, dans les tours et les clochers de la forêt prodigieuse. La voix de la grande rivière avait commencé de se faire entendre. Elle annonçait le temps de la drave.

Accompagné d'un interprète, un ingénieur de la compagnie était venu la veille chez le vieux maître-draveur, pour demander ses services.

Les pourparlers avaient été longs et durs, entrecoupés de silences hostiles et de protestations violentes contre cet étranger qui le commanderait, dans son propre pays, lui, seigneur et maître des longs trains de bois que, durant tant d'années, il avait conduits, sous la pique de fer, dans les cris et les tumultes de l'eau révoltée.

Mais les signes que lui avaient faits Joson et Marie, et, surtout, l'image apparue de la grande rivière, le visage et l'appel de cette route par où s'était écoulée sa vie, tout cela l'avait calmé.

Il avait fini par consentir.

Mais, ce soir-là, veille du départ, tout ce qu'il avait eu la faiblesse de taire lui remontait au cœur. Au feu de cette lampe qui allumait des escarbilles en ses regards, il avait l'air d'un forgeron martelant ses pensées de fer.

Après le récurage, il avait demandé à Marie de lui faire un petit bout de lecture, dans l'espoir que les mots des livres l'apaiseraient, peut-être.

Mais, voilà que, de cette diable de lecture, étaient sortis des mots en armes, et qu'avec eux toutes les voix du pays, de la montagne, des champs et des bois s'étaient engouffrées chez lui, ébranlant son âme et sa maison comme une bourrasque d'automne.

«Des étrangers sont venus! Ils ont pris presque tout le pouvoir . . .»

Menaud se rappela la visite de l'Anglais la veille . . .

«Une race qui ne sait pas mourir . . .»

Il se promenait de long en large, maintenant, répétait ces mots-là, s'arrêtait brusquement, faisait de grands gestes comme s'il se fût battu contre lui-même, contre sa propre servilité.

Marie, elle s'était rassise à son métier.

Et l'on n'entendait plus que le frappement du ros qui tassait la tissure entre les fils de la chaîne.

Un rythme la berçait de droite à gauche. De ses deux bras harmonieusement levés l'un après l'autre, elle semblait battre la mesure à quelque mystérieuse musique, cependant qu'à la trame de cette lourde étoffe grise, elle insérait toute la chaleur de son être pour son père, pour Joson, qu'elle protégerait ainsi contre le froid qui glace là-bas le cœur des hommes.

C'était sa manière à elle de dire à chaque coup de manchette: «Une race qui ne sait pas mourir!»

Ce qu'elle faisait là, sa mère et bien d'autres femmes l'avaient fait avant elle, entremêlant aux laines de subtils sentiments de force, de résistance, et des prières même.

Et peut-être aussi, dans la navette légère, la belle voyait-elle passer un songe d'amour, parfois . . .

Vers les huit heures, le chien se mit à grogner.

Quelqu'un secoua ses pieds sur le palier du seuil et cogna. C'était le Délié, le prétendant, depuis les Fêtes.

Marie ouvrit la porte et dit tout simplement: «Entre! Il y a une chaise icitte pour toi.»

Puis elle se mit à rougir.

Depuis quelque temps, au sortir de l'église surtout, elle avait senti que les yeux du Délié s'arrêtaient sur elle. Aussi sa chair s'en était-elle émue, comme s'émeuvent les arbres du printemps quand le soleil les réchauffe d'amour.

Il prit une chaise; elle, son travail.

Mais le dialogue silencieux qu'échangeaient son cœur et la pensée de son père, ainsi qu'une laine fragile, s'était rompu.

Text and context

Usually classified as a *roman de la terre*, *Menaud, maître-draveur* is a relatively late example of a genre of writing that takes rural Quebec as its setting and is concerned with the survival of the francophone population as a race apart, thanks to its distinct language, faith and traditional rural lifestyle. Its author, Félix-Antoine Savard, worked as a parish priest from the mid-1920s to the mid-1940s, ministering both in rural areas like those depicted in this novel, and in the new settlements established in Abitibi in the Depression years of the 1930s. His education (Classical Studies and then training for the priesthood in Chicoutimi) and his experiences as a priest made him part of the traditional intellectual élite of his generation. He shared their distrust of industrialization and urbanization, and retained a belief in the land as a key to the salvation of the race. Yet *Menaud, maître-draveur* is no simple celebration of the agricultural way of life. In tracing one man's tragic decline from being a master log-driver to an obsessed and confused old man, the narrative also tells of a community that has passed from one form of domination to another and a race whose claims on the territory remain a distant dream.

The function of this early passage in the novel is primarily that of exposition. The text is constructed as a series of layers of reference to the present moment of action, to recent events and to the more distant past. These open up the contradictions and conflicts that motivate the subsequent development of the plot and are common to many examples of the *roman de la terre* .

The third-person narration of the evening spent by Menaud and his daughter closes with the arrival of le Délié, Marie's suitor, which introduces a note of discord into the father–daughter relationship. Into this scene the narrator inserts three analepses. The first of these gives a brief history of Menaud's married life. The second and third are flashbacks to a visit from the forestry company's engineer and his interpreter, and the awkward negotiations which ensued ('entrecoupés de silences hostiles et de protestations violentes' (l. 39)). Menaud's emotional response to this visit is heightened by this two-stage flashback, recounted in the third person yet adopting his perspective on 'cet étranger' (l. 40), representative of 'foreign' power on his soil.

This extract, and the novel as a whole, is strangely dominated by *Maria Chapdelaine* (1916), the novel from which Marie reads to her father on the eve of his departure for the mountains. It is perhaps symptomatic of Quebec's colonial relationship to France and then to Britain that this work, probably the most widely read 'French-Canadian' novel, was written by a French author, Louis Hémon. Savard's use of *Maria Chapdelaine* as an intertext encourages the reader to make the comparison between these two texts, twenty years apart, a process that is explicitly demonstrated in the chosen passage. In the preceding, opening section of the novel, Marie had been reading Hémon's text to Menaud, her presumably illiterate father. Menaud is now reflecting on a key phrase from the text, 'une race qui ne sait pas mourir' (l. 1), taken from the section where Maria hears three 'voices' that persuade her to marry a fellow settler and so contribute to the survival of her people, rather than emigrating with her second suitor to the manufacturing towns of the United States. This phrase structures the rest of the passage, appearing five times and acting as a refrain that binds the short sections together. In the new context of Savard's text the reference to 'une race qui ne sait pas mourir' is at once a declaration of traditionalist nationalism (Quebec must preserve its language, faith and rural way of life in order to survive) and an ironic pointer. Menaud's family, as a microcosm of the race, will be diminished by the death of Menaud's son and Menaud's own descent into dementia, as the local population see more and more of the territory around them and the resources within it being taken over by anglophone capitalists. Twenty years after the publication of Hémon's text, the appeal to traditionalism and isolationism to ensure the survival of the race seems all the more desperate.

Nevertheless the effect of the phrase in the text, used by narrator and protagonist alike, is dramatic. The first three uses occur in quick succession, like the incantation of a chant or a spell, accompanied first by images of fire: 'cette parole flambait . . . comme un feu d'abatis dans la clairière du printemps' (l. 2); then by the allusion to a jet, or rush of sap: 'ces mots d'où jaillissaient' (l. 5); and third by the image of flight: 'laissant ses regards voler' (l. 11), which is reinforced later with references to 'ailes' and 'élan' (l. 30). With the fourth repetition of the quotation, the effect of the words on Menaud moves from the metaphorical and psychological to the physical as he begins to enact his agitation with 'de grands gestes' (l. 61), so leading the reader to expect some decisive action to follow. At this point the narrator turns to Marie, whose weaving itself becomes tied up with the sense of movement within the passage. In contrast to the sudden movements of her father, Marie's body is taken up with the rhythmical swaying of her weaving, the narrator representing her (feminine) domestic activity as a complement to her father's desire for action. By reintroducing the quote from Hémon a fifth time, the narrator draws Marie's weaving, and by extension, the role of women, into the struggle for survival of the Quebec people. As if to close the section down with a diminuendo, Marie's movements are described as 'entremêlant aux laines de subtils sentiments de force, de résistance, et de prières même' (l. 74), moving back from a suggestion of physical resistance to mental or spiritual resistance. The spirit of resistance that builds up in the passage is triggered by the coincidence between the nationalist discourse of *Maria Chapdelaine* and Menaud's imminent departure for the mountains to work as log-driver for the anglophone-owned timber company which holds the logging rights on the tracts of forest in the Appalachian mountains to the north-west of Mainsal.

Menaud and his daughter are represented as being receptive to voices and sounds which come from a diverse range of sources: the literary text read aloud ('cette diable de lecture' and 'des mots en armes' (l. 53)); the sound of the north wind which inspires Menaud with its 'paroles magiques' and 'philtres embaumés'(l. 27); the sound of the forest linked metaphorically with church bells; the summoning call of 'la grande rivière' (l. 35); and 'quelque mystérieuse musique' (l. 67) which seems to inhabit Marie as she weaves. The voices and sounds to which they respond and which seem to represent their moral and spiritual values suggest a world view which combines some elements of Christianity and literary culture with a spiritual identification with nature in its wild state. Nature imagery appears throughout the passage, whether to describe Menaud's physical appearance or his thought patterns, or to suggest the strength of Marie's sexual attraction to le Délié, her suitor, assuring the connection in the reader's mind between the protagonists and their environment.

The use of the quotations from *Maria Chapdelaine* and the similar patterns of imagery which build on the bond between father and daughter would seem to suggest that the male and female are in sympathy with one another, similarly in tune with nature and embodying a certain form of Quebec nationalism. And yet the passage introduces two points of conflict, one of which relates to the past and one to the future. Menaud's late wife figures in the text as an obstacle to Menaud's deepest instinct, the love of freedom, an obstacle from which her death has finally released him (l. 24). The second point of conflict is also represented by a female character – Marie – since her chosen suitor, le Délié, accepts and supports anglophone economic interests in the region. His arrival causes the breaking of the 'laine fragile' (l. 89) that had united the thoughts of father and daughter.

Savard's representation of Menaud draws on two distinctive models of masculinity which have become part of Quebec's popular image of its own past, and which recur in many of the *romans de la terre*. By instinct and inclination he is a *coureur des bois*, the archetypal free male in Quebec, who, from the earliest days of colonization, lived from his knowledge of the land, as guide, as fur trader, living beyond the reach of the laws of the colony and in close contact with the aboriginal population. Up in the mountains Menaud can still dream of liberty, independence and domination. Yet he has spent his married life confined to clearing and cultivation of the land in the narrow stretch of farmland between the St Lawrence and the mountains, to the north of Quebec City. The harsh, but monotonous lifestyle of the *habitant* has left its mark on Menaud, 'le colorant des mêmes ocres et des mêmes gris que les maisons, les rochers et les terres de Mainsal' (l. 14). In contrast to this life bound to the soil, the life of the *coureur des bois* is suggested by images of flight, height and distance, Menaud being 'toujours prêt . . . à s'évader du regard vers le bleu des monts' (l. 25). Yet though the life of the *coureur des bois* is associated in the text with freedom from constraint, and positively connoted through the imagery employed, any idealism is undercut by the brief reminders of the economic context. For in 1930s Quebec Menaud can be neither 'roi' nor 'seigneur' nor 'maître' of the mountains (ll. 32, 41). His desire to work on the mountain rivers outweighs his repugnance at working for the Anglo-Canadian timber company. Menaud's position is, then, symptomatic of that of the francophone population of Quebec: he feels dispossessed in his own land, a land exploited for its resources by a whole series of 'Anglais' (l. 58), be they British, Canadian or from the United States. For Savard's contemporaries the terms 'roi' and 'seigneur' would have been reminiscent of the Quebec people's colonial and feudal past (the seigneurial system of land-ownership lasted in Quebec until 1854). The term 'maître', on the other hand, had a particularly topical resonance as part of the nationalist historian Abbé Groulx's 1937 call for the Quebec people to become 'maîtres chez nous'. To today's reader, Menaud's desire for independence, bound to fail in the 1930s, may seem prophetic rather than dated. For while the nature of Quebec nationalism has seen many transformations, the question of sovereignty remains alive.

Further reading

Savard, Félix-Antoine, *L'Abatis* (Montreal: Fides, 1943).

Boivin, Aurélien, 'Présentation' to Félix-Antoine Savard, *Menaud, maître-draveur* (Montreal: Bibliothèque québécoise, 1992), pp. 7–20.

Brochu, André, 'Félix-Antoine Savard. Menaud ou l'impossible fête', *L'Instance critique 1961–73* (Montreal: Leméac, 1974), pp. 247–74.

Grandpré, Pierre de and Duhamel, Roger, in Pierre de Grandpré (ed.), *Histoire de la littérature française du Québec*, tome II (1900–1945), (Montreal: Librairie Beauchemin, 1968), pp. 273–80.

Hémon, Louis, *Maria Chapdelaine* (Montreal: Bibliothèque québécoise, 1990).

Purdy, Anthony, *A Certain Difficulty of Being* (Toronto: McGill-Queen's University Press, 1990), Chapter 2.

Ricard, François, *L'Art de Félix-Antoine Savard dans 'Menaud, maître-draveur'* (Montreal: Fides, 1972).

Robidoux, Réjean and Brochu, André, *Le Roman canadien du vingtième siècle* (Ottawa: Editions de l'Université d'Ottawa, 1966), pp. 33–43.

Smart, Patricia, *Writing in the Father's House. The Emergence of the Feminine in the Quebec Literary Tradition* (Toronto: University of Toronto Press, 1991), Chapter 2.

Language and style

This linguistic commentary will concentrate upon the treatment of a number of themes and images present in the passage and upon the characterization of two members of the Menaud household, father and daughter, who are its focus.

The first major theme is that of silence and speech, the first aspect of which is evoked by the ambient atmosphere of the setting, one of calm and quietness, e.g. 'un long silence' (l. 9), 'le soir immobile . . . la campagne endormie' (l. 10). But it is particularly evident in Menaud himself, whose complex characterization occupies about two-thirds of the passage (ll. 1–62). On the one hand, he is subject to a brooding silence, e.g. 'une âme sage . . . le goût des choses calmes, profondes . . . la surface tranquille' (l. 17). On the other, he is troubled by pent-up energy and emotion within himself, e.g. 'cette force grave, patiente . . . une passion sauvage' (l. 18). This contradiction in his character is epitomized in his late wife's ambition for him: – 'enraciner au sol ce fier coureur des bois' (l. 19). It is this suppressed energy and love of the wilderness which responds to the quotation from *Maria Chapdelaine*, repeated five times in the passage, which his daughter has previously read to him and with which he strongly identifies: 'une race qui ne sait pas mourir'. The power of the words is seen in such expressions as 'cette parole flambait dans l'humble maison' (l. 2); 'ces mots d'où jaillissaient une force, une jeunesse' (l. 5). Later he asks his daughter 'de lui faire un petit bout de lecture, dans l'espoir que les mots des livres l'apaiseraient' (l. 51). However, the search for peace is not fulfilled – 'cette diable de lecture' with its 'mots en armes' (l. 53) disturbs him greatly, 'ébranlant son âme', and makes him only too aware of his helplessness (l. 62). Yet the words of the book are not the only voices he hears. Reinforcing the words of the book are other words, ranging from 'les paroles magnifiques' of the mountains (l. 27), to 'La voix de la grande rivière' (l. 34), to the climax with 'toutes les voix du pays, de la montagne, des champs et des bois' (l. 54). The message from the book, the mountains and all of nature is clear and direct. Menaud has no difficulty understanding or communicating with nature. However, when it comes to communicating with the company engineer (l. 39), the situation is quite different. Not only is an interpreter required – because they speak different languages enshrining the inequality of the *langue dominante* and the *langue dominée* – but the communication is by no means easy, e.g. 'Les pourparlers avaient été longs et durs, entrecoupés de silences hostiles et de protestations violentes' (l. 39). Later Menaud accuses himself of having had 'la faiblesse de taire' things he should have said (l. 48).

Three other themes criss-cross the theme of silence and speech. First, nostalgia for the wilderness is underlined by the recurrent use of the word 'regard', e.g. 'il contempla longtemps la campagne endormie, laissant ses regards voler jusqu'aux horizons lointains' (l. 10, also ll. 26, 50). The adjective 'long' which occurs eight times in this section constitutes the second of these subsidiary themes. It serves to underscore the general atmosphere of life in the Menauds' community and Menaud's existence itself and, because of the double reference, succeeds in making Menaud himself a microcosm of his beloved wilderness: Quebec, e.g. 'les six longs mois d'hiver' (l. 7, also ll. 31, 41); Menaud, e.g. 'un long silence' (l. 9, also ll. 11, 20, 60); the distressing interview with the company engineer is characterized thus: 'Les pourparlers avaient été longs et durs' (l. 39). Linked to this recurrent use of 'long' is the use of 'lointain', with a similar value: 'laissant ses regards voler jusqu'aux horizons lointains' (l. 11). The third theme involves the use of the adjective 'dur', which has a similar cohesive function to 'long' and is in fact linked to it in l. 39, with reference to the negotiations with the engineer (quoted above). Describing Menaud's life, it occurs in ll. 13 and 17: 'La vie dure'. An alternative, 'âpre', occurs with reference to the land: 'il avait défriché cette âpre terre' (l. 25).

The section of the passage devoted to Menaud contains a number of images, which are significant as much in their tenors as in their vehicles. The significance of sounds and words has already been pointed out in the definition of Menaud's character. Four of the images have 'parole'/'mots'/'voix' as their tenors, e.g. 'Voilà maintenant que cette parole flambait dans l'humble maison comme un feu d'abatis dans la clairière du printemps' (l. 2); 'Il se tenait là, fixé sur ces mots d'où jaillissaient une force, une jeunesse, quelque chose de comparable au printemps miraculeux de Mainsal' (l. 5, also l. 58 (quoted above)). Similarly, another of the key words, 'regards', is the tenor of another of the images: 'laissant ses regards voler jusqu'aux horizons lointains, et revenir ainsi que des engoulevents au nid de ses pensées' (l. 11). From the point of view of the vehicle, the natural world is represented in all but one of the images and emphasizes Menaud's obsession with nature. The seasons feature prominently – spring (ll. 3, 6 quoted above), 'sous la surface tranquille . . . on devinait . . . tel un fleuve du printemps . . . l'amour de son pays' (l. 20, and suggested l. 10 (quoted above)); autumn l. 55 (quoted above). The reference to nighthawks is echoed in the fairly traditional image '[i]l avait retrouvé ses ailes' (l. 30). The remaining image drawn from nature is 'les cloches du printemps s'étaient mises à sonner là-bas, dans les tours et les clochers de la forêt prodigieuse' (l. 33), and evokes the religious, mystical attitude Menaud feels for the forest, which is also suggested in 'le vent du Nord venait lui verser au cœur les paroles magiques et les philtres embaumés' (l. 26). After the visit of the engineer, the imagery takes on a quite different aspect, e.g. '[Menaud] avait l'air d'un forgeron martelant ses pensées de fer' (l. 50): the earlier 'nid de ses pensées' (l. 12), with its evocation of freedom in nature, is replaced by an anvil for his 'pensées de fer'. The contrast between Menaud's yearning for the wilderness and his being rooted in Mainsal is emphasized by the contrasts between the colour terms used, e.g. 'La vie dure . . . le colorant des mêmes ocres et des mêmes gris que les maisons, les rochers et les terres de Mainsal' (l. 13); '[Menaud] toujours prêt . . . à s'évader du regard vers le bleu des monts' (l. 25).

The pace of the text changes with the description of Marie (ll. 62–89). A series of contrasts and parallels between the depiction of father and daughter emerge. Whereas the description of her father had focused on his past and his desire to follow his instincts into the mountains as soon as he could (l. 28), the narrative involving Marie is very much based in the present. However, sounds are an important element of the characterization of both of them. Whereas the sounds and voices of nature had inspired and tempted her father, it is the sounds of domesticity (the shuttle and the weaving machine) and her heart (her love of the family and nascent love for le Délié) that dominate Marie's life: 'Un rythme la berçait . . . harmonieusement . . . elle semblait battre la mesure à quelque mystérieuse musique' (l. 66), 'chaque coup de manchette' (l. 71, also l. 64). Whereas the sounds affecting her father were external to him and tended to disturb him, Marie assumes the rhythms of her work and is in harmony with them. Another contrast between father and daughter is seen in the resignation of her father to living in Mainsal and Marie's contentment and protective instinct (l. 69). The material she is weaving may be grey (compare the colours in Menaud's life), but it is being woven to provide warmth and protection for her menfolk. The refrain that had obsessed her father is repeated now, but perhaps with a narrower interpretation: now 'la race' (l. 71) may refer to just her family. Another link with her father occurs in the imagery connected with Marie: spring figures again – 'Aussi sa chair s'en était-elle émue, comme s'émeuvent les arbres du printemps quand le soleil les réchauffe d'amour' (l. 85). The image – 'le dialogue silencieux qu'échangeaient son cœur et la pensée de son père, ainsi qu'une laine fragile, s'était rompue' (l. 88) – not only underlines the domestic side of her nature but also prefigures a serious rupture between her and her father later on. These similarities, contrasts and potential conflicts between father and daughter – sounds and the forest, in particular – emphasize their identity with their 'race' and their different aspirations and provide the structure and cohesion of the passage.

Chapter 27

Gabrielle Roy

Bonheur d'occasion (Montreal: Boréal, 1993), pp. 381–4. First published Montreal: Société des éditions Pascal, 1945.

Et elle décida: «Je vais me rendre à l'hôpital.» Elle chercha ses chaussures sous le lit, ses bas. Elle arriva à la commode où se trouvait son chapeau. Elle n'arrivait plus à se rappeler où elle avait mis son manteau. Elle cherchait à se souvenir désespérément, faisait le tour de la pièce du regard et recommençait encore. Ses pauvres vêtements . . . elle en avait honte . . . Honte de s'en aller ainsi se remettre entre les mains d'étrangers . . . Et pourtant, un instinct plus fort, tout occupé à défier l'atroce emprise de la douleur, lui conseillait de partir comme elle était, à peine vêtue . . . Enfin, elle trouva son manteau, elle s'en couvrit, elle partit, chancelante, ne démêlant pas vraiment par quels moyens elle s'y prendrait pour se rendre à l'hôpital et espérant à demi ne jamais y arriver. Sur le seuil, elle se heurta à la voisine qui amenait la sage-femme.

Quelques instants plus tard, recouchée dans son lit, elle pensa avec tristesse, avec une profonde gêne: «Ça y est; je dois être rendue à l'hôpital.» Toujours elle avait eu horreur des hôpitaux. Elle imaginait des lumières brutales, une mise en scène terrible, des étrangers autour d'elle . . . Elle n'avait pu se résigner à y entrer même selon l'avis du médecin, à la naissance de Philippe, qui avait été dure. Mais cette fois, elle n'avait pas dû y échapper.

Peu à peu pourtant, à l'odeur, au bruit, elle reconnaissait l'atmosphère de son logis. Un léger soupir de satisfaction lui échappa. Elle risqua un coup d'œil, chercha à se remettre dans le présent, à donner une signification à ce qui se passait autour d'elle. Deux femmes s'activaient dans la chambre. «Des inconnues, quand même!» se dit-elle.

Voilà ce qui lui avait toujours été le plus pénible. Etre livrée au regard, à l'assistance d'autrui. Avoir si effroyablement besoin de secours. Elle essayait de ramener un pli du drap, une couverture sur elle.

Une inconnue? Non pourtant, elle reconnaissait maintenant le visage incliné vers elle. C'était le visage qu'elle avait entrevu à la naissance de Daniel, de la petite Gisèle aussi.

Des mains fortes l'aidaient, l'humiliaient profondément. Mais sa pensée, par instants, détachée du présent, flottait, s'en allait, cherchant des souvenirs épars. Dans les années passées, elle coulait, filait comme un bateau à la dérive qui aperçoit le paysage à reculons, très vite, parfois toute une vaste courbe, parfois un seul point de la rive, clair, précis, saillant. Elle fuyait sur ce bateau emporté, redescendant à une allure vertigineuse ce courant de sa vie qu'elle avait montée si lentement, au prix de si grandes difficultés, et des choses qu'elle avait à peine remarquées au cours du premier voyage lui apparaissaient nettement. Mais tout défilait sans s'ordonner et trop vite pour qu'elle s'y reconnût. Et plus les visions se mêlaient, se superposaient, moins elle comprenait. Il y avait elle, troublée, radieuse, très douce, fiancée à Azarius. Et revoyant cette jeune fille vêtue de mousseline claire, certain jour d'été, au bord du Richelieu limpide, elle eût pu lui sourire vaguement comme à une étrangère dont la rencontre est agréable, sans importance, purement fortuite. Et puis, il y avait elle tout aussitôt, soudain vieillie, qui acceptait le sacrifice d'Eugène . . . Mais, non, elle luttait contre Eugène. Elle luttait pour un peu d'argent. Un peu d'argent qu'il lui enlevait et avec lequel elle devait acheter des vêtements, de la nourriture. Et elle était de nouveau sur la rive du Richelieu: sa robe d'été bruissait encore au vent léger de là-bas et ses cheveux emmêlés, sentant le foin, les fleurs, lui fouettaient le visage . . . Mais voici qu'elle marchait, marchait par les rues du faubourg, cherchant une maison où elle pourrait accoucher . . . Et puis, il fallait se hâter de finir une robe de mariage. Pour Florentine qui allait épouser Emmanuel? . . . Non, c'était avant le départ de Florentine, c'était au temps où ils étaient secourus par l'assistance publique. . . . Elle cousait pour apporter sa part aux dépenses du ménage . . . Il ne fallait pas être longtemps malade . . . Elle perdrait ses clientes . . . Mademoiselle Elise voulait sa robe tout de suite . . . Mon Dieu, il fallait pourtant se lever et achever cette robe . . . Le brusque effort qu'elle tenta déchaîna une vague de douleur aigüe. Maintenant, elle était penchée sur un lit d'hôpital. Qui donc allait mourir? Qui donc souffrait tant? Où était-elle? Daniel? Ne pouvait-elle rien pour calmer la douleur de cet enfant? Ou la sienne? Leurs souffrances semblaient s'être réunies, fondues dans sa propre chair . . . Et puis, un faible cri lui parvint. Elle s'abattit sur l'oreiller. Et presque aussitôt, à travers des épaisseurs d'ombre, une voix:

– Vous avez vu ça, madame Lavallée! Pas une plainte. Pas même une petite plainte. Courageuse comme madame Lacasse, il y a en pas gros.

«Pas une plainte», songea Rose-Anna. Qui donc avait déjà prononcé ces mots? Puis elle se souvint: c'était la sage-femme qui avait assisté sa mère. «Pas une plainte . . .» Rose-Anna se sentit plus près de sa mère, soudain, qu'elle ne l'avait jamais été. Une certaine fierté, une sorte de courage gonflèrent son cœur, comme si, étrangement, une force nouvelle venait de lui être transmise par le souvenir de la vieille madame Laplante.

Son esprit vacillait entre le sommeil et mille petites préoccupations qui l'assaillaient déjà, qu'elle savait le temps venu de reprendre. Elle allongea la main pour indiquer un tiroir de la commode où la sage-femme trouverait des vêtements de nouveau-né. Elle avait toujours eu tout prêt: des petites robes ni ornées ni soyeuses, mais propres et chaudes.

Et anxieuse, subitement dévorée de crainte, elle demanda à voir l'enfant. Toujours cette peur de donner naissance à un enfant mal conformé.

– Un beau garçon, dit la sage-femme. Délicat, mais bien vivant. Six livres, je dirais, dit-elle, le soupesant entre ses bras ronds.

Et Rose-Anna eut un éblouissement, un désir éperdu de le tenir dans ses bras. Enfin lavé, roulé dans un édredon, il lui fut apporté. Les petits poings fermés sortaient un peu de la couverture. Sur les joues satinées tremblait l'ombre des cils blonds, fins comme du duvet. La fragilité d'un nouveau-né l'avait toujours profondément émue. Elle s'abandonna enfin au repos, un bras supportant le tout petit être qui dormait. Elle se sentait vidée de douleur, de toute profonde tristesse. Après chaque maternité, il lui arrivait de se retrouver ainsi, le cœur alangui, et courageuse en même temps, comme si elle venait de puiser encore à la source mystérieuse, intarissable de sa jeunesse. Il lui sembla que ce n'était pas son douzième enfant qu'elle tenait contre elle, mais le premier, l'unique. Et pourtant, cette tendresse ravie n'excluait point les autres enfants. Elle les entendit entrer un peu plus tard, ramenés par Yvonne qui les avait conduits à la promenade après classe. Enivrés de grand air et de liberté, ils réclamaient leur souper. Rose-Anna se surprit à diriger la sage-femme qui selon la coutume du faubourg, remplirait l'office de bonne aussi bien que de garde-malade.

Il y a du rôti froid et du pain, murmura-t-elle. Vous ferez manger les enfants. Et vous verrez à ce que leurs vêtements soient prêts pour l'école demain matin. Y a souvent des petits accrocs à raccommoder.

Text and context

The extract is taken from a chapter towards the end of the novel and recounts the birth of a twelfth child to Rose-Anna Lacasse. While the image of the mother at the heart of a large family is a common motif in Quebec literature, both in the *roman de la terre* and in post-war texts, the representation of childbirth is far less common. The centrality of the mother-figure to Quebec literature results from two linked influences: the teachings of the Catholic church and the survivalist ideology which stressed the importance of sustaining a high birth-rate among the French-speaking population to ensure their continued existence as one of the two 'founding peoples' of Canada. Yet in a society where the Virgin Mary symbolized perfect motherhood, the female body, sexuality and reproduction were by definition impure, and the church's guidance on conjugal love was couched largely in terms of sin. The resulting ambivalence towards the child-bearing woman is evident in the chosen passage.

The structure of the extract can be seen as a scene in three parts: first Rose-Anna is shown on her own, terrified at the prospect at giving birth alone; the central section relates the process of childbirth, and the accompanying mental journey into the past; finally, with the birth, of the child, Rose-Anna returns to the present, with the strength to continue. The reader follows Rose-Anna through the process by sharing her thought processes and impressions. The effect of this close focus is, rather paradoxically, that the reader is almost taken by surprise by the abrupt appearance of the baby: 'Et puis, un faible cri lui parvint' (l. 59). Rather than the physical experience of the birth, the passage is concerned with the emotions and the metaphysical significance of the event.

In order to achieve this close insight into the mind (if not the body) of Rose-Anna, Roy uses a narrative form which largely moulds itself to Rose-Anna's consciousness thanks to a number of devices, discussed in detail in the 'Language and style' commentary. This passage is narrated in the third person, but, as is true throughout the novel, the narrative voice is not that of a standard omniscient narrator. The passage quickly moves from the physical to the psychological. The subjectivity of the passage then becomes more strongly marked as the passage takes on some of the characteristics of a stream of consciousness in which the content and the structure of the protagonist's mental experience take over. This is evident in the sometimes contradictory statements which reflect Rose-Anna's state of mind, as in her confusion about whether or not she has gone to hospital and whether or not she recognizes the two women present. The subjectivity of the account is also obvious in the internal perspective from which we see her actions and the actions of others. The external world only penetrates her consciousness with difficulty. Once the child is born it is as if Rose-Anna resurfaces and rejoins the present. This part of the extract marks a return to a more coherent, chronological account of a sequence of events, together with generalizing statements about Rose-Anna's experience of maternity: 'Elle avait toujours eu tout prêt' (l. 72); 'La fragilité d'un nouveau-né l'avait toujours profondément émue' (l. 81).

The longest paragraph in the extract, which is framed by the awareness of the 'stranger's' hands at the beginning and her voice at the end, focuses the most closely on Rose-Anna. First it describes her mental state and then represents that mental state by moving towards a form of interior monologue as it progresses, as Rose-Anna retreats within herself to cope with the pain and its public exposure. The sentences imitate a chain of thoughts and memories, with links and repetitions as the thoughts clarify or move on: 'Et puis, il y avait elle tout aussitôt, soudain vieillie, qui acceptait le sacrifice d'*Eugène* . . . Mais non, elle *luttait* contre *Eugène*. Elle *luttait* pour *un peu d'argent. Un peu d'argent* qu'il lui enlevait' (l. 42) (emphases added). Occasionally the language adopts the form of free indirect discourse, mimicking her thoughts: 'Qui donc allait mourir? Qui donc souffrait tant? Où était-elle? Daniel?' (l. 56.) The effect of the flow of thoughts is jerky and incoherent (frequent use of ellipses to demarcate one thought from the next; a pattern of *enchaînement* which relies on free association; the collapsing of chronology which results in an inability to situate herself in time (who is alive, who dead); sudden shifts of focus introduced simply with 'Et puis' (ll. 42, 49, 59); 'Maintenant' (l. 55); 'Mais voici qu'elle (l. 47), conveying Rose-Anna's lack of control over the thoughts or her body. The immediacy and rawness of her memories ('tout défilait sans s'ordonner et trop vite pour qu'elle s'y reconnût') (l. 36) contrast somewhat with the extended image of a boat floating, flowing, fleeing (l. 30) used by the narrator to prepare the reader in a rather more poetic way for the stream of thoughts which follow.

In thematic terms, the image of the boat adrift on the water associates the birth process, as the child moves down the birth canal, with the reverse flow of Rose-Anna's thoughts, reviewing moments of her life as if at a turning point or perhaps in the face of death. Throughout the passage, and in the novel as a whole, Roy establishes a close link between birth and death. Indeed, even at the moment of birth, Rose-Anna is mentally elsewhere, imagining herself by the bed of her dying son, who died in hospital the night before she went into labour (l. 55). Helpless in the face of his suffering, Rose-Anna's physical pain, his agony and her anguish all become one, and the birth and the death are seamlessly joined in her body. The association between birth and death has various layers of significance. In terms of the plot of *Bonheur d'occasion*, the coincidence of Daniel's death and the new baby's birth dramatically heightens the connection between the two, but both infantile mortality and death in childbirth were still common enough in Quebec to make women view each pregnancy with some apprehension. Within this passage there are signs that Rose-Anna is not only preoccupied with death (the merging together of Daniel's suffering with her own), but that she may even desire death (if that is how one interprets the line: 'espérant à demi ne jamais y arriver' (l. 10)). The repeated pattern of hardship and loss means that death may indeed represent the only escape, for there is no way back to that younger, glorious self, glimpsed by the river. So while her return to life after the birth is positive in part, it cannot wipe out the memory for the reader of the confrontation with mortality and reflections on the ultimate pointlessness of existence. Yet the extract does close with Rose-Anna's temporary reconciliation with her life, both for reasons of necessity (feeding, clothing and finding shelter for the children), and because of the strength of her maternal feelings which are renewed with the sight and touch of her newborn son.

By concentrating on the mental and emotional journey of childbirth, Roy has chosen not to dwell on the physical processes, perhaps unintentionally reproducing the norms of good taste and orthodox Catholic morality of Quebec in the 1940s. She does, however, make it clear to the reader that her protagonist has internalized a deep sense of shame about the body, which may explain Rose-Anna's own strategies for coping with the birth. A feeling of shame is evident on a number of levels. Rose-Anna is ashamed of her body, feeling the need to cover it up (first with her coat and then with the bedclothes) (ll. 8, 24). She is ashamed of the pain of childbirth and of giving in to its domination. The general approval of such an attitude (the need to suffer in silence) is made explicit by the midwife's words, 'Pas même une petite plainte' (l. 61) and by Rose-Anna's brief sense of pride in remembering that her own mother (a mother of fifteen) had been praised in the same way (l. 65). Rose-Anna is ashamed of her poverty and, as with her body and her pain, does her best to conceal it. The cleanliness of her baby clothes, the provision of food for the children's meal indicate the importance of retaining dignity in the presence of strangers (l. 70). The act of childbirth accentuates all these feelings of shame as it exposes her to others, makes her reliant upon others, strangers by definition because they see her, her poverty and her suffering from the outside, hence the striking juxtaposition in 'Des mains fortes l'aidaient, l'humiliaient' (l. 29). While Rose-Anna feels her resistance to be a sign of strength ('une force nouvelle' (l. 67)), the reader might also judge that such fear of others and shame for self only serve to intensify Rose-Anna's isolation and her acceptance of her rotten lot in life, both in terms of gender and class.

In this extract maternity is not idealized, nor is it totally undermined or subverted as it will be in a novel such as Blais's *Une saison dans la vie d'Emmanuel* (see Chapter 28 below) where the mother figure is mute, reduced to an animal-like state by the combined hardships of farm life and repeated pregnancies. Rose-Anna displays an instinctive maternal love, which temporarily restores her, putting her in touch both with her elderly mother and her own youth ('comme si elle venait de puiser encore à la source mystérieuse, intarissable de sa jeunesse' (l. 85)). This account of a birth has the effect of making this birth symbolic of all the births which Rose-Anna has experienced – a series of life-threatening events which have brought her to consider the meaning of life and death, which take her close to death and then return her brutally to life – emerging both weakened and strengthened.

Further reading

Roy, Gabrielle, *Alexandre Chenevert* (Montreal: Stanké, 1954).
—— *La Montagne secrète* (Montreal: Stanké, 1961).
—— *Rue Deschambault* (Montreal: Boréal, 1993).

Bessette, Gérard, *Une littérature en ébullition* (Montreal: Editions du Jour, 1968).
Blais, Jacques, 'L'unité organique de *Bonheur d'occasion*', *Etudes françaises* 6, 1 (February 1970), 25–50.
Bourbonnais, N., 'Gabrielle Roy: la représentation du corps féminin', *Voix et images* XIV, 1, 40 (Autumn 1988), 72–89.
Brochu, André, 'Gabrielle Roy. Thèmes et structures dans *Bonheur d'occasion* ', *L'Instance critique 1961–73* (Montreal: Leméac, 1974), pp. 206–46.
Lewis, Paula Gilbert, 'La dernière des grandes conteuses: une conversation avec Gabrielle Roy', *Etudes littéraires*, 17, 3 (Winter 1984), 563–76.
Ricard, François, *Gabrielle Roy* (Montreal: Fides, 1975).
Smart, Patricia, *Writing in the Father's House. The Emergence of the Feminine in the Quebec Literary Tradition* (Toronto: University of Toronto Press, 1991), Chapter 5.

Language and style

Of the two major modes in which the passage is composed – narrative, i.e. the events surrounding the birth of Rose-Anna's twelfth child, and psychological analysis, i.e. the depiction of Rose-Anna's psychological state – it is the latter that dominates. Rose-Anna's fears, memories and aspirations, in particular her anxieties about the present and her confusion about the past, are described and suggested throughout the passage.

The first paragraph focuses on the loneliness and isolation of Rose-Anna in the last moments before giving birth and her fear at the prospect of the birth itself. This is especially conveyed by the repetition of the subject pronoun 'elle', which occurs eleven times in nine sentences, and even in those clauses where the subject pronoun is not explicitly expressed it is 'elle' which is understood. No other personal pronoun appears; the only other subjects mentioned also refer to Rose-Anna ('ses vêtements', 'la honte', 'un instinct'). Rose-Anna is entirely alone. Her anxiety and confusion are emphasized by the piling up of short clauses introduced by 'elle', and later the present participles, as she searches here and there in all the nooks and crannies and furniture of her room for her going-out clothes, and experiences uncertainty as to what course of action to take. Her confusion is prefigured and symbolized in the early sentences of the paragraph by the use of 'arriver' and 'chercher' in chiasmus, 'chercher – arriver – arriver – chercher' and by the fact that both words have two values, one physical ('to arrive' and 'to look for' respectively) and the other abstract ('(not) to succeed' and 'to try to'). After a long sentence depicting her indecision, the paragraph comes to an abrupt end as she bumps into the midwife. The sense of isolation and confusion extends beyond the first paragraph to the next four, and is reinforced by a number of other features. The disembodiment of the midwife and her assistant, who 's'activaient dans la chambre' (l. 21), removes the possibility of genuine human contact: they are not referred to by name or as people but as 'le visage' (l. 26), 'Des mains fortes' (l. 29), 'une voix' (l. 60). Moreover there is no real communication between Rose-Anna and the two visitors: Rose-Anna does not actually talk to them – 'se dit-elle' (l. 22), 'songea Rose-Anna' (l. 63) – until some time after the birth, and even then it is a matter of 'murmura-t-elle' (l. 93). She does not reply when the midwife (presumably) speaks to her (l. 76), and the helpers talk to each other as if she is not there (l. 61).

The picture of Rose-Anna's wretchedness and embarrassment at her poverty is brought out in the emotive vocabulary used in the first few paragraphs: in the first paragraph 'désespérément', 'pauvres', 'honte/honte', 'atroce emprise de la douleur'; in the next 'tristesse', 'profonde gêne', 'horreur', 'brutales', 'terrible'; in the fourth 'pénible', 'effroyablement'; and in the fifth 'l' [Rose-Anna] humiliaient profondément'.

It is at this point in the passage that the narrative perspective begins to shift. It continues to shift throughout these early paragraphs, as far as l. 68. The perspective is sometimes from within the main character, and sometimes from without. Sometimes the readers are shown her outside appearance and actions; at others they are shown and invited to share the inner turmoil that Rose-Anna is suffering; at yet others they find themselves in an in-between perspective. Lying on her bed of child-labour her mind travels in many directions, unaware of chronology and how to interpret the events. It is this combination of stream of consciousness and free indirect discourse that is especially apparent in the longest and pivotal paragraph of the passage, beginning l. 29. The extended image of the boat seems too literary and sophisticated in its structure for Rose-Anna, especially when the concentration of detail in the sentence beginning l. 31 is taken into account. But after the *points de suspension*, the perspective does change and free indirect discourse becomes much more obvious. The image of the boat meanders throughout the first third of the paragraph, suggesting at first any boat on any water-course, until Rose-Anna manages to identify the Richelieu and sees herself on the bank as a young girl. The image reaches its climax at that point, where Rose-Anna is described: 'Il y avait elle, troublée, radieuse, très douce' (l. 38). Here the double meaning of 'troublée' may seal together the image and Rose-Anna: 'troublée' not only suggests Rose-Anna's nervousness at her engagement, but also the murky, muddled nature of the water in the river, thereby symbolizing Rose-Anna's present and future. Rose-Anna's desperate determination to make sense out of her confused state of mind is brought out by a series of verbs denoting mental activity – 'remarquer', 'reconnaître', 'comprendre' – all within three lines (ll. 36–8). The uncertainty of her grip on reality is underlined by the large number of contrasts introduced by 'mais' and 'pourtant' not only in this paragraph but throughout the passage ('mais' occurs in ll. 16, 29, 36, 47, 76, 87; 'mais non' in l. 43; 'non' in l. 50; 'pourtant' in ll. 6, 18, 87; 'non pourtant' in l. 26) and by the group of verbs denoting confusion, e.g. 'sans s'ordonner' (l. 37), 'se mêlaient, se superposaient' (l. 37); 'vacillait' (l. 69).

Relief from her wretched current state is provided by memories of that earlier period on the bank of the Richelieu. A powerful, dense description of her as a young girl is given – 'cette jeune fille vêtue de mousseline claire . . . sa robe d'été bruissait encore au vent léger de là-bas et ses cheveux emmêlés, sentant le foin, les fleurs, lui fouettaient le visage' (l. 39). The poetry of that period is underlined by the use of alliteration (fricatives) before the picture dies away ('foin' – 'fleurs' – 'fouettaient' – 'visage'). The contrast between the 'robe d'été', with the carefreeness and smells it evoked, and the other 'robe' she was making later for Mademoiselle Elise, with the remembrance of being ill and trying to provide for the family, is emphasized by the proximity of the two references. This long paragraph, like the first, also finishes abruptly – 'un faible cri lui parvint' (l. 59) – bringing her sharply back from her rêverie to reality.

After this paragraph, narrative takes over and the scene finishes with Rose-Anna at last attempting to communicate with the helpers and looking after the needs of her other children.

One or two other stylistic devices used by Gabrielle Roy deserve mention. Repetition as a cohesive device occurs on a number of occasions, e.g. 'elle en avait honte . . . Honte de s'en aller ainsi' (l. 5), 'visage' (l. 26), 'luttait' (l. 43), 'un peu d'argent' (l. 44), 'marchait' (l. 48), 'plainte' (four times from l. 61). The author also has a predilection for apposed doublets (without *et*): subjects, e.g. 'Une certaine fierté, une sorte de courage gonflèrent son cœur' (l. 66): objects, e.g. 'Elle chercha ses chaussures sous le lit, ses bas' (l. 1, also ll. 25, 45, 47, 78, 87); indirect objects (l. 23); adverbial expressions, e.g. 'Peu à peu pourtant, à l'odeur, au bruit, elle reconnaissait l'atmosphère de son logis' (l. 18, also l. 12); infinitives (l. 20); prepositional expressions (ll. 27, 82); adjectives (ll. 72, 86); past participles (l. 79); relative clauses (l. 69); clauses (ll. 29, 30, 31, 38). Apposed triplets are also quite common: objects, e.g. 'Elle imaginait des lumières brutales, une mise en scène terrible, des étrangers autour d'elle' (l. 14); adjectives (l. 41); present participles (l. 8); clauses (ll. 3, 8). Adjectives are used in quartets, e.g. 'des petites robes ni ornées ni soyeuses, mais propres et chaudes' (l. 72, also l. 38). Interestingly all these devices, which are frequently used in the third-person narrative and stream of consciousness sections, are absent from the section in paragraph 6 where free indirect discourse predominates.

Chapter 28

Marie-Claire Blais

Une saison dans la vie d'Emmanuel (Montreal: Boréal, 1991), pp. 67–72. First published Montreal: Editions du Jour, 1965.

Abandonnés par notre pauvre mère qui lorsqu'elle n'était pas aux champs ou à l'écurie à soigner sa jument atteinte de consomption (dont l'odeur était un peu comparable à la mienne aujourd'hui, je dois l'avouer) dialoguait avec ses morts, tous alignés les uns à côté des autres sur le vieil harmonium rongé par les rats (seul héritage de Grand-Père Napoléon qui aimait jouer des hymnes la nuit pour faire enrager ma chaste grand-mère), morts du mois de novembre, morts des longues soirées d'hiver – ma mère les appelait un à un des ténèbres où ils ronflaient avec bien-être, dans sa mauve chemise de nuit, quelques cheveux épars sur son front toujours humide, cette triste femme contemplait avec douceur les enfants, les bébés au sourire édenté, des vieilles photographies mille fois regardées . . .

«Ah! suppliait-elle, d'une faible voix, Hector, pourquoi m'as-tu abandonnée? Est-ce que tu m'entends? Gemma! Gemma! tu avais à peine un jour, lorsque tu es partie. M'entends-tu, Gemma?»

Mais à mesure que les heures passaient, ma mère confondait les noms, les événements, et les morts valsaient confusément devant ses yeux. (Elle pensait à Gemma, mais sans le savoir, elle voyait Olive à la place, le petit crâne sanglant d'Olive écrasée sous la charrue de mon père. Et Gemma? Ah! Le jour de sa première communion, oui disparue, comme ça, dans sa robe de dentelle!)

Gemma, Barthélémy, Léopold, elle avait encore les chaussons de laine de ce lointain Barthélémy qu'elle n'était pas sûre d'avoir mis au monde, mais qu'importe! Et Léopold, une année, il ne restait qu'une année, et il sortait du séminaire. Léopold qui avait tant de talent! Ah!

Mais Dieu avait pris Léopold d'une curieuse façon. Par les cheveux, comme on tire une carotte de la terre.

En revenant d'une joviale tuerie de lapins et de renards, les frères aînés trouvèrent pendus, à la branche d'un arbre solitaire – qui donc? le squelettique Léopold dans sa robe de séminariste, balancé par le vent, mort, bien mort, prêt à écorcher comme les proies qu'ils tenaient à la main, d'un geste triomphal. «Mon Dieu, soupirèrent-ils en chœur, *en voilà une idée le vendredi saint!* J'ai toujours pensé qu'il avait les idées noires, celui-là!» Mais enivrés par la chasse, la bière et le vent qui leur fouettait les tempes, les aînés décrochèrent Léopold de son arbre (je dois ajouter ici que Léopold était si brillant qu'à l'âge de dix ans, il récitait par cœur des passages de la Bible qu'il ne comprenait pas du tout, et écrivait des épitaphes en latin . . . J'ai hérité moi-même de l'esprit aventureux de mon frère, et comme lui, je laisserai derrière moi des reliques qui pourriront dans la poussière, *la poussière des temps*, si l'on veut – car à part notre cher curé, et le Frère Théodule qui me fait subir en ce moment le martyre du thermomètre . . . qui donc pourrait lire ma prose en latin?) Ainsi, ils le décrochèrent de l'arbre, et le jetant comme un sac de pommes de terre sur leur dos les aînés rentrèrent allègrement chez nous, nous montrant leur gibier, dont le cher Léopold au cou pris dans la corde de sa ceinture.

«Malédiction! Oh, malédiction!», dit mon père, et il cracha par terre. Seule ma mère versa ces larmes funèbres si bienfaisantes pour Léopold.

Donc – abandonnés par notre mère, orphelins errants au visage barbouillé de soupe, et au derrière cuit par les coups – (c'était au temps où Héloïse faisait la soupe, et s'écriait à toute minute, debout sur sa chaise: «Maman, le chat est dans la soupe!») Fortuné et moi avions commencé notre descente en enfer. Tragiquement marqués par l'exemple de notre frère Léopold, nous avons tenté des suicides que nous n'avons jamais réussis jusqu'au bout, car Héloïse nous trahissait toujours par un cri de joie avant que l'un de nous ait franchi le seuil de l'éternité. «Maman, maman, le couteau à pain, maman! ah! le sang coule, maman.» Il y eut la tentation de l'eau (comme il faisait bon de se jeter dans le puits l'été, et être repêché par la bretelle de ma culotte, par la main toujours alerte de ma grand-mère!) et ensuite, le feu. Nous avons mis le feu partout, misérables oisifs que nous étions. Ma grand-mère venait à peine de tailler des rideaux dans ses draps, que nous les regardions flamber. Ils flambaient délicieusement d'ailleurs, et pour la première fois, j'eus l'impression d'avoir réussi quelque chose. Mon père dut nous mettre à l'école, ne pouvant garder avec lui sur ses champs déjà si stériles – deux incendiaires . . . *Après l'école, écoutez-moi toutes, femmes, après l'école c'est la maison de correction!*

Ma mère se plaignait que la vie était dure, et les hommes cruels.

– Je ne veux plus entendre un mot, dit mon père. *Je fume!*

Il fumait, et son tabac répandait l'odeur de tous les cadavres de la famille . . . Mais le Septième et moi avions beaucoup de respect pour *l'heure de fumerie* de mon père. Assis à chaque bout de la table, les mains sur les genoux, notre livre de lecture éparpillé par terre (quelle maladie apprendre à lire, à la fin, c'est ma grand-mère qui l'apprit la première) mais gardant le souvenir sonore de ces *ba*, de ces *bou ba bin bon beu* que nous avions effleurés du regard sur le tableau de l'école (ah! la chère école, toujours menacée de s'écrouler sous le vent et la neige, et la menue flamme du poêle qui nous réchauffait, mais avec prudence . . .). Nous regardions jaillir de la fumée ces lettres géantes, les *o*, les *i* et les *c* (et quelques notes de musique) que mon père formait de sa bouche ignorante, lui qui ne pouvait pas lire son nom, même écrit en majuscules. Notre père écrivait ainsi des romans, des contes qu'il ne lirait jamais, car de sa pipe sortait l'illustration brumeuse de mes œuvres futures. C'est ainsi que je devins un poète. J'en pris la solennelle décision le soir même, assis avec Fortuné sur le même banc de latrines, qui, à l'échange et à l'usure, dorlotait nos fesses d'une agréable chaleur. Non seulement mon père fumait, mais les aînés, assis autour de mon père, les jambes allongées dans leur salopette bleue, remuant les doigts de pied de leurs chaussettes de laine (qu'ils n'enlevaient que tous les six mois, et encore n'était-ce que pour la santé de ma grand-mère), eux aussi laissaient mourir dans leurs barbes noires de frêles soupirs de volupté – mais rien d'autre, sinon des *eh* et des *oh* et parfois un léger bâillement qui ressemblait à une mouche. Mais comme je leur ai toujours reproché dans ma sagesse précoce: ils n'avaient pas assez d'imagination pour dire autre chose.

Text and context

Treating as it does the themes of rural life, the family, and institutionalized Catholicism, Blais's text can seen both to return to and to subvert the norms of the *roman de la terre*, the traditional French-Canadian 'cultural text' of which Savard's *Menaud, maître-draveur* (see Chapter 28 above) is a late example.[1] The choice of narrative form of this passage is one instance of the modernity of *Une saison dans la vie d'Emmanuel*. The novel is narrated partly by a third-person narrator, partly in the third person, but as if from the perspective of the newborn eponymous hero, and partly in the first person by the young poet, Jean Le Maigre. This combination of narrative voices marks a break from the traditional third-person narrative of the rural novel and makes the reader more aware of the potential complexities of the work. It is from the so-called 'autobiographie' of Jean Le Maigre, written as he dies of tuberculosis in the infirmary of the novitiate, that the extract is taken. The very notion of a passage devoted to the artist's discovery of his vocation would be incongruous in the *roman de la terre*. By introducing such a figure into the harsh and isolating rural setting, Blais turns the genre on its head.

This extract illustrates Blais's subversive approach to the cultural text in her treatment of several central themes. The family, the traditional symbol of French-Canadian survivalism, is represented here from Jean Le Maigre's perspective. His mother ('notre pauvre mère' (l. 1), 'cette triste femme' (l. 9)) is not the strong centre of the family, but rather the object of his pity. Mentally and emotionally absent from her living family, she can only find the strength to care for the livestock or mourn her dead children, strangely more real to her than the surviving children. It is significant that in this passage her only direct speech is addressed to her dead children, and that Jean Le Maigre subsequently informs the reader of the confused state of his mother's thoughts: 'Elle pensait à Gemma, mais sans le savoir, elle voyait Olive à la place' (l. 15), this narrative correction repeating the pattern elsewhere in the novel where the mother remains largely silent, the voiceless victim of years of domestic and sexual

1 For further discussion of the *roman de la terre* and its place in the development of Quebec literature see Chapter 25.

servitude. The figure of the father is a caricature of the patriarchal male, laying down the law ('écoutez-moi toutes, femmes' (l. 59)), an unquestioned role model for the stupid elder sons (referred to collectively as 'les aînés'), who imitate his every action, but he is mocked by Jean Le Maigre for his ignorance ('lui qui ne pouvait pas lire son nom, même écrit en majuscules' (l. 71)). Somewhat paradoxically, the one figure who does attempt to impose the values of the traditional Catholic family is the grandmother whose care and surveillance over the children is repeatedly mentioned in the passage ('la main toujours alerte de ma grand-mère' (l. 53)), but who also was the first in the family to teach herself to read (l. 65) and to this extent represents a link with the modern age. In terms of the family structure, then, the parents' generation constitute the denial of liberation and of individuality, whereas the grandmother is an ambiguous figure, at once traditionalist and aware of the liberating potential of learning.

The brutality and lack of humanity which characterizes many of the family members in this passage is directly associated by Jean Le Maigre's narration with the rural lifestyle which surrounds them. The grotesque representation of 'les aînés' makes this particularly clear. His elder brothers' response to their discovery of Léopold's suicide shows their dehumanization, as his dead body is debased to the level of the game they have just been hunting: 'prêt à écorcher comme les proies qu'ils tenaient à la main' (l. 27); 'le jetant comme un sac de pommes de terre sur leur dos' (l. 38); 'nous montrant leur gibier, dont le cher Léopold' (l. 40). Rural life in Blais's text is not associated with life, renewal and continuity, but rather with death (of the many dead children it is perhaps the death of the infant Olive, 'le petit crâne sanglant d'Olive écrasée sous la charrue de mon père' (l. 16) which is the most shocking to the reader), sterility ('ses champs déjà si stériles' (l. 58)), disease (consumption, from which both the mother's mare and Jean Le Maigre suffer (l. 2)), and the weakening of the bond with the past, metonymically suggested by the reference to 'le vieil harmonium rongé par les rats (seul héritage de Grand-Père Napoléon)' (l. 4).

The status of the third key element in the rural novel, the Catholic faith, is both affirmed and undermined in Jean Le Maigre's account. Catholicism is present in the passage on a number of levels. There are direct references to God (both in the form of blasphemy and general explanation), to the church's representatives: 'notre cher curé' (l. 36); 'le Frère Théodule' (l. 36); to church ceremony: '[la] première communion' (l. 18); to the institutions of the church, such as the seminary (l. 21) and the school (the Catholic Church being the main provider of education in Quebec until the reforms of the *révolution tranquille*); to the discourse of Catholicism, evident in Jean Le Maigre's use of terms such as 'notre descente en enfer' (l. 47), 'le seuil de l'éternité' (l. 50), 'le martyre' (l. 37) to describe events in his own life. By being the sole source of education for the rural francophone population, the church can be seen to have represented an escape route for the more academically able children, preparing them for a life in one of the many church institutions. Yet in Jean Le Maigre's narrative, as in the novel as a whole, some unsettling patterns would seem to emerge. The unexplained death of Gemma happened to take place on the day of her first communion (l. 17). Léopold's unexplained suicide happened near the end of his time at the seminary, where he had been an exceptional pupil (l. 21). He was found in his seminarist's robe, and the state of his body suggests he may have been dead (and so missing) some time ('le squelettique Léopold', 'mort, bien mort' (l. 26)). Jean Le Maigre's own situation while writing his autobiography is referred to in passing and adds to the slight unease of the reader: 'le Frère Théodule qui me fait subir en ce moment le martyre du thermomètre. . .' (l. 36), a reference which becomes all the more disturbing in retrospect when later one learns how le Frère Théodule has acted out a variety of sexual perversions on boys in his care, and apparently hastened a number of deaths. These references in the passage serve to destabilize the image of the Church as an escape route from rural poverty. Neither the family structure nor that of the Church acts to protect these children from suffering and in this they both seem to explain the pessimism of Blais's fictional universe. What might have seemed to the reader initially as a possible escape route for the rural youth (education) in fact turns out to be rather a riskier choice. The father's equation of school with punishment ('*après l'école c'est la maison de correction*' (l. 00)) suddenly seems more accurate than at first sight. The Church owns the tools that might enable Quebec's youth to revolt, but it also proceeds to pervert those in its care and leads many to their death.

The particular form of rebellion which Blais's text explores is that of the writer. Clearly a writer must first acquire literacy, and in this passage literacy is the preserve of the school (and so of the Church), but as it spreads it also penetrates the home. The last section of the passage represents the invasion of everyday, wretched reality by literature, as the two brothers decipher letters, words, images in their father's smoke rings (l. 69). This ability to transform the base elements of their daily life into something other unites the brothers and connects them to the dead brother Léopold, similarly gifted as a writer. As writers they can at least transform the world in their poems, in their fantasies, and so can refuse to live a life of unquestioning continuity and repetition. Clearly, in Jean Le Maigre's view, this ensures their superiority over the rest of their family: 'ils n'avaient pas assez d'imagination pour dire autre chose' (l. 83). But while the family's blinkered pursuit of collective survival is rejected in favour of an individual rebellion, it is clear from the context of this passage (the autobiography of a dying adolescent), that the prospect for the young writer/rebel is bleak, doomed to leaving 'des reliques' (l. 35) to a very limited potential readership: 'qui donc pourrait lire ma prose en latin?' (l. 37).

In terms of its structure, this passage is typified by Jean Le Maigre's love of parentheses and detours. As he aims to explain to the reader the birth of his vocation, he is repeatedly sidetracked into anecdotes and reflections on his, and his brother's, 'descente en enfer' (l. 47). The first long sentence ('Abandonnès . . . ') lacks a main verb and so leaves the brothers' 'abandonment' hanging in the air for a further two pages, while the mother's obsession with her dead children and the suicide of Léopold are related. Only then is the reader told that abandonment by the mother led the brothers on their downward spiral (playing with death, playing with fire (l. 55)) that results in their father's decision to send them to school.

As will have been evident at a first reading of the passage, Blais does not employ the techniques of mimetic realism. Her text is complex, employing parody, paradox, and the grotesque in order to revisit and subvert the norms of Quebec traditionalism. The passage is devastating in terms of its exposure of prejudice, sadism, repression and universal, inescapable human suffering. And yet the experience of reading the extract is not one of unrelieved despair. The parody of the 'cultural text' allows the reader to distance him- or herself and recognize the limitations of traditionalism. Paradoxes are both thematic (the father being the unwitting origin of Jean Le Maigre's vocation) and stylistic (the use of oxymoron as in 'une joviale tuerie' (l. 25)). The use of exaggeration and caricature, as in the creation of the nameless series of grunting older brothers, adds humour to the passage. The juxtaposition of the elevated and the basic (discovering one's vocation as a poet on a shared toilet seat (l. 75)) has an ironic effect and serves to avoid sentimentality or idealism. There is black humour in the lengthy passage describing Léopold's fate, which makes it seem gratuitous, grotesque, absurd, rather than unrelievedly tragic. Just as Jean Le Maigre's writings will transform and poeticize reality, so the paradoxes, grim humour and shock effects of Blais's writings help the reader to read more into the text than a simple narrative and recognize the real targets of her writing.

Further reading

Blais, Marie-Claire, *Les Nuits de l'Underground* (Montreal: Boréal, 1990).
—— *Le Sourd dans la ville* (Montreal: Boréal, 1996).
—— *L'Ange de la solitude* (Montreal: VLB, 1989).

Cancalon, Elaine D., '*Une saison dans la vie d'Emmanuel* : le discours du conte', *Voix et images* 43 (Fall 1989), 102–10.
Goldmann, Lucien, 'Note sur deux romans de Marie-Claire Blais', in *Structures mentales et création culturelle* (Paris: Editions Anthropos, 1970), pp. 353–64.
Green, Mary Jean, *Marie-Claire Blais* (New York: Twayne Publishers, 1995).
Laurent, Françoise, *L'Œuvre romanesque de Marie-Claire Blais* (Montreal: Fides, 1986).
Marcotte, Gilles, *Le Roman à l'imparfait: Essais sur le roman québécois d'aujourd'hui* (Montreal: La Presse, 1976), pp. 93–137.
Nadeau, Vincent, *Marie-Claire Blais: Le Noir et le tendre. Etude d''Une saison dans la vie d'Emmanuel', suivi d'une bibliographie critique* (Montreal: Les Presses de l'Université de Montréal, 1974).
Paradis, Suzanne, *Femme fictive, femme réelle: le personnage féminin dans le roman féminin canadien français (1884–1966)* (Quebec: Editions Garneau, 1966).

Language and style

In many ways the first sentence (ll. 1–10) is a microcosm of the whole book and of the passage under review in particular. It contains bathos, description, humour and contains the major themes covered in the passage/book: the harsh life led by the family – and animals – in rural Quebec, comfortless religion (epitomized by the hymns played by the grandfather to annoy the grandmother), the worlds of the living and the dead inter-linked, an obsession with death, the ugliness of humans (mother and babies). Linguistically, too, the first sentence is typical of the passage as a whole, with its graphic detail, especially its use of short adjectives and adjectival expressions and embedded adverbial expressions, and its use of repetition. Overall a depressing atmosphere is created, relieved to a certain extent by the ironic humour which occurs in parentheses.

Parentheses play an unusually significant role in the passage – there are nine of them – and they are generally the result of some association of ideas in the narrator's, Jean le Maigre's, mind. In the first sentence they are used to contain asides reflecting on earlier incidents with humorous intent, e.g. the donkey's smell compared to Jean himself at the time of writing (l. 2); the honourable legacy left by the grandfather mocked by being used to annoy his wife (l. 5). There are a number of similar examples later in the passage, e.g. Léopold's recitations from the Bible are devalued because of his incomprehension of what he is reading (l. 31); Héloïse's soup making (l. 45); Jean's being saved in undignified manner from the well (l. 52); the older brothers and their socks (l. 78). Elsewhere parentheses are also used to arouse pity, e.g. with reflections on the dead siblings (l. 15); relating the difficulty of learning to read (l. 65); describing nostalgia for school (l. 67).

Imagery serves a similar purpose, making the grotesque events recounted more palatable by presenting them in a burlesque manner, e.g. the occasion when it is said that the dead

Léopold hanging in the tree by his hair has been taken by God in the same way as a carrot is pulled from the ground (l. 23); the description of his body being carried by his brothers like a sack of potatoes (l. 39) and being dumped unceremoniously in front of the family like 'gibier' (l. 40) – indeed Léopold is as much part of the game-bag as the animals. The snoring and yawning of the older brothers is compared to a fly (l. 82). These images reveal how little value is attached to human life: it is reduced to the level of vegetables, animals, insects.

Attitudes towards death are further demonstrated in such oxymorons as 'joviale tuerie' (l. 25) and the dismissive way in which the older brothers refer to Léopold hanging by his hair in a tree (l. 28). Jean le Maigre refers to 'un cri de joie [from Héloïse] avant que l'un de nous ait franchi le seuil de l'éternité' (l. 50), as well as the earlier implication that the dead are happy (l. 8) – free from the horror of living. Death pervades the passage – the word 'mort' is repeated three times in the first paragraph and twice in close proximity in l. 27.

Playing a very similar role to the asides contained in parentheses is another feature which adds vigour and drama to the extract: the insertion of passages of direct speech in the narrative, which act as concrete illustrations of the point currently being made. The comment of the older brothers on the death of Léopold has already been mentioned (l. 28). There is the catalogue of dead babies rehearsed by the mother, also the father's outburst at another death (l. 42); Héloïse's soup making (l. 45) and her reaction to the boys' suicide attempts (l. 50 already referred to), the father's threat to the boys (l. 57) and his autocratic behaviour (l. 59).

At a deeper stylistic level is the evocative power of the graphic vocabulary. The youthful narrator casts his eye over the events he is recounting with minute attention to detail, some incongruous, but all picturesque and contributing to the macabre atmosphere of the episode. Among the most significant lexical features is the fact that a very large proportion of nouns in the passage are accompanied by an adjective. Taking the second half of the first paragraph (ll. 7–10), it is possible to have a glimpse of the device, and to see that some of the details provided are almost supernumerary: Jean's mother's 'chemise de nuit' is 'mauve' (do we need to know that?), her 'quelques cheveux' are 'épars' (that almost goes without saying), her forehead is 'toujours humide', she is a 'triste femme', the babies have 'un sourire édenté', the photographs are 'vieilles' and 'mille fois regardées'. What is still more striking, because of its departure from the norm, is the number of cases where an adjective precedes its noun, e.g. 'ma chaste grand-mère' (l. 6), 'sa mauve chemise de nuit' (l. 8), 'ce lointain Barthélémy' (l. 19), 'une joviale tuerie de lapins' (l. 25), 'le squelettique Léopold' (l. 26, also ll. 54, 68, 74, 76, 80). The 'bouche ignorante' of his father (l. 71) is yet another unorthodox use of an adjective – a transferred epithet. Very closely linked to the use of adjectives is that involving present and past participles. The above-normal frequency of their use adds to the graphic detail already provided by the adjectives. An additional effect which they create is the impression of density of composition, of much detail being packed into a small space. A past participle starts the passage and five others occur in the first paragraph alone (ll. 2, 4, 10); in all another nineteen examples occur (ll. 17, 18, 26, 27, 30, 40, 44, 45, 48, 64, 65, 68, 72, 75). Present participles are fewer but still significantly frequent (ll. 16, 25, 38, 40, 43, 44, 58, 66, 78). At regular intervals throughout the passage single-word adverbs are used to add a somewhat ironic tone to the text, e.g. 'les morts valsaient confusément devant ses yeux' (l. 15), 'les aînés rentrèrent allègrement chez nous, nous montrant leur gibier, dont le cher Léopold au cou pris dans la corde de sa ceinture' (l. 39, also 'tragiquement' (l. 47), 'délicieusement' (l. 56)).

The narrator in this extract of the novel is Jean le Maigre, writing in the first person.

However, occasionally the grief of his mother over her tragically lost children is also heard in free indirect discourse, e.g. 'Gemma? Ah! Le jour de sa première communion, oui disparue, comme ça, dans sa robe de dentelle!' (l. 17) and 'Barthélémy qu'elle n'était pas sûre d'avoir mis au monde, mais qu'importe! Et Léopold, une année, il ne restait qu'une année, et il sortait du séminaire. Léopold qui avait tant de talent! Ah!' (l. 20). This gives added intensity to the sections, especially with the repetition of 'année'. Repetition plays an identical role when 'morts' is repeated almost like an incantation on two occasions (ll. 3–6 and 27 (see above)).

From the point of view of structure, what is immediately striking is the high number of minor sentences in the narrative (excluding speech and parentheses within sentences). There are eight (plus eight simple sentences, five compound, seven complex and five compound-complex). The first minor sentence, ll. 1–10, is unusually long for a minor sentence and is left incomplete. It breaks off to allow the long parenthetical catalogue of deaths in the family and does not resume until l. 44. The other minor sentences, all except one of which occur in the review of the deaths of Jean's siblings, contribute to the effect of free indirect discourse. The exclamations and questions illustrate the mother's anguished despair as she reviews the deaths. The other minor sentence is similar in structure and purpose to the first and provides an introduction to and summary of Jean's and Fortuné's excursions into literacy via the pipe smoke of their father and brothers (l. 64), just as the first provided insights into the deaths of the family, which would occupy the text until this next section.

Marie-Claire Blais's style is a mixture of careful, detailed organization on the one hand and spontaneity and irony on the other. The switching between narrative modes, the associations of ideas and digressions (exploited in the parentheses) lead to a style very reminiscent of stream of consciousness.

Chapter 29

Michel Tremblay

La Grosse Femme d'à côté est enceinte (Montreal: Bibliothèque québécoise, 1990), pp. 226–31. First published Montreal: Leméac, 1978.

Quand Josaphat-le-Violon arriva vers six heures moins quart, Albertine avait la tête dans le fourneau du poêle à charbon et arrosait une gigantesque dinde dont la peau commençait à prendre une belle couleur dorée. «Hé, que ça va être bon, c'te p'tite dinde-là!». Elle n'entendit pas le coup de sonnette ni le cri de la grosse femme: «Bartine, ça sonne!» et Josaphat-le-Violon entra dans la maison suivi de Laura, sa fille, qui se tenait les jambes serrées et marchait presque en se contorsionnant. «Vite, vite, popa, laissez-moé passer, ça a pas de bon sens, j'ai les yeux qui me flottent dedans!» Laura traversa la salle à manger en courant, sans jeter un coup d'œil dans la chambre de sa cousine. «Allô, ma tante!» (Elle avait l'habitude d'appeler Albertine et la grosse femme «ma tante» à cause de la différence d'âge qui les séparait et aussi parce que, élevée à Saint-Jérôme, elle avait connu les deux femmes très tard. Elle appelait d'ailleurs Victoire «grand-moman», alors qu'en fait la vieille femme n'était que sa tante.) Elle bouscula Albertine en passant derrière elle pour se rendre à la salle de bains. Celle-ci hurla de peur et tomba sur ses genoux, la tête presque dans la marmite. «Allô, ma tante! X'cusez-moé, j'ai envie!» «Mon Dieu, que tu m'as fait peur! Ousque t'étais, donc, toé! Par ousque t'es rentrée?» Josaphat-le-Violon l'aida à se relever après avoir déposé son étui à violon et un gros sac de provisions sur la table de la cuisine. «Par la porte, Albertine, par la porte!» Ils entendirent la grosse femme rire. Albertine se frottait les genoux. «C'est pas une fille que vous avez, c't'un cyclone!» Sans répondre, Josaphat-le-Violon montra le sac sur la table. «J'vous ai apporté des oranges.» Albertine glissa le nez dans le sac, huma. «Des belles oranges! Marcel va-t'être content!» Elle sortit une orange du sac et la colla sur son nez et sa bouche. «D'où c'est qu'y'viennent, en temps de guerre, les oranges?» «Bartine, bonyeu, y poussent à'même place!» Josaphat-le-Violon se détourna et se dirigea vers la chambre de la grosse femme. «J'y'ai pas encore dit bonjour . . .» Le début de bonne humeur d'Albertine tomba d'un coup. «Bon . . . y va aller minoucher sa grosse préférée, encore . . .»Elle entendit les becs sonores et le bruit des springs quand le vieil homme s'assit au chevet de la femme de Gabriel. «C'est ça, restez collé là pendant que j'm'échine à faire vot'souper!» Sa cousine sortit de la salle de bains en riant après avoir tiré la chasse d'eau. «J'espère que vous vous êtes pas faite mal, ma tante! Mais j'vous ai pas poussée ben fort, j'pense que c'est plus la surprise qui vous a coupé les jambes . . . » Albertine s'était de nouveau pliée en deux pour pousser la marmite dans le fourneau. «T'es ben grosse, Laura! Si tu continues à engraisser de même, tu vas avoir l'air de ta tante ça s'ra pas long!» Albertine savait que Laura détestait qu'on lui parle de son obésité. Elle lui remettait la monnaie de sa pièce, un sourire méchant au bord des lèvres. En se redressant, elle se frotta les reins, puis jeta un coup d'œil en direction de sa cousine qu'elle n'avait pas encore regardée. «Toé-si tu l'attends pour la fin de juin, j'suppose?» Laura s'était assise au bout de la table de la cuisine et jouait avec un cendrier vide. «Ouan, comme ma tante!» Albertine essayait de se plier par en arrière. «Pis comme à peu près toutes les femmes d'la rue! J'ai jamais vu autant de femmes enceintes en même temps, moé!» «C'est normal, c'est l'été . . . » «C'est pas l'été, c'est le printemps.» «J'ai lu un article dans *Le Canada*, l'aut'jour ousqu'y disaient que le monde, en Amérique du Nord, y viennent presque toutes au monde en été rapport à l'hiver qui est trop longue . . . » «Pis, que c'est que ça change?» «Ben, ma tante . . . L'hiver, quand y fait trop frette trop longtemps, ça donne envie de se réchauffer un peu . . . Pis quand on se réchauffe, hein, ben . . . » «Pis y parlent de t'ça dans'journaux! On aura tout vu! C'est pas assez que les femmes d'la rue se cachent même pus d'être en famille, v'là rendu qu'y parlent de quand c'est que les enfants se font dans'es'journaux!» Attendre un bébé avait toujours été vaguement honteux pour les femmes de la ville et elles dissimulaient habituellement leur gros ventre sous un corset qui les étouffait et des vêtements très amples qui déguisaient leur silhouette. Même la grosse femme avait porté un corset pendant ses premières grossesses, malgré son embonpoint. Et quand une femme «un peu trop enceinte» passait dans la rue Mont-Royal, les regards se détournaient comme si elle avait été un objet obscène, honteux, et il se trouvait toujours une grenouille de bénitier ou un mangeux de balustres pour lui dire: «Le dernier mois, d'habetude, les femmes restent chez eux . . . » Et c'était vrai. Plutôt que de subir les reproches muets qu'elles pouvaient lire dans tous les regards qu'elles croisaient, les femmes restaient chez elles pendant les dernières semaines de leur grossesse. Elles-mêmes finissaient par ressentir une certaine gêne d'être déformées et bousculées par ce paquet d'énergies, cette vie si puissante qui se préparait à sortir d'elles. Ecrasées par cette religion monstrueuse qui défendait toute sorte de moyen de contraception, cette religion fondée sur l'égoïsme des hommes, pour servir l'égoïsme des hommes, qui méprisait les femmes et en avait peur au point de faire de l'image de la Mère, la Vierge Marie, Mère de Dieu, une vierge intacte et pure, inhumaine créature sans volonté et surtout sans autonomie qui s'était retrouvée un jour enceinte sans l'avoir désiré, par l'opération de l'Esprit-Saint (qu'on osait représenter sous la forme d'un oiseau! enceinte d'un oiseau, la Mère de Dieu!) et qui avait enfanté sans avoir besoin de mettre au monde, insulte ultime faite au corps des femmes; gavées par les prêtres de phrases creuses autant que cruelles où les mots «devoir» et «obligations» et «obéissance» prédominaient, ronflants, insultants, condescendants, les femmes canadiennes-françaises, surtout celles des villes, avaient fini par ressentir une honte maladive d'être enceintes, elles qui n'étaient pas dignes, comme l'autre, de mettre un enfant au monde sans qu'un homme, leur propriétaire et maître, leur passe dessus et qui, surtout, n'avaient pas le droit de se dérober à leur «devoir», à leurs «obligations» parce qu'elles devaient «obéissance» à ce merveilleux outil du destin que leur avait fourni directement la Volonté de Dieu: leur mari. La religion catholique, en un mot, niait la beauté de l'enfantement et condamnait les femmes à n'être *jamais* dignes puisque la mère de leur Dieu, l'image consacrée de la Maternité, n'avait été qu'un entrepôt temporaire d'où l'Enfant n'était ni entré ni sorti. Albertine souleva le couvercle du chaudron où bouillait encore la soupe et se mit à brasser énergiquement le liquide fumant pour se donner une contenance. «Si ça continue de même, j'les achèterai pus, les journaux!» «Juste l'Oratoire?» «Même Saint Joseph me déprime!» Elle remit le couvercle en faisant le plus de bruit possible. «Aide-moé à mettre la table, chus tu-seule comme un coq-dinde!» Josaphat-le-Violon avait pris la main de sa nièce dans ses grosses pattes calleuses de menuisier et il la regardait avec un bon sourire. «As-tu lu, aujourd'hui?» «Non, mon oncle, j'arrive pas à me concentrer assez.» «Trop de va-et-vient dans'maison?» «Non, c'est pas ça, tout le monde est parti sauf Bartine . . . Mais . . . on dirait que j'ai moins le goût que j'avais. Le bébé grouille souvent, pis j'pars dans mes rêveries.» «Toujours le Mexique?» «Non. Des rêveries plus sérieuses.» «Faut pas. La baie d'Acapulco t'a toujours aidée à continuer . . .» «Mais j'la verrai jamais, mon oncle! Tant que j'ai réussi à me faire accroire que j'finirais par y aller un jour, même si au fond j'savais que c'tait pas vrai, ça allait, mais là . . .» La grosse femme retira sa main des pattes de son oncle et arrangea un peu ses cheveux qui lui tombaient sur le front. «Y sèchent mal . . . Si au moins mes rêves étaient moins fous! Si au moins j'rêverais d'aller à la baie des Chaleurs ou ben donc à Percé, ça s'rait moins pire! Mais non! Acapulco!» «Ton sang indien te donne le goût des voyages, c'est normal!» «Mon sang indien, ça fait longtemps qu'y'a déviré en p'tite eau, mon oncle!» «C'est la première fois que j'te vois déprimée de même depuis le mois de décembre. Y'est-tu arrivé quelqu'chose avec Gabriel?» «Ben non . . . J'arais juste envie de me lever, mon oncle, de me traîner jusqu'au balcon, de m'assir pis de r'garder le soleil du printemps en face au lieu de guetter ses reflets dans la vitre du châssis de madame Chagnon, au troisième étage! Chus tannée de rêver d'Acapulco pis d'être même pas capable de me lever pour aller m'assir su'l'balcon!» «Ecoute . . . écoute . . . A soir, après le souper, Edouard, Gabriel, pis moé, on va essayer de te transporter su'l'balcon . . . Y fait assez chaud . . . Une p'tite heure ou deux à'bonne air du printemps, ça va t'aérer les esprits!» Cette fois ce fut la grosse femme qui prit une patte de Josaphat-le-Violon dans ses mains potelées. «Avec du Coke pis des chips?» «Avec toute c'que tu voudras.» «Allez-vous jouer la Méditation de *Thaïs*, pour moé?» «J'vas essayer.»

Text and context

This extract is an interesting counterpart to the passage from Roy's *Bonheur d'occasion* (see Chapter 27 above) because of the number of parallels that can be drawn. First, the texts are both set in working-class districts of Montreal in the Second World War (Roy's text in 1940, and Tremblay's in May 1942); second, both passages deal with maternity, both including a pregnant woman in her forties; finally, both raise questions about the prevailing moral and ideological climate. Yet the two passages were written over thirty years apart and striking differences emerge.

At first sight this extract looks distinctive. This episode, like all the others in the novel, combines third-person narration and dialogue in one uninterrupted paragraph. The dialogue is not attributed to named speakers, but its source is always clear either because of frequent use of terms of address by the speakers ('mon oncle', 'Bartine'), because of the sequence of responses or because of the content of the comments. This layout is common to each of the sixty-seven episodes that compose the text and together form an account of a day in the life of an extended family and of the street on which they live on the Plateau Mont-Royal. An initial reading of the passage confirms that this is a text which uses the language of Quebec. Indeed Tremblay was one of the first Quebec writers to use *joual* (the French of working-class eastern Montreal) in his plays and this passage demonstrates how a Montreal voice can be adopted in the novel. The sections of third-person narration use a higher register, the past historic main tenses suggesting a break with the oral mode, yet the presence of some features of Quebec French – 'le bruit des springs' (l. 28) rather than *des ressorts*; 'mangeux de balustres' (l. 57), a pejorative phrase for a sanctimonious person, and synonym for 'une grenouille de bénitier' (l.57) – maintain the Quebec identity of the text.

The combination of the lack of paragraph breaks or attribution of direct speech and the use of Quebec French enhances the immediacy of the dialogue and gives the text a certain theatricality. This theatricality is also evident in the use of arrivals and exits (Josaphat-le-Violon and his daughter Laura both appearing for the first time in the novel (l. 5) and injecting vitality into the domestic routine), in the sense of movement which produces moments of visual comedy (Albertine almost falling into her cooking pot (l. 15)), in the mixture of moods (comedy, pathos, tenderness and anger) emerging from the interactions between the different characters, and finally in the use of space which delineates and juxtaposes the territory of the two central women protagonists, Albertine and her sister-in-law, 'la grosse femme'.

In this passage (and throughout much of the novel) the two women are rooted in their respective domains (Albertine in the kitchen and 'la grosse femme' in her bed), which creates the effect of a split stage as the narrative is told first from the perspective of the kitchen (with 'la grosse femme' as a 'voice off', calling to Albertine or laughing at an overheard joke) and then moves to the relative privacy of the bedroom. In contrast to the air of vitality brought into the scene by the arrival of Josaphat-le-Violon and Laura, the domestic scene which they enter is enclosed and imprisoning. The women's relationship to these spaces symbolizes their entrapment within their social and biological roles. The unnamed 'grosse femme' of the title is literally immobilized in her bed by the combination of her advanced stage of pregnancy and her obesity, but the social stigma attached to the pregnant older woman in 1940s Quebec means that she is expected to hide herself from public view until after the birth. Albertine's physical confinement in the kitchen at the heart of the domestic space, represented in the text by the frequent references to her work at the stove, confirms her role as housewife.

Neither woman is reconciled to her condition in life, but neither of them is ready or able to break out of her entrapped state. Albertine's response to the world is essentially negative, both a victim and perpetrator of the traditional Catholic ideology of her time (this is made particularly clear in the exchange with Laura about the reproductive life of French-Canadians). Her unhappiness with her own situation is expressed through bitterness, resentment and a lack of self-worth. This negativity is projected onto those around her so that she is quick to undermine (as in the comment to Laura about her obese tendencies (l. 34)), to envy others (her bitter response to Josaphat's favouring of 'la grosse femme', 'sa grosse préférée' (l. 27)), and to impose her own negative feelings about sex and the female body onto others. Food is her one remaining pleasure (the sight of the turkey (l. 3), the smell of the oranges (l. 22)) and the only topic on which Albertine comments positively in the whole passage. Blind to her own oppression, she treats her fellow women with hostility, and becomes the uncomprehending butt for others' teasing (Josaphat's jokes have the effect of gentle put-downs). In contrast to this Martha/martyr figure, 'la grosse femme' is less embittered, for while she is equally, if not more trapped in the home, she does have desires and dreams of transcendence.

Dreams and the imagination represent a strategy for escaping the humdrum routines of daily life and the social restrictions of 1940s Quebec society. To 'la grosse femme', the bay at Acapulco (l. 94) is the perfect antithesis to Quebec, signifying exoticism (unlike Percé and la Baie des Chaleurs on the Gaspé peninsular in Quebec (l. 100)), the liberation of the mind and the body. It may seem paradoxical that this immobilized woman is capable of contemplating escape to an alternative, idealized life, whereas her sister-in-law has no such resources. But 'la grosse femme' differs from her sister both racially (she has some Indian blood) (l. 101) and in terms of her feelings about sexuality and maternity. To this extent she can be seen as less complicit in the traditional French-Canadian ideology. However, in this passage 'la grosse femme' is finding it more and more difficult to escape, either through her daydreams or through literature, as her physical situation becomes increasingly restrictive. The extract does close with a reaffirmation of the dream of freedom, but because of the combination of the sublime (represented by Massenet's 'Méditation' from *Thaïs* (l. 113)) and the physical (crisps and Coke on the balcony (l. 112)) the tone is one of anticlimax and ambiguity.

As a result of the prominence of dialogue, of movement and gesture within the passage, the reader is encouraged to hear and see the scene, largely unaware of a narratorial presence. There are, however, two narratorial interventions which interrupt the flow of action. The first of these is simply explanatory, situating Laura in the network of family relationships. The second comes in the midst of the discussion between Albertine and Laura about the reproductive life of French-Canadians. At first it seems as if Tremblay has slipped clumsily into didactic mode, with the aim of demystifying the cult of the Virgin Mary and criticizing the patriarchal ethos of the Church for the benefit of the modern-day reader. Yet on closer reading the narrator's outburst seems to exemplify the position of this narrator within Tremblay's text. The narrator, by pointing out the degree to which the protagonists are the victims of a certain ideology, and then by giving a critique of that ideology in recognizably post-

révolution tranquille[1] and pro-feminist terms, establishes a distance between the action and its narration. The narrator does 'know' more than the protagonists, because of this retrospective angle. Yet the narrator almost acquires the status of another protagonist. The attack on the Church is conducted in terms which are not measured and rational, but which are passionate and vivid. The language is that of the bar or the street, with elements of the harangue, with humour, repetition for rhetorical effect, and irony. This narrator is speaking in anger, responding to Albertine's deeply ingrained acquiescence with the Church's teachings on the shamefulness of the female body, not so much to refute her views, but to explain their real source. The effect may well be didactic, but the form allows the anger and the sorrow to be voiced from a perspective close to that of the community of the Plateau Mont-Royal.

Further reading

Tremblay, Michel, *Les Belles Sœurs* (Montreal: Leméac, 1989).

—— *Thérèse et Pierrette à l'école des Saints-Anges* (Montreal: Leméac, 1980).

Cambron, Micheline, *Une société, un récit. Discours culturel au Québec, 1967–76* (Montreal: l'Hexagone, 1989).

David, Gilbert and Lavoie, Pierre (eds), *Le Monde de Michel Tremblay* (Montreal/Carnières Morlanwelz: Cahiers de Théâtre Jeu/Editions Lansman, 1993).

Duchaine, Richard, *Ecriture d'une naissance: naissance d'une écriture. 'La Grosse Femme d'à côté est enceinte' de Michel Tremblay* (Quebec: Nuit blanche éditeur, 1994).

Laurendeau, P., 'Théâtre, roman et pratique vernaculaire chez Michel Tremblay', *Présence francophone* 31 (1988), 5–19.

Reid, G. J., 'An eye for an ear: *Fifth Business* and *La Grosse Femme d'à côté est enceinte*', *Studies in Canadian Literature* 14, 2 (1989), 128–49.

Sarkany, Stéphane, 'Le modèle d'inscription du "framéricain" chez Michel Tremblay', *Présence francophone* 32 (1988), 21–31.

Sirois, Antoine, *Mythes et symboles dans la littérature québécoise* (Montreal: Tryptique, 1992).

Language and style

Three distinct modes of discourse are apparent in this passage: first, the narrative – the arrival of Josaphat-le-Violon, which leads to the complaints of Albertine and 'la grosse femme' – second, the narrator's invective against the Catholic view of child-bearing, and third, the conversational passages. The narrative section is located mainly in the first half of the passage (ll. 1–50) but also briefly in the last few lines; the polemical section in lines 51–83. Each mode is expressed in a distinctive tone.

It is instructive to compare the sentence structure of the two modes in which the narrator directly addresses the readership, the narrative and polemical sections. Of the twenty-nine sentences constituting the narrative, fourteen are simple in structure, seven compound, three complex and five compound-complex. The first two sentences contain the largest number of clauses, two main and two subordinate clauses; the first is the only sentence to begin with a subordinate clause. In the eight sentences with subordinate clauses, there is a total of eleven such clauses, seven relative, two temporal, one causal, one with 'alors que'. The narrative therefore consists principally of sentences built from main clauses with only a minimum of

1 For further discussion of the *révolution tranquille* see Chapter 25.

subordinate clauses. The main clauses tend to be short, and the majority of these sentences involve action – description or intellectual speculation is rarely expressed. Probably the most striking characteristic of the sentences is that except for two cases (ll. 1 and 37), the first item is the subject, making for a direct uncomplicated storyline. The narrative is carried along by the verbs, which have a particularly important role to play. The impression produced by the narrative section is one of economic use of language, undemanding structures, straightforward story-telling. This contrasts strongly with the polemical section, which, through a subtle combination of moral invective and specific reference to conditions evoked in the narrative, attacks the attitude of the Roman Catholic Church towards child-bearing.

Here the sentences are completely different in structure. Of the eight sentences, two are simple in structure, none compound, three complex and three compound-complex. Although the narrative section is much longer than the polemical section, the latter contains many more subordinate clauses. In fact, there are twenty subordinate clauses, all except three of which are relative. The relative clauses add detail after detail to a passage which is already highly coloured by adjectives, in contrast to the previous section where adjectives were comparatively rare. Initial elements also differ: whereas subjects were almost invariably in first position in the narrative, on one occasion it is a subordinate clause, on another it is 'plutôt' + infinitive, on another a series of past participles; and in one instance where a subject begins the sentence, it is an infinitive. The effect is to produce a slightly higher register in this section than in the narrative section. Particularly significant is the sentence, beginning in l. 63, which is the pivot of the section. A complex sentence, it contains twelve subordinate clauses, all except one of which are relative. These combine to form a sentence both oratorical and rhetorical in tone, the message of which – the responsibility of the Church in inflicting a slave-like position upon women – is left ringing in the reader's ears. The sentence begins with a powerful participle describing the fate of French-Canadian women, 'écrasées', then a pejorative adjective denouncing the Roman Catholic religion, 'monstrueuse'; 'religion' is further pilloried by being repeated. Indeed it is through repetition in particular that this sentence achieves its condemnatory effect: not only is 'religion' repeated, but so are 'l'égoïsme des hommes', 'Mère', 'vierge', 'sans', 'devoir', 'obligations', 'obéissance'. Other stylistic devices used in this sentence to enhance its rhetorical tone include the use of apposition, e.g. 'au point de faire de l'image de la Mère, la Vierge Marie, Mère de Dieu, une vierge intacte et pure, inhumaine créature' (l. 66, also l. 70); series of expressions, e.g. 'où les mots «devoir» et «obligations» et «obéissance» prédominaient, ronflants, insultants, condescendants' (l. 73, also l. 65 already quoted); reprise, 'les femmes canadiennes-françaises, surtout celles des villes, avaient fini par ressentir une honte maladive d'être enceintes, elles qui n'étaient pas dignes' (l. 74); suspense reinforced by inversion, '«obéissance» à ce merveilleux outil du destin que leur avait fourni directement la Volonté de Dieu: leur mari' (l. 79); sarcasm, 'l'Esprit-Saint (qu'on osait représenter sous la forme d'un oiseau! enceinte d'un oiseau, la Mère de Dieu!' (l. 69)); embedded expressions (l. 75 quoted above but which continues 'comme l'autre, de mettre un enfant au monde'); symmetry, e.g. 'bousculées par ce paquet d'énergies, cette vie si puissante . . . Ecrasées par cette religion monstrueuse qui défendait toute sorte de moyen de contraception, cette religion. . . . ' (l. 63) and subsequently continues 'gavées par les prêtres . . . ' (l. 72). This is further enhanced by the passion engendered by the vocabulary, where some of the most emotive words used in the novel occur: 'écrasées', 'monstrueuse', 'méprisait', 'inhumaine créature', 'insulte ultime', 'gavées', 'cruelles', 'insultants', 'honte maladive', 'merveilleux outil du destin – leur mari'. The effect of this outpouring of fierce condemnation in this sentence is crushing.

Light relief is provided by the third section, which is conversational. Tremblay portrays his characters as using linguistic features associated with *joual*, the distinctive sociolect of Montreal. The following features have been identified. First, from a grammatical point of view: consistent non-use of the negative particle *ne* (*ne* does not occur at all in the mouths of the protagonists), 'y' is used as a universal pronoun – representing masculine singular (l. 27), masculine plural (ll. 44, 48, 50, 98), feminine plural (ll. 24, 45), third-person indirect object (l. 26), impersonal *il* (ll. 46, 104, 110); however, the impersonal pronoun is occasionally omitted (e.g. l. 94); 'tu' occurs as a disjunctive form (l. 103). The conjunction 'où' takes on non-standard forms, both as interrogative e.g. 'ousque' = *où* (l. 16) (but 'où' also occurs in l. 23) or relative, e.g. 'un article . . . ousqu'y disaient . . '. (l. 44). Less common features, also diverging from the norms of standard French, are the use of 'des' before a plural adjective, e.g. 'des belles oranges' (l. 22), the agreement of a past participle with a preceding indirect object, e.g. 'j'espère que vous vous êtes pas faite mal' (l. 31), assigning feminine gender to 'hiver' (l. 45), 'eux' for 'elles', e.g. 'les femmes restent chez eux' (l. 58). Another feature of note is the choice of second person pronouns in the context of the family. The following patterns emerge: 'vous' is used when a young female addresses her father (l. 7), her older cousins (whom she calls aunts, see l. 9) (ll. 15, 31, 32, 33), an older female, her uncle (Josaphat) (ll. 20, 29, 113); 'tu' is used, as in standard French, when an older relative is addressing a younger one (ll. 16 *et passim*).

Second, from a phonological point of view, various devices are used to convey the pronunciation habits of the protagonists. Tremblay makes regular use of apostrophes to represent the omission of mute *e* and other vowel sounds, e.g. in *ce/cet/cette* (ll. 3, 20, 112), in *de* (ll. 42, 49), in the future/conditional of *être* (l. 100), in *petit* (ll. 4, 102, 110), in *quelque chose* (l. 104), in *regarder* (l. 105), in subject pronouns *tu*, *je* consistently (*tu* at l. 103 is a disjunctive form (see above)); 'v'là' for *voilà* (l. 50), 't'ça' for *tout ça* (l. 48). From time to time, an apostrophe marks the omission of the definite article, e.g. 'à'même place' (ll. 25, 48). 'Vot'' and 'aut'' occur (l. 30 and l. 44 respectively) and 'su'l'balcon' (ll. 108, 110). Apostrophes are also used to indicate other peculiarities of pronunciation: 'x'cusez' (l. 15). The practice becomes so habitual that occasionally inappropriate use occurs, e.g. 'c't'un cyclone' (l. 20). Aphaeresis occurs in 'Bartine' (l. 5). Elision leads onto ellipsis, e.g. 'rapport à' for *par rapport à* (l. 45), 'Toé-si' = *toi aussi* (l. 39). A false liaison/hiatus blocker is recorded – 'Marcel va-t'être content' (l. 22). In addition to the use of apostrophes, other orthographies are used to indicate typical *joual* departures from standard pronunciation, some of which are, of course, also typical of the popular French of France: 'arais' (*aurais*), 'assir' (*asseoir*), 'ben' (*bien*), 'pis' (*puis*), 'pus' (*plus*), 'j'vas' and the regular use of 'moé' and 'toé' for the disjunctive pronouns. Also typical of *joual* are 'moman' and 'popa' for *maman* and *papa*, and 'frette' (l. 47) for *froid*.

Finally the atmosphere of Montreal is still further confirmed by the use of certain lexical items (words, expressions and interjections/expletives): e.g. 'bonyeu' (l. 24) = good God, 'châssis' (l. 106) = window, 'coq-dinde' (l. 88) = stupid person, 's'échiner' (l. 30) = to slave away, 'une grenouille de bénitier' (l. 57), 'un mangeux de balustres' (l. 57), both of which = a sanctimonious person, 'minoucher' (l. 27) = to say sweet nothings to, 'ouan' (l. 40) = yes, 'tanner' (l. 107) = to be dog tired, 'j'ai les yeux qui me flottent dedans' (l. 7) = I'm bursting for the loo.

It is Tremblay's ability to switch style and register and to blend conversation and narrative so skilfully, integrating the passage as a whole (at one point the use of anglicisms typical of conversation spills over into the narrative ('le bruit des springs'(l. 27)) which is the notable stylistic feature of the passage as a whole.

Chapter 30

Antonine Maillet

Pélagie-la-Charrette (Montreal: Bibliothèque québécoise, 1990), pp. 309–13. First published Montreal: Leméac, 1979.

. . . Et j'ai du grain de mil, et j'ai du grain de paille, et j'ai de l'oranger, et j'ai du tri, et j'ai du tricoli, et j'ai des allumettes, et j'ai des ananas, j'ai de beaux . . . j'ai de beaux . . . j'ai de beaux oiseaux.

Pélagie s'est arrachée à sa botte de paille et elle marche, oui, elle marche, le bras enroulé sur un pieu de ridelle comme autour du mât . . . là-bas, en haute mer, il s'avance, son Beausoleil, il revient vers elle, vers Grand'Pré. Son long voyage s'achèvera là, dans sa terre natale, où il la rejoindra, il l'a promis. Elle l'attendra sous les pommiers en fleurs, en ce nouveau printemps de leur vie. Et cette fois, plus rien ne l'arrachera à lui, elle a accompli son œuvre, elle a répondu aux vœux des aïeux. Oui, cette fois . . .

Sa fille Madeleine, Catoune, Célina, Jeanne Aucoin, Agnès Dugas, toutes les femmes d'Acadie n'ont d'yeux que pour ce sourire de bien-aise qui triomphe sur le visage de Pélagie, la Pélagie-la-Charrette qui fait de toutes ses forces les derniers pas qui la séparent de sa terre d'origine. Encore un souffle, encore un tout petit souffle et Grand'Pré sera là, en face de la baie Française qu'on appelle désormais *Bay of Fundy*.

Quelques jours plus tard, Pierre à Pitre grimpa jusqu'à la dernière branche d'un chêne solitaire et hucha:

– La mer!

Enfin! c'était elle, la baie, la baie où se mirait sur une rive le fort Beauséjour, et sur l'autre tout le bassin des Mines. Pélagie avançait presque d'un pas ferme, devançant les autres, haletant de toute sa poitrine. Demain, Beauséjour. Les Cormier et les Girouard en frétillaient; Jeanne Aucoin s'en serrait le ventre.

– Je ferons en premier la cérémonie d'enterrement des morts, qu'elle dit. Jamais je croirai qu'ils rendront point nos morts après vingt-cinq ans.

– Et nos caves pour nous y rebâti', qu'ajouta François à Pierre à Pierre à Pierrot.

Et les champs, et les barques, et les aboiteaux. Ils repartiront de rien, s'il faut, mais ils repartiront chez eux, et renoueront le passé à l'avenir.

Déjà les Basques sortaient leurs musiques, l'Acadie tout entière rentrait en chantant ... quand le Sauvage, parti en éclaireur, revint avec la nouvelle: Beauséjour était occupé, à demeure. De même que tout l'isthme de Chignectou.

Les charrettes, sur le coup, cessèrent de respirer. Pélagie fut la première à reprendre son souffle pour demander:

– Et la Grand'Prée?

Grand'Pré était désert, brûlé et désert, depuis le jour fatal de septembre 1755. Par superstition, ou par crainte de Dieu, on n'avait pas osé s'y installer, personne. On avait laissé là, abandonné aux goélands et aux herbes sauvages, ce bourg jadis prospère et animé de la rive française.

Comme un cimetière antique ...

Comme un berceau à la dérive ...

Tous les yeux se détournèrent du sud-sud-ouest, et avisèrent le nord.

Sauf Pélagie.

Elle restait là, comme un sphinx de pierre, murmurant pour elle seule des mots qui s'inscrivaient à mesure dans le ciel ... Cette Grand'Prée qui n'était point pour ses enfants, ne serait point non plus pour les enfants des autres. Personne n'y ferait son nid, jamais ... jamais ...

Puis levant la tête et le poing au ciel, elle hucha aux générations à venir:

– Vous y reviendrez en pèlerinage pour y fleurir les tombes de vos aïeux. Je le dis à tous les LeBlanc, les Bourg, les Bourgeois, les Landry, les Cormier, les Giroué, les Belliveau, les Allain, les Maillet et les fils d'Acadie qui sont aveindus d'exil dans des charrettes à bœufs. Je le dis à tous les enfants du pays. Touchez point à la Grand'Prée, mais gardez-en mémoire au fond des cœurs et des reins.

Et pour illustrer son dire devant son peuple affaissé aux pieds des charrettes, elle arracha son mouchoir de col, l'ouvrit tout grand au vent, en replia lentement les quatre coins, puis l'enfouit dans la poche de son tablier.

– Je l'emporte au fond de mon devanteau, ma Grand'Prée, qu'elle articula, personne viendra me l'arracher une troisième fois.

Et dans sa poche de devanteau, elle enfouit aussi des mots, des mots anciens aveindus à cru de la goule de ses pères et qu'elle ne voulait point laisser en hairage à des gots étrangers; elle y enfouit des légendes et des contes merveilleux, horrifiques ou facétieux, comme se les passait son lignage depuis le début des temps; elle y enfouit des croyances et coutumes enfilées à son cou comme un bijou de famille qu'elle laisserait à son tour en héritage à ses descendants; elle enfouit l'histoire de son peuple commencée deux siècles plus tôt, puis ballottée aux quatre vents, et laissée moribonde dans le ruisseau ... jusqu'au jour où un passant la ramasserait, et la ravigoterait, et la rentrerait de force au pays; elle y enfouit ses pères et ses fils engloutis dans le Dérangement, son fils Jean égaré dans la forêt sauvage de la Pennsylvanie, et qui seul ne retrouverait peut-être pas le chemin du retour; elle y enfouit le capitaine de la *Grand'Goule*, son héros, son rêve impossible qui ne l'atteindrait point sur les rives de la Grand'Prée . . . Car tu comprends, Beausoleil, ils nous l'avont pris, notre Grand'Prée, avec ses pommiers en fleurs, et sa morue fraîche, et ses fraises de bois. Ils nous avont pris nos terres et nos bâtiments. Asteur, il nous faut encore un coup embourrer l'Acadie dans l'étoffe du pays, l'enfouir dans nos coffres, et la faire grimper un peu plus vers le nord . . . Mais, toi, Beausoleil, tu resteras au chaud dans ma poche de devanteau, au creux de mon ventre, Broussard dit Beausoleil qui a illuminé ma marche vers le pays à la tête de mon peuple.

. . . Son peuple. Pour la première fois, Pélagie s'aperçut que sa famille sortie de Géorgie dans une charrette, rendue en Acadie était devenue un peuple. En dix ans, elle avait raflé à la terre d'exil des tribus entières de ses pays et payses et les avait ramenées à leurs terres par la porte d'en-derrière.

Surtout n'éveillez pas l'ours qui dort.

Rentrez chacun à votre chacunière sur la pointe des pieds et attendez le temps qu'il faut. On a bien attendu en Géorgie, dans les Caroline, en Marilande, et tout le long de la Nouvelle-Angleterre, attendu que passe la première charrette pour y accrocher la sienne. On pourra de même attendre sur le marchepied de son logis que la porte s'ouvre et que la maison se vide. Attendre que la terre se réchauffe, que la mer se calme, que les mémoires s'émoussent. Attendre que les plantes regerment dans les champs et les potagers saccagés.

Alban à Charles à Charles laissa Pélagie poursuivre sa pensée jusqu'au bout. Puis s'essuyant le front, il l'avisa:

– Je sons icitte dans les marais de Tintamarre, qu'il dit. C'est point un endroit pour y creuser des caves ou planter des piquets de cabanes. Je ferions peut-être mieux de songer à lever le pied.

– Oui, qu'elle fit, monter vers le nord.

– Le Sauvage conte qu'y en a plusieurs des nôtres au fond des anses et des baies, dans les bois, à l'abric.

– A l'abric chez eux, en Acadie.

Alban à Charles à Charles baissa les yeux et se tut. Mais Pélagie l'entendit tout de même. Il lui disait que l'Acadie, ça n'existait plus; qu'il n'y aurait plus désormais que des Acadiens.

Pélagie leva la tête et sourit à Alain Girouard:

– Quoi c'est que ça peut faire? qu'elle dit. C'est les hommes qui faisont la terre, et point la terre qui fait les hommes. Là où c'est que je marcherons, nous autres, il faudra bien qu'ils bailliont un nom à l'endroit. Je l'appellerons l'Acadie. Par rapport que j'allons la rebâti', tu vas ouère, j'allons la rebâti' à grandeur du pays.

Alban avisa Pélagie, puis leva un sourcil dans un petit hé, hé!

Puis c'est elle qui cria:

– Remettez les charrettes en marche!

Mais quand elle voulut bouger la sienne, elle trouva les quatre roues enfoncées dans les marais de Tintamarre.

Et Pélagie se souvint des marais de Salem.

A Salem, sa charrette s'était arrachée par miracle à la glaise des marais. L'Acadie sortie d'exil était réellement née, comme le premier homme, du limon de la terre. A Tintamarre . . . Beausoleil arriverait-il à temps pour sauver sa charrette une seconde fois?

Text and context

In 1755 the British authorities in Halifax (Nova Scotia) began a series of deportations of the francophone population living on fertile farmland along the coast of what is now Nova Scotia, New Brunswick and Prince Edward Island. About 11,000 of a population of 13,000 were driven out of what they called Acadie, many being deported by ship to British colonies all the way along the eastern seaboard of North America. Just as the defeat on the Plains of Abraham in 1759 was to mark the end of the period of New France, so *le grand dérangement* of the deportation came to symbolize the end of a golden age. Maillet's *Pélagie-la-Charrette*, which established an Acadian voice among the literature of francophone North America, tells of the return from exile, a generation later, of a group of Acadians. During a ten-year journey northwards through the continent they suffer death, illness, imprisonment and the risk of being sold into slavery, but they also gather in strength, as new families join their wagons to the trail. At the head of the group is the matriarchal figure of Pélagie-la-Charrette, who, with her wagon, comes to symbolize the struggle of a conquered people to reclaim its identity and its place in Canada. The chosen passage recounts their discovery that what was Acadie is now occupied by British settlers.

The northward route that dominates the narrative contrasts with the westward movement of pioneers and fortune seekers that one normally associates with the image of a wagon trail in North America. For unlike the attraction of the unknown western frontier, the return to Acadie is a journey back home, in search of roots and traditions. Their arrival home is announced by the sight of the bay (the Bay of Fundy), of le fort Beauséjour and the bassin des Mines (l. 21). Once again in sight of their 'terre d'origine', the Acadians feel they can return to their traditional way of living in this landscape, evoked by the refrain: 'Et les champs, et les barques, et les aboiteaux' (l. 28).[1] But the hope of rebuilding their lives is dashed when their Indian scout returns to report that their former homes (Beauséjour, l'isthme de Chignectou) are occupied, or, in the case of la Grand'Pré, Pélagie's spiritual home, in ruins (l. 36). Their continued existence as a people will depend not on a territorial identity (and indeed there is no longer any definable territory called Acadie), but rather on a cultural identity. Pélagie understands Alban Girouard's expression as saying that: 'l'Acadie, ça n'existait plus; qu'il n'y aurait plus désormais que des Acadiens' (l. 101). La Grand'Pré stands as a symbol to underline the difference between the survival of the Acadian people

1 'Les aboiteaux' refer to the dikes constructed by the Acadians to drain the marshy coastal land.

and that of the population of what is now Quebec. Whereas Quebeckers retained their language, their religion and the *code de Paris*,[2] Acadie had been wiped off the map, its people unrecognized as a French-speaking minority. Maillet's text is at once a tribute to and an expression of this unrecognized minority. In its turn it re-enacts the transmission of this oral tradition for modern-day Acadians, and by transforming it into written form, declares its survival to a much wider francophone community.

If the place names stand as memorials to the Acadian past, the family names indicate the way forward. The passage shows two of the ways that the genealogical coherence of the Acadian people is recalled. Pélagie, when addressing her people, lists their names: 'Je le dis à tous les LeBlanc, les Bourg, les Bourgeois, les Landry, les Cormier, les Giroué, les Belliveau, les Allain, les Maillet et les fils d'Acadie qui sont aveindus d'exil dans des charrettes à bœufs' (l. 49). Since the Acadians are descended from a core of about forty settler families, this use of listing has the effect of reinforcing a sense of cultural identity. Second, the designation of Acadians by their paternal lineage ('Alban à Charles à Charles' (l. 91)) or their maternal lineage in the case of women, binds the generations together in a chain which both looks back and also leads on into the future. Indeed the novel mirrors the patterns of lineage in its own narrative structure. While the main narrative recounts the return from exile in the 1770s, a second layer of story-telling is set in 1880, with Pélagie's descendant Pélagie-la-Gribouille as the protagonist, and a third layer of story-telling has a modern-day (1979) first-person narrator who inserts herself at the end of the chain ('l'Histoire . . . continue encore dans la bouche de mon cousin Louis à Bélonie' (p. 15)), so emphasizing the continuity of the oral tradition which has held a minority culture together.

As Pélagie symbolically gathers up the tales, the words, the customs and the history of her reborn people, she is in fact conserving them as an oral tradition. The importance of the oral tradition for the survival of an Acadian culture proved to be crucial since the once high levels of literacy of the Acadian people dropped rapidly as a result of the period of exile in English-speaking colonies and the lack of provision for any French-language schooling on their return. The ways that this passage draws upon an oral culture makes it an interesting parallel to Michel Tremblay's *La Grosse Femme d'à côté est enceinte* (see Chapter 29 above). To read Maillet is to hear a distinctive Acadian voice. This voice does not express itself in the modern-day *chiac* of New Brunswick francophones, but rather uses older forms and vocabulary which date back to the eighteenth century. Other aspects of the text contribute to its spoken quality. As seen in the stylistic commentary, the narrative voice moves between Pélagie's own words and thoughts, and a slightly more distanced voice, both of which use Acadian terms. The narrative is bound together with other features of an oral culture, with sayings such as 'Surtout n'éveillez pas l'ours qui dort' (l. 83), or with refrains like the opening three lines of the passage which echo the calls of pedlars or market traders selling their wares: 'et j'ai des allumettes, et j'ai des ananas, j'ai de beaux . . . j'ai de beaux . . . j'ai de beaux oiseaux' (l. 2).

While Acadian oral traditions are an important component of Maillet's literary style, the imagery and intertextual elements encourage the reader to see parallels with the Old Testament account of the history of the Jews. A number of parallels can be found in this extract. The journey back from exile echoes that of the Israelites returning from slavery in Egypt to the Promised Land. Like the Israelites, the Acadians seem to have supernatural guidance,

2 The *code de Paris* was a particular version of French civil law.

'Beausoleil qui a illuminé ma marche vers le pays' (l. 76) being reminiscent of the pillar of fire and the pillar of smoke which guided them on their way. The reference at the end of the passage to the 'marais de Salem' (l. 114) (where the Acadians were saved from drowning in the marshes by the intervention of the semi-fantastic figure of Beausoleil), recalls the miraculous passage through the Red Sea. Pélagie herself can be read as a matriarchal equivalent of Moses. Like him, she arrives in sight of the Promised Land, but then dies (Pélagie dies just after the end of this extract). Like Moses, Pélagie passes on guidance to her people (in her exhortation to them to honour la Grand'Pré as a sacred site, a memorial to the past, and in her recommendation to hold on to their culture and to settle further north (l. 75)). By echoing the biblical story, Maillet can be seen to enhance the status of Pélagie and to liken the return of the Acadians from exile not only to the Old Testament return from Egypt, but by extension to the diaspora and the founding of modern Israel. At the same time, by basing the rebirth of the Acadian people on a matriarchal figure, rather than the patriarch of Judaeo-Christian tradition, Maillet is perhaps offering the Acadians a different model of heritage and of tradition, one that relies not on patriarchal values but on the maternal principle and feminine values. This view is reinforced by the emphasis in the text on the maternal body – 'au creux de mon ventre' (l. 76) and women's clothing – 'sa poche de devanteau' (l. 59) – on a feminine notion of inheritance – 'des croyances et coutumes enfilées à son cou comme un bijou de famille' (l. 63) – and on non-conflictual values – 'Surtout n'éveillez pas l'ours qui dort' (l. 83). On their return, the Acadian people were confronted with patriarchal power in the form of the British administration. Powerless to resist them by military or political means, the form of resistance that they developed can indeed be understood as representing a different, feminine model of cultural assertion.

Further reading

Maillet, Antonine, *La Sagouine. Pièce pour une seule femme* (Montreal: Leméac, 1986).
—— *Cent Ans dans les bois* (Montreal: Leméac, 1981).
—— *Le Huitième Jour* (Montreal: Leméac, 1986).

Dinwoodie, C., 'Where is Acadia?', *British Journal for Canadian Studies* 1, 1 (1986), 15–29.
Drolet, Bruno, *Entre dune et aboiteaux . . . un peuple. Etude critique des œuvres d'Antonine Maillet* (Montreal: les Editions Pleins Bords, 1975).
Finney, James de, 'Antonine Maillet: un exemple de réception littéraire régionale', *Revue d'histoire littéraire du Québec et du Canada français* 12 (Summer-Autumn 1986), 17–33.
Fitzpatrick, Marjorie, A., 'Antonine Maillet: the search for a narrative voice', *Journal of Popular Culture* 15, 3 (Winter 1981), 4–13.
Griffiths, Naomi, *The Contexts of Acadian History* (Kingston and Montreal: McGill-Queen's University Press, 1992).
Moulaison, Glenn, 'La lecture idéologique de *Pélagie-la-Charrette*', *Revue de l'Université de Moncton* 21, 2 (1988), 33–45.
Smith, Donald, *Voices of Delivrance. Interviews with Quebec and Acadian Writers* (Toronto: Anansi, 1986).

Language and style

The most striking feature of this passage stylistically is the role or position of the narrator in the development of the storyline. It soon emerges that her identity does not remain constant. At times she is the objective narrator; it is with this function that she moves the story along, e.g. 'Quelques jours plus tard, Pierre à Pitre grimpa jusqu'à la dernière branche d'un chêne solitaire' (l. 17, also ll. 33, 54, 79, 91, 100, 109, 112). At other times the narrator seems to be an unseen but sympathetic companion on the trek to Acadie, sharing the hopes and disappointments of the journey. This is the case when she reacts to certain situations, e.g. 'Pierre à Pitre . . . hucha: La mer!' and the narrator exclaims: 'Enfin! c'était elle, la baie, la baie' (l. 20) and when she adds to the list of items, begun by François à Pierre à Pierre, which the travellers wish to repair (l. 28). This identification with the protagonists goes a stage further through the frequent use of free indirect discourse. In this guise she identifies with Pélagie. This happens in the second paragraph, which begins with an impartial description of Pélagie, but quickly becomes a proclamation of her aspirations, finishing with a merging of identities, in the words 'Oui, cette fois . . '. (l. 10). A very similar situation arises in ll. 44–7. There is in fact a regular switching between free indirect discourse and a slightly more dispassionate voice. For example, in the third paragraph, ll. 11–14 are the narrator's own words, but ll. 14–16, with the change to the future tense, align her squarely with Pélagie once again. A similar situation occurs later in the passage. In l. 71 the use of 'tu' in a section of highly emotive discourse from the narrator signals a change of perspective: the narrator becomes Pélagie for a few lines (ll. 72–8), finishing with 'mon peuple' and then switches back to her original persona with 'son peuple' (l. 79). This switching of identity leads to situations where it is not altogether clear who is actually speaking, the more so since no graphological indications are provided. For example, when l. 83 warns, in the words of one of the Acadian sayings which is repeated throughout the novel, 'Surtout n'éveillez pas l'ours qui dort' and l. 84 advises 'Rentrez chacun à votre chacunière', the identities of the narrator and Pélagie become indistinguishable. This constantly changing narratorial perspective reaches its climax in sections where the narrator, though distinct from Pélagie, nonetheless uses the language of the Acadians herself. The closeness of the narrator's identity with the people whose history she is telling means that their language becomes her language. It is in the section beginning l. 59 that the linguistic link between narrator and protagonists becomes most obvious. Pélagie's dramatic gesture of embracing all the members of the group through the symbol of the folded scarf thrust into her apron pocket (l. 56) leads on to a desire to protect the language which is likewise buried in her apron pocket, not only the language (note the dense use of Acadian terms at this point (ll. 60, 61)), but also the legends, tales, beliefs, customs, the whole history of her people and their heroes. The lists of names given on occasions (ll. 11, 50, 85 – place names – and to a lesser extent l. 22) echo the lists of warriors found in early epic poetry and emphasize the unity and identity of the group.

The Acadian variety of French presented here has a number of characteristics which distinguish it from standard French. Acadian pronunciation is suggested: by the use of apostrophes to mark the loss of final sounds, e.g. 'rebâti'' (ll. 27, 107 twice), by 'abric' for *abri* (ll. 98, 99), 'goule' for *gueule* (l. 60), 'ouère' for *voir* (l. 107). The passage contains a number of Acadian lexical items, from the narrator as well as from the Acadians themselves (in fact more from the narrator), e.g. 'aboiteaux' = dikes (l. 28), 'aveindus' = arrived (ll. 51, 60), 'Asteur' = at present (l. 74), 'chacunière' = home (l. 84), 'devanteau' = apron (ll. 39, 57; but compare 'tablier' (l. 56)), 'gots' = throats (l. 61), 'hairage' = inheritance (l. 60; but compare 'héritage' (l. 64)), 'icitte' = here (l. 93) 'pays et payses' = countrymen and women (l. 81). The pronoun 'je' is used as a first person plural pronoun, as well as for first person singular, e.g. 'Je ferons en premier la cérémonie d'enterrement des morts' (l. 25, also ll. 93, 94, 105, 106, 107). Irregular verbs at times have distinctive forms (showing a tendency towards regularization) – first person plural of the present tense of *être*, 'je sons' (l. 93), third person plural of the present tense of *avoir*, e.g. 'ils nous l'avont pris' (l. 72, also l. 73), of *faire*, 'faisont' (l. 104), of the present subjunctive of *bailler*, 'ils bailliont' (l. 106).

The use of Acadian linguistic features by the narrator as well as by the protagonists, the sharing of the Acadians' aspirations by the narrator, the merging of the narrator's speech with that of the protagonists, all contribute to the oral nature of the narrative. This is clear from the eulogy of Acadian language delivered in ll. 59 and following, particularly the reference to beliefs and customs being 'enfilées à son cou comme un bijou de famille'. A number of stylistic devices, typical of oral rather than written story-telling, reinforce this effect. Alliteration, an aid to remembering text, occurs on a number of occasions, e.g. 'On pourra de même attendre sur le marchepied de son logis que la porte s'ouvre et que la maison se vide. Attendre que la terre se réchauffe, que la mer se calme, que les mémoires s'émoussent' (l. 87, also ll. 28, 67, 79), as do the use of deictics, e.g. 'là-bas' (l. 5), 'là' (ll. 15, 38, 44), 'Déjà' (l. 30), post-positioning of nouns, e.g. 'il s'avance, son Beausoleil, il revient vers elle' (l. 5, also ll. 20, 37), and apposition (ll. 13, 70, 72, 76). Repetition is widely used in the passage, the most striking examples being of particular words, e.g. 'enfouit' eight times (between l. 56 and l. 75), 'attendre' six times (between l. 84 and l. 89). Other elements are repeated: prepositions (l. 6), adverbs (ll. 8, 52), nouns (ll. 20, 59), negative particles (l. 47), clauses (ll. 6, 28). Repetition of names focuses attention on the person in question, e.g. Pélagie (l. 13), Beausoleil (l. 72). Linked to repetition is the use of doublets, e.g. present participles (l. 22), triplets, e.g. adjectives (l. 36), verbs (l. 67, reinforced by alliteration), objects (l. 72), infinitives (l. 74), parallel clause structures (ll. 9, 23). Strategic positioning of certain words binds the text tightly together – for example, 'arracher', a powerful physical verb, occurs twice at the beginning of the passage, once to show Pélagie's determination (l. 4) and again to show her devotion to Beausoleil (l. 9), and again at the end with reference to escaping the treacherous marshes of Salem (l. 115).

The oral nature of the text is also emphasized by the use of graphological devices, which correspond to breaks in oral delivery or change of tone. This is achieved through frequent use of 'points de suspension' (on ten occasions, e.g. ll. 10, 31, 40, 41). Minor sentences are rarely used in the narrative itself, but when they are, they have a poignant effect: of hope, e.g. 'Demain, Beauséjour' (l. 22), of disappointment (l. 32); this is especially so at l. 40 when they are combined with 'points de suspension', presented as complete paragraphs and contain both bleak and hopeful imagery to describe the deserted area of Grand'Pré:

> Comme un cimetière antique . . .
> Comme un berceau à la dérive . .

The last aspect to be considered links in with the previous – the use of imagery. This tends to take the form of short similes. Two of the four remaining (three others have already been mentioned) relate to Pélagie: in the first (l. 5), she is described as walking, 'le bras enroulé sur un pieu de ridelle comme autour du mât' suggesting that her enterprise is as great as any seafaring adventure (and is therefore worthy of captain Beausoleil); in the second which occurs immediately after the two similes relating to Beauséjour, she is compared to a sphinx (l. 44), aloof from her fellow travellers. The final simile – 'L'Acadie sortie d'exil était réellement née, comme le premier homme, du limon de la terre' (l. 115) – implies that for the Acadians nationhood, triumph, is born out of slime, adversity.

Chapter 31

Régine Robin

La Québécoite (Montreal: Typo, 1993), pp. 184–90. First published Montreal: Editions Québec/Amérique, 1983.

Le dimanche en été, ils traîneraient de longues heures autour du marché Jean-Talon. Ils adoreraient ça. Elle aurait l'impression par moments d'être à Naples ou en Sicile. Lui aussi pourrait avec de l'imagination par moments revoir les marchés de petites villes du Paraguay. Ce serait des piles de tomates, de choux-fleurs, de poivrons, des paniers d'osier pleins de bleuets ou de fraises, des amoncellements de laitues. Plus loin de l'ail en natte, des oignons rouges, des oignons blancs, de l'échalote, des herbes fines. Ça sentirait bon le fenouil, le serpolet et la menthe sauvage au milieu des mouches et des guêpes, entre les melons d'eau un peu sûrs et des figues de Barbarie venues on ne sait d'où. Plus loin encore des fleurs, des plantes vertes, des senteurs suaves au-dessus des voix italiennes ou grecques. Joyeux tohu-bohu au milieu duquel ils auraient le sentiment d'être chez eux, s'extasiant devant tous les étalages, devant le miel et les confitures naturelles, devant les bocaux d'ail sauvage aussi bien que devant la lavande en sachets.

Ils monteraient toutes leurs provisions, et iraient chez Milano chercher leurs pâtes fraîches, leurs olives et du féta. Ils retourneraient déjeuner à la pizzeria où ils se seraient connus, puis se baladeraient dans le quartier, autour du parc Jarry, ou le long de la Main descendant jusqu'à Beaubien, Rosemont, voire Laurier, rencontrant des amis italiens, latino-américains ou québécois. Ils reviendraient chez eux, feraient l'amour sur le tapis du salon. Elle aimerait les mots doux murmurés à son oreille en espagnol. Elle se mettrait ensuite à son piano, ce vieux piano d'occasion mais aux tonalités cristallines, et y resterait des heures dans le calme des fins d'après-midi. Il l'écouterait calé au fond de sa chaise berçante, sa pipe d'amsterdamer à la main, des tas de journaux latino-américains clandestins jonchant le plancher du salon.

Métro République, une station importante. Tout le monde changeait. On devait ensuite emprunter un long couloir pour accéder à la direction «Mairie des lilas». On se réunissait le dimanche sur la place par tous les temps. A quinze ans les itinéraires ne sont pas originaux. Tous sur les grands boulevards jusqu'aux Italiens. République devant la Toile d'Avion ou devant l'hôtel moderne. Plus tard, tu attendis de longues heures Janos. Vous vous étiez donné rendez-vous. Il rêvait depuis longtemps d'une bonne choucroute. Tu avais retenu une table «chez Jenny». Tu arrivas en avance, te commandant un pastis pour tromper l'attente, fumant tes gauloises l'une après l'autre avec nervosité. Tu avais connu Janos à Budapest au conservatoire en automne. Il était professeur de musique et personne ne savait jouer Kodaly ou Bartok comme lui, au piano, au violon, au violoncelle. Il avait traversé les événements de 1956 sans trop d'embûches, ne comprenant rien, ne vivant que pour sa musique, pour cette ville qu'il aimait tant, pour la maison qu'il occupait à «Rozja Domb», la colline des roses et qui avait un charme fou ouvrant sur un jardin aux haies de lilas et de rosiers grimpants, ne vivant que pour fouler les feuilles mortes dans l'île Marguerite et voir passer les bateaux sur le Danube. Janos tardait. Tu ne savais que penser. De la table où tu attendais tristement, tu regardais la place de la République. Il pleuvait. Parapluies, pardessus, flaques et freins devant les feux. Tu regardais ce Paris de la fin de ton adolescence. Déjà errante. A Paris ou à Budapest? A quoi bon! Janos ne vint pas ce soir-là, ni aucun autre soir. Il rentra précipitamment à Budapest. Il t'écrira beaucoup plus tard. Il avait fui sachant que s'il venait te voir, ce soir-là, il lâcherait tout pour toi, son pays, sa maison, le conservatoire et la musique. Tu restais seule de longues heures «chez Jenny» à la République. Lorsque tu sortis de là, ayant réglé l'addition, ayant commandé pour la forme une choucroute à laquelle tu ne touchas pas, tu pris le métro. Métro République, direction Porte des Lilas. Jamais plus les lilas de la colline des roses à Budapest, jamais plus le regard enfantin de Janos. Les villes se cherchent et se répondent dans la nuit. Parfois, elles se ressemblent. Paris ou Budapest.

Budapest ou Paris. Ou Montréal. Quelle importance! Quelque part dans l'imaginaire de la ville!

Le texte m'échappe. Je le sens glisser. Sécrétions de pittoresque, épanchements. Nostalgies de deux sous. Illusions de l'enracinement. Ce personnage encore une fois m'échappe. Je finis par me laisser prendre à son histoire. Je finis par croire à la réalité de Mime Yente et de son chat Bilou, je finis par vouloir suivre une intrigue, un semblant d'histoire avec un début et une fin. Je finis par vouloir un brin d'ordre, de logique, un lieu quoi. Vivre à petits pas, à petits feux. Le temps à se traîner jour après jour. Les courses à faire. Pardon. Magasiner. Enfilement de gestes, miettes de ville, de vide, de vie. Je finis par avoir la nostalgie du récit. Où la mener? Elle ne peut tout de même pas habiter tous les quartiers de Montréal. La promener longtemps ainsi dans la ville aux soirs chagrins, aux ombres resserrées? Du marché Jean-Talon à Verdun, de Pointe-aux-Trembles au Vieux-Montréal? En attente, brisée? Lui donner des amants de toutes les nationalités et après? Restera l'exil, l'éternel sentiment d'être ailleurs, déracinée. Montréal ou Paris, Budapest ou Jitomir ou New York. Les villes se cherchent et se répondent dans la nuit. Parfois elles se ressemblent. Quelle importance! Quelque part dans l'imaginaire de la ville.

Je me sens totalement piégée par elle. Elle finit par me prendre par la main, par me guider. Si je lui compose tel visage, si je lui donne tel destin, elle se rebiffe. C'est elle qui finit par commander. Elle veut sa place, toute sa place. Elle n'accepte pas d'être une ombre, un simple support à l'écriture. Non. Elle sort du papier, elle entraîne son barbudo. Mime Yente et Bilou dans cette émergence. Elle me fait la nique. Elle s'installe. Oui, s'installer. Rester quelque part. La tentation des races pures, des beaux passeports, des généalogies, des «moi mes ancêtres ici, il y a deux cents, trois cents ans, moi ma noblesse qui remonte au temps des croisades, moi cette terre, mes aïeux la travaillaient . . . » A d'autres! On connaît. Je n'ai pas d'aïeux. Tous morts à Auschwitz et avant anonymes, des petits, des obscurs, des sans-grades. Pas d'aïeux, des ailleurs, oui, elle m'échappe. Fatiguée sans doute de cette course folle à travers la ville, de ce roman qu'elle n'arrive pas à terminer.

faux messies et
faux récits

Oui, la fatigue. Budapest ou Paris, Paris ou Budapest ou Montréal. Qu'importe! Cela n'a pas de fin.

Le vendredi soir serait consacré à Mime Yente. On se rendrait à Snowdon, on lui apporterait des fleurs. Elle allumerait les bougies de la Menorah et on fêterait gaiement le sabbat. Mime Yente remplirait une coupe de vin puis déclamerait en hébreu sa pipe d'amsterdamer à la main «Le soir se fit, puis le matin; ce fut le sixième jour. Ainsi furent terminés les cieux et la terre et toute leur armée. Dieu avait achevé, le septième jour, l'œuvre faite par lui et il se reposa, le septième jour de toute l'œuvre qu'il avait faite. Dieu bénit le septième jour et le proclama saint parce qu'en ce jour il se reposa de l'œuvre entière qu'il avait créée en la faisant.» On dînerait fastueusement aux bougies de la Menorah. La tante mettrait les petits plats dans les grands. On se régalerait de *gefilte fish*, de *Knödles*, de blinis à la crème sûre et de stroudle. Le tout arrosé de thé, car le samovar de Jitomir serait perpétuellement de la partie, Bilou sous la table ramassant les miettes et se blottissant contre les pieds des uns et des autres. Mime Yente aurait tout de suite adopté ce «barbudo» aux yeux noirs sortis des prisons de Stroesner. Il lui aurait raconté ses luttes, ses victoires et ses défaites, elle lui aurait raconté par le menu l'Ukraine, les pogroms de Petliura, sa fuite à Londres et le procès Schwartzbard à Paris. Ils se seraient parfaitement compris. Des anciens combattants un peu sur la touche, un peu grognards. Ils auraient bien d'autre chose en commun, la pipe et l'amsterdamer par exemple. Le vendredi soir, elle jouerait pour Mime Yente des airs anciens et du Chopin pour Bilou en pelote sur les partitions en haut à droite. Ils évoqueraient la situation politique dans le monde, en Amérique latine, au Canada et au Québec. Ils n'en finiraient pas d'évoquer le passé.

– Vous devriez déménager, dirait régulièrement Mime Yente. C'est trop humide là-bas. Vous devriez trouver quelque chose dans le quartier tout près d'ici. Ils ne répondraient pas, attachés qu'ils seraient au marché Jean-Talon, aux pizzerias du coin et aux épiceries italiennes à leurs yeux irremplaçables.

– On verra plus tard, répondrait-elle entre deux verres de thé. On verra plus tard. Ils quitteraient Mime Yente assez tard dans la soirée, ayant une longue trotte par bus et métro pour rentrer. Les soirs d'été, ils marcheraient à pied jusqu'à l'intersection de Sherbrooke et de Saint-Laurent ne prenant le bus que pour monter la Main. Ou alors par d'autres itinéraires compliqués, ils s'en reviendraient à la maison à pied. Ils aimeraient marcher dans la ville à l'écoute de ses langues, de ses métamorphoses, de ses bruits. De Snowdon, ils rejoindraient Victoria par Lacombe qu'ils suivraient très loin dans le nord, rêvant de maisons de pierre ou de brique, voyant dans la nuit des intérieurs encore brillamment éclairés avec de beaux abat-jour à franges et des plantes vertes devant les fenêtres. Ils longeraient ainsi Victoria jusqu'à Van Horne et parfois au-delà jusqu'au cœur du quartier juif.

Spaghetti ville — Bagel ville
Royal Bank — Brown Derby
Pharmaprix — Fiducie Victoria

Partout des boucheries kascher, des synagogues, des maisons de prières et des congrégations. La Bagelerie Van Horn, l'épicerie Budapest et le marché Aviv. Puis ils longeraient Outremont, les belles maisons le long du parc Pratt. Ce serait le silence. Le quartier endormi redeviendrait populaire au-delà. Ils prendraient par le nord remontant la rue Saint-Laurent jusque chez eux. Ce serait une très longue promenade prenant des allures de bout du monde. Ils ne l'entreprendraient que certaines nuits d'été, de ces nuits au vent léger, accompagnés de senteurs de lilas à la fin de juin ou de roses plus tard, des senteurs des jardinets entourant les maisons. Ils ne se sentiraient totalement eux-mêmes qu'en marchant, en traversant les différents quartiers.

Text and context

Finding one's way around the narrative layers of *La Québécoite* is like finding one's bearings in an unknown city. Doubtless the similarity is intended, as Robin's text deals with the situation of those who live between two or more cultures, and explores the difficulties of identity and of expression which result from that experience. Robin's own cultural origins (born in France to Polish-Jewish parents) and her choice as an adult of living and writing in Montreal make her *une écrivaine migrante*, one of a number of 'new Quebeckers' whose writing has opened up Quebec literature to greater cultural diversity in the last twenty years.[1] The chosen extract is a relatively straightforward section of narrative, but it illustrates the

1 The Haitian-born writer Dany Laferrière is also one of these new Quebeckers. See Chapter 24 above for an analysis of one of his texts set in Haiti.

interweaving of the different narrative paths and the sense of disorientation that this can create in the reader.

There are three levels of narrative in the novel. At the first level the female narrator refers to herself both as 'je' and 'tu', the latter being used in a section devoted to the recollection of a teenage love affair in Paris (l. 29), and 'je' referring to the narrator engaged in writing her novel. The narrator/novelist then creates a second level of narrative, in which she constructs three different scenarios, each one imagining how a woman from Paris, simply identified as 'elle', settles into three different 'lives' in Montreal. In this extract the third fictional life story is being told, the protagonist, 'elle', having a relationship with a Paraguayan political exile and living in the Italian immigrant quarter near the marché Jean-Talon in northern Montreal. The status of these three scenarios as fictional variations is conveyed by the use of conditional verb forms. This woman protagonist in turn is writing a novel, in her case a novel about an elderly Jewish immigrant in Montreal, Mortre Himmelfarb, who is planning a lecture series on eastern European Jewish history. This third level of narrative is only evident in the chosen extract in the phrase

faux messies et
faux récits (l. 84)

that acts as an echo referring back to Mortre Himmelfarb's work on the false messiahs who inspired fanatical followers in the sixteenth and seventeenth centuries. In this phrase the falsity of the messiahs' claims is linked by the narrator to the inevitable untruthfulness and incompleteness of all narratives.

At times the relationship between sections of text resembles a collage. In addition to three narrative strands, the novel also includes extracts from television schedules, a restaurant menu and lists of names, either of underground stations or, as in this passage, of shops and businesses. The brief example in the passage, with its striking typographical layout, draws attention to the distinctive cultural mix evident on the streets of Montreal. The column arrangement (ll. 125–8) interrupts the linearity of the narrative. Like a collage, the novel cannot be read as a coherent, comprehensive account, but requires the reader to put together the different components and question their status and meaning. While the use of a fragmented narrative and of collage effects makes the reading of the novel difficult, other features act like echoes and links between the sections. In this passage these echoes are provided by references to music by Polish and Hungarian composers (Chopin, Kodály and Bartok (ll. 35, 107)), to plants (roses and lilac), and by the repetition with variations of lists of place names, in a way which both links them and suggests their interchangeability: 'Paris ou Budapest. Budapest ou Paris. Ou Montréal' (ll. 49, 86). Roses and lilac weave their way through the different urban settings, not only in descriptions, but also in the choice of place names ('"Rozja Domb", la colline des roses' (l. 38); 'Rosemont'; 'Porte des Lilas'; in Budapest, Montreal and Paris respectively). These patterns of repetition work like a leitmotiv in the text, not so much symbolizing a deeper, unifying meaning, but rather providing a pattern in a complex and fragmentary text.

The links and overlaps between sections help to highlight a number of common concerns or traits. As the title of the novel suggests, with its play on the word *Québécoise*, one of the novel's central themes is that of identity. (The created word 'Québécoite' combines the notion of *se tenir coi(te)* with the word *Québécoise* to suggest the silencing of the migrant (or immigrant) female voice in Quebec.) All the protagonists relate to two or more cultures but they respond in a variety of ways to this split or plural identity. The 'je' narrator (together with her 'tu' self), the 'elle' protagonist, her aunt Mime Yente, and her fictional protagonist, Himmelfarb, are all Jewish. The latter two, members of the older generation, both identify strongly with their original eastern European Jewish culture, Mime by her marking of the sabbath (l. 88), her samovar and Yiddish cuisine, Himmelfarb by his teaching of eastern European Jewish history. Mime Yente's identification with her Yiddish roots can be seen as a way of resisting cultural assimilation. But it can also be understood as part of a process of 'ghettoization', whereby ethnic groups choose to retreat into the safety of a small community (here the anglophone Jewish quarter of Snowdon), effectively accepting their position on the margins of Quebec society.

For the younger generation ('je/tu' and 'elle'), the Holocaust has destroyed any easy identification with a lost Yiddish past. In her recollection of her affair with Janos in the late 1950s, the narrator refers to herself as 'Déjà errante' (l. 44), which is suggestive of the term *le Juif errant* and the diaspora of Jews throughout the world. The present-day narrator, reflecting on the difficulty of locating her protagonist in Montreal creates her as a perpetual wanderer and outsider: '. . . et après? Restera l'exil, l'éternel sentiment d'être ailleurs, déracinée' (l. 67). The sense of rootlessness comes not only from the constant movement between countries, languages and cultures, but also from a specific rupture with the past: 'Je n'ai pas d'aïeux. Tous morts à Auschwitz et avant anonymes' (l. 80). The sections of narrative which relate to the narrator's past in Paris have a spatial connection with a key moment in the history of Parisian Jews. Each of the three parts of the novel refers to the metro stations of one of three lines, numbers 6, 8 and 10. In the chosen extract, the metro line used is line 8, which triggers a childhood recollection of the Bastille, as well as these memories of Place de la République. The three lines cross at la Motte-Picquet Grenelle, the nearest station to the site of the infamous Vél d'Hiv raid, in the course of which over 12,000 Jews were rounded up, and later sent to Auschwitz.[2] The association of place and event is underlined by another leitmotiv that is repeated elsewhere in the novel: 'Après Grenelle. Je ne sais plus. La ligne se perd dans ma mémoire' (pp. 73, 166, 204). It is this trauma which lies at the heart of the text, the unnameable place where the three lines cross and where the lives of the different narrators and protagonists both take their meaning and lose their sense of origin, among the dead of Auschwitz.

Allusions to the history of the Jews in the twentieth century remind the reader that Nazi actions were often carried out by colluding French citizens, motivated both by anti-Semitism and the desire for the survival of the French nation. In *La Québécoite*, nationalism, be it Québécois, French or any other, is tainted by history. And by opening the text up to other kinds of oppression and exclusion (the Stroessner regime (l. 101) which lasted in Paraguay till 1989, Soviet oppression in Hungary in 1956, pogroms in Eastern Europe (l. 103)), Robin indicates the need to think differently about rigid national identities and more fluid, shifting identities, about questions of exclusion and inclusion. In the context of post-*révolution tranquille* Quebec, the discourse of Quebec separatism in the 1970s was perceived by many immigrants as being narrowly nationalistic and therefore hostile to cultural difference. Against this background, the rootless individual takes up a position that Robin refers to elsewhere as 'l'entre-deux', so undermining the monolithic nature of identity based on place, race or nationality.

2 The raid is named after the Vélodrome d'hiver in Paris, since demolished, which served as a collection point for the Jews as they were rounded up during the night of the 16–17 July 1942.

The passage explores the tension between the marginalized person's desire to belong, to be *chez soi*, and the attraction of mobility. The opening two paragraphs of the passage offer a euphoric description of the way in which the 'elle' protagonist and her Paraguayan partner feel 'chez soi' in the Jean-Talon district. From the abundance and variety of exotic and local produce, to the racial mix of their friends, to their own love making, this section speaks to the reader in terms of plurality and cultural exchange. But later in the passage, after the account of Mime Yente's nostalgic re-creation of her lost Yiddish culture, the couple establish a different relationship to the city, a relationship symbolized by their varied routes across Montreal: 'Ils aimeraient marcher dans la ville à l'écoute de ses langues, de ses métamorphoses, de ses bruits' (l. 119). Their mobility in the urban environment suggests the desire to resist any permanent inclusion in the anglophone Jewish 'ghetto' of the Snowdon district of western Montreal. But even this freer pattern of movement does not quite correspond to the position of the migrant writer. As her own plots attempt to draw the narrative and the reader into their realist web, the narrator breaks: 'Le texte m'échappe. Je le sens glisser' (l. 56). Only by disturbing our reading can Robin underline the fictional and artificial nature of her novel and of *all récits*. And only by destabilizing the different models of identity which are represented in the text does Robin give the reader a sense of what it might mean to occupy the shifting spaces of *l'entre-deux*.

Further reading

Robin, Régine, *Le Naufrage du siècle* suivi de *Le Cheval blanc de Lénine* (Montreal: XYZ, 1995).
—— *L'Immense Fatigue des pierres. Biofictions* (Montreal: XYZ, 1996).

Chapman, Rosemary, *Siting the Quebec Novel* (Bern: Peter Lang, 2000), Chapter 4.
Frédéric, Madeleine, 'L'écriture mutante dans *La Québécoite* de Régine Robin', *Voix et images* 48 (1991), 493–502.
Harel, Simon, 'La parole orpheline de l'écrivain migrant', in Pierre Nepveu and Gilles Marcotte (eds), *Montréal imaginaire. Ville et littérature* (Montreal: Fides, 1992).
Milot, Louise and Lintvelt, Jaap (eds), *Le Roman québécois depuis 1960: méthodes et analyses* (Quebec: Presses de l'Université Laval, 1992).
Potvin, Claudine, 'La (dé)construction de la mémoire: *La Québécoite* de Régine Robin', in Lucie Lequin and Maïr Verthuy (eds), *Multi-culture, multi-écriture: la voix migrante au féminin en France et au Canada* (Paris: L'Harmattan, 1996), pp. 261–74.
Purdy, Anthony, 'Altérité, authenticité, universalité: Dany Laferrière et Régine Robin', in 'Le Récit québécois depuis 1980', ed. Irène Oore and Betty Bednarski, *Dalhousie French Studies* 23 (Fall–Winter 1992), 51–9.
Simon, Sherry, L'Hérault, Pierre, Schwartzwald, Robert and Nouss, Alexis, *Fictions de l'identitaire au Québec* (Montreal: XYZ, 1991).

Language and style

Robin calls her text a collage (p. 207) and gives an insight into her method of composition, when, using the voice of one of her narrators, she says,

> elle y remplirait des pages de poésie en yiddish au fil de l'inspiration – tantôt attaquant une autre portion de pizza, c'est un mot, une assonance qui s'imposerait brutalement, tantot au détour d'une cigarette écrasée dans le cendrier, c'est une image qui prend

corps, une analogie, une comparaison, tantot c'est tout un passage qui arriverait comme ça. Elle ne raturerait jamais au départ. Elle attendrait quelques jours avant de lire. Puis, travaillerait ces images, ces mots, ces assemblages, ces structures.

(p. 62)

This approach to composition is evident at a number of levels. By using a variety of narratorial voices the author presents an array of personalities to prosecute the novel (see 'Text and context' above). There is also a variety of settings in the passage, juxtaposed next to each other without any overt transition – scene one (ll. 1–24) set in the Italian immigrant district of Montreal, scene two set in Paris (ll. 25–55) and, after an interlude on the power of nostalgia, scene three (ll. 71–137) set in the Jewish district of Montreal. Similarly, a key theme of this passage, epitomized in the expression 'Joyeux tohu-bohu'(l. 11) and evoked from beginning to end, namely delight in cosmopolitan diversity and richness, adds yet another layer to the collage effect. This theme, with its corollary the search for identity when confronted with such diversity, is regularly conveyed by accumulating large numbers of concrete nouns and thereby creating an atmosphere of physical and sensuous intensity: through place names, Montreal with its streets and districts (ll. 1, 16, 54, 64, 117, 120, 130), Paris with its streets and metro stations (ll. 25, 43, 44, 50, 52, 54, 86), Budapest (ll. 34, 44, 45, 51, 53, 54, 68, 86), Naples and Sicily (l. 2), Paraguay (l. 4), London (l. 103), Ukraine and Petliura (l. 102), Jitomir (l. 69), New York (l. 69), Latin America, Canada and Quebec (l. 108); through the names of flowers, fruit and vegetables with their smells (ll. 4–10), and of foodstuffs (ll. 12, 15, 97); and through reference to religious rites (l. 89), insects (l. 8), musical instruments (l. 35), composers (l. 35), shops and other buildings (ll. 112, 121, 128). More directly, the joyous nature of the hubbub is brought out through the references to different languages (ll. 10, 20) and nationalities (ll. 18, 23) and specifically in 'Ils aimeraient marcher dans la ville à l'écoute de ses langues, de ses métamorphoses, de ses bruits' (l. 119) and by implication in 'Ils ne se sentiraient totalement eux-mêmes qu'en marchant, en traversant les différents quartiers' (l. 136). The equal validity of the places mentioned as foci of identity is brought out in the interchangeability of the order of names when combined, 'Paris ou Budapest' (ll. 44, 52, 86), 'Budapest ou Paris' (ll. 54, 86) or extended in 'Montréal ou Paris, Budapest ou Jitomir ou New York' (l. 68, less so in l. 86). As the narrator says, 'Les villes se cherchent et se répondent dans la nuit. Parfois elles se ressemblent' (l. 69). Another leitmotiv, involving items included in the enumerations and enhancing the interchangeability of the locations, concerns roses and lilac, occurring with reference to the three major sites of the narrative, Paris (ll. 26, 50), Budapest (ll. 38, 39), Montreal (l. 56). Even in the interlude, enumeration occurs: 'Sécrétions de pittoresque, épanchements. Nostalgies de deux sous. Illusions de l'enracinement' (l. 56).

The collage effect and accompanying hubbub are conveyed linguistically too. The disorientation experienced by the narrator/author as she grapples with the value of different tenses is expressly described when she says, 'Sais-je exactement où je la [the narrative] conduis, perdue entre ces conditionnels, ces présents et ces imparfaits?' (p. 138). Scene one is expressed through the conditional tense, scene two the imperfect and scene three a return to the conditional. In the first paragraph, there is a piling up of detail – six simple sentences interspersed with three minor sentences. The absence of verbs in two of the minor sentences (ll. 6, 9) together with the enumeration of vegetables and flowers, has the same effect as a photograph, freezing a situation in time. The simple sentences tend to have similar structures, subject pronoun preceding verb in initial position, e.g. 'Ils adoreraient ça' (l. 1), 'Elle aurait l'impression' (l. 2), 'Lui aussi pourrait . . . revoir' (l. 3), again suggesting disconnected details. Of the first twelve sentences of scene two, three are minor and nine simple, again with subject pronouns being mainly in initial position, producing the same disconnected effect as in scene one. Although scene three begins in a different mode, the reader being introduced to the self-questioning of the narrator/author, the structure of the first twelve sentences, three minor, seven simple, one compound and one complex, again, as in the other two scenes, presents a disjointed, staccato effect. Even in the interlude a similar combination of simple and minor sentences occurs (indeed minor sentences outnumber major ones). The narrator/author talks of 'les mots tronqués, les mots traversés, les mots scindés' (p. 79); the same qualities can be applied, perhaps even more aptly, to the sentence structure of the passage, dislocated, lacking links.

The repetitions of words, phrases and sentences also add to the collage effect, like ready-made lexical blocks to be inserted into the text at appropriate moments: roses and lilac, 'Paris ou Budapest' have already been mentioned. 'Les villes se cherchent et se répondent dans la nuit. Parfois, elles se ressemblent' occurs twice (ll. 49, 69) as does, following close after it, 'Quelle importance! Quelque part dans l'imaginaire de la ville!' (ll. 54, 70). The impression created is one of sameness in diversity, of human differences between members of a greater humanity. Repetition occurs regularly and, with less thematic significance, throughout the passage: 'on verra plus tard' (l. 114); 'je finis par' occurs four times (l. 58) and reappears three times further on (ll. 72, 74, 109); there are also repetitions of prepositions ('devant' (ll. 12, 29); 'pour' (l. 37); 'jusqu'à' (l. 124)), of adverbs ('jamais plus' (l. 50); un peu' (l. 104)), of 'moi' (l. 78), of nouns ('piano' (l. 20), 'soir' (l. 45), 'place' (l. 74), 'ville' (l. 125), 'nuits' (l. 134), 'senteurs' (l. 134)), verbs ('s'installer' (l. 77), 'échapper' (ll. 38, 56, 82), 'prendre/entreprendre' (l. 131)), of adjectives ('petits' (l. 61), 'faux' (l. 84)), of present participles ('ne vivant que pour . . . '. (l. 37)).

Robin's narrator's concern and sensitivity for words (see the statement from p. 79 quoted above) is illustrated through a number of stylistic devices, the purpose being to highlight her ability to manipulate her lexical material. These devices are particularly concentrated in the interlude (ll. 56–86) where the narrator/author discusses composition. Word play, 'Je n'ai pas d'aïeux . . . Pas d'aïeux, des ailleurs' (l. 80), rhyme, 'faux messies et faux récits' (l. 84), alliteration, 'Parapluies, pardessus, flaques et freins devant les feux' (l. 42), 'miettes de ville, de vide, de vie' (l. 62 also l. 35), are all employed to that end. Doublets and parallel constructions occur innumerable times, e.g. 'Si je lui compose tel visage, si je lui donne tel destin' (l. 73), 'Vivre à petits pas, à petits feux' (l. 61, also ll. 60, 62, 65, 69, 70, 72, 112, 134). Present participles are particularly noticeable used in this way, e.g. 'Tu arrivas en avance, te commandant un pastis pour tromper l'attente, fumant tes gauloises l'une après l'autre' (l.32, also ll. 17, 37, 48, 99, 115, 132). Triplets also occur in large numbers, e.g. 'personne ne savait jouer Kodaly ou Bartok comme lui, au piano, au violon, au violoncelle' (l. 35, also ll. 58, 60, 78, 92, 112, 129); quartets too are frequent, e.g. 'La tentation des races pures, des beaux passeports, des généalogies, des «moi mes ancêtres ici . . . »' (l. 77, also ll. 47, 63 (questions), 102, 108). A triplet of present participles occurs: '[Janos] ne comprenant rien, ne vivant que pour sa musique, pour cette ville qu'il aimait tant, pour la maison qu'il occupait à «Rozja Domb» . . . ne vivant que pour fouler les feuilles mortes' (l. 36). There is one example of an initial inversion plus doublet: 'Restera l'exil, l'éternel sentiment d'être ailleurs' (l. 67).

The scenes that constitute the collage are bursting with detail – details that are compressed but vibrant, tripping over each other in the long sentences, standing out starkly in the minor ones. The scenes depicted are rich and dense evocations of Paris and Montreal, the descriptions of markets and shops, sights and smells, noises and people all contributing to a sensuous but 'joyeux tohu-bohu'. The frequent use of many stylistic devices in the sentence structure – abundant enumerations, present participles, repetitions, doublets and triplets – underscores this graphic impression.

Chapter 32

Jacques Poulin

Volkswagen Blues (Montreal: Leméac/Actes Sud, 1998), pp. 279–84. First published Montreal: Editions Québec/Amérique, 1984.

Les fantômes de San Francisco

– Il est fait moitié en acier et moitié en rêve, dit Jack.

– C'est le plus beau que j'aie vu de toute ma vie, dit la fille.

– Quand j'étais petit, je pensais qu'il était en or. J'étais sûr qu'il avait été construit avec l'or qu'on avait découvert en Californie.

Ils parlaient du Golden Gate Bridge, qu'ils apercevaient au loin sur la droite, émergeant d'une masse de brouillard, tandis qu'ils s'engageaient sur un autre pont, le Bay Bridge, pour traverser la baie qui les séparait de San Francisco.

Le voyage touchait à sa fin.

Ils étaient partis de Gaspé, où Jacques Cartier avait découvert le Canada, et ils avaient suivi le fleuve Saint-Laurent et les Grands Lacs, et ensuite le vieux Mississippi, le Père des Eaux, jusqu'à Saint Louis, et puis ils avaient emprunté la Piste de l'Oregon et, sur la trace des émigrants du 19e siècle qui avaient formé des caravanes pour se mettre à la recherche du Paradis Perdu avec leurs chariots tirés par des bœufs, ils avaient parcouru les grandes plaines, franchi la ligne de partage des eaux et les montagnes Rocheuses, traversé les rivières et le désert et encore d'autres montagnes, et voilà qu'ils arrivaient à San Francisco.

La ville était couverte de brouillard.

L'homme et la fille ne savaient pas où aller. En sortant du pont, ils prirent une rue qui suivait les quais; la rue, qui s'appelait L'Embarcadero, les conduisit à diverses installations pour touristes: le Fisherman's Wharf, la Cannery (un vieil immeuble en briques aménagé en boutiques et magasins), une petite plage, un vieux fort, un musée maritime, un club de yacht, un parc nommé Victoria Square et enfin le Palace of Fine Arts, vestige d'une exposition internationale tenue en 1915.

Ils flanèrent sur les quais et dans les boutiques, mais il y avait vraiment trop de touristes . . . et de gens qui cherchaient à vendre des choses aux touristes; les uns et les autres, au bout d'un moment, leur parurent insupportables et ils se réfugièrent sur la petite plage.

Ils s'assirent dans le sable.

L'île d'Alcatraz était en face d'eux. Et lorsqu'ils se retournaient pour voir la ville, ils apercevaient les *cable cars* qui bringuebalaient sur la pente abrupte de la rue Hyde, avec leur chargement de touristes, en faisant résonner le cling-clang insolite de leur clochette à chaque intersection. Au flanc de la colline, les teintes pastel des maisons adoucissaient le paysage.

La fille enleva ses «running shoes» et s'avança au bord de la baie. Elle demeura quelques instants immobile, les pieds dans l'eau et les yeux fixés sur les murs beiges de la vieille prison d'Alcatraz. Puis elle revint vers l'homme qui était resté assis dans le sable avec le chat sur ses genoux, et elle vit qu'il regardait lui aussi vers l'île.

– C'est la fin de l'été, mais l'eau est aussi froide que sur la Côte Nord! dit-elle. A quoi pensiez-vous?

– Je pensais à Burt Lancaster, dit-il.

– A cause du film *les Oiseaux d'Alcatraz*?

– Bien sûr. Et aussi parce que c'est un acteur que Théo aimait beaucoup. Mon frère aimait aussi John Wayne, Gary Cooper, Alan Ladd, Randolph Scott, Kirk Douglas . . . Et vous, à quoi pensiez-vous?

– Aux Indiens. Ils se sont emparés de la prison en 1969 et ils ont déclaré que l'île était un territoire indien.

Elle souriait.

– Et qu'est-ce qui est arrivé? demanda l'homme.

– Les policiers ont établi un blocus autour de l'île, dit-elle, et ensuite . . .

Elle écarta les bras en signe d'impuissance et, pivotant sur ses pieds nus, elle se tourna vers la ville et fit une profonde révérence. Son geste semblait dire que les Indiens perdaient toujours, qu'ils avaient perdu cette fois encore et qu'il n'y avait rien à faire. C'était le destin ou quelque chose de ce genre.

– Tout de même, dit-elle. C'est une belle ville!

– Oui, mais il fait froid! dit l'homme. On s'en va?

Le soleil n'arrivait pas à percer le brouillard et ils frissonnaient à cause de l'humidité qui les pénétrait jusqu'aux os.

Ils se hâtèrent de regagner le Volkswagen. L'homme s'installa au volant. Après avoir jeté un coup d'œil sur une carte de la ville, il décida de rouler un moment dans Bay Street, mais il tourna à droite et prit Columbus lorsqu'il vit un panneau signalant que le quartier de North Beach se trouvait dans cette direction. Le nom de North Beach évoquait pour lui des souvenirs liés aux beatniks et à Jack Kerouac.

On the Road était un des livres que la Grande Sauterelle avait «empruntés» au cours du voyage parce qu'il était mentionné dans le dossier de police de Toronto. Elle l'avait trouvé en version française dans une bibliothèque de Kansas City; elle le connaissait déjà, mais elle avait eu du plaisir à le relire. «Qui n'a pas relu, n'a pas lu», disait-elle. Pour sa part, l'homme avait préféré garder intact le souvenir de sa première lecture: il se souvenait d'un voyage ayant les allures d'une fête continuelle, qui était raconté dans un style puissant et enchevêtré comme les routes immenses de l'Amérique; alors il s'était contenté de relire la préface, dans laquelle il avait souligné cette phrase:

> La route a remplacé l'ancien «trail» des pionniers de la marche vers l'Ouest; elle est le lien mystique qui rattache l'Américain à son continent, à ses compatriotes.

Ils virent tout de suite que North Beach était un quartier très spécial, alors ils abandonnèrent le vieux Volks sur le parking du Safeway, au coin de Chesnut, et ils mirent des chandails de laine pour aller à pied dans l'avenue Columbus. Même s'il avait grandi depuis le début du voyage, le chat noir acceptait encore de se balader dans le capuchon de la Grande Sauterelle; il avait trouvé une nouvelle position: au lieu de dormir en boule au fond du capuchon, il se tenait debout, les pattes et le menton appuyés sur l'épaule de la fille.

Ils passèrent devant un immeuble en briques rouges qui abritait la bibliothèque du quartier. Un peu plus loin, sur la gauche, il y avait un parc appelé Washington Square.

– Ah oui, dit l'homme, Kerouac venait souvent par ici.

Il parlait comme si Jack Kerouac était une vieille connaissance; à la vérité, il n'avait lu que deux de ses livres et quelques articles sur lui dans des revues.

– Une fois, il avait acheté un gallon de vin blanc, dit-il. Le vin qu'il préférait était du Tokay, une marque bon marché. Alors il s'est amené dans le parc avec sa petite cruche de Tokay et il s'est mis à boire. Il s'est assis au pied d'un arbre et il a bu jusqu'à ce qu'il ne reste plus une goutte de vin, et ensuite il était complètement soûl et il s'est endormi dans l'herbe.

Washington Square était un parc ordinaire, un carré de verdure avec des arbres, des bancs, quelques monuments et un coin pour les enfants, mais tout à coup, avec la présence de Kerouac, tout était transformé. Des formes suspectes étaient allongées dans l'herbe. A cause du brouillard, l'herbe était certainement mouillée, et pourtant il y avait des vieux et des *bums* qui étaient étendus et dormaient, enveloppés dans des journaux ou des couvertures de toile. Le parc était envahi par les fantômes du passé.

Text and context

Like the extract from Maillet's *Pélagie-la-Charrette*, this passage is concerned with the end of a journey. Whereas in Maillet's text the journey is the return home to Canada of an exiled population, in Poulin's novel the two protagonists are travelling outwards from Canada on a journey which takes them across the American continent to San Francisco. The direction of this journey suggests both an opening out towards the rest of the North American continent and a recognition on the part of Quebeckers that they too are North Americans. In many ways their route represents the successive waves of exploration, settlement and migration across North America. It starts from Gaspé, where the French explorer Jacques Cartier first landed in July 1534 (l. 9). It continues on via the Great Lakes to the Mississippi (retracing the steps of seventeenth-century French explorers, such as Brûlé, Radisson and La Salle). Then the route heads west on the Oregon Trail and branches south-west to California, as wagon loads of emigrants had done in the 1860s, and as those fleeing from the effects of the Depression and the drought years were to do in the 1930s (l. 12). But in addition to recalling the routes, and the expectations of pioneers and travellers, the protagonists have personal reasons for crossing the continent. For Jack, his motivation is primarily to search for his brother whom he has not seen for twenty years. For Pitsémine, referred to in this passage by her nickname 'la Grande Sauterelle', the journey is a chance to learn more about the history of the aboriginal peoples of North America. In so doing, she hopes to gain a better understanding of her own identity as a *métisse*, her mother being a Montagnais Indian and her father white. A final layer of references which accompanies their journey across the American continent is provided by a range of written accounts, biographical, historical and literary, which la Grande Sauterelle and Jack read and cite as they travel west.

As this complex layering of trails/routes suggests, the journey is at once a journey forwards and a journey into the past, a past that is composed of many different and competing interests which Poulin manages to highlight by his choice of genre and protagonists. Jack and la Grande Sauterelle have certain things in common (they are both Quebeckers, both francophone, both can speak English), but their difference in terms of race, sex and age has a far greater effect on the way they respond to America. The passage opens with the protagonists' response to the best-known symbol of San Francisco, the Golden Gate Bridge. Jack and la Grande Sauterelle then walk through the tourist area adjoining San Francisco Bay before turning their backs on the city to look out across the bay to Alcatraz Island. Finally they drive through the streets of San Francisco and, because of its association with Jack Kerouac, follow a sign to the North Beach district, where they find their way on foot to Washington Square. Each of these stages on the journey raises questions about the kind of America they, and those before them, have discovered.

Like the sight of Grand'Pré in *Pélagie-la-Charrette*, the sight of the Golden Gate Bridge symbolizes more than the end of a journey. While Grand'Pré was at once a place of origin and a monument to the past of a small displaced community, the Golden Gate Bridge has come to represent a dream of freedom and prosperity for millions wishing to share the American Dream. The combination of the material ('acier') and the ideal ('rêve'), evoked in Jack's opening comment about the bridge (l. 1), can be applied more widely to popular images of America, and more specifically of the west. For early explorers, trading routes, the exploitation of natural resources and territorial expansion were motives as powerful as any missionary zeal or search for an earthly paradise. For later migrants, the flight from poverty and the aspiration to share in Californian wealth were just as inspiring as the desire for individual or collective freedom.

The ideals of personal freedom and mobility which are common to the different versions of the American Dream that appear in the course of the novel are undermined by being juxtaposed with the material realities of the United States. In this passage the end of the road, San Francisco Bay, appears to the two travellers as over-commercialized, where traders and tourists dominate, feeding off each other in a cycle that stresses the materialistic rationale of the modern-day tourist industry, which converts geographical and historical sites into heritage trails. Jack and la Grande Sauterelle's distaste for the base materialism of such commercialism is expressed by their return to sit on the beach looking out over the bay (l. 27). Here the dreams of freedom are undermined as the two gaze at Alcatraz Island. Their initial responses differ sharply, highlighting the cultural and political space between them. For Jack, the immediate association that the old prison walls bring to mind is a Hollywood image (that of Burt Lancaster in *Birdman of Alcatraz* (l. 41)) and by extension the string of other (white, anglophone, male) Hollywood stars whom his brother Théo admired. While la Grande Sauterelle is able to anticipate Jack's train of thought (being as it is typical of mainstream white North American popular culture), her personal response is to recall the part played by Alcatraz in the history of American Indian militancy (l. 46). Between 1969 and 1971, North American Indians occupied the island, claiming territorial rights over it. The significance of this and other occupations (including that of the village of Wounded Knee in 1973) was to provide a focus for the American Indian Movement's questioning of the policy of assimilation and an assertion of their right for self-determination. As usual in the novel, la Grande

Sauterelle is aware of how any site, event or historical figure can take on different, often contradictory meanings, according to whether they are seen from within the dominant ideology or from its margins.

The final stage of this encounter with San Francisco opens up a further frame of reference. As they start to drive around the city, Jack sees a place name that reminds him of Jack Kerouac, which introduces *On the Road*, a book which he knows his brother Théo had with him on his own travels. By referring to *On the Road* (l. 65), Poulin is inviting the reader to read *Volkswagen Blues* at once as a continuation of the genre and as a deviation from it. *On the Road* (published in 1957) was hugely successful in the States because it seemed to articulate the energy and the individualism of the beat generation. Jack cites Kerouac's definition of the road as 'le lien mystique qui rattache l'Américain à son continent, à ses compatriotes' (l. 75). Road novels and road movies have both been used as vehicles to explore and reinvent masculinist models of national identity. But Poulin's rewriting of the road novel in the 1980s is an attempt to move beyond such an understanding of national identity. In this extract, Kerouac's figures survive only as ghostly memories from a generation earlier, hence the title of this chapter, 'Les fantômes de San Francisco'. And when Jack and la Grande Sauterelle walk through Washington Square on Kerouac's trail, they find a number of old men and drop-outs sleeping rough, like some forgotten débris of the beat generation (l. 99). This can be read as a pointer to the outcome of Jack's own search. His brother Théo, whom he and la Grande Sauterelle eventually track down, turns out to be reduced to an amnesiac, a paralysed version of the heroic figure in Jack's head.

Volkswagen Blues is far from an *On the Road* for Quebeckers. The sense of anticlimax, the cold and the damp which greet them in San Francisco further undermine Jack's tendency to romanticism and nostalgia. Hollywood images are juxtaposed with an account of the defeat of the Indian occupation of Alcatraz. Kerouac's journey, remembered by Jack as 'une fête continuelle' (l. 70), contrasts with the sight of old men sleeping rough in Washington Square. And yet, if these initial impressions seem negative, there is a more positive implication, which is the possibility for la Grande Sauterelle and Jack to reassess ('relire') (l. 68) America, and the many different versions of its past. Equally, this will allow them to rethink their own identity as Quebeckers in a Quebec which will no longer look exclusively in on itself, but open out towards the wider world.

Further reading

Poulin, Jacques, *Les Grandes Marées* (Montreal: Bibliothèque québécoise, 1990).

—— *Le Vieux Chagrin* (Montreal/Arles: Leméac/Actes Sud, 1989).

—— *La Tournée d'automne* (Montreal: Leméac, 1993).

Chassay, Jean-François, *L'Ambiguïté américaine. Le roman québécois face aux Etats-Unis* (Montreal: XYZ Editeur, 1995).

Hébert, Pierre, *Jacques Poulin: la création d'un espace amoureux* (Ottawa: Les Presses de l'Université d'Ottawa, 1997).

'Jacques Poulin', Special Issue of *Voix et images* XV, 1 (Autumn 1989).

Miraglia, Anne Marie, *L'Ecriture de l'Autre chez Jacques Poulin* (Candiac, Quebec: Les Editions Balzac, 1993).

Morency, Jean, *Le Mythe américain dans les fictions d'Amérique. De Washington Irving à Jacques Poulin* (Quebec: Nuit blanche éditeur, 1994).

Socken, P. G., *The Myth of the Lost Paradise in the Novels of Jacques Poulin* (London/Toronto: Associated University Presses, 1993).

Language and style

Jack's opening statement – 'Il [Golden Gate Bridge] est fait moitié en acier et moitié en rêve' (l. 1) – provides in a nutshell a major stylistic theme of the passage, the contrast between precise, solid detail and less tangible fantasy. On the one hand, the events are described almost like diary entries. The visit to San Francisco and the journey through the city are recorded with detailed precision. Names of bridges (ll. 5, 7), streets (ll. 19, 31, 61, 79), districts (l. 62), parks (ll. 22, 85, 95), buildings (ll. 20, 23, 78) occur regularly throughout. The directions taken by the travellers are precisely given, as if following a map (compare 'Après avoir jeté un coup d'œil sur une carte de la ville' (l. 60)): e.g. 'ils apercevaient au loin sur la droite' (l. 5), 'il décida de rouler un moment dans Bay Street, mais il tourna à droite et prit Columbus' (l. 61, also ll. 6, 18, 29, 61, 84). Detailed descriptions are given of buildings, e.g. 'la Cannery (un vieil immeuble en briques aménagé en boutiques et magasins)' (l. 20), 'le Palace of Fine Arts, vestige d'une exposition internationale tenue en 1915' (l. 23). Their colours are particularly mentioned, e.g. 'les teintes pastel des maisons adoucissaient le paysage' (l. 32), 'les murs beiges de la vieille prison' (l. 35), 'un immeuble en briques rouges' (l. 84). A film title (l. 42), the names of actors (ll. 41, 44), the history of Alcatraz (l. 46), references to tourists (ll. 20, 25, 31) all provide an atmosphere of authenticity and factual exactitude, as do the references to the cold water (l. 39) and weather (l. 56).

On the other hand, we learn nothing of the appearance of the protagonists, and a sense of unreality, reflecting the title of the chapter, is engendered by a series of allusions. As a child Jack had fantasized that the bridge was built of gold (l. 3). But much more importantly, the character of Jack Kerouac hovers like a ghost over the protagonists, e.g. 'Le nom de North Beach évoquait pour lui des souvenirs liés aux beatniks et à Jack Kerouac' (l. 62, also ll. 64, 87, 88). His ghost-like presence transforms the park (l. 97) – there were 'formes suspectes' (l. 97) and 'Le parc était envahi par les fantômes du passé' (l. 100).

The link between these two contrasting aspects of the passage, leading from reality into memory and fantasy, is formed by the fog, which is mentioned on a number of occasions, and which, as in a film, transports the reader from one world into another, e.g. the 'Golden Gate Bridge, qu'ils apercevaient au loin sur la droite, émergeant d'une masse de brouillard' (l. 5, also ll. 57, 98).

A number of English terms are used in the text, in addition to the names of monuments. These are signalled in a variety of seemingly arbitrary ways – sometimes in italics, e.g. '*cable cars*' (l. 30), '*bums*' (l. 99), sometimes in *guillemets*, e.g. '«running shoes»' (l. 34); '«trail»' (l. 74) occurs in the quotation from Kerouac), sometimes without any external indication, e.g. 'cling-clang' (l. 31), 'gallon' (l. 90).

In his reaction to Jack Kerouac's *On the Road*, the protagonist Jack recalls its 'style puissant et enchevêtré comme les routes immenses de l'Amérique' (l. 71). It is interesting to gauge whether such a description can be applied to this text. The answer is, as so often, 'yes and no'. 'No', because the style of *Volkswagen Blues* can in no way be called 'puissant'. It is in fact non-descript, a simple account of a journey, expressed in ordinary vocabulary, with no grandiose analyses or descriptions. In fact this is mirrored in the characterization of the two protagonists, who are largely anonymous in this passage (apart from the mention of 'Jack' in the first line, they are consistently referred to as 'l'homme' and 'la fille'; ironically the cat seems to have a more significant presence (ll. 37, 79–83)). Nothing is learnt about their appearance or their characters from the text. Their speeches rarely stretch for more than a single line – the only relatively long speeches occurs towards the end of the extract when Jack is recounting an episode from his hero's life (ll. 90–4); consequently nothing which might individualize the protagonists is to be discovered there.

However, if the vocabulary is far from 'puissant', the syntax does have something of the 'enchevêtré' about it. This may be demonstrated by examining the syntactic structure of the passage. A definite pattern emerges in the first half of the text. Longer paragraphs are regularly separated by paragraphs consisting of a single line, e.g. ll. 5–7/l. 8/ll. 9–16/l. 17/ll. 18–27 (two paragraphs)/l. 28/ll. 29–38. There is almost a regularity about the number of lines involved, the longer paragraphs or sections generally consisting of between eight and twelve lines, and the one-line paragraphs pointing to the next phase of the action. From l. 39 there follows a passage with nine short speeches, interspersed with a description of accompanying paralinguistic gestures (l. 51), and after that, with the entry of Jack Kerouac onto the scene, a series of longer paragraphs – and another pattern. Where previously the alternation had been one of length, here it is one of substance – descriptions of the route taken by the protagonists alternate with references and memories of the author.

The 'enchevêtrement' of the first half of the text is not restricted to the short/long alternation, but can be demonstrated within the paragraphs themselves. The first long paragraph is complex in structure (main clause with three subordinate clauses), the second compound-complex (main + subordinate + main + main + subordinate + main + main), reflecting the complicated route followed by the nineteenth-century emigrants; the third begins with a simple sentence but follows it with another compound-complex sentence (main + subordinate + subordinate + main), containing considerable enumeration of buildings; the fourth is also compound-complex; the fifth to a certain extent mirrors the third (simple + complex). There is therefore an 'enchevêtrement' of clauses within the sentences, and in addition many adverbial expressions which enhance still further the interlocking and intertwining effect of the passage. This pattern of sentences with complicated structures and many adverbial elements is repeated in the third (Jack Kerouac) section. Two passages stand out as being particularly dramatic in structure and content. The first is 'ils avaient parcouru les grandes plaines, franchi la ligne de partage des eaux et les montagnes Rocheuses, traversé les rivières et le désert et encore d'autres montagnes' (l. 14), where the past participles and symmetrical phrases compressed together convey the demands of the journey. The second is

> Elle écarta les bras en signe d'impuissance et, pivotant sur ses pieds nus, elle se tourna vers la ville et fit une profonde révérence. Son geste semblait dire que les Indiens perdaient toujours, qu'ils avaient perdu cette fois encore et qu'il n'y avait rien à faire.
> (l. 51)

Here the three clauses of the first sentence, all linked by 'et' and therefore separated from each other, express a certain lack of dynamism, which contrasts with the next sentence, where the three clauses introduced by 'que' and repeating 'perdaient/perdu' reflect the girl's despair at the eternal tragedy of the Indians. No other sentences contain such passion.

«Qui n'a pas relu, n'a pas lu» (l. 68) is in many ways the guiding principle for all the linguistic commentaries undertaken in this book. This statement made by the girl is to a certain extent corroborated by the man, who has at least read the preface to *On the Road* more than once (l. 72). It is only by reading and rereading that stylistic features, patterns and techniques emerge. Living the text, through constant rereading, helps us understand what makes it *live* itself.

Index

For Product Safety Concerns and Information please contact our EU representative GPSR@taylorandfrancis.com
Taylor & Francis Verlag GmbH, Kaufingerstraße 24, 80331 München, Germany

www.ingramcontent.com/pod-product-compliance
Lightning Source LLC
Chambersburg PA
CBHW081356090726
47908CB00011B/2688
9780415198400